Blackstone's Police Manual

General Police Duties

Blackstone's Police Manual

Volume 4

General Police Duties

2018

Glenn Hutton

BA, MPhil, FCIPD

Gavin McKinnon

LLB, LLM, MSt (Cantab), CMgr

and

Paul Connor

Cert Ed (FE), PG Cert Ed (ODE), LLB

Consultant Editor: Paul Connor

OXFORD
UNIVERSITY PRESS

OXFORD

UNIVERSITY PRESS

Great Clarendon Street, Oxford, OX2 6DP,
United Kingdom

Oxford University Press is a department of the University of Oxford.
It furthers the University's objective of excellence in research, scholarship,
and education by publishing worldwide. Oxford is a registered trade mark of
Oxford University Press in the UK and in certain other countries

© Oxford University Press, 2017

The moral rights of the authors have been asserted

First Edition published in 1998
Twentieth Edition published in 2017

Impression: 1

Published in the United States of America by Oxford University Press
198 Madison Avenue, New York, NY 10016, United States of America

British Library Cataloguing in Publication Data

Data available

ISBN 978-0-19-880613-4

Printed in Great Britain by
Bell & Bain Ltd., Glasgow

Foreword for 2018 Blackstone's Police Manuals

The police service currently faces a series of challenges; from the changes that police forces must make to deliver savings and reduce crime to the increasing complexity of the threats to national security, public safety and public order. Underpinning the ability of officers to deal effectively with these challenges is the knowledge and understanding of relevant law and procedure and the ability to apply this on a daily basis. This understanding is the cornerstone in providing a professional policing service.

The College of Policing plays a vital role in the development of police officers and staff, helping them to obtain and retain the skills and knowledge they need to fight crime and protect the public. The College has a remit to develop, maintain and test standards to ensure suitability for promotion. Part of this responsibility requires the College to ensure a comprehensive and relevant syllabus is produced. As such, the College works alongside Oxford University Press to ensure these Manuals are an accurate and up-to-date source of information and that they reflect what is required by people working across policing.

The *Blackstone's Police Manuals 2018* are the definitive reference source and official study guide for the national legal examination which all candidates must successfully pass in order to be promoted to sergeant or inspector. Their content is derived from evidence gathered from operational sergeants and inspectors alongside input from the wider police service. Whilst they are primarily designed to support officers seeking to progress their careers in preparing for their promotion examinations, they also provide a reference point for officers and staff seeking to continue their professional development and maintain their knowledge as a professional in policing. If you are using these Manuals to prepare for your promotion examinations I would like to take this opportunity to wish you the very best of luck in your studies, and I hope these books will assist you in progressing your career within the police service.

Alex Marshall
Chief Executive Officer
of the College of Policing

Preface

The *Blackstone's Police Manuals* are the only official study guides for the Police Promotion Examinations—if the law is not in the Manuals, it will not be in the exams.

All the Manuals include explanatory keynotes and case law examples, providing clear and incisive analysis of important areas. As well as covering basic law and procedure they take full account of the PACE Codes of Practice and human rights implications. They can also be used as a training resource for police probationers, special constables and PCSOs, or as an invaluable reference tool for police staff of all ranks and positions.

By its very nature, policing covers a wide and widening range of activities. As society gets more complex and demanding, so too does the job of those who police it. Add to that the enormous political dimension, and it is no surprise that the legislative framework governing policing delivery has grown in depth and breadth. As a result, *General Police Duties* necessarily contains a wide range of powers, offences and considerations.

The 2018 edition has been edited and updated to incorporate all recent legislative changes and the revised PACE Codes of Practice. The legislation containing significant changes to the contents of the Manual includes the Anti-social Behaviour, Crime and Policing Act 2014, the Serious Crime Act 2015, the Criminal Justice and Courts Act 2015, the Deregulation Act 2015, the Counter-Terrorism and Security Act 2015 and the Criminal Procedure Rules 2015. This edition also includes a number of recent criminal cases decided by the appellate courts.

The aim of this Manual is to take this shifting and growing body of law and analyse the essential elements in a practical and pragmatic context—without losing the specific meaning and applicability along the way. If we have achieved that, it is thanks to the contributions of the many police officers and staff, lawyers and practitioners who have helped in the development of this Manual, now in its nineteenth edition; if we haven't, it is not for the want of trying.

Oxford University Press are always happy to receive any useful written feedback from any reader on the content and style of the Manual, especially from those involved in or with the criminal justice system. Please email this address with any comments or queries: police.uk@ oup.com.

The law is stated as at 1 June 2017.

Acknowledgements

Blackstone's Police Manuals have become firmly established as a 'household name' in the context of police law for which they are the leading text in England and Wales. Their growth and refinement year on year is a result, not simply of Parliament and the legislators, but also of the many and varied contributions of the Manuals' wide readership.

Thanks are due to all (except perhaps the legislators) and there is never space to mention everyone individually.

In particular, thanks to the staff of the Legal Services Department of the College of Policing (CoP) and Examinations and Assessment. The monthly Digest produced by the Legal Services Department is an invaluable reference and the informative syllabus review conducted by Examinations and Assessment has helped to shape the content and style of the Manual.

Thanks to George Cooper (Northamptonshire Police), Stuart K. Fairclough (Metropolitan Police), Paul Murphy (Greater Manchester Police) and Kevin Whitehouse (West Midlands Police).

Our thanks, as always, to all the staff involved in the production of the Manual in the Academic and Professional Law Department at Oxford University Press, especially Peter Daniell, Amy Baker, Gemma Wilkins and Pam Birkby. Special thanks also to Sonal, Priya, Jayna and Rosalie for their continued support and forbearance.

Glenn Hutton, Paul Connor and Gavin McKinnon

Contents

PART III General Police Duties **235**

Table of Cases

Table of Statutes

Table of Statutory Instruments

Table of Codes of Practice

Table of European Legislation

Table of Home Office Circulars

Table of International Treaties and Conventions

How to use this Manual

Volume numbers for the Manuals

The 2018 Blackstone's Police Manuals each have a volume number as follows:

Volume 1: *Crime*
Volume 2: *Evidence and Procedure*
Volume 3: *Road Policing*
Volume 4: *General Police Duties*

The first digit of each paragraph number in the text of the Manuals denotes the Manual number. For example, chapter 2.3 is chapter 3 of the *Evidence and Procedure* Manual and chapter 4.3 is chapter 3 of the *General Police Duties* Manual.

All index entries and references in the Tables of Legislation and the Table of Cases, etc. refer to paragraph numbers instead of page numbers, making information easier to find.

Material outside the scope of the police promotion examinations syllabus—blacklining

These Manuals contain some information which is outside the scope of the police promotion examinations. A full black line down the margin indicates that the text beside it is excluded from Inspectors' examinations.

PACE Code Chapters

The PACE Codes of Practice have been taken out of the appendices and are now incorporated within chapters in the main body of the Blackstone's Police Manuals. A thick grey line down the margin is used to denote text that is an extract of the PACE Code itself (i.e. the actual wording of the legislation) and does not form part of the general commentary of the chapter.

The PACE Codes of Practice form an important part of the police promotion examinations syllabus and are examinable for both Sergeants and Inspectors. They are not to be confused with 'blacklined' content that is excluded from the syllabus for Inspectors' examinations (see 'Material outside the scope of the police promotion examinations syllabus—blacklining').

Length of sentence for an offence

Where a length of sentence for an offence is stated in this Manual, please note that the number of months or years stated is the maximum number and will not be exceeded.

Any feedback regarding content or other editorial matters in the Manuals can be emailed to police.uk@oup.com.

Police Promotion Examinations Rules and Syllabus Information

The rules and syllabus for the police promotion examinations system are defined within the Rules & Syllabus document published by College of Policing Selection and Assessment on behalf of the Police Promotion Examinations Board (PPEB). The Rules & Syllabus document is published annually each September, and applies to all police promotion assessments scheduled for the calendar year following its publication. For example, the September 2017 Rules & Syllabus document would apply to all police promotion assessments held during 2018.

The document provides details of the law and procedure to be tested within the National Police Promotion Framework Step 2 Legal Examination, and also outlines the rules underpinning the police promotion examination system.

All candidates who are taking a police promotion examination are strongly encouraged to familiarise themselves with the Rules & Syllabus document during their preparation. The police promotion examination rules apply to candidates undertaking the National Police Promotion Framework.

The document can be downloaded from the Development Section of the College of Policing website, which can be found at <http://www.college.police.uk>. Electronic versions are also supplied to all force examination officers.

If you have any problems obtaining the Rules & Syllabus document from the above source, please contact the Candidate Administration Team via the 'Contact us' section of the College of Policing website (see above).

Usually, no further updates to the Rules & Syllabus document will be issued during its year-long lifespan. However, in exceptional circumstances, the College of Policing (on behalf of the PPEB) reserves the right to issue an amended syllabus prior to the next scheduled annual publication date.

For example, a major change to a key area of legislation or procedure (e.g. the Codes of Practice) during the lifespan of the current Rules & Syllabus document would render a significant part of the current syllabus content obsolete. In such circumstances, it may be necessary for an update to the syllabus to be issued, which would provide guidance to candidates on any additional material which would be examinable within their police promotion examinations.

In such circumstances, an update to the Rules & Syllabus document would be made available through the College of Policing website, and would be distributed to all force examination contacts. The College of Policing will ensure that any syllabus update is distributed well in advance of the examination date, to ensure that candidates have sufficient time to familiarise themselves with any additional examinable material. Where possible, any additional study materials would be provided to candidates free of charge.

Please note that syllabus updates will only be made in *exceptional* circumstances; an update will not be made for every change to legislation included within the syllabus. For further guidance on this issue, candidates are advised to check regularly the College of Policing website, or consult their force examination officer, during their preparation period.

PART ONE

Police

The Police and the Policing Family

4.1.1 Introduction

The police service is constantly changing and evolving. In recent times we have seen the operation of a voluntary redundancy scheme for police officers (which came into effect in January 2013). Add to this the implementation of accelerated and direct entry routes to the ranks of inspector and superintendent and the fact that serving constables can be promoted to inspector within two years, new joiners can be promoted to inspector in three years, and the first cohort of officers to join at the rank of superintendent began their training in November 2014 and you can see ample evidence of such change and evolution. The Appointment of Chief Officers of Police (Overseas Police Forces) Regulations 2014 (SI 2014/2376), which came into effect in October 2014, even make it possible for those who have been or are serving in approved overseas police forces, and in approved ranks in those forces, to be appointed as chief officers in police forces in England and Wales.

Another radical change is contained in the Policing and Crime Act 2017, whereby civilian volunteers will be delegated police powers for the first time to assist in technical investigations in areas such as cyber crime.

However, there remains much that is unique about the status of police officers, and their role is distinct from that of an employee in many regards.

4.1.2 Acting Ranks

Many police powers are restricted to officers holding particular ranks. In particular, there are occasions when the Police and Criminal Evidence Act 1984 requires officers of certain ranks to perform roles. The 1984 Act recognises that there may be occasions when officers of the appropriate rank are not readily available and so in limited circumstances allows officers of a lower rank to perform their roles.

Section 107 of the Police and Criminal Evidence Act 1984 sets out occasions when an officer of a lower rank can perform the functions that usually require a higher rank. Section 107 states:

(1) For the purpose of any provision of this Act or any other Act under which a power in respect of the investigation of offences or the treatment of persons in police custody is exercisable only by or with the authority of a police officer of at least the rank of superintendent, an officer of the rank of chief inspector shall be treated as holding the rank of superintendent if—
(a) he has been authorised by an officer holding a rank above the rank of superintendent to exercise the power or, as the case may be, to give his authority for its exercise, or
(b) he is acting during the absence of an officer holding the rank of superintendent who has authorised him, for the duration of that absence, to exercise the power or, as the case may be, to give his authority for its exercise.
(2) For the purpose of any provision of this Act or any other Act under which such a power is exercisable only by or with the authority of an officer of at least the rank of inspector, an officer of the rank of sergeant shall be treated as holding the rank of inspector if he has been authorised by an officer of at least the rank of superintendent to exercise the power or, as the case may be, to give his authority for its exercise.

The only mention of officers performing the higher rank of sergeant in the Police and Criminal Evidence Act 1984 is to be found in s. 36. Section 36 states:

(3) No officer may be appointed a custody officer unless he is of at least the rank of sergeant.

(4) An officer of any rank may perform the functions of a custody officer at a designated police station if a custody officer is not readily available to perform them.

However, in *Vince* v *Chief Constable of Dorset Police* [1993] 1 WLR 415, Steyn LJ made it clear that s. 36(4) should only be an exception and 'that it was not intended that chief constables would be entitled to arrange matters so that as a matter of routine officers below the rank of sergeant performed the functions of custody officers'.

4.1.2.1 Temporary Promotion

Regulation 6 of the Police (Promotion) Regulations 1996 (SI 1996/1685) deals with temporary promotion. Regulation 6 states:

> A member of a police force who is required to perform the duties of a higher rank may, even if there is no vacancy for that rank, be promoted temporarily to it, but, in the case of promotion to the rank of sergeant or inspector only if he is qualified for the promotion under regulation 3.
>
> A member of a police force who is successful in the written paper under Part I of the qualifying assessment, and who has commenced the period of work-based assessment under Part IIB of the qualifying assessment, shall, at the commencement of the work-based assessment, be temporarily promoted to the rank of sergeant or inspector as the case may be.

4.1.3 Employment Status and Conditions of Police Officers

Police officers are not 'employees' for *most* purposes as they are not employed under contracts as such; they are public office holders (*Fisher* v *Oldham Corporation* [1930] 2 KB 364 and also *Sheikh* v *Chief Constable of Greater Manchester Police* [1990] 1 QB 637). Consequently a number of employment rights do not apply to police officers. For example, they cannot bring claims for wrongful dismissal (these are *contractual* claims) and they are prevented by statute from claiming unfair dismissal.

However, for some purposes (e.g. sex and race discrimination) chief officers are treated *as if they are employers* of their officers. This has caused difficulties in practice and these categories have become blurred even further by recent events. So, for instance, some non-Home Office police officers *do have* a contract for service with their 'employer' (e.g. British Transport Police (*Spence* v *British Railways Board* [2001] ICR 232)).

Some of the Police Reform Act 2002 rules allow individuals who are employees in the strict sense to potentially be placed outside the full statutory protection for employees (by the Employment Rights Act 1996, s. 200) because they have the powers and privileges of constables.

For some purposes, statutes refer to the European concept of 'workers' which, being a wider concept than 'employees', often *does* apply to the police. This expression can be found in the Working Time Regulations 1998 (SI 1998/1833) which are an example of police officers being treated as though they were employees working under a contract of employment. One effect of this is that officers can rely on the annual leave year that is agreed from time to time by the force, something which has a knock-on effect on issues such as pension entitlements (*Hyman* v *Chief Constable of South Wales Police* [2003] Po LR 166). 'Workers', are generally protected under the Public Interest Disclosure Act 1998 and this is a further area of importance to police officers (**see para. 4.1.21**).

The practical importance of all this lies in the fact that the police have had to be given their own statutory framework for dealing with complaints, conduct and efficiency (**see chapter 4.2**). In April 1999, significant changes were made to the procedures governing the performance and conduct of, and complaints against, police officers. These changes have been further extended by amendments to the general employment laws and changes to the police conduct and complaints framework. The Police Regulations 2003 (SI 2003/527) cover a number of areas that are central to the performance of police duties and good governance, as well as placing restrictions on the private lives of officers. The Police (Amendment No. 3) Regulations 2012 (SI 2012/1960) amend the 2003 Regulations which specifically restrict the business interests an officer and their relatives can have.

4.1.3.1 Voluntary Severance for Police Officers

Regulation 14A of the Police Regulations 2003 allows the Secretary of State to create a voluntary early retirement scheme allowing officers to leave the service with a severance package. This has been implemented in several police forces in England and Wales.

4.1.4 Part-time Appointments

Regulation 5 of the Police Regulations 2003 allows a chief constable, after consultation with local representatives of the staff associations, to appoint an officer to perform part-time service in *any rank*. The relevant timescales involved were amended (by the Police (Amendment No. 4) Regulations 2012 (SI 2012/2712)) so that, currently, part-time officers may give notice in writing of their intention to be re-appointed as a full-time member and will be appointed within *two months* of the date on which the notice is received by the force, where there is a suitable vacancy, or when *four months* have elapsed since the day the notice was received, or from an earlier date if reasonably practicable.

4.1.5 Personal Records

The Police Regulations 2003 place a requirement on the chief constable to keep a personal record of each member of his/her force. Regulation 15(2) specifies that the record must contain:

- a personal description of the member;
- particulars of place and date of birth;
- particulars of marriage or civil partnership (if any) and children (if any);
- if applicable a record of service in any branch of the military or civil service;
- a record of service (if any) in any other police force and of transfers (if any) from one police force to another;
- a record of whether the officer passed or failed any qualifying examination at which he/she was a candidate;
- a record of service in the police force and the date on which the officer ceased to be a member of the police force with the reason thereof.

The record must also include particulars of all promotions, postings, removals, injuries received, periods of illness, commendations, rewards and sanctions other than cautions imposed under reg. 35 of the Police (Conduct) Regulations 2012 (SI 2012/2632).

4.1.6 Periods of Duty and Travelling Time

Regulation 22 of the Police Regulations 2003 allows the Home Secretary to determine the normal periods of duty of a member of a police force, the authority to specify the periods allowed for refreshment, the variable shift arrangements which may be operated by a force, the manner and timing of the publication of duty rosters and the matters to be contained therein.

'Travelling time' may be treated as duty under the same Regulation. In this context 'travelling time' means time spent by members of a police force in travelling to and from their home where they are required to perform their normal daily period of duty in more than one tour of duty, between two tours, or where they are recalled to duty between two tours of duty, in consequence of their recall. The Home Secretary may confer on the chief officer discretion to fix a limit on the travelling time which is to be treated as duty and allow discretion to fix a limit on the amount of the expenses which may be reimbursed in respect of travelling time.

4.1.7 Overtime, Public Holidays and Rest Days

Regulation 25 of the Police Regulations 2003 permits the Home Secretary to determine the circumstances and manner in which a member of a police force shall be compensated in respect of overtime incurred when officers begin work earlier than their rostered time without 'due notice' and have completed their normal daily period of duty, or remain on duty after their tour of duty ends, or are recalled between two tours of duty. For the purposes of this regulation, 'due notice' means notice given at least eight hours before the revised starting time of the rostered tour of duty in question. 'Recall' does not include a warning to be in readiness for duty if required.

The Home Secretary can confer on the chief officer discretion to fix the day on which a period commences for the purposes of the determination, to fix the period within which time off in compensation for overtime is to be granted, and the discretion to allow time in addition to that specified in the determination to be taken into account in computing any period of overtime.

Likewise, reg. 26 allows the Home Secretary to determine the circumstances and manner in which a member of a police force shall be granted leave or otherwise compensated in respect of time spent on duty on days which a member of a police force has elected to treat as public holidays, or rostered rest days.

4.1.8 The Police Federation and Trade Union Membership

Part III of the Police Act 1996 makes provision for the establishment and maintenance of police representative institutions.

Section 59 provides for the continued existence of the Police Federation and specifies that it may represent a police officer in any proceedings brought under regulations made under s. 50(3) (e.g. efficiency and conduct; **see chapters 4.2 and 4.3**) or an appeal from such proceedings.

The Secretary of State may make Regulations in relation to matters concerning the Federation (s. 60(1)), e.g. the Police Federation Regulations 1969 (SI 1969/1787), as amended.

Provision is made under s. 61 for a Police Negotiating Board to represent the interests of persons and bodies who between them maintain the police forces in Great Britain in relation to:

- hours of duty
- leave
- pay and allowances
- pensions
- clothing, equipment and accoutrements.

Section 64 of the Police Act 1996 states:

(1) Subject to the following provisions of this section, a member of a police force shall not be a member of any trade union, or of any association having for its objects, or one of its objects, to control or influence the pay, pensions or conditions of service of any police force.

> **KEYNOTE**
>
> Where a person was a member of a trade union before becoming a member of a police service, he/she may, with the consent of the chief officer of police, continue to be a member of that union during the time of his/her service (s. 64(2)).

Section 64 also states:

(5) Nothing in this section applies to membership of the Police Federations, or of any body recognised by the Secretary of State for the purposes of this section as representing members of police forces who are not members of those Federations.

4.1.9 Special Constables

The terms under which special constables may be appointed and deployed are set out in the Special Constables Regulations 1965 (SI 1965/536). The Police Act 1996 covers how officers can be deployed, as well as allowing special constables to use their constabulary powers in forces throughout England and Wales. Amendments in 2006 brought special constables into line with regular officers, and allow greater flexibility in their deployment. Police Regulations also apply to special constables.

4.1.10 Extending the Policing Family

A feature of the Police Reform Act 2002 lies in what has been called the 'extended police family'. It has been recognised that police officers can spend too much time tied up with administrative or non-core tasks which, in turn, has led to the employment of civilian support staff in specific roles, for example as detention and escort officers, and giving them relevant powers to let them carry out their jobs. This allows police officers time to concentrate on the core policing tasks that require the full range of powers and training that police officers can offer, and provide the public with additional reassurance by having more officers visible and out working in the community.

Part 4 of the Police Reform Act 2002 introduced some novel developments in the law regulating policing powers by potentially extending some of those powers to a whole range of non-police individuals. These individuals will be designated in a particular role(s) or title(s) specifically used in the legislation. They will be given a number of different titles, including the titles specifically used in the legislation (such as Investigating Officers and Detention Officers). The whole system works by allowing the relevant chief officer to confer certain powers on different groups of people by designating or accrediting them. The chief officer does not *have* to confer any powers on any such groups and he/she can decide to confer only a reduced number of powers or to place further limitations on those powers: the Act simply gives the chief officer the freedom and flexibility to do so.

4.1.11 Who Manages or Employs People with Police Powers?

A good starting point is to consider who the relevant person's employer is. Some roles created under the Act (such as Police Community Support Officers) can only be carried out by police employees; if you do not work directly for the police, you cannot have these powers or perform these roles. In other roles (Detention Officers and Escort Officers), the person does not necessarily have to be employed by the police. If the person is not employed by the force, their employer must have a contract with the relevant Police and Crime Commissioner. These people will have their powers contained in a 'designation' from the relevant chief officer.

Another group of people who can have powers conferred on them by a chief officer are not employees of either the police or a contractor. These people are 'accredited' with powers that can only come from their accreditation under a statutory Community Safety Accreditation Scheme. In order to perform *any* of the roles and exercise *any* of the powers under part 4 of the Act, an individual must be employed by somebody, because it is through the person's employer that the chief officer or the relevant constable can exercise a degree of control over those auxiliary staff who are not directly employed by the police. Therefore, if you are unemployed or self-employed, the legislation will not allow you to have these powers or to carry out any of the relevant functions.

4.1.12   The 'Chain of Control'

There is a sort of 'chain of control' linking the individual to a chief constable. The further along the chain people are, the less control a chief officer has over them and therefore the fewer powers they can be given under the Act. In the case of staff directly employed by a particular police force, they will have a contract of employment with their own force as will any member of non-sworn civilian staff. Moving down the chain you find individuals who are not police employees but are employed by an outside organisation which itself has a contract with the police. Examples would be security companies providing prisoner escort services. These employees can be given more limited powers and roles under the Act. Further still along the chain are people employed by entirely independent non-police organisations. These people could be working for any number of local businesses or organisations within a police area and the Act allows a chief officer to accredit their employees with limited policing powers.

4.1.13   Designated Police Employees

The first group of people who can be empowered under part 4 of the Police Reform Act 2002 are those employed by the police and under the direction and control of their chief officer. These police employees can be 'designated' under s. 38 by their chief officer as *one or more* of the following:

- Police Community Support Officers (PCSOs)
- Investigating Officers
- Detention Officers
- Escort Officers.

No one may be designated in these roles unless the chief officer is satisfied that they are a suitable person to carry out the designated functions, are capable of carrying out those functions effectively and have received adequate training. Adequate training is not defined but it would have to cover the exercise and performance of the relevant powers and duties to be conferred on the person (see s. 38(4)). Considerable weight was given to these safeguards and the restrictions on any use of force (**see para. 4.1.20**) during the passage of the Police Reform Bill through Parliament, and the provision of effective training was seen as an essential measure to the proper functioning of this new framework.

Because these designated staff are employees of the relevant force, the chief officer is responsible for dealing with reports of misconduct and complaints against them in the normal way. However, the Independent Police Complaints Commission (IPCC) also has jurisdiction over any such allegations or complaints.

4.1.14 Powers Conferred on Designated Police Employees

The specific powers that can be conferred by the chief officer on these designated employees depend on which designated role(s) they are given. The powers are set out in sch. 4 to the Police Reform Act 2002. Schedule 4 is itself divided into further parts, 1 to 4, with each part containing a number of statutory powers. Helpfully the parts of sch. 4 correspond to the four roles set out in the list at **para. 4.1.13** so that the respective powers under parts 1 to 4 and the relative designated employee roles look like this:

Person	Powers
PCSO	Part 1
Investigating Officer	Part 2
Detention Officer	Part 3
Escort Officer	Part 4

The powers set out in sch. 4 are numerous but they do follow a degree of common sense considering the requirements of the roles they cover. For example, it makes sense for an Investigating Officer to be given investigative powers such as powers of entry, search and seizure and powers to arrest suspects during an interview where further offences are revealed. Similarly, Detention Officers need powers to fingerprint and search prisoners. People already employed by the police in certain roles can be designated under this part of the Act (e.g. scenes of crime officers can be given powers of entry and search).

The Police and Justice Act 2006, s. 7 allows for a standard set of Community Support Officer (CSO) powers and duties. The powers will be determined by an order from the Secretary of State. The full list of powers is summarised in **appendix 4.1**.

When a chief constable first designates a person as a PCSO, he/she is required to ensure that the person has received adequate training in the exercise of the standard powers that are in force at that time (s. 38(5B) of the Police and Reform Act 2002).

4.1.15 Disorder Penalty Notices

The Criminal Justice and Police Act 2001 provides powers for fast-track resolution of some lower level criminal offences. This system relies on the issuing of penalty notices, though they are generally referred to as disorder penalty notices rather than fixed penalty notices. The power to issue penalty notices is among those that can be conferred on a designated person under sch. 4 to the Police Reform Act 2002. The heading to s. 1 in the statute refers to 'on the spot' penalties. This is misleading as no payment will be required before 21 days (under s. 5). Section 3 sets out the form of the fixed penalty notice and the amounts permissible. The Secretary of State may add to this list by statutory instrument and may specify different amounts for people of different ages (s. 3(1A)).

The offences which are subject to the fixed penalty scheme are set out in s. 1, along with the relevant penalties which are set out in the relevant statutory instrument issued under the 2001 Act. This has been amended several times since the initial Order was made in 2002 and the most up-to-date version should be consulted (a summary of the offences and relevant penalties is set out in **appendix 4.2**).

4.1.15.1 Power to Issue Penalty Notices

The power to issue such notices in respect of the s. 1 offences is set out at s. 2. Basically, s. 2 allows a police officer in uniform (if away from a police station) or one that has been authorised by his/her chief officer (if at a police station) to give a person aged 10 or over a penalty notice if he/she has reason to believe that the person has committed a s. 1 offence. A person given a penalty notice will have the option of requesting to be tried in the normal way or of paying the penalty within the suspended enforcement period. The right to request trial is intended as a safeguard of the defendant's right to a fair trial under Article 6 of the European Convention on Human Rights. If the person fails to pay within that period, a sum of one and a half times the amount of the penalty may be enforced against him/her as a fine. After the suspended enforcement period ends, proceedings may be brought against the person in the normal way for the relevant offence(s). Where a penalty notice is given to a person under the age of 16, the relevant chief officer of police must notify such parent or guardian as he/she thinks fit (Penalties for Disorderly Behaviour (Amendment of Minimum Age) Order 2004 (SI 2004/3166)). Any such notification must be in writing and must include a copy of the penalty notice and may be served by giving it to the parent or guardian personally or sending it to the parent or guardian at his/her usual or last-known address by first-class post before the end of the period of 28 days beginning with the date on which the penalty notice was given (see Article 3 of the 2004 Order).

If it transpires that a notification has been sent to a person who is not a parent or guardian of the person receiving the penalty notice (or that it would have been more appropriately sent to someone else), the chief officer can cancel the original notification and send out a fresh one (Article 4).

Where a parent or guardian of a young penalty recipient is notified in this way, then (unless the notification is cancelled) he/she is liable to pay the penalty under the original notice (Article 5). Full details surrounding the proposed operation of the whole scheme are available in the form of guidance from the Home Office under s. 6.

4.1.16 Employees of Contracted-out Businesses

Although their employee status is the source of control over these employees' activities and performance, the first thing to note is that employees of contracted-out businesses are *not* employed by the police force. Where a police force has entered into a contract for the provision of services relating to the detention or escorting of people in custody, s. 39 of the Police Reform Act 2002 allows the chief officer to designate employees *of the contractor* as either Detention Officers or Escort Officers or both. As such these people may be given some or all of the powers of those roles set out in parts 3 and 4 of sch. 4 to the Act (**see appendix 4.1**). These contracted-out personnel *cannot* be given the powers of PCSOs and Investigating Officers as they are employees of the contractor, *not* police employees.

Before designating anyone under this part of the Act, a chief officer must be satisfied that the person:

- is a suitable person to carry out the functions for which he/she is to be designated;
- is capable of effectively carrying out those functions; and
- has received adequate training in the carrying out of those functions and in the exercise of those powers and duties to be conferred on him/her (s. 39(4)).

As with the police employees given powers under parts 1–4 of sch. 4, significant emphasis was placed on these safeguards in securing the passage of the Police Reform Bill through Parliament, in particular, the provision of effective training. Further weight was given to the reassurances provided by the restrictions on the use of force (**see para. 4.1.20**).

If an employee stops being an employee of the contractor, or the contract between the employer and the police comes to an end, any designation ceases to have effect (s. 39(13)). Section 39 also allows for regulations to be made regarding the handling of complaints and misconduct issues arising out of the functions of designated employees.

4.1.17 Accredited Employees

Further still along the chain of control linking the force with the employee are those people who are simply employed by local businesses and employers in the relevant police area. Those businesses do not have to have an existing contract with the force or the Police and Crime Commissioner and their employees only gain their accreditation from powers conferred under a Community Safety Accreditation Scheme (CSAS).

A CSAS is a scheme set up and maintained by a chief officer for the purposes of:

- contributing to community safety and security;
- combating crime and disorder, public nuisance and other forms of anti-social behaviour.

4.1.18 Community Safety Accreditation Schemes

Before establishing a CSAS, a chief officer must consult with the Police and Crime Commissioner maintaining that force and every local authority any part of whose area lies within his/her force (s. 40(4)). In the case of the Metropolitan Police the commissioner must consult the Deputy Mayor of London for Policing and Crime. Any CSAS must also appear in the policing plan of any force. A CSAS must contain provisions for making arrangements with local employers carrying on business (including those carrying out statutory functions) for the supervision of any of their employees who become accredited under the scheme (s. 40(8)). In addition, it is the duty of the chief officer to ensure that the employers of the persons on whom powers are conferred have established and maintain satisfactory arrangements for handling complaints relating to the carrying out of functions under the scheme (s. 40(9)). This is all the more important as the accredited employees will have no formal individual link with the force, either directly (as in the case of designated police employees under parts 1 to 4 of sch. 4) or indirectly (as with employees of contracted-out businesses whose employees are designated under parts 3 and 4 of the schedule).

Under a CSAS, s. 41 of the Police Reform Act 2002 allows a chief officer to accredit people with certain policing powers. These powers are set out in sch. 5 to the Act and in **appendix 4.1**.

4.1.19 General Considerations for Designated or Accredited Employees

Designated or accredited employees empowered under the Police Reform Act 2002 exercising any powers granted thereunder in relation to any person must produce their authority to that person if requested to do so (s. 42(1)). Their powers are only exercisable if the employee is wearing the relevant uniform as determined or approved by the chief officer and identified or described in the designation/accreditation (s. 42(2)). Any designation or accreditation will specify the extent, nature and duration of the powers conferred by it and also any uniform that the employee is required to wear. In the case of an accredited employee (i.e. acting under the authority of sch. 5 of the Act), he/she must also be wearing an appropriate badge as specified by the Secretary of State in the manner or place specified (s. 42(2)). Given the nature of some investigative functions carried out by Investigating Officers, a police officer of or above the rank of inspector may direct an Investigating Officer not to wear a uniform for the purposes of a particular operation (s. 42(2A)). If such a direction is given, s. 42(2) will not apply in relation to *that* Investigating Officer for the purposes of *that* operation. The officer giving this direction not to wear uniform must be from the same force as the chief officer who appointed the Investigating Officer under s. 38.

A chief officer of police may modify or withdraw an employee's designation or accreditation *at any time* simply by giving the employee notice (s. 42(3)). This power of revocation or amendment is absolute and there is no requirement for any misconduct or poor performance on the part of the employee. If a designation or accreditation is modified or withdrawn, the chief officer must send a copy of the notice to the relevant employer (see s. 42(5) and (6)). The Secretary of State can add to the relevant police powers that are extended to designated or accredited employees in a much simpler and quicker format in some circumstances and reference should be made to the most up-to-date version of the various schedules.

Any liability for civil wrongs (torts) arising out of conduct in the course of an employee's designation or accreditation will be apportioned jointly between the police force, the employer and the individual (see s. 42).

4.1.20 Use of Force

There are two main sources of a designated employee's power to use reasonable force. The first source is the specific power granted under sch. 4 to the Police Reform Act 2002 as discussed at **para. 4.1.14**. The second source is to be found in s. 38(8) of the Act. This provides that if a designated employee has a power which, if exercised by a constable, would have a further power to use reasonable force then the designated employee will also have the same entitlement to use reasonable force. For instance, where a constable is exercising powers under the Police and Criminal Evidence Act 1984 where the consent of another person other than a police officer is not needed (e.g. most powers of arrest, search and seizure), s. 117 gives the officer a power to use reasonable force if necessary. If a designated Investigating Officer uses a power to enter premises following an arrest (sch. 4, para. 18), he/she will be entitled to use reasonable force if necessary because a constable using the same power to enter and search would also have the power to use reasonable force. However, given the sensitivities around the use of force by the police and other agents of the State, there are further restrictions on the use of force by a designated employee. If, as in the above example, the designated employee uses force to enter premises, that power can *only* be used:

- in the company *and* under the supervision of a constable, or
- for the purpose of saving life or limb or preventing serious damage to property. (s. 38(9))

It is unlikely that the requirements of s. 38(9) would be satisfied by a merely passive physical presence by a constable at a time when the power is exercised and the legislation envisages some form of active and effective supervision by the constable. Similarly, any designated employee using these powers will need to be able to show how the various criteria were met by the particular circumstances at the time.

The general rules and restrictions on the use of force will apply in these cases (**see para. 4.4.3.3**) and any use of force by a designated employee will come under close scrutiny, particularly where that person is a Detention Officer or Escort Officer employed by a contracted-out business under s. 39.

4.1.21 The Public Interest Disclosure Act 1998 and 'Whistle Blowing'

The Public Interest Disclosure Act 1998 was introduced to help create an atmosphere where workers both feel and *are* able to report certain cases of wrongdoing at work, primarily to their employers, but to outside bodies or individuals if appropriate. Often described as 'whistle blowing', the reporting of criminal, unlawful, dangerous or damaging practices and situations has been protected by the 1998 Act for most workers for several years provided the Act's conditions are complied with. The legislation distinguishes between internal disclosures to the relevant employer and disclosures made to external bodies or individuals including the police with the emphasis firmly on *internal* disclosure. It would clearly not be appropriate on all occasions when an employee believes something is amiss at work for that to be reported to an outside body, for instance by selling the story to the press or passing the information straight to an MP. The Act therefore differentiates between different types of situation which may need to be reported. These distinctions are less important where the employer *is* the police but it is still necessary to consider the relevant statutory procedure. Many employers have published detailed reporting procedures for making disclosure. In some areas of employment, the Secretary of State has made regulations prescribing those people and bodies to whom some disclosures can be made where appropriate. Examples are the IPCC and HM Revenue and Customs (under the Public Interest Disclosure (Prescribed Persons) Order 2014 (SI 2014/2418)).

The Act works by inserting various provisions into the Employment Rights Act 1996 resulting in a fairly detailed piece of legislation which is beyond the scope of this Manual.

4.1.22 Protected Disclosures

Section 43B of the Employment Rights Act 1996 refers to 'protected disclosures'. These are generally disclosures made in accordance with the Act of information which, in the reasonable belief of the maker, tends to show *one or more* of the following:

- a criminal offence has been committed, is being committed or is likely to be committed;
- a person has failed, is failing or is likely to fail to comply with any legal obligation to which he/she is subject;
- a miscarriage of justice has occurred, is occurring or is likely to occur;
- the health or safety of any individual has been, is being or is likely to be endangered;
- the environment has been, is being or is likely to be damaged;
- information tending to show any matter falling within any one of the preceding paragraphs has been, is being or is likely to be deliberately concealed.

The likelihood of some of the issues covered above arising is possibly greater in a policing or criminal justice environment than elsewhere.

It is immaterial that the relevant failure reported occurs or would occur outside the United Kingdom (s. 43B(2)). As discussed at **para. 4.1.21**, the disclosure should generally be made to the employer or other responsible or prescribed person. However, if:

- the employee reasonably believes that he/she will be subjected to a detriment by the employer if the disclosure is made, or
- there is no relevant or prescribed person and the employee reasonably believes that it is likely that evidence relating to the failure will be concealed or destroyed if a disclosure is made, or
- the employee has previously made a disclosure of substantially the same information to the employer or prescribed person

then he/she may make a protected disclosure to someone else.

But even if the above conditions are met, the employee must make any disclosure in good faith, must not be acting for personal gain and must reasonably believe that the information (and any allegation contained in it) is substantially true and it must be reasonable in all the circumstances of the case for him/her to make the disclosure (s. 43G). In determining whether it was reasonable to make the disclosure in all the circumstances here, regard will be had in particular to the identity of the person receiving it, the seriousness of the reported failure, any breach of confidentiality by the employee and the circumstances of any earlier disclosure.

If the relevant failure is of an exceptionally serious nature and the employee reasonably believes that the information (and any allegation contained in it) is substantially true, he/she may make a protected disclosure, in good faith and not for personal gain, to an external person provided it is reasonable in all the circumstances to do so (s. 43H). Again, all the circumstances, and particularly the identity of the external party, will be relevant in determining whether it was reasonable to make the disclosure. It is important to note that, if the making of the disclosure would itself amount to an offence, the disclosure *will not* be protected. An example of where this might be the case is under the Regulation of Investigatory Powers Act 2000, s. 19 (disclosing information as to the existence or non-existence of an interception warrant (**see para. 4.18.4**)).

For the purposes of part IVA (Protected Disclosures), a police officer is to be treated as an employee (s. 43KA).

As well as making the workplace safer and more open to scrutiny, the 1996 Act creates a number of key rights for individuals. For instance, it makes the dismissal of an employee automatically unfair if the reason (or principal reason if there is more than one) for the dismissal is that the employee made a protected disclosure (s. 103A). While the Code of Conduct under the Police (Conduct) Regulations 2012 has always placed officers under a duty to report wrongdoing by fellow officers, there has not been any form of statutory protection for those who do so. Additionally, an employee also has the right under the Act not to be subjected to any other detriment by his/her employer (e.g. being disciplined, denied perks or promotion) on the grounds that he/she has made a protected disclosure (s. 47B). Employees can bring a complaint to the employment tribunal in respect of these matters and the usual statutory ceiling on the amount of the compensatory award that the tribunal can make is removed.

Complaints and Misconduct

4.2.1 Introduction

Police complaints and misconduct has always been a complex area of police law and procedure.

One of the key points to emerge from the 2005 Taylor Review of police officer disciplinary arrangements was the need to shift the emphasis and culture in police misconduct matters towards an environment focused on development and improvement as opposed to one focused on blame and punishment. Additionally, the report stressed the importance of carrying out a full assessment of the alleged conduct at an early stage with a view to then implementing a proportionate and non-bureaucratic response.

Misconduct is defined as a breach of the Standards of Professional Behaviour (**see para. 4.2.2**); gross misconduct means a breach of the Standards of Professional Behaviour so serious that dismissal would be justified. Unsatisfactory performance or unsatisfactory attendance mean an inability or failure of a police officer to perform the duties of the role or rank he/she is currently undertaking to a satisfactory standard or level.

A series of statutory instruments provides the performance and misconduct framework:

- The Police (Performance) Regulations 2012 (SI 2012/2631) set out the procedures for dealing with cases of unsatisfactory performance or attendance of police officers.
- The Police (Conduct) Regulations 2012 (SI 2012/2632) set out the procedures for dealing with cases of misconduct or gross misconduct. The Conduct Regulations contain the 'Standards of Professional Behaviour' that police officers are expected to maintain.
- The Police (Complaints and Misconduct) Regulations 2012 (SI 2012/1204) provide the link between the misconduct procedures for police officers of all ranks and special constables, and the police complaints system governed by the provisions in sch. 3 to the Police Reform Act 2002.
- The Police Appeals Tribunals Rules 2012 (SI 2012/2630) set out the procedures for an appeal to a police appeals tribunal and the grounds on which a police officer or special constable can appeal against a finding and/or a particular outcome from the Conduct and Performance Regulations.

The Home Office issued Home Office Circular 23/2012, *Changes to the police complaints system and procedures for dealing with police officer misconduct and unsatisfactory performance*, which came into effect on 16 November 2012.

The Police (Complaints and Conduct) Regulations 2013 (SI 2013/281) have strengthened the role and powers of the Independent Police Complaints Commission (IPCC), particularly with regard to compelling officers to attend interviews, including those who have witnessed an event, not just officers whose conduct is under investigation.

On 12 January 2015 new regulations which prevent police officers from resigning or retiring if they are subject to an allegation that could lead to dismissal came into force.

4.2.2 The Standards of Professional Behaviour

The Standards of Professional Behaviour provide the yardstick by which the conduct of police officers is judged. They apply to police officers of all ranks, special constables, and to those subject to suspension. They are not intended to describe every situation but rather to set a framework which enables everybody to know what type of conduct by a police officer is acceptable and what is unacceptable. The standards are:

- **Honesty and Integrity**: Police officers are honest, act with integrity and do not compromise or abuse their position.
- **Authority, Respect and Courtesy**: Police officers act with self-control and tolerance, treating members of the public and colleagues with respect and courtesy. Police officers do not abuse their powers or authority and respect the rights of all individuals.
- **Equality and Diversity**: Police officers act with fairness and impartiality. They do not discriminate unlawfully or unfairly.
- **Use of Force**: Police officers only use force to the extent that it is necessary, proportionate and reasonable in all the circumstances.
- **Orders and Instructions**: Police officers only give and carry out lawful orders and instructions. Police officers abide by police regulations, force policies and lawful orders.
- **Duties and Responsibilities**: Police officers are diligent in the exercise of their duties and responsibilities.
- **Confidentiality**: Police officers treat information with respect and access or disclose it only in the proper course of police duties.
- **Fitness for Duty**: Police officers when on duty or presenting themselves for duty are fit to carry out their duties and responsibilities.
- **Discreditable Conduct**: Police officers behave in a manner which does not discredit the police service or undermine public confidence, whether on or off duty. Police officers report any action taken against them for a criminal offence, conditions imposed by a court or the receipt of any penalty notice.
- **Challenging and Reporting Improper Conduct**: Police officers report, challenge or take action against the conduct of colleagues which has fallen below the standards of professional behaviour.

4.2.3 The Role of the Police Friend

At all stages of the misconduct or performance proceedings (including any interview during an investigation into misconduct), police officers have the right to consult with and be accompanied by a police friend.

The police friend can be a police officer, a police staff member, or a person nominated by the police officer's staff association. A person asked to be a police friend is entitled to refuse, and cannot be appointed to act if he/she had any involvement in that particular case.

The police friend can:

- advise the police officer concerned throughout the proceedings under the Police (Conduct) Regulations 2012 or Police (Performance) Regulations 2012;
- unless the police officer concerned has the right to be legally represented and chooses to be so represented, represent the police officer concerned at the misconduct proceedings, performance proceedings, appeal meeting, a special case hearing or at a police appeals tribunal;
- make representations to the 'appropriate authority' concerning any aspect of the proceedings under the Conduct or Performance Regulations;
- accompany the police officer concerned to any interview, meeting or hearing which forms part of any proceedings under the Conduct or Performance Regulations.

The 'appropriate authority' under the Performance Regulations is the chief officer of police, who may delegate any of his/her functions to a police officer of at least the rank of chief inspector or a police staff member who is of at least a similar level of seniority to a chief inspector.

A police friend who has agreed to accompany a police officer is entitled to take a reasonable amount of duty time to fulfil those responsibilities and is considered to be on duty when attending interviews, meetings or hearings.

Subject to any timescales set out in the Conduct or Performance Regulations, at any stage of a case, up to and including a misconduct meeting or hearing or an unsatisfactory performance meeting, the police officer concerned or his/her police friend may submit that there are insufficient grounds upon which to base the case and/or that the correct procedures have not been followed, clearly setting out the reasons and submitting any supporting evidence. It will be for the person responsible for the relevant stage of the case to consider any such submission and determine how best to respond to it, bearing in mind the need to ensure fairness to the police officer concerned.

At a misconduct meeting, hearing or special case hearing under the Conduct Regulations or the Performance Regulations where the police friend attends, he/she may:

(a) put the police officer concerned's case;
(b) sum up that case;
(c) respond on the police officer concerned's behalf to any view expressed at the meeting;
(d) make representations concerning any aspect of the proceedings;
(e) confer with the police officer concerned;
(f) in a misconduct meeting or hearing, ask questions of any witness, subject to the discretion of the person(s) conducting that hearing.

A police officer is entitled to be legally represented at a misconduct hearing or special case hearing (in cases that fall to be dealt with under the Conduct Regulations) or a third stage performance meeting (for dealing with an issue of gross incompetence under the Performance Regulations). Where he/she decides to be so represented, the police friend can also attend and may consult with the police officer concerned, but will not carry out functions (a)–(d) and (f) described above.

Where a police officer is arrested or interviewed in connection with a criminal offence committed while off duty that has no connection with his/her role as a serving police officer, then the police friend has no right to attend the criminal interview.

4.2.4 Death or Serious Injury Matters

A death or serious injury (DSI) matter is defined in s. 12 of the Police Reform Act 2002. Where there is an investigation into a DSI case and there is no complaint or indication of any conduct matter, the investigation will focus on the circumstances of the incident. However, where during the course of the investigation into the DSI matter there is an indication that a person serving with the police may have committed a criminal offence or behaved in a manner that would justify the bringing of disciplinary proceedings, the DSI matter will be reclassified as a recordable conduct matter (or complaint if appropriate) and dealt with accordingly.

4.2.5 Misconduct Procedures

The procedures are intended to provide a fair, open and proportionate method of dealing with alleged misconduct and to encourage a culture of learning and development.

Where the conduct is linked to a complaint, recordable conduct matter or DSI matter the appropriate authority is required to follow the provisions in the Police Reform Act 2002, the accompanying Police (Complaints and Misconduct) Regulations 2012 and the IPCC statutory guidance which set out how complaints by members of the public are to be dealt with.

Probationer constables are not subject to the procedures for dealing with unsatisfactory performance, since there are separately established procedures for dealing with the performance of student police officers. However, they are subject to the misconduct procedures. The chief officer has discretion whether to use the misconduct procedures or the procedures set out at reg. 13 of the Police Regulations 2003 (Discharge of Probationer) as the most appropriate means of dealing with a misconduct matter. In exercising this discretion regard should be had to whether the officer admits the conduct or not. Where the misconduct in question is not admitted then in most, if not all, cases the matter will fall to be determined under the misconduct procedures. If the reg. 13 procedure is used, the student police officer should be given a fair hearing (i.e. an opportunity to comment and present mitigation) under that procedure.

4.2.5.1 Suspension or Change of Duty

Suspension is not a formal misconduct outcome and does not suggest any prejudgement. The period of suspension should be as short as possible and any investigation into the conduct of a suspended police officer should be made a priority. The decision to suspend a police officer will only be taken where there is an allegation of misconduct/gross misconduct and:

- an effective investigation may be prejudiced unless the police officer is suspended; or
- the public interest, having regard to the nature of the allegation and any other relevant considerations, requires that the police officer should be suspended; and
- a temporary move to a new location or role has been considered but is not appropriate in the circumstances.

A temporary move to a new location or role must always be considered first as an alternative to suspension. While suspended, a police officer ceases to hold the office of constable and, in the case of a member of a police force, ceases to be a member of a police force, save for the purposes of the misconduct proceedings.

The police officer or his/her police friend may make representations against the initial decision to suspend (within seven working days beginning with the first working day after being suspended) and at any time during the course of the suspension if he/she believes the circumstances have changed and that the suspension is no longer appropriate.

The police officer should be told exactly why he/she is being suspended or being moved to other duties and this should be confirmed in writing. If suspension is on public interest grounds, it should be clearly explained, so far as possible, what those grounds are. The use of suspension must be reviewed at least every four weeks, and sooner where facts have become known which suggest that suspension is no longer appropriate. In cases where the suspension has been reviewed and a decision has been made to continue that suspension, the police officer must be informed in writing of the reasons why. Suspension must be authorised by a senior officer although the decision can be communicated to the police officer by an appropriate manager.

In cases where the IPCC is supervising, managing or independently investigating a matter, the appropriate authority will consult with the IPCC before making a decision whether to suspend or not. It is the appropriate authority's decision whether to suspend a police officer or not. The appropriate authority must also consult the IPCC before making the decision to allow a police officer to resume his/her duties following suspension (unless the suspension ends because there will be no misconduct or special case proceedings or because these have concluded) in cases where the IPCC is supervising, managing or independently investigating a case involving that police officer.

The Standards of Professional Behaviour continue to apply to police officers who are suspended from duty. The appropriate authority can impose such conditions or restrictions on the police officer concerned as are reasonable in the circumstances, e.g. restricting access to police premises or police social functions.

4.2.5.2 Assessment of Misconduct

The initial assessment when an allegation of misconduct is made is conducted by the appropriate authority, and the purpose of the initial assessment is to:

- ensure a timely response to an allegation or an issue relating to conduct;
- identify the police officer subject to the allegation and to eliminate those not involved;
- ensure that the most appropriate procedures are used.

If it is not possible to make an immediate assessment, a process of fact finding should be conducted but only to the extent that it is necessary to determine which procedure should be used. It is perfectly acceptable to ask questions to seek to establish which police officers may have been involved in a particular incident and therefore to eliminate those police officers who are not involved.

Even if the person making the assessment has decided that the matter is not potentially one of misconduct he/she should consider whether there are any developmental or organisational issues which may need to be addressed by the individual (e.g. through management action) or the organisation.

Where an allegation is made which indicates that the conduct of a police officer did not meet the standards set out in the Standards of Professional Behaviour, the appropriate authority must decide whether, if proven or admitted, the allegation would amount to misconduct or gross misconduct. The assessment will also determine whether, if the matter was referred to misconduct proceedings, those proceedings would be likely to be a misconduct meeting (for cases of misconduct) or a misconduct hearing (for cases of gross misconduct or if the police officer concerned has a live final written warning at the time of the assessment and there is a further allegation of misconduct).

If new evidence emerges, a fresh assessment can be made. The matter may be moved up to a level of gross misconduct or down to a level of misconduct.

Unless there are good reasons to take no action, there are two ways by which line managers can deal with matters which have been assessed as potential misconduct: management action or disciplinary. The purpose of management action is to deal with misconduct in a timely, proportionate and effective way that will: command the confidence of staff, police officers, the police service and the public; identify any underlying causes or welfare considerations; improve conduct; and prevent a similar situation arising in the future.

Where an appropriate manager decides at the severity assessment that management action is the most appropriate and proportionate way to deal with an issue of misconduct, there will be no requirement to conduct a formal investigation and therefore no requirement to give a written notice to the police officer concerned in accordance with the provisions in the Conduct Regulations. Where at a later stage, either following the investigation or on withdrawal of the case (under reg. 20 of the Conduct Regulations or reg. 7 of the Police (Complaints and Misconduct) Regulations 2012), an appropriate manager decides to take management action, written notice of this will be given to the police officer as soon as possible. Management action is not to be confused with management advice. Management advice is a disciplinary outcome that can only be imposed following a misconduct meeting or hearing.

Where it is felt that management action is not appropriate to deal with the alleged breach of the Standards of Professional Behaviour an investigation into the alleged misconduct may be necessary. Where, in cases of potential misconduct, management action is not considered appropriate, there will be an investigation under the Conduct Regulations and in cases where the allegation amounts to one of gross misconduct, the matter will always be investigated.

4.2.5.3 Written Notification to Officer

Written notification will be given to the police officer concerned by the investigator appointed to investigate the case, advising the officer that his/her conduct is under investigation—either under reg. 15 of the Conduct Regulations or under reg. 16 of the Complaint Regulations in the case of complaints subject to special requirements (during an investigation into a complaint if it appears to the person investigating that there is an indication that a person to whose conduct the investigation relates may have committed a criminal offence, or behaved in a manner which would justify the bringing of disciplinary proceedings, the person investigating must certify the investigation as one subject to special requirements (para. 19A of sch. 3 to the Police Reform Act 2002)).

The written notice will:

- inform the police officer that there is to be an investigation of his/her potential breach of the Standards of Professional Behaviour and inform the police officer of the name of the investigator who will investigate the matter;
- describe the conduct that is the subject of the investigation and how that conduct is alleged to have fallen below the Standards of Professional Behaviour;
- inform the police officer concerned of the appropriate authority's (or investigator's in a matter dealt with under the 2002 Act) assessment of whether the conduct alleged, if proved, would amount to misconduct or gross misconduct;
- inform the police officer of whether, if the case were to be referred to misconduct proceedings, those would be likely to be a misconduct meeting or misconduct hearing;
- inform the police officer that if the likely form of any misconduct proceedings changes, the police officer will be notified of this together with the reasons for that change;
- inform the police officer of his/her right to seek advice from his/her staff association or any other body, and whom the police officer may choose to act as his/her police friend;
- inform the police officer that if his/her case is referred to a misconduct hearing or special case hearing, he/she has the right to be legally represented by a relevant lawyer. If the police officer elects not to be so represented he/she may be represented by a police friend. The notice will also make clear that if he/she elects not to be legally represented he/she may be dismissed or receive any other disciplinary outcome without being so represented;
- inform the police officer that he/she may provide, within ten working days of receipt of the notice (unless this period is extended by the investigator), a written or oral statement relating to any matter under investigation and he/she (or his/her police friend) may provide any relevant documents to the investigator within this time;
- inform the police officer that while he/she does not have to say anything, it may harm his/her case if he/she does not mention when interviewed or when providing any information within the relevant time limits something which he/she later relies on in any misconduct proceedings or special case hearing or at an appeal meeting or police appeals tribunal.

The written notification may be provided to a manager (including by email) to give to the police officer concerned or, where appropriate and with the agreement of the police friend, the notice may be given to the police friend to give to the police officer concerned. In both cases the notice must be given to the police officer in person. Alternatively, the notice can be posted by recorded delivery to his/her last known address. The responsibility for ensuring that the notice is served rests with the investigator (in cases dealt with under the 2002 Act) or the appropriate authority. In both cases it is the investigator who must cause the officer concerned to be given the written notice. Therefore while the appropriate authority may do it, the responsibility for ensuring that the notice is served rests with the investigator.

Where the IPCC is conducting an independent or managed investigation the responsibility for ensuring that the police officer is provided with the written notification (as soon as practicable) rests with the investigator appointed or designated to conduct that investigation.

4.2.5.4 Investigation

The purpose of an investigation is to:

- gather evidence to establish the facts and circumstances of the alleged misconduct;
- assist the appropriate authority to establish on the balance of probabilities, based on the evidence and taking into account all of the circumstances, whether there is a case to answer in respect of either misconduct or gross misconduct or that there is no case to answer;
- identify any learning opportunities for the individual or the organisation.

In cases which are not being managed or dealt with by the IPCC, the appropriate authority should ensure that a proportionate and balanced investigation is carried out as soon as possible after any alleged misconduct comes to the appropriate authority's attention and that the investigation is carried out as quickly as possible allowing for the complexity of the case. It is therefore crucial that any investigation is kept proportionate to ensure that an overly lengthy investigation does not lead to grounds for challenge. Where the investigation identifies that the issue is one of performance rather than misconduct, the police officer should be informed as soon as possible that the matter is now being treated as a performance issue.

The investigator is required to notify the police officer of the progress of the investigation at least every four weeks from the start of the investigation.

The investigator (under the Conduct Regulations or the 2002 Act) has a duty to consider the suggestions submitted to him/her. The investigator should consider and document reasons for following or not following any submissions made by the police officer or his/her police friend with a view to ensuring that the investigation is as fair as possible. The suggestions may involve a further suggested line of investigation or further examination of a particular witness. The purpose is to enable a fair and balanced investigation report to be prepared and, where appropriate, made available for consideration at a misconduct meeting/hearing and to negate the need (except where necessary) for witnesses to attend a meeting/hearing.

4.2.5.5 Interviews during Investigation

It will not always be necessary to conduct a formal interview with the police officer subject to the investigation. In some cases, particularly involving low level misconduct cases, it may be more appropriate, proportionate and timely to request a written account from the police officer. The police officer must attend the interview when required to do so and it may be a further misconduct matter to fail to attend.

If the police officer concerned or his/her police friend is not available at the date or time specified by the investigator, the police officer may propose an alternative time. Provided that the alternative time is reasonable and falls within a period of five working days beginning with the first working day after that proposed by the investigator the interview must be postponed to that time.

Where a police officer is on certificated sick leave, the investigator should seek to establish when the police officer will be fit for interview. It may be that the police officer is not fit for ordinary police duty but is perfectly capable of being interviewed. Alternatively the police officer concerned may be invited to provide a written response to the allegations within a specified period and may be sent the questions that the investigator wishes to be answered.

Where a police officer is alleged to have committed a criminal offence a normal criminal investigation will take place, with the police officer being cautioned in accordance with the

PACE Code of Practice. Where the matter to be investigated involves both criminal and misconduct allegations, it should be made clear to the police officer concerned at the start of the interview whether he/she is being interviewed in respect of the criminal or misconduct allegations. This may be achieved by conducting two separate interviews, although this does not prevent the responses given in respect of the criminal interview being used in the misconduct investigation and therefore a separate misconduct interview may not be required.

Care should be taken when conducting a misconduct interview where the police officer is also the subject of a criminal investigation in respect of the same behaviour, as anything said by the police officer concerned in the misconduct interview when not under caution and used in the criminal investigation could be subject to an inadmissibility ruling by the court at any subsequent trial. At the beginning of a misconduct interview or when asking a police officer to provide a written response to an allegation, the police officer shall be reminded of the warning contained in reg. 15(1)(h) of the Conduct Regulations (or reg. 16(1)(h) of the Complaint Regulations for cases dealt with under the 2002 Act).

Prior to an interview with a police officer who is the subject of a misconduct investigation, the investigator must ensure that the police officer is provided with sufficient information and time to prepare for the interview. The information provided should always include full details of the allegations made against the police officer, including the relevant dates and places of the alleged misconduct if known. The investigator should consider whether there are good reasons for withholding certain evidence obtained prior to the interview and if there are no such reasons the police officer should normally be provided with all the relevant evidence obtained. The police officer will then have the opportunity to provide his/her version of the events together with any supporting evidence he/she may wish to provide. The police officer will be reminded that failure to provide any account or response to any questions at this stage of the investigation may lead to an adverse inference being drawn at a later stage.

Interviews do not have to be electronically recorded but if they are the person being interviewed shall be given a copy upon request. If the interview is not electronically recorded a written record or summary of the discussion must be given to the person being interviewed. The police officer concerned should be given the opportunity to check and sign that he/she agrees with the summary as an accurate record of what was said and should sign and return a copy to the investigator. Where a police officer refuses or fails to exercise his/her right to agree and sign a copy this will be noted by the investigator. The police officer may make a note of the changes he/she wants to make to the record and a copy of this will be given to the persons conducting the hearing/meeting along with the investigator's account of the record.

Other than for a joint criminal/misconduct investigation interview it will not be necessary for criminal-style witness statements to be taken. In misconduct investigations an agreed and signed written record of the information supplied will be sufficient.

4.2.5.6 Investigation Report and Supporting Documents

At the conclusion of the investigation the investigator must as soon as practicable submit his/her report of the investigation setting out an accurate summary of the evidence that has been gathered. It will also include a recommendation whether in the opinion of the investigator there is a case to answer in respect of misconduct or gross misconduct or whether there is no case to answer.

The appropriate authority shall make a decision based on the report and determine whether there is a case to answer in respect of misconduct or gross misconduct or that there is no case of misconduct to answer (reg. 19 of the Conduct Regulations). If it is decided that there is no case of misconduct to answer, management action may still be appropriate. In matters involving a complaint, where the complaint was subject to a local or supervised investigation under the 2002 Act, the decision of the appropriate authority may be subject to an appeal by the complainant to the IPCC. Similarly in cases where an investigation into a complaint, recordable conduct matter or DSI matter has been conducted under para. 18 (managed) or 19 (independent) of sch. 3 to the 2002 Act, the IPCC has the power to make recommendations and give directions as to whether there is a case to answer. If no further action is to be taken then it is good practice that the investigation report or part of the investigation report that is relevant to the police officer should be given, subject to the harm test, to the police officer on request.

4.2.5.7 Action Prior to Misconduct Meetings/Hearings

In cases where it is decided that there is a misconduct case to answer, the appropriate authority will need to determine whether the matter can be dealt with by means of immediate management action without the need to refer the case to a misconduct meeting. This will be particularly appropriate in cases where the police officer concerned has accepted that his/her conduct fell below the standards expected of a police officer and demonstrates a commitment to improve his/her conduct in the future and to learn from that particular case. In addition the appropriate authority will need to be satisfied that this is the case and that management action is an adequate and sufficient outcome having regard to all the circumstances of the case.

Where the appropriate authority consider that there is a case to answer in respect of misconduct and that management action would not be appropriate or sufficient (for example because the police officer has a live superintendent's warning issued under the previous procedures or the misconduct is serious enough to justify a written warning being given), a misconduct meeting/hearing should be arranged and the police officer shall, subject to the harm test, be given a copy of the investigation report (or the part of the report which is relevant to him/her), any other relevant documents gathered during the course of the investigation and a copy of his/her statement to the investigator.

In determining which documents are relevant, the test to be applied will be that under the Criminal Procedure and Investigations Act 1996, namely whether any document or other material undermines the case against the police officer concerned or would assist the police officer's case.

Where a determination has been made that the conduct amounts to gross misconduct, the case shall be referred to a misconduct hearing (or special case hearing if appropriate). The appropriate authority will also provide the police officer with a notice containing the matters discussed at reg. 21(1)(a) of the Conduct Regulations, including the particulars of the behaviour that is alleged to have fallen below the standards in the Standards of Professional Behaviour.

It is important to note that in cases where the misconduct to be considered was identified as a direct result of a complaint, any decision by the appropriate authority to hold or not to hold a particular misconduct proceeding may be subject to an appeal by the complainant. The appropriate authority, having made its decision on the outcome of the investigation into the complaint and whether there is a case to answer in respect of misconduct or gross misconduct, will notify the complainant of its determination and inform the complainant of his/her right of appeal. The police officer subject of the investigation into his/her conduct should be informed of the determination of the appropriate authority but also informed that the appropriate authority's decision could be subject to an appeal by the complainant to the IPCC. The appropriate authority should then wait until either a 28 plus 2 days period that the complainant may appeal in has elapsed or an appeal has been received and decided by the IPCC before serving the written notice described above confirming how the proceedings are to be dealt with. There is no requirement to wait until the period the complainant has in which to appeal has elapsed in cases where the appropriate authority has determined that the case should be dealt with at a misconduct hearing or a special case hearing.

No final decision can be taken by the appropriate authority in the case of a recordable conduct matter where the IPCC is considering whether to recommend or direct that an appropriate authority take particular misconduct proceedings unless the appropriate authority intends to refer the matter to a misconduct hearing or special case hearing.

Within 14 working days (unless this period is extended by the person conducting the misconduct meeting/hearing for exceptional circumstances) beginning with the first working day after being supplied with the investigator's report and relevant documents and written notice, the police officer will be required to submit in writing:

- whether or not he/she accepts that the behaviour described in the particulars amounts to misconduct or gross misconduct as the case may be;
- where he/she accepts that his/her conduct amounts to misconduct or gross misconduct as the case may be, any written submission he/she wishes to make in mitigation;
- where he/she does not accept that his/her conduct amounts to misconduct or gross misconduct as the case may be, or he/she disputes part of the case, written notice of the particulars of the allegations he/she disputes and his/her account of the relevant events and any arguments on points of law he/she wishes the person conducting the meeting or hearing to consider.

The police officer concerned will also (within the same time limit) provide the appropriate authority and the person conducting the misconduct meeting or hearing with a copy of any document he/she intends to rely on at the misconduct proceedings. In addition, at a misconduct hearing the persons conducting that hearing have the right to have a relevant lawyer available to them for advice at the hearing.

The police officer shall be informed of the name of the person holding the meeting/hearing together with the name of any person appointed to advise the person conducting the meeting/hearing as soon as reasonably practicable after they have been appointed. The police officer may object to any person hearing or advising at a misconduct meeting or hearing within three working days starting with the first working day after he/she was notified of the person's name.

If the police officer concerned submits a compelling reason why such a person should not be involved in the meeting/hearing, a replacement should be found and the police officer will be notified of the name of the replacement and the police officer concerned will have the same right to object to that person. The police officer concerned may object to a person conducting a misconduct meeting or hearing or advising at such proceedings if, for example, the person has been involved in the case in a way that would make it difficult to make an objective and impartial assessment of the facts of the case.

4.2.5.8 Documents for the Meeting/Hearing

The person conducting the misconduct meeting/hearing shall be supplied with:

- a copy of the notice supplied to the police officer that sets out the fact that the case was to be referred to a misconduct meeting/hearing and details of the alleged misconduct etc.;
- a copy of the investigator's report or such parts of the report as relate to the police officer concerned, any other relevant documents gathered during the course of the investigation and a copy of any statement made by the officer;
- the notice provided by the police officer setting out whether or not the police officer accepts that his/her conduct amounts to misconduct or gross misconduct, any submission he/she wishes to make in mitigation where the conduct is accepted, and where he/she does not accept that the alleged conduct amounts to misconduct or gross misconduct or he/she disputes part of the case, the allegations he/she disputes and his/her account of the relevant events; any arguments on points of law submitted by the police officer concerned

as well as any documents he/she intends to rely on at the meeting/hearing, submitted under reg. 22 of the Conduct Regulations;

- where the police officer concerned does not accept that the alleged conduct amounts to misconduct or gross misconduct as the case may be or where he/she disputes any part of the case, any other documents that in the opinion of the appropriate authority should be considered at the meeting/hearing;
- any other documents that the persons conducting the meeting/hearing request that are relevant to the case.

4.2.5.9 Witnesses

Generally speaking, misconduct meetings and hearings will be conducted without witnesses. A witness will only be required to attend a misconduct meeting/hearing if the person conducting or chairing the meeting/hearing reasonably believes his/her attendance is necessary to resolve disputed issues in that case.

The appropriate authority and the officer concerned shall inform each other of any witnesses they wish to attend, including brief details of the evidence those persons can provide and their addresses. They should attempt to agree which witnesses are necessary to deal with the issues in dispute.

The appropriate authority shall supply the persons conducting the proceedings with a list of the witnesses agreed between the parties or, where there is no agreement, the lists provided by both the officer and the appropriate authority. The person conducting a misconduct meeting or the chair of a misconduct hearing will decide whether to allow such witnesses. The person conducting or chairing the misconduct proceedings may also decide that a witness other than one on such lists should be required to attend (if his/her attendance is considered necessary).

In special cases (fast track) no witnesses, other than the officer concerned, will provide evidence at the hearing.

4.2.6 Misconduct Proceedings

There are two types of misconduct proceedings:

- A misconduct meeting for cases where there is a case to answer in respect of misconduct and where the maximum outcome would be a final written warning.
- A misconduct hearing for cases where there is a case to answer in respect of gross misconduct or where the police officer has a live final written warning and there is a case to answer in respect of a further act of misconduct. The maximum outcome at this hearing would be dismissal from the police service without notice.

It is important that misconduct hearings are only used for those matters where the police officer has a live final written warning and has potentially committed a further act of misconduct that warrants misconduct proceedings or the misconduct alleged is so serious that it is genuinely considered that, if proven or admitted, dismissal from the police service would be justified.

4.2.6.1 Timing for Holding Meetings/Hearings

A misconduct meeting shall take place not later than 20 working days beginning with the first working day after the date on which the documents and material for the meeting have been supplied to the police officer under reg. 21 of the Conduct Regulations. Misconduct hearings shall take place not later than 30 working days beginning with the first working day after the date the documents for the hearing have been supplied to the police officer concerned. The time limit for holding a misconduct meeting or a misconduct hearing can be extended if in the interests of justice the person conducting or chairing the misconduct proceedings considers it appropriate to extend beyond that period.

In order to maintain confidence in the misconduct procedures it is important that the misconduct meetings/hearings are held as soon as practicable and extensions to the time-scales should be an exception rather than the rule.

4.2.6.2 Purpose of Misconduct Meeting/Hearing

The purpose of a formal misconduct meeting/hearing is to:

- give the police officer a fair opportunity to make his/her case having considered the investigation report, including supporting documents, and to put forward any factors the police officer wishes to be considered in mitigation (in addition to the submission which must be sent in advance to the person conducting or chairing the meeting/hearing for his/her consideration);
- decide if the conduct of the police officer fell below the standards set out in the Standards of Professional Behaviour based on the balance of probabilities and having regard to all of the evidence and circumstances;
- consider what the outcome should be if misconduct is proven or admitted. Consideration will be given to any live written warnings or final written warnings (and any previous disciplinary outcomes that have not expired) and any early admission of the conduct by the police officer.

4.2.6.3 Misconduct Meeting/Hearing—Non-senior Officers

A misconduct meeting for non-senior officers (police officers up to and including the rank of chief superintendent and all special constables) will be heard by a police officer (or other member of a police force) of at least one rank above the police officer concerned. However, in the case of a special constable, the member of the police force must be a sergeant or above or a senior human resources professional. Alternatively, a police staff member who, in the opinion of the appropriate authority, is a grade above that of the police officer concerned can be appointed, but not if the case substantially involves operational policing matters.

A misconduct hearing for non-senior officers will consist of a three person panel. The chair will always be a legally qualified person from 1 January 2016.

4.2.6.4 Misconduct Hearings in Public

Where a misconduct hearing (not misconduct meetings) arises from a case where the IPCC has conducted an independent investigation (in accordance with para. 19 of sch. 3 to the 2002 Act) and the IPCC considers that because of its gravity or other exceptional circumstances it would be in the public interest to do so, the IPCC may, having consulted with the appropriate authority, the police officer concerned, the complainant and any witnesses, direct that the whole or part of the misconduct hearing will be held in public. The IPCC has published criteria for deciding when such cases will be held in public and a copy of this is available on the IPCC website at <http://www.ipcc.gov.uk>.

In November 2014 the Home Secretary launched a consultation on increased transparency via a far greater number of cases potentially being held in public. The intention is that misconduct hearings for higher level cases that could lead to dismissal will be public by default. This includes both misconduct hearings and special case hearings but does not include lower level misconduct meetings, which the government does not propose to make public. Appeals hearings held by Police Appeals Tribunals will also be made public by default.

Legally qualified chairs replaced the senior officer who previously chaired the panel of a disciplinary hearing from 1 January 2016, and the chief officer in a special case hearing. There is no proposed change to the composition of panels for senior officers, or for misconduct meetings or appeal hearings.

4.2.6.5 Joint Meetings/Hearings

Cases may arise where two or more police officers are to appear before a misconduct meeting or hearing in relation to apparent failures to meet the standards set out in the Standards of Professional Behaviour stemming from the same incident. In such cases, each police officer may have played a different part and any alleged misconduct may be different for each police officer involved. It will normally be considered necessary to deal with all the matters together in order to disentangle the various strands of action, and therefore a single meeting/hearing will normally be appropriate.

A police officer may request a separate meeting/hearing if he/she can demonstrate that there would be a real risk of unfairness to that police officer if his/her case was dealt with in a joint meeting/hearing. It is for the person conducting the meeting or the chair of a misconduct hearing to decide if a separate meeting or hearing is appropriate.

4.2.6.6 Meeting/Hearing in Absence of Officer Concerned

It is in the interests of fairness to ensure that the misconduct meeting/hearing is held as soon as possible. Thus a meeting/hearing may take place if the police officer fails to attend. In cases where the police officer is absent (e.g. through illness or injury) a short delay may be reasonable to allow him/her to attend. If this is not possible or any delay is considered not appropriate in the circumstances the persons conducting the meeting/hearing may allow the police officer to participate by telephone or video link. In these circumstances a police friend will always be permitted to attend the meeting/hearing to represent the police officer in the normal way (and in the case of a misconduct hearing the police officer's legal representative where appointed).

If a police officer is detained in prison or other institution by order of a court, there is no requirement on the appropriate authority to have the officer concerned produced for the purposes of the misconduct meeting/hearing.

4.2.6.7 Conduct of Misconduct Meeting/Hearing

It will be for the persons conducting the meeting/hearing to determine the course of the meeting/hearing in accordance with the principles of natural justice and fairness. They will have read the investigator's report together with any account given by the police officer concerned during the investigation or when submitting his/her response under reg. 22 of the Conduct Regulations. They will also have had the opportunity to read any relevant documents attached to the investigator's report.

Any document or other material that was not submitted in advance of the meeting/hearing by the appropriate authority or the police officer concerned may still be considered at the meeting/hearing at the discretion of the persons conducting the meeting/hearing. Where any such document or other material is permitted to be considered, a short adjournment may be necessary to enable the appropriate authority or police officer concerned, as the case may be, to read or consider the document or other material and consider its implications.

Where there is evidence at the meeting or hearing that the police officer concerned, at any time after being given written notice under reg. 15 of the Conduct Regulations (or reg. 16 of the Complaint Regulations), failed to mention when interviewed or when making representations to the investigator or under reg. 22 of the Conduct Regulations, any fact relied on in his/her defence at the meeting/hearing, being a fact which in the circumstances existing at the time the police officer concerned could reasonably have been expected to mention when questioned or providing a written response, the persons conducting the meeting/hearing may draw such inferences from this failure as appear appropriate.

Where a witness does attend to give evidence, any questions to that witness should be made through the person conducting the meeting or in the case of a misconduct hearing the chair. This does not prevent the person conducting the meeting or the chair in a misconduct hearing allowing questions to be asked directly if he/she feels that is appropriate. It is for the persons conducting the meeting/hearing to control the proceedings and focus on the issues to ensure a fair meeting/hearing.

The persons conducting misconduct meetings/hearings will consider the facts of the case and will decide (on the balance of probabilities) whether the police officer's conduct amounted to misconduct, gross misconduct (in the case of a misconduct hearing) or neither. Where proceedings are conducted by a panel any decision shall be based on a majority (the chair having the casting vote where there is a panel of two or four) if necessary. If the meeting decides that the police officer's conduct did not fall below the standards expected then as soon as reasonably practicable (and no later than five working days beginning with the first working day after the meeting or hearing) the police officer shall be informed and no entry will be made on his/her personal record.

4.2.6.8   Standard of Proof

In deciding matters of fact misconduct meetings/hearings must apply the standard of proof required in civil cases, that is, the balance of probabilities. Conduct will be proved on the balance of probabilities if the persons conducting the meeting/hearing are satisfied by the evidence that it is more likely than not that the conduct occurred.

4.2.6.9   Outcomes of Meetings/Hearings

If the persons conducting the misconduct meeting/hearing find that the police officer's conduct did fail to meet the Standards of Professional Behaviour, they will then determine the most appropriate outcome. In considering the question of outcome the persons conducting the meeting/hearing will need to take into account any previous written warnings (imposed under the Police (Conduct) Regulations 2012 but not superintendent's warnings issued under the previous procedures) that were live at the time of the initial assessment of the conduct in question, any aggravating or mitigating factors and have regard to the police officer's record of service, including any previous disciplinary outcomes that have not been expunged in accordance with reg. 15 of the Police Regulations 2003. The persons conducting the meeting/hearing may (only if deemed necessary and at their discretion) receive evidence from any witness whose evidence would in their opinion assist them in this regard.

The persons conducting the meeting/hearing are also entitled to take account of any early admission of the conduct on behalf of the police officer concerned and attach whatever weight to this he, she or they consider appropriate in the circumstances of the case.

In addition, the police officer concerned and his/her police friend (or where appropriate legal representative) will be given the opportunity to make representations on the question of the most appropriate outcome of the case. The appropriate authority also has the opportunity to make representations as to the most appropriate outcome.

4.2.6.10   Outcomes Available at Misconduct Meetings/Hearings

The meeting/hearing may record a finding that the conduct of the police officer concerned amounted to misconduct and take no further action or impose one of the following outcomes:

- **Management advice**—The police officer will be told the reason for the advice, that he/she has a right of appeal, and the name of the person to whom the appeal should be sent.

- **Written warning**—The police officer will be told the reason for the warning, that he/she has a right to appeal, and the name of the person to whom the appeal should be sent, and that the warning will be put on his/her personal file and remain live for 12 months from the date the warning is given. This means that any misconduct in the next 12 months is likely to lead to (at least) a final written warning.
- **Final written warning**—The police officer will be told the reason for the warning, that any future misconduct may result in dismissal, that he/she has a right to appeal and the name of the person to whom the appeal should be sent, and that the final written warning will be put on his/her personal file and remain live for 18 months from the date the warning is given. This means that only in exceptional circumstances will further misconduct (that justifies more than management advice) not result in dismissal. (In exceptional circumstances only, the final written warning may be extended for a further 18 months on one occasion only.)

At a misconduct hearing, in addition to the three outcomes above, the persons conducting the hearing will also have available the outcomes of:

- **Dismissal with notice**—The notice period will be determined by the persons conducting the meeting subject to a minimum of 28 days.
- **Dismissal without notice**—Dismissal without notice will mean that the police officer is dismissed from the police service with immediate effect.

Where the persons conducting a misconduct hearing find that the police officer's conduct amounted to gross misconduct and decide that the police officer should be dismissed from the police service, that dismissal will be without notice. Where a police officer appears before a misconduct hearing for an alleged act of gross misconduct, and the persons conducting the hearing find that the conduct amounts to misconduct rather than gross misconduct, then (unless the police officer already has a live final written warning) the disciplinary outcomes available to the panel are those that are available at a misconduct meeting only.

4.2.6.11   Notification of the Outcome

In all cases the police officer will be informed in writing of the outcome of the misconduct meeting/hearing. This will be done as soon as practicable and in any case within five working days beginning with the first working day after the conclusion of the misconduct meeting/hearing. The notification in the case of a misconduct meeting will include notification to the police officer concerned of his/her right to appeal against the finding and/or outcome and the name of the person to whom any appeal should be sent. In the case of a police officer who has attended a misconduct hearing, the notification will include his/her right of appeal to a police appeals tribunal against any finding and/or outcome imposed. In cases involving a complainant, where the complaint was the subject of a local or supervised investigation the appropriate authority will be responsible for informing the complainant of the outcome. In cases managed or independently investigated by the IPCC, the IPCC will be responsible for informing the complainant of the outcome.

4.2.6.12   Expiry of Warnings

Notification of written warnings issued, including the date issued and expiry date, will be recorded on the police officer's personal record, along with a copy of the written notification of the outcome and a summary of the matter. Where a police officer has a live written warning and transfers from one force to another, the live warning will transfer with the police officer and will remain live until the expiry of the warning and should be referred to as part of any reference before the police officer transfers.

Where a police officer who has a live written warning or final written warning takes a career break in accordance with Police Regulations, any time on such a break will not count towards the 12 months (in the case of a written warning) or 18 months (in the case of a final written warning) or 36 months (in the case of an extended final written warning) that the warning is live.

4.2.6.13 Attendance of Complainant or Interested Person at Misconduct Proceedings

Where a misconduct meeting/hearing is being held as a direct result of a public complaint, the complainant or interested person will have the right to attend the meeting/hearing as an observer up until the point at which disciplinary action is considered (in addition to attending as a witness if required to do so). This right is subject to the right of the chair or person conducting the proceedings to exclude or impose conditions on the complainant's or interested party's attendance to facilitate the proper conduct of proceedings and to exclude him/her while evidence is being given, the disclosure of which to the complainant or interested party would be contrary to the harm test. He/she may be accompanied by one other person and, if he/she has a special need, one further person to accommodate that need (e.g. an interpreter, sign language expert etc.).

A complainant and any person accompanying the complainant will be permitted to remain in the meeting/hearing up to and including any finding by the persons conducting the meeting/hearing, after having given evidence (if appropriate). The complainant and any person accompanying the complainant will not be permitted to remain in the meeting/ hearing while character references or mitigation are being given or the decision of the panel as to the outcome is being given. However, the appropriate authority will have a duty to inform the complainant of the outcome of any misconduct meeting/hearing whether the complainant attends or not.

The persons conducting a misconduct meeting/hearing will have the discretion to allow a witness (who is not a complainant or interested person) who has attended and given evidence at the meeting/hearing to remain or to ask him/her to leave the proceedings after giving his/her evidence.

4.2.6.14 IPCC Direction and Attendance at Meetings/Hearings

Where the IPCC exercises its power (under para. 27 of sch. 3 to the 2002 Act) to direct an appropriate authority to hold a misconduct meeting/hearing, this will also include a direction as to whether the proceedings will be a misconduct meeting or hearing. In making such a direction the IPCC will have regard to the severity assessment that has been made in the case and been notified to the police officer concerned.

Where a misconduct meeting/hearing is to be held following:

- an investigation managed or independently investigated by the IPCC; or
- a local or supervised investigation where the IPCC has made a recommendation under para. 27(3) of sch. 3 to the Police Reform Act 2002 that misconduct proceedings should be taken and the recommendation has been accepted by the appropriate authority; or
- the IPCC has given a direction under para. 27(4) of that schedule that misconduct proceedings shall be taken,

the IPCC may attend the misconduct meeting/hearing to make representations. Such representations may be an explanation why the IPCC has directed particular misconduct proceedings to be brought or to comment on the investigation. Where the IPCC is to attend a misconduct hearing, it may instruct a relevant lawyer to represent it.

4.2.7 Right of Appeal

A police officer has a right of appeal against the finding and/or the outcome imposed at a misconduct meeting. The appeal is commenced by the police officer concerned giving written notice of appeal to the appropriate authority, clearly setting out the grounds for the appeal within seven working days beginning with the first working day after the receipt of the notification of the outcome of the misconduct meeting (unless this period is extended by the appropriate authority for exceptional circumstances). The police officer has the right to be accompanied by a police friend.

The police officer concerned may only appeal on the grounds that:

- the finding or disciplinary action imposed was unreasonable;
- there is evidence that could not reasonably have been considered at the misconduct meeting which could have materially affected the finding or decision on disciplinary action; or
- there was a serious breach of the procedures set out in the Regulations or other unfairness which could have materially affected the finding or decision on disciplinary action.

4.2.7.1 Appeal following Misconduct Meeting—Non-senior Officers

An appeal against the finding and/or the outcome of a misconduct meeting will be heard by a member of the police service of a higher rank or a police staff manager who is considered to be of a higher grade than the person who conducted the misconduct meeting. A police staff manager should not be appointed to conduct the appeal if the case substantially involves operational policing matters. A police officer or police staff member may be present to advise the person conducting the appeal on procedural matters. The person determining the appeal will be provided with the following documents:

- the notice of appeal from the police officer concerned setting out his/her grounds of appeal;
- the record of the original misconduct meeting;
- the documents that were given to the person who held the original misconduct meeting;
- any evidence that the police officer concerned wishes to submit in support of his/her appeal that was not considered at the misconduct meeting.

The person appointed to deal with the appeal must first decide whether the notice of appeal sets out arguable grounds of appeal. If he/she determines that there are no arguable grounds he/she shall dismiss the appeal and inform the police officer concerned accordingly setting out his/her reasons. Where the person appointed to hear the appeal determines that there are arguable grounds of appeal and the police officer concerned has requested to be present at the appeal meeting, the person appointed to conduct the proceedings will hold a meeting with the police officer concerned. Where the police officer fails to attend the meeting, the person conducting the appeal may proceed in the absence of the police officer concerned.

The person conducting the appeal may consider:

- whether the finding of the original misconduct meeting was unreasonable having regard to all the evidence considered or if the finding could now be in doubt due to evidence which has emerged since the meeting;
- any outcome imposed by the misconduct meeting which may be considered as too severe or too lenient having regard to all the circumstances of the case;
- whether the finding or outcome could be unsafe due to procedural unfairness and prejudice to the police officer (although the person conducting the appeal must also take into account whether the unfairness or prejudice could have materially influenced the outcome).

The person determining the appeal may confirm or reverse the decision appealed against. Where the person determining the appeal decides that the original disciplinary action imposed was too lenient he/she may increase the outcome up to a maximum of a final written warning. An appeal is not a repeat of the misconduct meeting. It is to examine a particular part of the misconduct case which is under question and which may affect the finding or the outcome.

The appeal will normally be heard within five working days beginning with the working day after the determination that the officer concerned has arguable grounds of appeal. The officer concerned can object to the person appointed to conduct the appeal in the same way as he/she could for the original misconduct meeting (**see para. 4.2.5.7**).

4.2.7.2 Appeal following Misconduct Hearing

Where a police officer has appeared before a misconduct hearing, any appeal against the finding or outcome is to the police appeals tribunal (**see paras 4.2.9 to 4.2.9.9**). The police officer should be informed that the police appeals tribunal can increase any outcome imposed as well as reduce or overturn the decision of the misconduct hearing or special case hearing.

Senior officers have the right to appeal against the finding and/or outcome of a misconduct meeting or hearing. The appeal in both cases will be made to the police appeals tribunal. The police officer should be informed that the police appeals tribunal can increase any outcome imposed as well as reduce or overturn the decision of the misconduct hearing or special case hearing.

4.2.8 Fast Track Cases ('Special Cases')

The operation of the fast-track misconduct procedures, referred to as 'special cases', is set out in part 5 of the Conduct Regulations. The special case procedures can only be used if the appropriate authority certifies the case as a special case, having determined that the 'special conditions' are satisfied or if the IPCC has given a direction under para. 20H(7) of sch. 3 to the Police Reform Act 2002.

The 'special conditions' are that there is sufficient evidence, in the form of written statements or other documents, without the need for further evidence, whether written or oral, to establish on the balance of probabilities that the conduct of the police officer concerned constitutes gross misconduct, and it is in the public interest for the police officer concerned to cease to be a police officer without delay.

These procedures are therefore designed to deal with cases where the evidence is incontrovertible in the form of statements, documents or other material (e.g. CCTV, DNA) and is therefore sufficient without further evidence to prove gross misconduct and it is in the public interest, if the case is found or admitted, for the police officer to cease to be a member of the police service forthwith. Even where the criteria for special cases are met there may be circumstances where it would not be appropriate to certify the case as a special case, for instance, where to do so might prematurely alert others (police officers or non-police officers) who are, or may be, the subject of an investigation.

In the case of non-senior officers the case will be heard by the police officer's chief constable (assistant commissioner in the Metropolitan Police) or in cases where the chief constable is an interested party or is unavailable, another chief constable or an assistant commissioner. The police officer will have a right of appeal under reg. 56 of the Conduct Regulations to a police appeals tribunal against any finding of gross misconduct and the disciplinary action imposed.

Where a matter that meets the criteria for using the special case procedures has arisen from a complaint by a member of the public, the complainant or interested person will have the right to attend the special case hearing as an observer subject to any conditions imposed by the person conducting proceedings under reg. 52(3) of the Conduct Regulations. Where a complainant or interested person is to attend a special case hearing he/she will be entitled to be accompanied by one other person and if the complainant or interested person has a special need, by one further person to accommodate that need. A complainant or interested person and any person accompanying the complainant or interested person will be permitted to remain in the hearing up to and including any finding by the person (or persons in the case of a senior officer) conducting the hearing. The complainant or interested person and any person accompanying the complainant or interested person will not be permitted to remain in the hearing while character references or mitigation are being given or the decision of the person conducting the hearing (or persons in the case of a senior officer) as to the outcome is being given. However, the appropriate authority will have a duty (in cases investigated locally or supervised by the IPCC) to inform the complainant or interested person of the outcome of the hearing whether the complainant or interested person attends or not.

There will be no oral witness testimony at the special case hearing other than from the police officer concerned. There will be copies of the notice given to the police officer, the certificate certifying the case as a special case, the notice the police officer has supplied in response, including any documents he/she provides in support of his/her case, a copy of the investigator's report or such parts of that report as relate to the police officer concerned, statements made by the police officer during the investigation, and in a case where the police officer concerned denies the allegation against him/her, copies of all statements and documents that in the opinion of the appropriate authority should be considered at the meeting.

The hearing may proceed in the absence of the police officer concerned, but the persons conducting the hearing should ensure that the police officer concerned has been informed of his/her right to be legally represented at the hearing or to be represented by a police friend where the police officer chooses not to be legally represented.

4.2.8.1 Special Case Process

Where the appropriate authority determines that the special conditions are satisfied and unless it considers that the circumstances are such as to make it inappropriate to do so, it shall certify the case as a special case and refer it to a special case hearing. The decision as to whether a case is suitable for using the fast-track procedure will be taken by the appropriate authority which must determine whether it believes the special conditions are satisfied having regard to the available evidence and any other relevant information.

If the appropriate authority decides that the special case procedures will not be used, it will refer the case back to the investigator if further investigation is required or to the appropriate authority to proceed under the standard procedures. If the appropriate authority decides that the special case procedures should be used, it will sign a 'Special Case Certificate' and will provide to the police officer concerned notice giving particulars of the conduct that is alleged to constitute gross misconduct and copies of:

- the Special Case Certificate;
- any statement the police officer may have made to the investigator during the course of the investigation;
- subject to the harm test:
  + the investigator's report (if any) or such parts of that report as relate to the police officer concerned, together with any documents attached to that report; and
  + any relevant statement or documents gathered during the course of the investigation.

The police officer concerned will also be told the date, time and place of the hearing and of his/her right to legal representation and to advice from a police friend. The date of the meeting will be not less than 10 working days and not more than 15 working days from the date the Special Case Certificate and other documents are provided to the police officer concerned.

Within seven working days of the first working day after the day on which the written notice and documents are supplied to the police officer concerned, the police officer shall provide a written notice to the appropriate authority of:

- whether or not he/she accepts that his/her conduct constituted gross misconduct;
- where he/she accepts that the conduct constituted gross misconduct, any submission he/she wishes to make in mitigation;
- where he/she does not accept that the conduct constituted gross misconduct;
  + the allegations he/she disputes and his/her version of the relevant events; and
  + any arguments on points of law he/she wishes to be considered by the person or persons conducting the meeting.

At the same time the police officer shall provide the person conducting or chairing the hearing with copies of any documents he/she intends to rely on at the hearing (in accordance with reg. 45).

4.2.8.2 Outcome of Special Case Hearing

Where the persons conducting the special case hearing find that the conduct of the police officer concerned constituted gross misconduct, they shall impose disciplinary action, which may be dismissal without notice, a final written warning (unless a final written warning has been imposed on the police officer concerned within the previous 18 months), or an extension of a final written warning.

Where the police officer concerned has received a final written warning within the 18 months prior to the assessment of the conduct then, in exceptional circumstances only, the final written warning may be extended by a further 18 months. An extension of a final written warning can occur once.

Where the persons conducting the hearing determine that the conduct does not amount to gross misconduct, then he, she or they may dismiss the case. Alternatively, he, she or they may return the case to the appropriate authority to be dealt with at a misconduct meeting or hearing (where there is a live final written warning) under the standard procedures. This may be because the persons conducting the hearing consider that the conduct is misconduct rather than gross misconduct. There is power under reg. 42 for the appropriate authority to remit the case to be dealt with under the standard procedures at any time prior to the start of the special case hearing. This might be because it considers that a particular witness whose evidence is crucial to the case and is disputed must be called to give oral testimony.

Where the police officer admits the allegation or the persons conducting the hearing find it proved on the balance of probabilities, then the persons conducting the hearing:

- shall have regard to the record of police service of the police officer concerned as shown on his/her personal record;
- may consider such documentary evidence as would, in their opinion, assist him, her or them in determining the question; and
- shall give the police officer concerned, and his/her police friend or relevant lawyer, an opportunity to make oral or written representations.

The police officer concerned shall be informed of the finding and any disciplinary action imposed or a decision to dismiss the case or revert it back to be dealt with under the standard procedures as soon as practicable and in any event shall be provided with written notice of these matters and a summary of the reasons within five working days beginning with the first working day after the conclusion of the hearing.

4.2.9 Appeals to the Police Appeals Tribunal

The Police Appeals Tribunal Rules 2012 govern the composition and operation of the Police Appeals Tribunal.

A police officer has a right of appeal to a police appeals tribunal against any disciplinary finding and/or disciplinary outcome imposed at a misconduct hearing or special case hearing held under the Conduct Regulations. Senior police officers, in addition, have the right to appeal to a police appeals tribunal against any disciplinary finding and/or outcome imposed at a misconduct meeting. A police officer may not appeal to a tribunal against a finding of misconduct or gross misconduct where that finding was made following acceptance by the officer that his/her conduct amounted to misconduct or gross misconduct (as the case may be). A police officer of a rank up to and including chief superintendent has a right of appeal to a police appeals tribunal against the finding and/or the following outcomes imposed following a third stage meeting under the Performance Regulations to dismiss or reduce in rank. In addition if the case has been dealt with at a stage three meeting, without having progressed through stages one and two, the police officer may appeal against redeployment to alternative duties, the issue of a final written improvement notice, or the issue of a written improvement notice.

4.2.9.1 Composition and Timing of Police Appeals Tribunals

Where the appeal is made by a police officer who is not a senior officer, the tribunal will consist of:

- a legally qualified chair drawn from a list maintained by the Home Office;
- a representative of the local policing body, i.e. the Police and Crime Commissioner's Office or the Mayor's Office for Policing and Crime in the Metropolitan Police Area (referred to collectively in law as 'the local policing body');
- a serving senior officer (ACPO rank); and
- a retired member of a police force who was a member of the Police Superintendents' Association of England and Wales or the Police Federation of England and Wales for Federated ranks.

A tribunal will take place as soon as reasonably practicable, no later than three months of the determination by a tribunal chair that a hearing should be held.

4.2.9.2 Grounds of Appeal

A police appeals tribunal is not a re-hearing of the original matter; rather its role is to consider an appeal based on specific grounds.

In the case of matters dealt with under the Police (Conduct) Regulations 2012 the grounds for appeal are:

- the finding or disciplinary action imposed was unreasonable; or
- there is evidence that could not reasonably have been considered at the misconduct meeting (in the case of senior police officers), the misconduct hearing or special case hearing (as the case may be); or
- there was a breach of the procedures set out in the Police (Conduct) Regulations 2012, the Police (Complaints and Misconduct) Regulations 2012, sch. 3 to the Police Reform Act 2002 or other unfairness which could have materially affected the finding or decision on disciplinary action.

In the case of matters dealt with under the Police (Performance) Regulations 2012 the grounds for appeal are:

- the finding of unsatisfactory performance or attendance or gross incompetence, or the outcome imposed, was unreasonable; or

- there is evidence that could not reasonably have been considered at the third stage meeting which could have materially affected the finding or decision on the outcome; or
- there was a breach of the procedures set out in the Police (Performance) Regulations 2012 or other unfairness which could have materially affected the finding or decision on the outcome; or
- where the police officer was required to attend a third stage meeting following a first and second stage meeting, the police officer concerned should not have been required to attend that meeting as his/her unsatisfactory performance or attendance was not similar to or connected with the unsatisfactory performance or attendance referred to in his/her final written improvement notice.

4.2.9.3   Notice of Appeal

Where a police officer wishes to appeal, he/she will need to give notice of his/her appeal in writing to the 'relevant local policing body'. The notice of appeal must be given within 10 working days, beginning with the first working day after the police officer is supplied with a written copy of the decision that he/she is appealing against. In cases where the police officer fails to submit his/her notice of appeal within the 10 working days period, he/she may, within a reasonable time after the end of that period, submit a notice of appeal which shall be accompanied by the reasons why it was not submitted within that period, and the reasons for the officer's view that it was served within a reasonable time after that period. The tribunal chair will then determine whether the appeal could have reasonably and practicably been submitted within the time limit.

4.2.9.4   Procedure on Notice of Appeal

As soon as reasonably practicable after receipt of a copy of the notice of appeal and in any case within 15 working days (beginning with the first working day following the day of such receipt) the chief constable shall provide to the relevant local policing body:

- a copy of the decision appealed against (namely the written judgment of the original panel/person);
- any documents that were available to the panel/person conducting the original hearing; and
- the transcript or part of the transcript of the proceedings at the original hearing requested by the appellant (a copy of the transcript (if applicable) shall also at the same time be sent to the appellant).

The appellant, within 20 working days beginning with the first working day following the day on which he/she is supplied with a copy of the transcript or, where no transcript is requested, within 35 working days (beginning with the first working day following the day on which the appellant gave notice of his/her appeal), shall provide to the relevant local policing body:

- a notice setting out the finding, disciplinary action or outcome appealed against and of his/her grounds for the appeal;
- any supporting documents;
- where the appellant is allowed to call witnesses (for appeals made only on the ground of there being evidence that could not reasonably have been considered at the original hearing and which could have materially affected the finding or outcome):
  - ✦ a list of any proposed witnesses; and
  - ✦ a witness statement from each of the proposed witnesses;
- if he/she consents to the appeal being determined without a hearing (that is, on the basis of the papers alone), notice in writing that he/she so consents.

In relation to the appellant, a 'proposed witness' is a person whom the appellant wishes to call to give evidence at the hearing, whose evidence was not and could not reasonably have been considered at the hearing and whose evidence could have materially affected the decision being appealed against.

4.2.9.5   Determination of an Appeal

Where the tribunal chair allows the appeal to go forward to a tribunal hearing the local policing body will be responsible for making the administrative arrangements prior to and at the tribunal and for ensuring that the members of the tribunal appointed to deal with the appeal are sent the papers together with a schedule of the documents that each of the members should have.

The tribunal chair who made the determination as to whether to allow the notice of appeal to proceed to a tribunal need not necessarily be the same tribunal chair who hears the subsequent appeal. However, the chair who makes the decision as to whether the appeal should be dealt with at a hearing or on the papers should be the chair appointed to hear the appeal itself.

Where an appeal has not been dismissed at the review stage, the tribunal chair shall determine whether the appeal should be dealt with at a hearing. It is expected that this decision will be made by the tribunal chair within ten working days of receiving the papers. If the appellant has not consented to an appeal being dealt with on the papers then a hearing shall be held. If the appellant has consented, the tribunal chair may determine that the appeal shall be dealt with without a hearing. If the appeal is to be dealt with at a hearing, the chair shall give the appellant and the respondent his/her name and contact address.

4.2.9.6   Legal and Other Representation

The appellant can be represented at a hearing by a relevant lawyer or a police friend. Where the appellant is represented by a lawyer the appellant's police friend may also attend.

4.2.9.7   Procedure at Hearing

Where the case is to be heard at a tribunal hearing, the chair of the tribunal shall cause the appellant and the respondent to be given written notice of the time, date and place of the hearing, at least 20 working days or such shorter period as may with the agreement of both parties be determined, before the hearing begins.

The tribunal chair will determine in advance of the tribunal whether to allow any witness that the appellant or respondent proposes to call to give evidence at the tribunal. Witnesses will only be permitted where the ground for appeal is that there is evidence that could not reasonably have been considered at the original hearing which could have materially affected the finding or decision on outcome. No witnesses shall give evidence at the hearing unless the chair reasonably believes that it is necessary for the witness to do so. Any witness that does attend the tribunal may be subject to questioning and cross questioning. It is for the tribunal to decide on the admissibility of any evidence, or to determine whether or not any question should or should not be put to a witness. A verbatim record of the evidence given at the hearing shall be taken; and the relevant local policing body shall keep such record for a period of not less than two years from the date of the end of the hearing.

The tribunal has discretion to proceed with the hearing in the absence of either party, whether represented or not, if it appears to be just and proper to do so. Where it is decided to proceed in the absence of either party the tribunal should record its reasons for doing so. The tribunal may adjourn the appeal as necessary.

The hearing shall be held in private. The tribunal may allow a person to attend the hearing as an observer for the purposes of training. On the application of the appellant or the respondent or otherwise, the tribunal chair may require any observer to withdraw from all or any part of the hearing.

4.2.9.8 Attendance of Other Persons

Where the matter to be dealt with at the appeal is related directly to a complaint made against the appellant or a conduct matter involving an interested party, the chair of the tribunal shall cause the complainant or interested party to be given notice of the time, date and place of the tribunal. The complainant or interested party may attend the tribunal as an observer. The complainant or interested party may be accompanied by one other person and in addition, if the complainant or interested party has a special need, by one further person to accommodate that need. Where the complainant or interested party or any person accompanying him/her is to give evidence at the tribunal, then he/she or any person accompanying him/her may not attend the hearing before that evidence is given. Where the appeal is a 'specified appeal' then the tribunal chair shall cause the IPCC to be notified of the time, date and location of the tribunal. In such cases the IPCC may attend as an observer.

4.2.9.9 Determination and Outcome of Appeal

A tribunal need not be unanimous in its determination of the appeal or of any other decision before it and may reach a decision based on a majority. Where a tribunal finds itself divided equally, the tribunal chair will have the casting vote.

A tribunal, when determining any disciplinary or unsatisfactory performance outcome imposed, may impose any outcome that the original panel/person could have imposed. The tribunal has the power to increase as well as reduce the outcome imposed by the original panel/person. The decision of the tribunal will normally be made on the day of the tribunal hearing.

The tribunal chair shall, within three working days of the tribunal determining the appeal, give written notice to the appellant of the tribunal's decision.

A police officer ordered to be reinstated in his/her former force or rank will be deemed to have served in his/her force and/or rank continuously from the date of the original decision to the date of reinstatement. Reinstatement means that the officer is put back in the role that he/she would have been in if not dismissed or reduced in rank.

4.3 | Unsatisfactory Performance and Attendance

4.3.1 Introduction

The formal procedures to deal with unsatisfactory performance and attendance are set out in the Police (Performance) Regulations 2012. These are referred to as 'UPPs' (and are referred to by that abbreviation in this chapter).

The aim of the procedures is to provide a fair, open and proportionate method of dealing with performance and attendance issues, encouraging a culture of learning and development for individuals and the organisation. Early intervention via management action should achieve the desired effect of improving and maintaining a police officer's performance or attendance to an acceptable level; however, in some cases it will be appropriate for managers to take formal action under the procedures. The procedures in the UPPs are largely the same whether applied to unsatisfactory performance or attendance (the differences that do exist are set out below). However, the issues that arise in attendance cases may be different from those in performance cases.

4.3.2 Applicability

The procedures apply to police officers up to and including the rank of chief superintendent, including special constables. However, given the nature of special constables as unpaid volunteers, initiation of such cases may be limited to those where the special constable either contests that his/her performance or attendance is unsatisfactory or agrees that it is unsatisfactory but expresses a desire to continue with his/her special constable duties. In other cases the special constable may choose to resign from his/her role as a special constable. In setting meeting dates and establishing panels, regard should be had to the nature of special constables as volunteers.

> **KEYNOTE**
>
> The procedures *do not apply* to student police officers during their probationary period. The procedures governing performance and attendance issues in respect of police students are determined locally by each force. These procedures are underpinned by reg. 13 of the Police Regulations 2003.

4.3.3 Ongoing Performance Assessment and Review

Every police officer should have some form of performance appraisal, commonly referred to as a 'performance and development review' (PDR). The PDR should be the principal method by which the police officer's performance and attendance are monitored and assessed. The activities and behaviours expected of a police officer in order to achieve his/her objectives should be in accordance with the relevant national framework which will form the basis of the police officer's role profile.

4.3.4   Sources of Information

Unsatisfactory performance or attendance will often be identified by the immediate line manager of the police officer as part of his/her normal management responsibilities. Where the police officer currently works to a manager who has no line management responsibility for him/her, it is the responsibility of that manager to inform the police officer's line manager of any performance or attendance issues he/she has identified. It is possible that line managers may be alerted to unsatisfactory performance or attendance on the part of one of their police officers as a result of information or complaint from a member of the public. Such cases must be dealt with in accordance with the established procedures for the handling of complaints.

The outcome of an investigation into a complaint alleging misconduct may identify an issue of unsatisfactory performance or attendance. Consequently, the appropriate authority may determine that there is no case to answer in respect of misconduct or gross misconduct but it may be appropriate to take action under the UPPs.

While the unsatisfactory performance and attendance procedures are internal management procedures, it may be necessary at times to inform public complainants of action taken with respect to the police officer to whom the complaint relates.

4.3.5   Management Action

There are some principles which should apply in management action:

- the line manager must discuss any shortcoming(s) or concern(s) with the individual at the earliest possible opportunity. It would be wrong for the line manager to accumulate a list of concerns about the performance or attendance of an individual and delay telling him/her about them until the occasion of the police officer's annual or mid-term PDR meetings;
- the reason for dissatisfaction must be made clear to the individual as soon as possible and there must be a factual basis for discussing the issues, i.e. the discussion must relate to specific incidents or omissions that have occurred;
- line managers should seek to establish whether there are any underlying reasons for the unsatisfactory performance or attendance;
- consideration should be given as to whether there is any health or welfare issue that is or may be affecting performance or attendance;
- in cases where the difficulty appears to stem from a personality clash with a colleague or line manager, or where for other reasons a change of duties might be appropriate, the police officer's line management may, in consultation with the appropriate human resources adviser, consider redeployment if this provides an opportunity for the police officer to improve his/her performance or attendance. Where a police officer is redeployed in this way, the police officer and his/her new line management should be informed of the reasons for the move and of the assessment of his/her performance or attendance in the previous role;
- the line manager must make it clear to the police officer that he/she is available to give further advice and guidance if needed;
- depending on the circumstances, it may be appropriate to indicate to the police officer that if there is no, or insufficient, improvement, then the matter will be dealt with under the UPPs;
- line managers are expected to gather relevant evidence and keep a contemporaneous note of interactions with the police officer;
- challenging unsatisfactory performance or attendance in an appropriate manner does not constitute bullying.

The above principles cover the position when a line manager first becomes aware of some unsatisfactory aspect of the police officer's performance or attendance and is dealing with the issue as part of normal line management responsibilities.

Such management action should be put on record. Particularly, the line manager should record the nature of the performance or attendance issue, the advice given, and steps taken to address the problems identified. Such action ensures continuity in circumstances where one or more members of the management chain may move on to other duties or the police officer concerned moves to new duties.

Ideally performance or attendance will improve and continue to an acceptable level. Where there is insufficient or unsustained improvement, it will then be appropriate to use the UPPs. The period of time agreed or determined by the line manager for the police officer concerned to improve his/her performance or attendance prior to using the UPPs must be sufficient to provide a reasonable opportunity for the desired improvement or attendance to take place and must be time limited.

4.3.6 Performance Issues

Police officers should know what standard of performance is required of them and be given appropriate support to attain that standard and managers should let a police officer know when he/she is doing well or, if the circumstances arise, when there are the first signs that there is a need for improvement in his/her performance.

KEYNOTE

Unsatisfactory performance (or attendance) is defined in reg. 4 of the UPPs as 'an inability or failure of a police officer to perform the duties of the role or rank he [or she] is currently undertaking to a satisfactory standard or level'.

There is no formula for determining the point at which a concern about a police officer's performance should lead to formal procedures under the UPPs being taken. Each case must be considered on its merits. However, the following points need to be emphasised:

- the intention of performance management, including formal action under the UPPs is to improve performance;
- occasional lapses should be dealt with in the course of normal management activity and should not involve the application of the UPPs, which are designed to cover repeated failures to meet such standards or more serious cases of unsatisfactory performance;
- managers should be able to demonstrate that they have considered whether management action is appropriate before using the UPPs.

4.3.7 Attendance Issues

Where the UPPs are used in relation to attendance matters, they will normally relate to periods of sickness absence such that the ability of the police officer to perform his/her duties is compromised. Other forms of absence unrelated to genuine sickness would normally be dealt with under the misconduct procedures, e.g. where a police officer's absence is unauthorised. Except where a police officer fails to cooperate, appropriate supportive action must be taken before formal action is taken under the UPPs. A failure by a police officer to cooperate will not prevent formal action being taken or continued. If supportive action is taken, the police officer cooperates and the attendance improves and is maintained at a satisfactory level, there will be no need to take formal action under the UPPs. Where police officers are injured or ill they should be treated fairly and compassionately. Managers should be able to demonstrate that they have acted reasonably in all actions taken at all stages of the attendance management process, including any action under the UPPs.

4.3.7.1 Monitoring Attendance

Line managers, in conjunction with the force's human resources department if necessary, are responsible for monitoring a police officer's attendance. A formal record of a police officer's period of illness will be kept in accordance with reg. 15 of the Police Regulations 2003. The force Occupational Health Service is an essential part of effective attendance management and should be involved as soon as any concerns about a police officer's attendance are identified. Where action is taken under the UPPs in respect of a police officer's attendance, the police officer may be referred to the Occupational Health Service for up-to-date information and advice at any stage within the procedure in accordance with force policy. This should enable the force to make an informed decision about a police officer's attendance. Where police officers do not attend appointments or otherwise fail to cooperate with the force's Occupational Health Service, an assessment will be made on the information available.

4.3.7.2 Action under the UPPs

Formal action under the UPPs may be taken in cases of both unacceptable levels of persistent short-term absences and long-term absences due to sickness and/or injury. In deciding whether to take action under the procedures, managers must consider all of the facts available to them, including:

- the nature of the illness, injury or condition;
- the likelihood of the illness, injury or condition (or some other related illness, injury or condition) recurring;
- the pattern and length of absence(s) and the period of good health between them;
- the need for the work to be done, i.e. what impact on the force's performance and workload the absence is having;
- the extent to which a police officer has cooperated with supportive management action;
- whether the police officer was made aware, in the earlier supportive action, that unless an improvement was made, action under the UPPs might be used;
- whether the selected medical practitioner (SMP) has been asked to consider the issue of permanent disablement and/or the police force is considering medical retirement;
- the impact of the Equality Act 2010 and the public sector equality duty.

4.3.8 Multiple Instances of Unsatisfactory Performance

A police officer can move to a later stage of the UPPs only in relation to unsatisfactory performance or attendance that is similar to or connected with the unsatisfactory performance or attendance referred to in any previous written improvement notice. Where failings relate to different forms of unsatisfactory performance or attendance it will be necessary to commence the UPPs at the first stage (unless the failing constitutes gross incompetence). If more than one UPP is commenced, then, given that the procedures will relate to different failings and will have been identified at different times, the finding and outcome of each should be without prejudice to the others.

There may be circumstances where procedures have been initiated for a particular failing and an additional failing comes to light prior to the first stage meeting. In such circumstances it is possible to consolidate the two issues at the first stage meeting provided that there is sufficient time prior to the meeting to comply with the notification requirements explained in more detail below.

4.3.9   The First Stage

Where a line manager decides that the UPPs are the most appropriate way of addressing the performance or attendance matter, he/she will notify the police officer in writing that he/she is required to attend a first stage meeting and include in that notification the following details:

- details of the procedures for determining the date and time of the meeting;
- a summary of the reasons why the line manager considers the police officer's performance or attendance unsatisfactory;
- the possible outcomes of a first stage, second stage and third stage meeting;
- that a human resources professional or a police officer (who should have experience of UPPs and be independent from the line management chain) may attend the meeting to advise the line manager on the proceedings;
- that if the police officer agrees, any other person specified in the notice may attend the meeting;
- that prior to the meeting the police officer must provide the line manager with any documentation he/she intends to rely on in the meeting; and
- the police officer's rights, i.e. his/her right to seek advice from a representative of his/her staff association and to be accompanied and represented at the meeting by a police friend.

KEYNOTE

The notice shall be accompanied by copies of related documentation relied upon by the line manager in support of the view that the police officer's performance or attendance is unsatisfactory. In advance of the meeting, the police officer shall provide the line manager with any documents on which he/she intends to rely in support of his/her case. Any document or other material that was not submitted in advance of the meeting may be considered at the meeting at the discretion of the line manager, ensuring fairness to all parties. However the presumption should be that such documents or material will not be permitted unless it can be shown that they were not previously available to be submitted in advance. Where such a document or other material is permitted to be considered, a short adjournment may be necessary to enable the line manager or the police officer, as the case may be, to read or consider the document or other material and consider its implications. The length of the adjournment will depend upon the case.

Wherever possible, the meeting date and time should be agreed between the line manager and the police officer. However, where agreement cannot be reached the line manager must specify a time and date. If the police officer or his/her police friend is not available at the date or time specified by the line manager, the police officer may propose an alternative time. Provided that the alternative time is reasonable and falls within a period of five working days beginning with the first working day after that specified by the line manager, the meeting must be postponed to that time. Once the date for the meeting is fixed, the line manager should send to the police officer a notice in writing of the date, time and place of the first stage meeting.

4.3.9.1   First Stage Meeting

At the first stage meeting the line manager will:

- explain to the police officer the reasons why the line manager considers that the performance or attendance of the police officer is unsatisfactory;

- provide the police officer with the opportunity to make representations in response;
- provide his/her police friend (if he/she has one) with an opportunity to make representations;
- listen to what the police officer (and/or his/her police friend) has to say, ask questions and comment as appropriate.

Where the line manager finds that the performance or attendance of the police officer has been satisfactory during the period in question, he/she will inform the police officer that no further action will be taken. Where having considered any representations by either the police officer and/ or his/her police friend, the line manager finds that the performance or attendance of the police officer has been unsatisfactory he/she shall:

- inform the police officer in what respects his/her performance or attendance is considered unsatisfactory;
- inform him/her of the improvement that is required in his/her performance or attendance;
- inform the police officer that, if a sufficient improvement is not made within the period specified by the line manager, he/she may be required to attend a second stage meeting;
- inform the police officer that he/she will receive a written improvement notice;
- inform the police officer that if the sufficient improvement in his/her performance or attendance is not maintained during the validity period of such notice he/she may be required to attend a second stage meeting.

4.3.9.2   Procedure following the First Stage Meeting

As soon as reasonably practicable, following the meeting, the line manager shall cause to be prepared a written record of the meeting and, where he/she found at the meeting that the performance or attendance of the police officer was unsatisfactory, a written *improvement notice*. The written record and any improvement notice shall be sent to the officer as soon as reasonably practicable after they have been prepared.

KEYNOTE

Improvement notices require a police officer to improve his/her performance or attendance and must state:

- in what respect the police officer's performance or attendance is considered unsatisfactory;
- the improvement in performance or attendance required to bring the police officer to an acceptable standard;
- a 'specified period' within which improvement is expected to be made; and
- the 'validity period' of the written improvement notice.

Specified Period

The 'specified period' of an improvement notice is a period specified by the manager conducting the meeting (having considered any representations made by or on behalf of the police officer) within which the police officer must improve his/her performance or attendance. It is expected that the specified period for improvement would not normally exceed *three months*. On the application of the police officer or otherwise (e.g. on the application of his/her line manager), the appropriate authority may extend the specified period; if it considers it appropriate to do so. In setting an extension to the specified period, consideration should be given to any known periods of extended absence from the police officer's normal role, e.g. if the police officer is going to be on long periods of pre-planned holiday leave, study leave, or is due to undergo an operation. The extension should not lead to the improvement period exceeding *12 months* unless the appropriate authority is satisfied that there are exceptional circumstances making this appropriate.

The written record supplied to the police officer should comprise a summary of the proceedings at that meeting. Any improvement notice must be accompanied by a notice informing the police officer of his/her right to appeal and the name of the person to whom the appeal should be sent. The notice must also inform the police officer of his/her right to submit written comments on the written record of the meeting and of the procedure for doing so.

The police officer may submit written comments on the written record not later than the end of seven working days after the date that he/she received it (unless an extension has been granted by his/her line manager). However, if the police officer has exercised his/her right to appeal against the finding or outcome of the first stage meeting, the police officer may not submit comments on the written record. It is the responsibility of the line manager to ensure that the written record, written improvement notice and any written comments of the police officer regarding the written record are retained together and filed in accordance with force policies.

4.3.9.3 Assessment of Performance or Attendance

It is expected that the police officer's performance or attendance will be actively monitored against the improvement notice and, where applicable, the action plan by the line manager throughout the specified period of the improvement notice. The line manager should discuss with the police officer any concerns that the line manager has during this period as regards his/her performance or attendance and offer advice and guidance where appropriate.

As soon as possible after the improvement notice period comes to an end, the line manager must formally assess the performance or attendance of the police officer during that period. If the line manager considers that the police officer's performance or attendance is satisfactory, the line manager should notify the police officer in writing of this. The notification should also inform the police officer that while the performance or attendance of the police officer is now satisfactory, the improvement notice is valid for a period of 12 months from the date printed on the notice so that it is possible for the second stage of the procedures to be initiated if the performance or attendance of the police officer falls below an acceptable level within the remaining period.

If the line manager considers that the police officer's performance or attendance is still unsatisfactory, the line manager should notify the police officer in writing of this. The line manager must also notify the police officer that he/she is required to attend a second stage meeting to consider these ongoing performance or attendance issues.

If the police officer has improved his/her performance or attendance to an acceptable standard within the specified improvement period, but then fails to maintain that standard within the 12 month validity period, it is open to the line manager to initiate stage two of the procedures. In such circumstances the line manager must notify the police officer in writing of his/her view that the police officer's performance or attendance is unsatisfactory as the police officer has failed to maintain the improvement and that as a consequence the police officer is required to attend a second stage meeting to discuss his/her failure to maintain a satisfactory standard of performance or attendance.

4.3.9.4 First Stage Appeals

A police officer has a right of appeal. However, any outcome of this first stage meeting will continue to apply up to the date that the appeal is determined. Therefore where the police officer contests the finding or outcome, he/she should continue to follow the terms of the improvement notice and any accompanying action plan pending the determination of the appeal. The notice of appeal must clearly set out the grounds and evidence for the appeal.

The grounds for appeal are:

- the finding of unsatisfactory performance or attendance is unreasonable;
- any of the terms of the improvement notice are unreasonable;
- there is evidence that could not reasonably have been considered at the first stage meeting which could have materially affected the finding of unsatisfactory performance or attendance or any of the terms of the written improvement notice;
- there was a breach of the procedures set out in the UPPs or other unfairness which could have materially affected the finding of unsatisfactory performance or attendance or the terms of the improvement notice.

On the basis of the above grounds of appeal, the police officer may appeal against the finding of unsatisfactory performance or attendance or the terms of the written improvement notice, those being:

- the respect in which the police officer's performance or attendance is considered unsatisfactory;
- the improvement which is required of the police officer; and/or
- the length of the period specified for improvement by the line manager at the first stage meeting.

KEYNOTE

At the first stage appeal meeting the second line manager will provide the police officer with the opportunity to make representations and provide his/her police friend (if he/she has one) with an opportunity to make representations. Having considered any representations by either the police officer and/or his/her police friend, the second line manager may confirm or reverse the finding of unsatisfactory performance or attendance or endorse or vary the terms of the improvement notice appealed against.

The second line manager may deal with the police officer in any manner in which the line manager could have dealt with him/her at the first stage meeting. Where the second line manager has reversed the finding of unsatisfactory performance or attendance he/she must also revoke the written improvement notice.

Within three working days of the day following the conclusion of the appeal meeting, the police officer will be given written notice of the second line manager's decision. If the second line manager is in a position to send a written summary of the reasons for that decision, this may also accompany the written notice of the decision. Any decision made that changes the finding or outcome of the first stage meeting will take effect by way of substitution for the finding or terms appealed against and as from the date of the first stage meeting.

4.3.10 The Second Stage

Initiation of the second stage *must* be for matters similar to or connected with the unsatisfactory performance or attendance referred to in the improvement notice issued at the first stage. Where, at the end of the period specified in an improvement notice, the line manager finds that the police officer's performance or attendance has not improved to an acceptable standard during that period or that the police officer has not maintained an acceptable level of performance or attendance during the validity period of the notice, the second line manager will notify the police officer in writing that he/she is required to attend a second stage meeting. The notification will state:

- the details of the procedures for determining the date and time of the meeting;
- a summary of the reasons why the line manager considers the police officer's performance or attendance unsatisfactory;
- the possible outcomes of a second stage and third stage meeting;
- that the line manager may attend the meeting;
- that a human resources professional or a police officer (who should have experience of UPPs and be independent from the line management chain) may attend the meeting to advise the second line manager on the proceedings;
- that if the police officer agrees, any other person specified in the notice may attend the meeting;
- that prior to the meeting the police officer must provide the second line manager with any documentation he/she intends to rely on in the meeting; and
- the police officer's rights, i.e. his/her right to seek advice from a representative of his/her staff association (in the case of a member of the police force) and to be accompanied and represented at the meeting by a police friend.

KEYNOTE
The notice must also include copies of related documentation relied upon by the line manager in support of the view that the police officer's performance or attendance continues to be unsatisfactory.

In advance of the meeting, the police officer shall provide the second line manager with any documents on which he/she intends to rely on in support of his/her case. Any document or other material that was not submitted in advance of the meeting may be considered at the meeting at the discretion of the second line manager, ensuring fairness to all parties. However, the presumption should be that such documents or other material will not be permitted unless it can be shown that they were not previously available to be submitted in advance.

The second line manager should explain that there is potentially a further stage to the procedures and that the maximum outcome of stage two is a final improvement notice. The second line manager will also explain that if the procedure is followed to the final stage, possible outcomes include dismissal, a reduction in rank (in the case of a member of a police force and in performance cases only), redeployment to alternative duties or an extended improvement notice (in exceptional circumstances).

4.3.10.1 Second Stage Meeting

At the second stage meeting the second line manager will:

- explain to the police officer the reasons why he/she has been required to attend a second stage meeting;
- provide the police officer with the opportunity to make representations in response;
- provide the police officer's police friend (if he/she has one) with an opportunity to make representations;
- listen to what the police officer (and/or his/her police friend) has to say, ask questions and comment as appropriate.

The second line manager may adjourn the meeting at any time if he/she considers it is necessary or expedient to do so. Where, having considered any representations by either the police officer and/or his/her police friend, the second line manager finds that the performance or attendance of the police officer has been unsatisfactory (either during the period specified in the written improvement notice or during the validity period of the written improvement notice) he/she shall:

- inform the police officer in what respect(s) his/her performance or attendance is considered unsatisfactory;
- inform the police officer of the improvement that is required in his/her performance or attendance;
- inform the police officer that, if a sufficient improvement is not made within the period specified by the second line manager, he/she may be required to attend a third stage meeting;
- inform the police officer that he/she will receive a final written improvement notice; and
- inform the police officer that if the sufficient improvement in his/her performance or attendance is not maintained during the validity period of such notice, he/she may be required to attend a third stage meeting.

4.3.10.2 Procedure following the Second Stage Meeting

A written record of the meeting and any improvement notice shall be sent to the officer as soon as reasonably practicable after they have been prepared.

Any improvement notice must be accompanied by a notice informing the police officer of his/her right to appeal and the name of the person to whom the appeal should be sent. The notice must also inform the police officer of his/her right to submit written comments on the written record of the meeting and of the procedure for doing so.

The police officer may submit written comments on the written record not later than the end of seven working days after the date that he/she received it (unless an extension has been granted by the second line manager following an application by the police officer).

4.3.10.3 Second Stage Appeals

A police officer has a right of appeal against the finding and the terms of the improvement notice imposed at stage two of the UPPs and against the decision to require him/her to attend the meeting. However, any finding and outcome of this second stage meeting will continue to apply up to the date that the appeal is determined. Therefore where the police officer contests the finding or outcome, he/she should continue to follow the terms of the improvement notice and any accompanying action plan pending the determination of the appeal. Any appeal should be made in writing to the senior manager within seven working days following the day of the receipt of the improvement notice. The notice of appeal must clearly set out the grounds and evidence for the appeal. The grounds for appeal are as follows:

- the finding of unsatisfactory performance or attendance is unreasonable;
- any of the terms of the improvement notice are unreasonable;
- there is evidence that could not reasonably have been considered at the second stage meeting which could have materially affected the finding of unsatisfactory performance or attendance or any of the terms of the improvement notice;
- there was a breach of the procedures set out in the Police (Performance) Regulations or other unfairness which could have materially affected the finding of unsatisfactory performance or attendance or the terms of the written improvement notice;
- the police officer should not have been required to attend the second stage meeting as the meeting did not concern unsatisfactory performance or attendance which was similar to or connected with the unsatisfactory performance or attendance referred to in the written improvement notice that followed the first stage meeting.

On the basis of the above grounds of appeal, the police officer may appeal against the finding of unsatisfactory performance or attendance, the decision to require him/her to attend the second stage meeting or the terms of the written improvement notice, those being:

- the respect in which the police officer's performance or attendance is considered unsatisfactory;
- the improvement which is required of the police officer;
- the length of the period specified for improvement by the second line manager at the second stage meeting.

KEYNOTE

The police officer has the right to be accompanied and represented by a police friend at the second stage appeal meeting.

Once a date for the meeting is fixed, the senior manager should send to the police officer a notice in writing of the date, time and place of the second stage appeal meeting together with the information required to be provided under reg. 24 of the Performance Regulations.

At the second stage appeal meeting the senior manager will provide the police officer with the opportunity to make representations, and provide his/her police friend (if he/she has one) with an opportunity to make representations. Having considered any representations by either the police officer and/or his/her police friend, the senior manager may make a finding that the officer should not have been required to attend the second stage meeting, and reverse the finding made at that meeting, confirm or reverse the finding of unsatisfactory performance or attendance or endorse or vary the terms of the improvement notice.

Any decision made that changes the finding or outcome of the second stage meeting will take effect by way of substitution for the finding or terms appealed against and as from the date of the second stage meeting.

4.3.11 The Third Stage

Where, at the end of the period specified in the final written improvement notice, the line manager finds that the police officer's performance or attendance has not improved to an acceptable standard during that period or that the police officer has not maintained an acceptable level of performance or attendance during the validity period of the notice, the line manager must notify the police officer in writing that he/she is required to attend a third stage meeting to discuss these issues. As soon as reasonably practicable thereafter, the senior manager must give a notice to the officer informing him/her:

- that the meeting will be with a panel appointed by the appropriate authority;
- the procedures for determining the date and time of the meeting;
- a summary of the reasons why the police officer's performance or attendance is considered unsatisfactory;
- the possible outcomes of a third stage meeting;

- that a human resources professional or a police officer (who should have experience of UPPs and be independent from the line management chain) may attend to advise the panel on the proceedings;
- that counsel or a solicitor may attend the meeting to advise the panel on the proceedings and on any question of law that may arise at the meeting;
- where the police officer is a special constable, inform him/her that a member of the special constabulary will attend the meeting to advise the panel;
- that if the police officer agrees, any other person specified in the notice may attend, e.g. a person attending for development reasons; and
- the police officer's rights, i.e. his/her right to seek advice from a representative of his/her staff association (in the case of a member of the police force) and to be accompanied and represented at the meeting by a police friend.

The notice must also include copies of related documentation relied upon by the line manager in support of the view that the police officer's performance or attendance continues to be unsatisfactory. It is important to note that a third stage meeting may not take place unless the officer has been notified of his/her right to representation by a police friend. The notice does not at this stage need to give the names of the panel members as these may not be known at the time of issue. However, as soon as the panel has been appointed by the appropriate authority, the appropriate authority should notify the police officer of the members' names.

The purpose of the meeting is for the panel to hear the evidence of the unsatisfactory performance or attendance and to give the police officer the opportunity to put forward his/her views. It will also be an opportunity to hear of any factors that are continuing to affect the police officer's performance or attendance and what the police officer considers can be done to address them.

Where the police officer has reached stage three following stages one and two (i.e. not a gross incompetence meeting), the possible outcomes of this stage three meeting are as follows:

- redeployment;
- reduction in rank (in the case of a member of a police force and for performance cases only);
- dismissal (with a minimum of 28 days' notice); or
- extension of a final improvement notice (in exceptional circumstances).

Where the panel grants an extension to the final improvement notice, it will specify a new period within which improvement to performance or attendance must be made. The 12-month validity period of the extended final improvement notice will apply in full from the date of extension. The panel may also vary any of the terms in the notice.

4.3.11.1 Stage Three Gross Incompetence Meetings

There may be *exceptional circumstances* where the appropriate authority considers the performance (not attendance) of the police officer to be so unsatisfactory as to warrant the procedures being initiated at the third stage. This would be as a result of a single incident of 'gross incompetence'. It is not envisaged that an appropriate authority would initiate the procedures at the third stage in respect of a series of acts over a period of time.

KEYNOTE

'Gross incompetence' is defined in the Police (Performance) Regulations 2012 as 'a serious inability or serious failure of a police officer to perform the duties of the rank or role he is currently undertaking to a satisfactory standard or level, to the extent that dismissal would be justified, except that no account shall be taken of the attendance of a police officer when considering whether he has been grossly incompetent'.

Where the appropriate authority determines it is appropriate to initiate the procedures at this stage, then the police officer must be informed in writing that he/she is required to attend a third stage meeting to discuss his/her performance. Where the appropriate authority has informed the police officer that he/she is to attend a third stage only meeting, it must, as soon as reasonably practicable, send the police officer a notice in writing which will include the following details:

- that the meeting will be with a panel appointed by the appropriate authority;
- the procedure for determining the date and time of the meeting;
- a summary of the reasons why the police officer's performance is considered to constitute gross incompetence;
- the possible outcomes of a third stage only meeting;
- that a human resources professional and a police officer (who should have experience of UPPs and be independent from the line management chain) may attend to advise the panel on the proceedings;
- that counsel or a solicitor may attend the meeting to advise the panel on the proceedings and on any question of law that may arise at the meeting;
- where the police officer is a special constable, inform him/her that a member of the special constabulary will attend the meeting to advise the panel;
- if the police officer agrees, any other person specified in the notice may attend, e.g. a person attending for development reasons; and
- the police officer's rights, i.e. his/her right to seek advice from a representative of his/her staff association (in the case of a member of the police force) and to be accompanied at the meeting by a police friend.

The purpose of the meeting is for the panel to hear the evidence of the gross incompetence and to give the police officer and his/her representative the opportunity to make representations on the matter.

The appropriate authority will explain that the police officer is required to attend the third stage meeting and that the possible outcomes of the stage three meeting are:

- redeployment to alternative duties;
- the issue of a final written improvement notice;
- reduction in rank (with immediate effect);
- dismissal (with immediate effect); or
- the issue of a written improvement notice (if the panel considers that there has been unsatisfactory performance and not gross incompetence).

4.3.11.2 Panel Membership and Procedure

The panel will comprise a panel chair and two other members and be appointed by the appropriate authority of the force in which the police officer is a member. At least one of the three panel members must be a police officer and one should be a human resources professional. Membership will be as follows:

- First panel member (chair): Senior police officer or senior human resources professional.
- Second panel member: Police officer of at least the rank of superintendent or human resources professional who in the opinion of the appropriate authority is at least equivalent to that rank.
- Third panel member: Police officer of at least the rank of superintendent or police staff member who in the opinion of the appropriate authority is at least equivalent to that rank.

As soon as the appropriate authority has appointed a third stage panel, it should arrange for copies of all relevant documentation to be sent to those members. In particular, any document:

- that was available to the line manager in relation to any first stage meeting;
- that was available to the second line manager in relation to any second stage meeting;
- that was prepared or submitted in advance of the third stage meeting;
- that was prepared or submitted following those meetings, i.e. improvement notices, action plans and meeting notes;
- relating to any appeal.

As soon as the appropriate authority has appointed a third stage panel, it must send the police officer written confirmation of the names of panel members. The police officer has the right to object to any panel members appointed by the appropriate authority and any such objection must be made in writing to the appropriate authority no later than three working days after receipt of the notification of the names of the panel members. The police officer must include the ground of his/her objection to any panel member in that submission. The appropriate authority must inform the police officer in writing whether it upholds or rejects an objection to a panel member. If the appropriate authority upholds the objection, a new panel member will be appointed as a replacement. As soon as practicable after any such appointment, the police officer will be informed in writing of the name of the new panel member. The appropriate authority must ensure that the requirements for the composition of the panel are met. The police officer may object to the newly appointed panel member in the same way whereupon the appropriate authority must follow the same procedure again.

4.3.11.3 Special Constables and Third Stage Meetings

In cases where the police officer is a special constable, as indicated above (**see para. 4.3.11**), the force will appoint a member of the special constabulary to attend the meeting to advise the panel (this is for the purpose of fairness). The special constable advising the panel must have sufficient seniority and experience of the special constabulary to be able to advise the panel. The special constable advising the panel can be a police officer serving in a different force. The special constable adviser will not form part of the panel and will not have a role in determining whether or not the police officer's performance or attendance is unsatisfactory. In arranging a third stage meeting involving special constables, due consideration should be given to the fact that special constables are unpaid volunteers and may therefore have full-time employment or other personal commitments.

4.3.11.4 Third Stage Meeting Dates and Timeframes

Any third stage meeting should take place no later than 30 working days after the date that the notification has been sent to the police officer. Within that timeframe, wherever possible, the meeting date and time should be agreed between the panel chair and the police officer. However, where agreement cannot be reached the panel chair must specify a time and date. If the police officer or his/her police friend is not available at the date or time specified by the panel chair, the police officer may propose an alternative time. Provided that the alternative time is reasonable and falls within a period of five working days beginning with the first working day after that specified by the panel chair, the meeting must be postponed to that time. If the panel chair considers it to be in the interests of fairness to do so, he/she may extend the 30 working day period within which the meeting should take place and the reasons for any such extension must be notified in writing to both the appropriate authority and the police officer. As soon as a date for the meeting is fixed, the panel chair should send to the police officer a notice in writing of the date, time and place of the third stage meeting.

4.3.11.5 Procedure on Receipt of Notice of Third Stage Meeting

Within 14 working days of the date on which a notice has been sent to the police officer (unless this period is extended by the panel chair for exceptional circumstances), the police officer must provide to the appropriate authority:

- a written notice of whether or not he/she accepts that his/her performance or attendance has been unsatisfactory or that he/she has been grossly incompetent, as the case may be;
- where he/she accepts that his/her performance or attendance has been unsatisfactory or that he/she has been grossly incompetent, any written submission he/she wishes to make in mitigation.

Where the police officer does not accept that his/her performance or attendance has been unsatisfactory or that he/she has been grossly incompetent or where he/she disputes part of the matters referred to in the notice that he/she has received, he/she shall provide the appropriate authority with a written notice of:

- the matters he/she disputes and his/her account of the relevant events; and
- any arguments on points of law he/she wishes to be considered by the panel.

The police officer shall provide the appropriate authority and the panel with a copy of any document he/she intends to rely on at the third stage meeting.

Before the end of three working days following the officer's compliance the senior manager and the officer shall each supply a list of proposed witnesses or give notice that they do not have any witnesses. Where witnesses are proposed, this must be accompanied by brief details of their evidence and their address. The officer should try to agree a list of witnesses with the senior manager. Where agreement has not been reached, the officer shall send to the appropriate authority his/her list of witnesses. As soon as reasonably practicable after any list of witnesses has been agreed or, in the case where no agreement could be reached, supplied to the appropriate authority, the appropriate authority must send the lists to the panel chair together with, in the latter case, a list of its proposed witnesses. The panel chair will consider the list of proposed witnesses and will determine which, if any, witnesses should attend the third stage meeting.

The panel chair can determine that persons not named in the list should attend as witnesses. No witnesses will give evidence at a third stage meeting unless the panel chair reasonably believes that it is necessary in the interests of fairness for the witness to do so, in which case he/she will:

- in the case of a police officer, cause him/her to be ordered to attend the third stage meeting;
- in any other case, cause him/her to be given notice that his/her attendance at the third stage meeting is necessary.

Such notices will include the date, time and place of the meeting.

Where a witness attends to give evidence then any questions to that witness should be made through the panel chair. This would not prevent the panel chair allowing questions to be asked directly if he/she feels that this is appropriate.

The documents or other material to be relied upon at the meeting are required to be submitted in advance. Any document or other material that was not submitted in advance of the meeting may be considered at the meeting at the discretion of the panel chair. However, the presumption should be that such documents or other material will not be permitted unless it can be shown that they were not previously available to be submitted in advance or that they relate to mitigation following a finding of unsatisfactory performance or attendance that was contested by the police officer.

4.3.11.6   At the Third Stage Meeting

At the third stage meeting the panel chair will conduct the meeting and will explain to the police officer the reasons why he/she has been required to attend a third stage meeting and provide the police officer with the opportunity to make representations in response. Where the case is one of gross incompetence and the police officer has opted for legal representation, the chair will provide the police officer's legal representative with the opportunity to make representations. If the officer has chosen not to be legally represented, they will provide the police officer's police friend (if they have one) with an opportunity to make representations. The panel chair has a duty to listen to what the police officer and/or police friend has to say, and ask questions as appropriate.

Having considered any representations by either the police officer and/or his/her police friend or (where applicable) the police officer's legal representative, the panel will come to a finding as to whether or not the performance or attendance of the police officer has been unsatisfactory or whether or not his/her behaviour constitutes gross incompetence, as the case may be. If there is a difference of view between the three panel members, the finding or decision will be based on a simple majority vote, but it will not be indicated whether it was taken unanimously or by a majority.

The panel must prepare (or cause to be prepared) its decision in writing which shall also state the finding. Where the panel has found that the police officer's performance or attendance has been unsatisfactory or that he/she has been grossly incompetent, the decision must also state the panel's reasons and any outcome which it orders.

As soon as reasonably practicable after the conclusion of the meeting, the panel chair shall send a copy of the decision to the police officer and the line manager. However, the police officer must be given written notice of the finding of the panel within three working days of the conclusion of the meeting. Where the panel has made a finding of unsatisfactory performance or attendance or gross incompetence the copy of the decision sent to the police officer must also be accompanied by a notice informing him/her of the circumstances in which and the timeframe within which he/she may appeal to a police appeals tribunal. A verbatim record of the meeting should be taken. The police officer must, on request, be supplied with a copy of the record.

4.3.11.7   Postponement and Adjournment of a Third Stage Meeting

If the panel chair considers it necessary or expedient, he/she may direct that the third stage meeting should take place at a different time from that originally notified to the police officer. The panel chair's alternative time may fall after the period of 30 working days. In the event that the panel chair postpones a third stage meeting he/she should notify the following relevant parties in writing of his/her reasons and the revised time and place for the meeting:

- the police officer;
- other panel members; and
- the appropriate authority.

KEYNOTE

Video Link

If the police officer informs the panel chair in advance that he/she is unable to attend the third stage meeting on grounds which the panel chair considers reasonable, the panel chair may allow the police officer to participate in the meeting by video link or other means. In cases where the police officer is absent (e.g. through illness or injury) a short delay may be reasonable to allow him/her to attend. If this is not possible or any delay is considered not appropriate in the circumstances then the persons conducting the meeting/hearing may allow the police officer to participate by telephone or video link. In these circumstances a police friend will always be permitted to attend the meeting/hearing to represent the police officer in the normal way (and, in the case of a gross incompetence meeting, the police officer's legal representative where appointed).

4.3.11.8   **Assessment of Final and Extended Final Improvement Notices Issued at the Third Stage**

Where the police officer has been issued with a final improvement notice or, in exceptional cases, the panel has extended a final improvement notice period, it is expected that the police officer's performance or attendance will be actively monitored by the line manager throughout the specified period of the final/extended final improvement notice. The line manager should discuss with the police officer any concerns that the line manager has during this period as regards his/her performance or attendance and offer advice and guidance where appropriate.

As soon as reasonably practicable after the specified period of the final/extended final improvement notice comes to an end, the panel will assess the performance or attendance of the police officer during that period. The panel chair must then inform the police officer in writing of the panel's conclusion following assessment, i.e. whether there has been sufficient improvement in his/her performance or attendance during the specified period. If the panel considers that there has been insufficient improvement the panel chair shall also notify the officer that he/she is required to attend another third stage meeting.

If, at the end of the validity period of the final/extended final improvement notice, the panel considers that sufficient improvement to the police officer's performance or attendance has not been made or maintained during this period, the panel chair will inform the police officer of the panel's assessment. Any such notification to the police officer must also include notification that he/she is required to attend a further third stage meeting. Where an officer is required to attend a further third stage meeting, the UPPs shall apply as if he/she were required to attend that meeting for the first time and following a second stage meeting.

As with the initiation of stages one and two for unsatisfactory performance or attendance, a further third stage meeting must relate to matters similar to or connected with the unsatisfactory performance or attendance or gross incompetence referred to in the final improvement notice extended or issued by the panel. The panel should (where possible) be composed of the same persons who conducted the previous third stage meeting. However, there may be cases where reconstitution of the panel is either inappropriate or not possible. In such circumstances the appropriate authority may substitute members as it sees fit subject to the requirements in **para. 4.3.11.2.** As soon as reasonably practicable after the appointment of any new panel members, the police officer should be notified in writing of the changes in panel membership. The police officer will have the opportunity to object to any new panel members.

A police officer may only be given an extension to a final improvement notice on one occasion. Therefore where the police officer is required to attend a reconvened third stage meeting and the panel finds that the police officer's performance or attendance continues to be unsatisfactory, the only outcomes available to the panel are redeployment, reduction in rank (only for a member of a police force and in performance cases) or dismissal (with notice).

In cases where a police officer was issued with an improvement notice (as opposed to a final improvement notice) for unsatisfactory performance at a gross incompetence third stage meeting, that written improvement notice will be equivalent to a written improvement notice issued at a first stage meeting. In that case the procedure for assessing the performance of the police officer will be the same as that following the first stage.

4.3.11.9 Third Stage Appeals

Following a third stage meeting, a police officer may be able to appeal to a police appeals tribunal. However, any finding and outcome of the third stage meeting will continue to apply up to the date that the appeal is determined.

4.3.12 Attendance at Each Stage of the Procedures and Ill-health

Attendance at any stage meeting is not subject to the same considerations as reporting for duty and the provisions of reg. 33 (sick leave) of the Police Regulations 2003 *do not apply*. An illness or disability may render a police officer unfit for duty without affecting his/her ability to attend a meeting. However, if the police officer is incapacitated, the meeting may be deferred until he/she is sufficiently improved to attend. A meeting will not be deferred indefinitely because the police officer is unable to attend, although every effort should be made to make it possible for the police officer to attend if he/she wishes to be present. For example:

- the acute phase of a serious physical illness is usually fairly short-lived, and the meeting may be deferred until the police officer is well enough to attend;
- if the police officer suffers from a physical injury (for instance a broken leg) it may be possible to hold the meeting at a location convenient to him/her.

Where such circumstances apply at a stage three meeting, the force may wish to consider the use of video, telephone or other conferencing technology. Where, despite such efforts having been made and/or the meeting having been deferred, the police officer either persists in failing to attend the meeting or maintains his/her inability to attend, the person conducting the meeting will need to decide whether to continue to defer the meeting or whether to proceed with it, if necessary in the absence of the police officer. The person conducting the meeting must judge the most appropriate course of action. Nothing in this paragraph should be taken to suggest that, where a police officer's medical condition is found to be such that he/she would normally be retired on medical grounds, the UPPs should prevent or delay retirement.

4.3.13 The Use of Records under UPPs

Records of any part of the UPPs should not be taken into account after an improvement notice has ceased to be valid. Equally, where a police officer appeals and that appeal is successful, the record of that procedure should not be taken into consideration in any future proceedings or for any other purpose.

4.3.14 Misconduct, Performance and Attendance Issues for Seconded Officers

The procedures set out in the UPPs cannot be applied by the organisation to which the police officer is seconded under s. 97 of the Police Act 1996. However, the procedures set out in the Regulations can be applied by the parent force in respect of conduct, performance or attendance while on secondment. Those responsible for managing police officers on secondment are expected to manage any issue of unsatisfactory performance or attendance or minor misconduct in a proportionate, fair and timely manner without returning an officer to his/her parent force. Only if it is necessary to institute the formal procedures should an officer be returned to force, in accordance with the principles and procedures expressed below.

Where an officer is on secondment under the Police (Overseas Service) Act 1945, with the Police Ombudsman for Northern Ireland or with the Police Service of Northern Ireland, then he/she can be dealt with by the receiving organisation under its disciplinary arrangements. However, on return to his/her force, he/she can still be dealt with under the disciplinary arrangements in respect of the same matters.

It is important that police officers on secondment are clear about who has line management responsibility for them. The line managers for such police officers must ensure that the police officer continues to have a PDR and is made aware of these arrangements for dealing with issues of misconduct or unsatisfactory performance or attendance.

Where there is no or insufficient improvement in the performance or attendance of the police officer, the seconded police officer's line manager should prepare a written report which details the nature of the unsatisfactory performance or attendance together with the remedial and other measures taken, and send this report to the head of the organisation to which the police officer is seconded (or his/her nominated representative). The head of the organisation (or nominated representative), in conjunction with the appropriate authority for the police officer concerned, will decide whether it is appropriate that the police officer concerned should be returned to his/her parent force or whether the unsatisfactory performance or attendance can be addressed with the police officer remaining on secondment. Where a police officer who has been returned to his/her parent force under this procedure continues to demonstrate the same pattern of unsatisfactory performance or attendance, the details of the unsatisfactory performance or attendance while on secondment may be used to inform the decision whether it is appropriate to use the UPPs.

In alleged cases of misconduct by a secondee, the organisation to which the police officer has been seconded will need to make an initial assessment of the allegation of misconduct. If that assessment determines that the matter can be dealt with by management action, the seconded officer's manager is expected to deal with the matter in this way. As part of this decision making process, it may be necessary for the line manager to contact the appropriate authority for the seconded officer to assist in determining the nature of the conduct and whether it should be investigated. In this regard, the appropriate authority will need to consider its obligations under the Police Reform Act 2002 and any requirement to refer a matter to the Independent Police Complaints Commission (IPCC).

However, where the line manager considers that an alleged breach of the Standards of Professional Behaviour is more serious and indicates that the police officer concerned may have committed a criminal offence, or behaved in a manner that would justify the bringing of disciplinary proceedings, the head of the organisation to which the police officer is seconded (or his/her nominated representative) will liaise with the appropriate authority from which the police officer concerned is seconded to assess whether the officer should be returned to the force while a preliminary assessment into the matter is conducted by the parent force. If, as a result of that preliminary assessment, the parent force considers it appropriate to issue a reg. 15 notice in relation to the matter, the officer must be returned to force.

Where it is determined by the appropriate authority for the seconded officer and the organisation to which he/she is seconded, that the conduct, if proved or admitted, would not justify the bringing of disciplinary proceedings, management action may still be taken where appropriate. At the conclusion of any disciplinary proceedings, where the police officer has been returned to the parent force, that force together with the organisation to which the police officer concerned was seconded will decide if it is appropriate for the police officer to be able to resume his/her secondment.

4.3.15   Vicarious Liability of Chief Officers

Section 88 of the Police Act 1996 originally provided that a chief officer will be vicariously liable for the 'torts' (civil wrongs) of his/her officers committed in the performance (or purported performance) of their duties. This meant that the chief officer was responsible for the payment of any damages arising out of a civil claim in respect of such a tort. The extent of this vicarious liability was wider than that imposed on employers generally (*Weir* v *Chief Constable of Merseyside Police* [2003] EWCA Civ 111).

However, despite the fact that the vicarious liability of chief officers was broader than that of any ordinary employer, its limitation to strictly actionable civil wrongs was felt to have led to some inequities, denying remedies to individuals while failing to impose full accountability on the relevant chief officers. The Police Reform Act 2002 clarified the position and amended s. 88 to provide that chief officers will be liable for the 'unlawful conduct' (as opposed to purely civil wrongs) of their officers and employees when acting as such (s. 102).

4.3.16   Other Regulations

In addition to the specific provisions for conduct, complaints and efficiency, there are several other sources of regulation that govern the employment and deployment of police officers.

4.3.16.1   Restrictions on Private Lives

The Police Regulations 2003 impose restrictions on the private lives of officers. Regulation 6 provides that the restrictions contained in sch. 1 shall apply to all members of a police force. It also provides that no restrictions other than those designed to secure the proper exercise of the functions of a constable shall be imposed by the chief officer of police on the private lives of members of a police force except such as may temporarily be necessary or such as may be approved by the Secretary of State after consultation with the Police Advisory Board for England and Wales.

Schedule 1

Schedule 1 provides that a member of a police force:

- shall at all times abstain from any activity which is likely to interfere with the impartial discharge of his/her duties or which is likely to give rise to the impression among members of the public that it may so interfere;
- shall in particular:
    + not take any active part in politics;
    + not belong to any organisation specified or described in a determination of the Secretary of State.

For this purpose the Secretary of State has determined that no member of a police force may be a member of the British National Party (BNP), Combat 18 or the National Front.

- shall not reside at premises which are not for the time being approved by the chief officer of police;
- shall not, without the previous consent of the chief officer of police, receive a lodger in a house or quarters with which he/she is provided, or sub-let any part of the house or quarters;
- shall not, unless he/she has previously given written notice to the chief officer of police, receive a lodger in a house in which he/she resides and in respect of which he/she receives an allowance under sch. 3, or sub-let any part of such a house;
- shall not wilfully refuse or neglect to discharge any lawful debt.

4.3.16.2 Business Interests

Some business interests preclude people from applying to be a police constable (reg. 7 of the Police Regulations 2003).

Regulation 8 provides that, if a member of a police force or a relative included in his/her family proposes to have, or has, a 'business interest', the member shall forthwith give written notice of that interest to the chief officer of police unless that business interest was disclosed at the time of the officer's appointment as a member of the force.

On receipt of such a notice, the chief officer shall determine whether or not the interest in question is compatible with the member concerned remaining a member of the force and shall notify the member in writing of his/her decision within 28 days.

If a business interest is felt to be incompatible, the chief officer may dispense with the member's services after giving him/her an opportunity to make representations. Regulation 7(2) provides that a member of a police force or relative has a business interest if:

- the member holds any office or employment for hire or gain or carries on any business;
- a shop is kept or a like business carried on by the member's spouse (not being separated) at any premises in the area of the police force in question or by any relative living with him/her at the premises where he/she resides; or
- the member, his/her spouse (not being separated) or any relative living with him/her has a pecuniary interest in any licence or permit granted in relation to liquor licensing, refreshment houses or betting and gaming or regulating places of entertainment in the area of the police force in question.

'Relative' includes a reference to a spouse, parent, son, daughter, brother or sister.

A police officer must notify his/her chief officer of any changes in a business interest.

4.3.17 Offences

The following criminal offences relate to the general abuse of public office and specific offences relating to police officers or impersonation of officers or officials.

4.3.17.1 Misconduct in a Public Office

OFFENCE: **Misconduct in a Public Office—*Common Law***
- Triable on indictment • Imprisonment at large

It is a misdemeanour at common law for the holder of a public office to do anything that amounts to a malfeasance or a 'culpable' misfeasance (*R* v *Wyat* (1705) 1 Salk 380).

Where there is clear evidence of one or more statutory offences, they should usually form the basis of the case, with the 'public office' element being put forward as an aggravating factor for sentencing purposes.

The use of the common law offence should therefore be limited to the following situations:

- where there is no relevant statutory offence, but the behaviour or the circumstances are such that they should nevertheless be treated as criminal;
- where there is a statutory offence but it would be difficult or inappropriate to use it. This might arise because of evidential difficulties in proving the statutory offence in the particular circumstances;
- because the maximum sentence for the statutory offence would be entirely insufficient for the seriousness of the misconduct.

KEYNOTE

This offence has also been described as 'A man accepting an office of trust concerning the public is answerable criminally to the King for misbehaviour in his office...by whomsoever and in whatever way the officer is appointed' (*R* v *Bembridge* (1783) 3 Dougl 327).

Such offences can only be tried on indictment and the court has a power of sentence 'at large', that is, there is no limit on the sentence that can be passed. This ancient common law oddity is both a civil wrong (tort) giving rise to an action for damages in the county and High Court, and a criminal offence which is triable on indictment and punishable by an unlimited term of imprisonment.

Given the wide scope of the 'offence' element, it can cover a multitude of transgressions by police officers, from mistreating prisoners to the improper use of criminal intelligence. The conduct can be separated into occasions of *mal*feasance and *mis*feasance. The first requires some degree of wrongful motive or intention on the part of the officer while the second is more likely to apply where there has been some form of wilful neglect of duty: both are difficult to prove.

The essence of both is generally an abuse of public power in bad faith (*Thomas* v *Secretary of State for the Home Office* [2000] Prison LR 188). There must at least be some real connection between the alleged misconduct and the public office, for instance where a man employed by a local council as a maintenance manager dishonestly caused his employees to carry out works on his girlfriend's premises (*R* v *Bowden* [1996] 1 WLR 98). Therefore, simply behaving badly while off duty would not of itself make a public office holder (such as a police officer) guilty of this offence (*Elliott* v *Chief Constable of Wiltshire* (1996) *The Times*, 5 December—disclosure of previous convictions from PNC to a newspaper capable of amounting to misfeasance). It may, however, make the relevant *chief officer* vicariously liable under other heads of law if the off-duty officer was purporting to rely on his/her status as a constable (*Weir* v *Chief Constable of Merseyside* [2003] EWCA Civ 111).

The key elements of the offence so far as it applies to public office holders (such as police officers) were set out by the Court of Appeal in *Attorney-General's Reference (No. 3 of 2003)* [2004] EWCA Crim 868. That case arose out of a death in police custody and the officers were charged with manslaughter by gross negligence, along with the alternative offence of misconduct in a public office. It was argued that misconduct in a public office is a 'conduct' crime, i.e. one where the acts (or omissions) themselves were the real consideration and not the consequences which those acts/omissions brought about (see *Crime*, chapter 1.2). Although reluctant to try to give an exhaustive definition of the offence, the Court of Appeal identified the elements of conduct and state of mind that must be proved in order to convict an officer of misfeasance, holding the main ingredients to be:

- Conduct (or omission) which involved the public office holder *acting as such*. In other words, this would need to arise from the actions (or omissions) of a police officer while acting in his/her capacity as a constable. A purely personal matter arising while the officer was off duty would not normally meet this first criterion.
- Evidence of wilful neglect and/or wilful misconduct. Simple inadvertence or accidental action/omission without more will not be enough.
- The degree of wilful neglect/misconduct must be such as to amount to an abuse of the public's trust in the office holder.
- Proof that the officer acted/omitted to act without any reasonable excuse or justification.

In the civil setting, even though there might be circumstances where officers could be criticised for failures, including incompetence, excess of zeal and even serious negligence, the absence of bad faith or deliberate misuse of power would generally mean that there is not enough to support an allegation of misfeasance (*Ashley* v *Chief Constable of Sussex* [2005] EWHC 415 (QB)).

The ingredients of the civil wrong are fully set out in *Three Rivers District Council* v *Governor and Company of the Bank of England (No. 3)* [2003] 2 AC 1. Their application, especially in the case of police officers, was discussed at length in *Cornelius* v *London Borough of Hackney* [2002] EWCA Civ 1073. In *Three Rivers*, Lord Steyn confirmed that the civil and criminal wrongs bore some resemblance. Although many of the earlier cases involved an element of corruption, this is not a requirement for the offence (*R* v *Dytham* [1979] QB 722). This offence might be committed where a police officer wilfully neglects to prevent a criminal assault (as in *Dytham*), or possibly where a supervisory officer fails to intervene in a situation where one of his/her officers is carrying out an unlawful act.

From the many authorities (especially *Bowden*) it is arguable that this offence could be extended in appropriate circumstances to misconduct of non-sworn employees such as those designated (or perhaps even those accredited) under the Police Reform Act 2002 (as to which see *Evidence and Procedure*, chapter 2.1).

The Court of Appeal has held that, where the police wrote to the registered keepers of vehicles believed to have been stolen in another country, informing those keepers that they may not be the legal owners, the person who imported and sold the vehicles *might* be able to bring a claim for misfeasance—much would depend on the state of mind and intentions of the relevant individual in acting as they did (*R Cruickshank Ltd* v *Chief Constable of Kent* [2002] EWCA Civ 1840).

4.3.17.2 Offences Relating to Impersonation

OFFENCE: **Impersonating a Police Officer—*Police Act 1996, s. 90(1)***
- Triable summarily • Six months' imprisonment

The Police Act 1996, s. 90 states:

(1) Any person who with intent to deceive impersonates a member of a police force or special constable, or makes any statement or does any act calculated falsely to suggest that he is such a member or constable, shall be guilty of an offence and liable …

OFFENCE: **Wearing or Possessing Uniform—*Police Act 1996, s. 90(2) and (3)***
- Triable summarily • Fine *(No specific power of arrest)*

The Police Act 1996, s. 90 states:

(2) Any person who, not being a constable, wears any article of police uniform in circumstances where it gives him an appearance so nearly resembling that of a member of a police force as to be calculated to deceive shall be guilty of an offence …

(3) Any person who, not being a member of a police force or special constable, has in his possession any article of police uniform shall, unless he proves that he obtained possession of that article lawfully and has possession of it for a lawful purpose, be guilty of an offence …

KEYNOTE

'Article of police uniform' means:

- any article of uniform, or
- any distinctive badge or mark, or
- any document of identification

usually issued to members of police forces or special constables (s. 90(4)).

OFFENCE: **Impersonating Designated or Accredited Person—*Police Reform Act 2002, s. 46(3)***

> • Triable summarily • Six months' imprisonment and/or a fine *(No specific power of arrest)*

The Police Reform Act 2002, s. 46 states:

> (3) Any person who, with intent to deceive—
> (a) impersonates a designated person, an accredited person or an accredited inspector,
> (b) makes any statement or does any act calculated falsely to suggest that he is a designated person, that he is an accredited person or that he is an accredited inspector, or
> (c) makes any statement or does any act calculated falsely to suggest that he has powers as a designated or accredited person or as an accredited inspector that exceed the powers he actually has,
> is guilty of an offence.

KEYNOTE

These offences are based on the corresponding offences for police officers.

4.3.17.3 Causing Disaffection among the Police

OFFENCE: **Causing Disaffection—*Police Act 1996, s. 91(1)***

> • Triable either way • Two years' imprisonment on indictment
> • Six months' imprisonment and/or a fine summarily *(No specific power of arrest)*

The Police Act 1996, s. 91 states:

> (1) Any person who causes, or attempts to cause, or does any act calculated to cause, disaffection amongst the members of any police force, or induces or attempts to induce, or does any act calculated to induce, any member of a police force to withhold his services, shall be guilty of an offence …

4.3.17.4 Corrupt or Other Improper Exercise of Police Powers and Privileges

Section 26 of the Criminal Justice and Courts Act 2015 makes it an offence for a police officer and certain other persons to improperly exercise the powers and privileges of the office of constable. It supplements and expands upon the existing common law offence of misconduct in public office.

The definition of a constable includes a constable of a Home Office police force in England and Wales as well as the British Transport Police, a special constable of a police force or the British Transport Police, and National Crime Agency officers designated with the powers and privileges of a constable.

Subsection (1) provides that a police constable commits an offence if he or she exercises the powers and privileges of a constable improperly and the officer knows or ought to know that it is improper. A person guilty of the offence is liable on conviction on indictment to a sentence of imprisonment for 14 years or a fine, or both.

Subsection (4) provides that a police constable exercises the powers and privileges of a constable improperly if the exercise of a power or privilege is for the purpose of achieving a benefit to the officer, or a benefit or detriment for another person, and that a reasonable person would not expect the power or privilege to be exercised for the purpose of achieving that benefit or detriment. Subsection (9) defines 'benefit' or 'detriment' as meaning any benefit or detriment, whether or not in money and whether or not permanent.

The improper exercise of a power or privilege for the purpose of the offence can refer to cases in which there is a failure to exercise a power or privilege, or there is a threat to exercise a power or privilege or to fail to do so, in each case for the purpose of achieving a benefit or detriment and in any of these cases a reasonable person would not expect the power or privilege to be exercised for the purpose of achieving that benefit or detriment.

This new offence does not affect what constitutes the common law offence of misconduct in public office in England and Wales or Northern Ireland.

4.3.18 Health and Safety

Because police officers are not 'employees' (they are holders of the office of constable), many of the statutory provisions regulating the workplace do not apply directly to them. The health and safety regime created by the Health and Safety at Work etc. Act 1974 applies principally to 'employees' and therefore did not cover police officers (though it clearly covers their non-sworn support colleagues who *are* employees). However, the Police (Health and Safety) Act 1997 made changes to the legislation by treating police officers for certain purposes relating to health and safety as if they were employees. Briefly, these areas include:

- the application of part 1 of the 1974 Act to the police;
- the right of police officers not to be subjected to a detriment in relation to health and safety issues, e.g. not to be punished for raising appropriate health and safety issues or undertaking duties as health and safety representatives (s. 49A of the Employment Rights Act 1996);
- the right of police officers not to be unfairly dismissed in relation to health and safety issues (s. 134A of the Employment Rights Act 1996).

Under the Health and Safety at Work etc. Act 1974, any prosecution of a chief officer of police for an offence under that Act will be brought against the office of chief constable rather than against the individual him/herself. This change to the law (brought in by the Serious Organised Crime and Police Act 2005) brings the position of a chief officer into line with that of police authorities and their liability for breaches of health and safety legislation in respect of police staff (who are their employees). However, a chief officer may also be prosecuted in a personal capacity if it can be shown that he/she personally consented to the commission of an offence or personally connived in its commission, or was personally negligent.

Powers of Arrest

PACE Code of Practice for the Statutory Power of Arrest by Police Officers (Code G)

> A thick grey line down the margin denotes text that is an extract of the PACE Code itself (i.e. the actual wording of the legislation). This material is examinable for both Sergeants and Inspectors.

4.4.1 Introduction

This chapter scrutinises a number of key features that are relevant to powers of arrest and introduces certain shared points regarding arrest procedures before examining specific powers in detail (and consequently, Code G of the Codes of Practice).

4.4.2 Human Rights—The Right to Liberty and Security

Arresting a person amounts to a deprivation of liberty and security and therefore engages Article 5 of the European Convention on Human Rights. Of course, a person may be deprived of their liberty for a number of legitimate and lawful reasons.

Article 5 of the Convention states:

1. Everyone has the right to liberty and security of person. No one shall be deprived of his liberty save in the following cases and in accordance with a procedure prescribed by law:
    (a) the lawful detention of a person after conviction by a competent court;
    (b) the lawful arrest or detention of a person for non-compliance with the lawful order of a court or in order to secure the fulfilment of any obligation prescribed by law;
    (c) the lawful arrest or detention of a person effected for the purpose of bringing him before the competent legal authority on reasonable suspicion of having committed an offence or when it is reasonably considered necessary to prevent his committing an offence or fleeing after having done so;
    (d) the detention of a minor by lawful order for the purpose of educational supervision or his lawful detention for the purpose of bringing him before the competent legal authority;
    (e) the lawful detention of persons for the prevention of the spreading of infectious diseases, of persons of unsound mind, alcoholics or drug addicts or vagrants;
    (f) the lawful arrest or detention of a person to prevent his effecting an unauthorised entry into the country or of a person against whom action is being taken with a view to deportation or extradition.

KEYNOTE

A person can only be deprived of his/her general right to liberty under one of the conditions set out on the permitted grounds in Article 5(1)(a)–(f), and even then that deprivation must be carried out in accordance with *a procedure prescribed by law*. Note that Article 5 does not provide any power to arrest or detain; it simply sets out certain circumstances where the general right to liberty may be interfered with by some existing lawful means.

The 'procedure' must be set out in the domestic law of the country and be recorded in such a way that people can appreciate the possible consequences of their actions and adapt their behaviour accordingly. If the legal authority used to deprive a person of his/her liberty is ambiguous or unclear, that may well provide grounds for challenge under Article 5.

Even if a lawful power is sufficiently clear and well established, the list of permitted grounds in Article 5(1) (a)–(f) will have to be construed narrowly by the courts (*Winterwerp* v *Netherlands* (1979–80) 2 EHRR 387).

Lawful Detention after Conviction

This exception allows a person to be detained after their conviction by a 'competent court', i.e. a court having the jurisdiction to try that particular case. People who have been so convicted may be detained in accordance with the order of the court. Clearly, if the court does not have the power to pass the relevant order, the exception at Article 5(1)(a) will not apply and any detention will potentially amount to a violation of Article 5.

Lawful Arrest or Detention for Non-compliance

The exception under Article 5(1)(b) allows for the detention or arrest of a person who has failed to comply with the *lawful* order of a court. Failing to pay a fine or to observe the conditions of an injunction would be examples of such non-compliance. The exception also extends to the arrest or detention in order to secure the fulfilment of any obligation prescribed by law. Such an obligation might include an obligation to provide a roadside breath specimen or to surrender documents relating to a vehicle. The circumstances of any arrest or detention will be examined by the courts which will need to consider whether the person was given a reasonable opportunity to comply with the order/obligation and whether the arrest or detention was a reasonable way to make sure that the order/obligation was met.

Lawful Arrest/Detention in Relation to an Offence

There are several aspects to the permitted grounds under Article 5(1)(c). The arrest/detention must first be lawful in itself. Any arrest/detention that is later shown to have been *unlawful* cannot be saved under any of the other headings. Even a lawful arrest/detention will only meet the requirements of Article 5(1)(c) if it can be shown to have been:

- effected for the purpose of bringing the person before the relevant 'competent legal authority' (i.e. a judge or magistrate) on reasonable suspicion that the person had committed an offence; or
- reasonably considered necessary to prevent the person committing an offence or from fleeing afterwards.

Where a person has been lawfully arrested for the purpose of bringing him/her before a competent legal authority, it is not necessary to show that he/she actually *was brought* before that authority (*Brogan* v *United Kingdom* (1989) 11 EHRR 117). It is the *purpose* of the arrest at the time that is relevant as opposed to its ultimate achievement. This accords with the provisions of s. 30(7) of the Police and Criminal Evidence Act 1984 which require an arrested person to be released if the grounds for detaining him/her cease to exist (**see para. 4.4.12**). Given the statutory status of a custody officer, he/she would probably not be a 'competent legal authority' for this purpose, which seems to be judicial in nature and requiring a degree of independence from the arresting authorities. However, it is hard to see how the expression 'competent legal authority' can be limited to judges and magistrates because Article 5(3) goes on to use a more restrictive expression (*judge or other officer authorised by law to exercise judicial power*) to define just such people. The lack of fit here between the wording and our own police and judicial roles is caused partly by the fact that those roles are different in nature from those in many other European Union countries.

'Reasonable suspicion' here will be assessed objectively and the court will look for 'the existence of facts or information which would satisfy an objective observer that the person may have committed the offence' (*Fox* v *United Kingdom* (1991) 13 EHRR 157).

Lawful Detention of Minors

This ground refers solely to 'detention' rather than arrest, although Article 5 seems to use the two expressions interchangeably in places (e.g. Article 5(4) in the following section). The initial detention must be lawful. A minor for these purposes is a person who has not attained the age of 18.

4.4.2.1 Procedure

Article 5 goes on to state:

2. Everyone who is arrested shall be informed promptly, in a language which he understands, of the reasons for his arrest and of any charge against him.
3. Everyone arrested or detained in accordance with the provisions of paragraph 1(c) of this Article shall be brought promptly before a judge or other officer authorised by law to exercise judicial power and shall be entitled to trial within a reasonable time or to release pending trial. Release may be conditioned by guarantees to appear for trial.
4. Everyone who is deprived of his liberty by arrest or detention shall be entitled to take proceedings by which the lawfulness of his detention shall be decided speedily by a court and his release ordered if the detention is not lawful.
5. Everyone who has been the victim of arrest or detention in contravention of the provisions of this Article shall have an enforceable right to compensation.

KEYNOTE

The right to be informed of the reason for arrest is already enshrined in our domestic law under s. 28 of the Police and Criminal Evidence Act 1984 (**see para. 4.4.3.1**). The wording of Article 5(2) strengthens that requirement by specifying that the information must be given in a language that the person understands.

The reason for requiring this information to be given would appear to be to allow the arrested person to challenge the arrest and subsequent detention (*X v United Kingdom* (1982) 4 EHRR 188). The ability to challenge the lawfulness of that detention (and presumably, the arrest) is itself a Convention right under Article 5(4).

Article 5(5) gives a person who is the 'victim' of an arrest or detention in contravention of the rest of the Article an enforceable right to compensation.

Where a person was being extradited to Spain, the hearing was entitled to conclude that a delay of over five years between an individual's arrest and his extradition did not render the extradition unjust or oppressive (*Owalabi v Court Number Four at the High Court of Justice in Spain* [2005] EWHC 2849 (Admin)).

4.4.3 Powers of Arrest—Common Points

An arrest involves depriving a person of his/her liberty to go where he/she pleases (*Lewis v Chief Constable of South Wales Constabulary* [1991] 1 All ER 206). In a criminal context an arrest will usually be to answer an alleged charge, but occasionally an arrest may be preventive (such as where a person is arrested in connection with a breach of the peace), it may be to take samples or fingerprints, to return someone to prison or bring him/her before a court.

While the courts may issue warrants ordering the arrest of certain individuals on occasions, police officers are not under any general duty to arrest without warrant and should always consider the use of alternative methods of dealing with the incident or matter.

The source of a power of arrest may come from:

- the conditions at the time (e.g. allowing an arrest under s. 24 of the Police and Criminal Evidence Act 1984);
- the provisions of the particular Act (e.g. s. 7 of the Bail Act 1976, absconding from bail; see *Evidence and Procedure*, para. 2.3.11);
- the provisions of an order (e.g. a court order or warrant; see *Evidence and Procedure*, para. 2.2.6);
- common law (e.g. breach of the peace; see para. 4.11.2).

An arrest begins at the time when the arresting officer informs the person of it or when his/her words or actions suggest that the person is under arrest (*Murray* v *Ministry of Defence* [1988] 1 WLR 692).

Where a power of arrest exists, any lawful arrest must be made for a proper purpose. In the past the courts have allowed the police some latitude in what amounts to a proper purpose, including bringing the person to a police station (*Holgate-Mohammed* v *Duke* [1984] AC 437) and to obtain a confession even after a complainant has withdrawn his/her initial complaint (*Plange* v *Chief Constable of Humberside* (1992) *The Times*, 23 March). The courts have even accepted an arrest based on force policy (*Al Fayed* v *Commissioner of Police of the Metropolis* [2004] EWCA Civ 1579).

The practice of arresting someone on a 'holding' offence was accepted by the Court of Appeal in *R* v *Chalkley* [1998] QB 848, provided the arresting officers had reasonable grounds for suspecting that the person had actually committed that offence. If that suspicion is present, then the fact that the officers making the arrest are doing so with the intention of investigating another, more serious offence does not render the arrest unlawful. If, however, there are no such grounds to suspect that the person had in fact committed the offence, or the officers know at the time of the arrest that there is no possibility of the person actually being charged with it, the arrest will be unlawful.

Section 30(7) of the Police and Criminal Evidence Act 1984 (in keeping with common law) requires that, if the grounds for detaining a person cease to exist before reaching a police station, the person must be released (see para. 4.4.12).

4.4.3.1 Information to be Given and Recorded on Arrest

When a person is arrested, it does not matter what power is being used or what the reason for arrest is, s. 28 of the Police and Criminal Evidence Act 1984 makes clear provision for the information that *must* be given to a person on arrest. Section 28 states:

(1) Subject to subsection (5) below, where a person is arrested, otherwise than by being informed that he is under arrest, the arrest is not lawful unless the person arrested is informed that he is under arrest as soon as is practicable after his arrest.
(2) Where a person is arrested by a constable, subsection (1) above applies regardless of whether the fact of the arrest is obvious.
(3) Subject to subsection (5) below, no arrest is lawful unless the person arrested is informed of the ground for the arrest at the time of, or as soon as is practicable after, the arrest.
(4) Where a person is arrested by a constable, subsection (3) above applies regardless of whether the ground for the arrest is obvious.
(5) Nothing in this section is to be taken to require a person to be informed—
(a) that he is under arrest; or
(b) of the ground for the arrest,
if it was not reasonably practicable for him to be so informed by reason of his having escaped from arrest before the information could be given.

4.4.3.2 Caution

The Police and Criminal Evidence Act 1984 Code of Practice, Code C, para. 10, requires that a person must be cautioned on arrest or further arrest (**see para. 4.4.6**).

There will be occasions where those involved with the custody and care of prisoners will overhear remarks by a defendant or will have comments made to them, which may be of relevance to the case in which the defendant is prosecuted. While such people may not be under a strict duty to administer the caution in the same way as police officers, the admissibility of the evidence will be tested against the general requirements of fairness and it might be appropriate to give a caution and/or to make a record of such comments as soon as possible (*R* v *Ristic* [2004] EWCA Crim 2107—prison officer giving evidence of incriminating remarks overheard by a defendant).

Where police officers are themselves being interviewed or investigated, the caution used in such cases will follow the general criminal one from Code C, with the inclusion of an element relating to a failure to make a written statement.

4.4.3.3 Use of Force

Section 117 of the Police and Criminal Evidence Act 1984 allows the use of reasonable force when making an arrest. Section 3 of the Criminal Law Act 1967 also allows the use of such force as is reasonably necessary in the arrest of people and the prevention of crime.

Whether any force used is 'reasonable' will be determined in the light of all the circumstances, including the circumstances as the arresting officer believed them to be at the time. Such force may even be lethal to the defendant. Where serious harm is caused by an arrest, the courts will consider the time that was available to the officer to reflect on his/her actions and whether or not he/she believed that the danger presented to others by failing to arrest the person outweighed the harm caused to the person by the arrest (*Attorney-General for Northern Ireland's Reference (No. 1 of 1975)* [1977] AC 105).

Use of excessive force, while amounting to possible misconduct and assault, does not render an otherwise lawful arrest unlawful (*Simpson* v *Chief Constable of South Yorkshire* (1991) 135 SJ 383).

4.4.4 PACE Code of Practice for the Statutory Power of Arrest by Police Officers (Code G)

This Code applies to any arrest made by a police officer after midnight on 12 November 2012.

1 Introduction

1.1   This Code of Practice deals with statutory power of police to arrest a person who is involved, or suspected of being involved, in a criminal offence. The power of arrest must be used fairly, responsibly, with respect for people suspected of committing offences and without unlawful discrimination. The Equality Act 2010 makes it unlawful for police officers to discriminate against, harass or victimise any person on the grounds of the 'protected characteristics' of age, disability, gender reassignment, race, religion or belief, sex and sexual orientation, marriage and civil partnership, pregnancy and maternity when using their powers. When police forces are carrying out their functions they also have a duty to have regard to the need to eliminate unlawful discrimination, harassment and victimisation and to take steps to foster good relations.

1.2   The exercise of the power of arrest represents an obvious and significant interference with the Right to Liberty and Security under Article 5 of the European Convention on Human Rights set out in Part I of Schedule 1 to the Human Rights Act 1998.

1.3   The use of the power must be fully justified and officers exercising the power should consider if the necessary objectives can be met by other, less intrusive means. Absence of justification for exercising the powers of arrest may lead to challenges should the case proceed to court. It could also lead to civil claims against the police for unlawful arrest and false imprisonment. When the power of arrest is exercised it is essential that it is exercised in a non-discriminatory and proportionate manner which is compatible with the Right to Liberty under Article 5.

1.4   Section 24 of the Police and Criminal Evidence Act 1984 (as substituted by section 110 of the Serious Organised Crime and Police Act 2005) provides the statutory power for a constable to arrest without warrant for all offences. If the provisions of the Act and this Code are not observed, both the arrest and the conduct of any subsequent investigation may be open to question.

1.5   This Code of Practice must be readily available at all police stations for consultation by police officers and police staff, detained persons and members of the public.

KEYNOTE

Code G points out that juveniles should not be arrested at their place of education unless this is unavoidable. When a juvenile is arrested at their place of education, the principal or their nominee must be informed.

4.4.5

2 Elements of Arrest under section 24 PACE

2.1 A lawful arrest requires two elements:

A person's involvement or suspected involvement or attempted involvement in the commission of a criminal offence;

AND

Reasonable grounds for *believing* that the person's arrest is necessary.
- both elements must be satisfied, and
- it can never be necessary to arrest a person unless there are reasonable grounds to suspect them of committing an offence.

2.2 The arrested person must be informed that they have been arrested, even if this fact is obvious, and of the relevant circumstances of the arrest in relation to both the above elements. The custody officer must be informed of these matters on arrival at the police station. See Code C paragraph 3.4.

(a) Involvement 'in the commission of an offence'

2.3 A constable may arrest without warrant in relation to any offence anyone:
- who is about to commit an offence or is in the act of committing an offence
- whom the officer has reasonable grounds for suspecting is about to commit an offence or to be committing an offence
- whom the officer has reasonable grounds to suspect of being guilty of an offence which he or she has reasonable grounds for suspecting has been committed
- anyone who is guilty of an offence which has been committed or anyone whom the officer has reasonable grounds for suspecting to be guilty of that offence.

2.3A There must be some reasonable, objective grounds for the suspicion, based on known facts and information which are relevant to the likelihood the offence has been committed and the person liable to arrest committed it.

4.4.5.1

KEYNOTE

For the purposes of this Code, 'offence' means any statutory or common law offence for which a person may be tried by a magistrates' court or the Crown Court and punished if convicted.

This Code does not apply to powers of arrest conferred on constables under any arrest warrant, for example, a warrant issued under the Magistrates' Courts Act 1980, ss. 1 or 13, or the Bail Act 1976, s. 7(1), or to the powers of constables to arrest without warrant other than under s. 24 of PACE for an offence. These other powers to arrest without warrant do not depend on the arrested person committing any specific offence and include:

- PACE, s. 46A, arrest of person who fails to answer police bail to attend police station or is suspected of breaching any condition of that bail for the custody officer to decide whether they should be kept in police detention which applies whether or not the person commits an offence under s. 6 of the Bail Act 1976 (e.g. failing without reasonable cause to surrender to custody);
- Bail Act 1976, s. 7(3), arrest of person bailed to attend court who is suspected of breaching, or is believed likely to breach, any condition of bail to take them to court for bail to be reconsidered;

- Children and Young Persons Act 1969, s. 32(1A) (absconding)—arrest to return the person to the place where they are required to reside;
- Immigration Act 1971, sch. 2, to arrest a person liable to examination to determine their right to remain in the United Kingdom;
- Mental Health Act 1983, s. 136, to remove person suffering from a mental disorder to place of safety for assessment;
- Prison Act 1952, s. 49, arrest to return person unlawfully at large to the prison etc. where they are liable to be detained;
- Road Traffic Act 1988, s. 6D, arrest of driver following the outcome of a preliminary roadside test requirement to enable the driver to be required to provide an evidential sample;
- common law power to stop or prevent a breach of the peace—after arrest a person aged 18 or over may be brought before a justice of the peace court to show cause why they should not be bound over to keep the peace—not criminal proceedings.

4.4.5.2 Reasonable Grounds to Suspect

Central to the criteria set out in s. 24 is the concept of 'reasonable grounds for suspecting'. The wording of s. 24 has yet to be developed by the courts, however the interpretation of and approach to the pre-existing legislation are helpful in understanding the concepts involved.

Tests of 'reasonableness' impose an element of objectivity and the courts will consider whether, in the circumstances, a reasonable and sober person might have formed a similar view to that of the officer. Failing to follow up an obvious line of inquiry (e.g. as to the ownership of property found in the possession of the defendant) may well provide grounds for challenging the exercise of a power of arrest (*Castorina* v *Chief Constable of Surrey* at **para. 4.4.5.3**).

4.4.5.3 The *Castorina* test

The key test for establishing the lawfulness of an arrest without warrant is set out in *Castorina* v *Chief Constable of Surrey* (1996) 160 LG Rev 241.

The *Castorina* test effectively has three stages:

(1) Did the arresting officer suspect that the person who was arrested was guilty of the offence (or about to commit etc.)?
(2) If so, was there reasonable cause (i.e. reasonable grounds) for the arresting officer's suspicion?
(3) If the answer to the two previous questions is in the affirmative, then the officer has a discretion which entitles him/her to make an arrest—was the arresting officer's exercise of his/her discretion reasonable in all the circumstances?

The first stage in the *Castorina* test is a subjective one in that it depends entirely on what was in the officer's mind at the time.

The second stage of the *Castorina* test is a purely objective one to be determined by the judge on facts found by the jury/court. This element means that it is not enough for the officer to claim reasonable suspicion in his/her own mind. A court will go on to look at whether there were reasonable grounds to suspect that an offence had been committed and that the person had committed it.

It is not uncommon for police officers to be called to a situation where, while there might be only one or two people responsible for an offence, it is unclear which of a group of people is the culprit. The Court of Appeal has confirmed that where an offence has been committed and one of only a small number of people could have committed it, there is no reason why each member or all the group members cannot be arrested (*Cumming* v *Chief Constable of Northumbria Police* [2003] EWCA Civ 1844). In the absence of any information that could or should enable the police to reduce the number further, the fact that a person is in a small group, one of whom must have committed the offence, can amount to reasonable grounds for suspecting him/her.

What about the opposite case where only one person had the opportunity to commit the offence? Is 'opportunity' alone enough to justify reasonable grounds for suspicion? The view of Auld J in *Al Fayed* v *Commissioner of Police for the Metropolis* [2004] EWCA Civ 1579 was that 'there is nothing in principle which prevents opportunity from amounting to reasonable grounds for suspicion. Indeed in some circumstances opportunity may be sufficient to found a conviction.'

However, merely being told to arrest someone by a more senior officer is not a reasonable ground for doing so (*O'Hara* v *Chief Constable of the Royal Ulster Constabulary* [1997] AC 286).

Facts and information relevant to a person's suspected involvement in an offence should not be confined to those which tend to indicate the person has committed or attempted to commit the offence. Before making a decision to arrest, a constable should take account of any facts and information that are available, including claims of innocence made by the person, which might dispel the suspicion. There is no need, however, for the officer to discount every possible defence or to seek complete proof of the relevant facts or circumstances before effecting an arrest (*Ward* v *Chief Constable of Avon and Somerset Constabulary* (1986) *The Times*, 26 June).

Examples of facts and information which might point to a person's innocence and dispel suspicion include those which relate to the statutory defence provided by the Criminal Law Act 1967, s. 3(1) which allows the use of reasonable force in the prevention of crime or making an arrest and the common law of self-defence. This may be relevant when a person appears, or claims, to have been acting reasonably in defence of themselves or others or to prevent their property or the property of others from being stolen, destroyed or damaged, particularly if the offence alleged is based on the use of unlawful force, e.g. a criminal assault.

When investigating allegations involving the use of force by school staff, the power given to all school staff under the Education and Inspections Act 2006, s. 93, to use reasonable force to prevent their pupils from committing any offence, injuring persons, damaging property or prejudicing the maintenance of good order and discipline may be similarly relevant. ACPO and the CPS have published joint guidance to help the public understand the meaning of reasonable force and what to expect from the police and CPS in cases which involve claims of self-defence. Separate advice for school staff on their powers to use reasonable force is available from the Department for Education.

(b) Necessity criteria

2.4 The power of arrest is <u>only</u> exercisable if the constable has reasonable grounds for *believing* that it is necessary to arrest the person. The statutory criteria for what may constitute necessity are set out in paragraph 2.9 and it remains an operational decision at the discretion of the constable as to:
- which one or more of the necessity criteria (if any) applies to the individual; and
- if any of the criteria do apply, whether to arrest, grant street bail after arrest, report for summons or for charging by post, issue a fixed penalty notice or take any other action that is open to the officer.

2.5 In applying the criteria, the arresting officer has to be satisfied that at least one of the reasons supporting the need for arrest is satisfied.

2.6 Extending the power of arrest to all offences provides a constable with the ability to use that power to deal with any situation. However applying the necessity criteria requires the constable to examine and justify the reason or reasons why a person needs to be arrested or (as the case may be) further arrested, for an offence for the custody officer to decide whether to authorise their detention for that offence.

4.4.5.4 **KEYNOTE**

For a constable to have reasonable grounds for *believing* it *necessary* to arrest, he/she is not required to be satisfied that there is no viable alternative to arrest. However, it does mean that in all cases, the officer should consider that arrest is the practical, sensible and proportionate option in all the circumstances at the time the decision is made. This applies to a person in police detention after being arrested for an offence who is suspected of involvement in a further offence and where the necessity to arrest them for that further offence is being considered.

2.7 The criteria in paragraph 2.9 below which are set out in section 24 of PACE as substituted by section 110 of the Serious Organised Crime and Police Act 2005 **are** exhaustive. However, the circumstances that may satisfy those criteria remain a matter for the operational discretion of individual officers. Some examples are given to illustrate what those circumstances may be and what officers might consider when deciding whether an arrest is necessary.

2.8 In considering the individual circumstances, the constable must take into account the situation of the victim, the nature of the offence, the circumstances of the suspect and the needs of the investigative process.

2.9 When it is practicable to tell a person why their arrest is necessary (as required by paragraphs 2.2 and 3.3), the constable should outline the facts, information and other circumstances which provide the grounds for believing that their arrest is necessary and which the officer considers satisfy one or more of the statutory criteria in sub-paragraphs (a) to (f) namely:

(a) to enable the name of the person in question to be ascertained (in the case where the constable does not know, and cannot readily ascertain, the person's name, or has reasonable grounds for doubting whether a name given by the person as his name is his real name):

An officer might decide that a person's name cannot be readily ascertained if they fail or refuse to give it when asked, particularly after being warned that failure or refusal is likely to make their arrest necessary. Grounds to doubt a name given may arise if the person appears reluctant or hesitant when asked to give their name or to verify the name they have given.

Where mobile fingerprinting is available and the suspect's name cannot be ascertained or is doubted, the officer should consider using the power under section 61(6A) of PACE (see Code D paragraph 4.3(e)) to take and check the fingerprints of a suspect as this may avoid the need to arrest solely to enable their name to be ascertained.

(b) correspondingly as regards the person's address:

An officer might decide that a person's address cannot be readily ascertained if they fail or refuse to give it when asked, particularly after being warned that such a failure or refusal is likely to make their arrest necessary. Grounds to doubt an address given may arise if the person appears reluctant or hesitant when asked to give their address or is unable to provide verifiable details of the locality they claim to live in.

When considering reporting to consider summons or charging by post as alternatives to arrest, an address would be satisfactory if the person will be at it for a sufficiently long period for it to be possible to serve them with the summons or requisition and charge; or, that some other person at that address specified by the person will accept service on their behalf. When considering issuing a penalty notice, the address should be one where the person will be in the event of enforcement action if the person does not pay the penalty or is convicted and fined after a court hearing.

(c) to prevent the person in question—

(i) causing physical injury to himself or any other person;

This might apply where the suspect has already used or threatened violence against others and it is thought likely that they may assault others if they are not arrested.

(ii) suffering physical injury;

This might apply where the suspect's behaviour and actions are believed likely to provoke, or have provoked, others to want to assault the suspect unless the suspect is arrested for their own protection.

(iii) causing loss or damage to property;

This might apply where the suspect is a known persistent offender with a history of serial offending against property (theft and criminal damage) and it is thought likely that they may continue offending if they are not arrested.

(iv) committing an offence against public decency (only applies where members of the public going about their normal business cannot reasonably be expected to avoid the person in question);

This might apply when an offence against public decency is being committed in a place to which the public have access and is likely to be repeated in that or some other public place at a time when the public are likely to encounter the suspect.

(v) causing an unlawful obstruction of the highway;

This might apply to any offence where its commission causes an unlawful obstruction which it is believed may continue or be repeated if the person is not arrested, particularly if the person has been warned that they are causing an obstruction.

(d) to protect a child or other vulnerable person from the person in question.

This might apply when the health (physical or mental) or welfare of a child or vulnerable person is likely to be harmed or is at risk of being harmed, if the person is not arrested in cases where it is not practicable and appropriate to make alternative arrangements to prevent the suspect from having any harmful or potentially harmful contact with the child or vulnerable person.

(e) to allow the prompt and effective investigation of the offence or of the conduct of the person in question.

This may arise when it is thought likely that unless the person is arrested and then either taken in custody to the police station or granted 'street bail' to attend the station later, further action considered necessary to properly investigate their involvement in the offence would be frustrated, unreasonably delayed or otherwise hindered and therefore be impracticable. Examples of such actions include:

(i) interviewing the suspect on occasions when the person's voluntary attendance is not considered to be a practicable alternative to arrest, because for example:

- it is thought unlikely that the person would attend the police station voluntarily to be interviewed.
- it is necessary to interview the suspect about the outcome of other investigative action for which their arrest is necessary, see (ii) to (v) below.
- arrest would enable the special warning to be given in accordance with Code C paragraphs 10.10 and 10.11 when the suspect is found:
  ~ in possession of incriminating objects, or at a place where such objects are found;
  ~ at or near the scene of the crime at or about the time it was committed.
- the person has made false statements and/or presented false evidence;
- it is thought likely that the person:
  ~ may steal or destroy evidence;
  ~ may collude or make contact with, co-suspects or conspirators;
  ~ may intimidate or threaten or make contact with, witnesses.

(ii) when considering arrest in connection with the investigation of an indictable offence, there is a need:

- to enter and search without a search warrant any premises occupied or controlled by the arrested person or where the person was when arrested or immediately before arrest;
- to prevent the arrested person from having contact with others;
- to detain the arrested person for more than 24 hours before charge.

(iii) when considering arrest in connection with any recordable offence and it is necessary to secure or preserve evidence of that offence by taking fingerprints, footwear impressions or samples from the suspect for evidential comparison or matching with other material relating to that offence, for example, from the crime scene.

(iv) when considering arrest in connection with any offence and it is necessary to search, examine or photograph the person to obtain evidence.

(v) when considering arrest in connection with an offence to which the statutory Class A drug testing requirements in Code C section 17 apply, to enable testing when it is thought that drug misuse might have caused or contributed to the offence.

(f) to prevent any prosecution for the offence from being hindered by the disappearance of the person in question.

This may arise when it is thought that:

- if the person is not arrested they are unlikely to attend court if they are prosecuted;
- the address given is not a satisfactory address for service of a summons or a written charge and requisition to appear at court because the person will not be at it for a sufficiently long period for the summons or charge and requisition to be served and no other person at that specified address will accept service on their behalf.

4.4.5.5

KEYNOTE

Arrested persons must be given sufficient information to enable them to understand they have been deprived of their liberty and the reason they have been arrested, as soon as practicable after the arrest, e.g. when persons are arrested on suspicion of committing an offence they must be informed of the nature of the suspected offence and when and where it was committed. Suspects must also be informed of the reason or reasons why arrest is considered necessary. Vague or technical language should be avoided. When explaining why one or more of the arrest criteria apply, it is not necessary to disclose any specific details that might undermine or otherwise adversely affect any investigative processes. For example, the conduct of a formal interview when prior disclosure of such details might give the suspect an opportunity to fabricate an innocent explanation or to otherwise conceal lies from the interviewer.

4.4.5.6

Paragraph 2.9 (a), (b) and (c)

Although a warning is not expressly required, officers should, if practicable, consider whether to issue a warning which points out the person's offending behaviour, and explains why, if the person does not stop, the resulting consequences may make his/her arrest necessary. Such a warning might:

- if heeded, avoid the need to arrest, or
- if ignored, support the need to arrest and also help prove the mental element of certain offences, e.g. the person's intent or awareness, or help to rebut a defence that he/she was acting reasonably.

A person who is warned that he/she may be liable to arrest if his/her real name and address cannot be ascertained, should be given a reasonable opportunity to establish his/her real name and address before deciding that either or both are unknown and cannot be readily ascertained or that there are reasonable grounds to doubt that a name and address the person given is his/her real name and address. He/she should be told why his/her name is not known and cannot be readily ascertained and (as the case may be) of the grounds for doubting that a name and address he/she has given is his/her real name and address, including, for example, the reason why a particular document the person has produced to verify his/her real name and/or address is not sufficient.

4.4.5.7

Paragraph 2.9(e)

The meaning of 'prompt' should be considered on a case by case basis taking account of all the circumstances. It indicates that the progress of the investigation should not be delayed to the extent that it would adversely affect the effectiveness of the investigation. The arresting officer also has discretion to release the arrested person on 'street bail' as an alternative to taking the person directly to the station. Having determined that the necessity criteria have been met and having made the arrest, the officer can then consider the use of street bail on the basis of the effective and efficient progress of the investigation of the offence in question. It gives the officer discretion to compel the person to attend a police station at a date/time that best suits the overall needs of the particular investigation. Its use is not confined to dealing with child care issues or allowing officers to attend to more urgent operational duties, and granting street bail does not retrospectively negate the need to arrest.

4.4.5.8

Paragraph 2.9(e)(i)

An officer who believes that it is necessary to interview the person suspected of committing the offence must then consider whether his/her arrest is necessary in order to carry out the interview. The officer is not required to interrogate the suspect to determine whether he/she will attend a police station voluntarily to be interviewed but the officer must consider whether the suspect's voluntary attendance is a practicable alternative for carrying out the interview. If it is, then arrest would not be necessary. Conversely, an officer who considers this option but is not satisfied that it is a practicable alternative, may have reasonable grounds for deciding that the arrest is necessary at the outset 'on the street'. Without such considerations, the officer would not be able to establish that arrest was necessary in order to interview.

Circumstances which suggest that a person's arrest 'on the street' would not be necessary to interview him/her might be where the officer:

- is satisfied as to the person's identity and address and that he/she will attend the police station voluntarily to be interviewed, either immediately or by arrangement at a future date and time; and
- is not aware of any other circumstances which indicate that voluntary attendance would not be a practicable alternative. See para. 2.9(e)(i)–(v).

When making arrangements for the person's voluntary attendance, the officer should tell the person:

- that to properly investigate his/her suspected involvement in the offence he/she must be interviewed under caution at the police station, but in the circumstances his/her arrest for this purpose will not be necessary if he/she attends the police station voluntarily to be interviewed;
- that if he/she attends voluntarily, he/she will be entitled to free legal advice before, and to have a solicitor present at, the interview;
- that the date and time of the interview will take account of the person's circumstances and the needs of the investigation; and
- that if the person does not agree to attend voluntarily at a time which meets the needs of the investigation, or having so agreed, fails to attend, or having attended, fails to remain for the interview to be completed, his/her arrest will be necessary to enable him/her to be interviewed.

When the person attends the police station voluntarily for interview by arrangement (as above), his/her arrest on arrival at the station prior to interview would only be justified if:

- new information coming to light after the arrangements were made indicates that, from that time, voluntary attendance ceased to be a practicable alternative and the person's arrest became necessary; and
- it was not reasonably practicable for the person to be arrested before he/she attended the station.
- If a person who attends the police station voluntarily to be interviewed decides to leave before the interview is complete, the police would at that point be entitled to consider whether the person's arrest was necessary to carry out the interview. The possibility that the person might decide to leave during the interview is therefore not a valid reason for arresting him/her before the interview has commenced. See Code C, para. 3.21.

4.4.5.9 Paragraph 2.9(e)(ii)

It should be remembered that certain powers available as the result of an arrest (e.g. entry and search of premises, detention without charge beyond 24 hours, holding a person incommunicado and delaying access to legal advice) only apply in respect of indictable offences and are subject to the specific requirements on authorisation as set out in PACE and the relevant Code of Practice.

4.4.5.10 Paragraph 2.9(e)(iii) and (iv)

The necessity criteria do not permit arrest solely to enable the routine taking, checking (speculative searching) and retention of fingerprints, samples, footwear impressions and photographs when there are no prior grounds to believe that checking and comparing the fingerprints etc. or taking a photograph would provide relevant evidence of the person's involvement in the offence concerned or would help to ascertain or verify his/her real identity.

The necessity criteria do not permit arrest for an offence solely because it happens to be one of the statutory drug testing 'trigger offences' (Code C, Note 17E) when there is no suspicion that Class A drug misuse might have caused or contributed to the offence (para. 2.9 (e)(v)).

3 Information to be given on Arrest

(a) Cautions—when a caution must be given

3.1 Code C paragraphs 10.1 and 10.2 set out the requirement for a person whom there are grounds to suspect of an offence to be cautioned before being questioned or further questioned about an offence.

3.2 Not used.

3.3 A person who is arrested, or further arrested, must be informed at the time if practicable, or if not, as soon as it becomes practicable thereafter, that they are under arrest and the grounds and reasons for their arrest.

3.4 A person who is arrested, or further arrested, must also be cautioned unless:

(a) it is impracticable to do so by reason of their condition or behaviour at the time;

(b) they have already been cautioned immediately prior to arrest as in paragraph 3.1

3.5 The caution, which must be given on arrest, should be in the following terms:

'You do not have to say anything. But it may harm your defence if you do not mention when questioned something which you later rely on in Court. Anything you do say may be given in evidence.'

Where the use of the Welsh Language is appropriate, a constable may provide the caution directly in Welsh in the following terms:

'Does dim rhaid i chi ddweud dim byd. Ond gall niweidio eich amddiffyniad os na fyddwch chi'n sôn, wrth gael eich holi, am rywbeth y byddwch chi'n dibynnu arno nes ymlaen yn y Llys. Gall unrhyw beth yr ydych yn ei ddweud gael ei roi fel tystiolaeth.'

3.6 Minor deviations from the words of any caution given in accordance with this Code do not constitute a breach of this Code, provided the sense of the relevant caution is preserved.

3.7 Not used.

KEYNOTE

The Caution

Nothing in this Code requires a caution to be given or repeated when informing a person not under arrest that he/she may be prosecuted for an offence. However, a court will not be able to draw any inferences under the Criminal Justice and Public Order Act 1994, s. 34, if the person was not cautioned.

If it appears a person does not understand the caution, the people giving it should explain it in their own words.

In addition to the caution being given on arrest, Code C, para. 10.5 states that a caution must be given on all other occasions before a person is charged or informed they may be prosecuted (see *Evidence and Procedure*, para. 2.10.2.2).

4 Records of Arrest

(a) General

4.1 The arresting officer is required to record in his pocket book or by other methods used for recording information:

- the nature and circumstances of the offence leading to the arrest
- the reason or reasons why arrest was necessary
- the giving of the caution
- anything said by the person at the time of arrest.

4.2 Such a record should be made at the time of the arrest unless impracticable to do. If not made at that time, the record should then be completed as soon as possible thereafter.

4.3 On arrival at the police station or after being first arrested at the police station, the arrested person must be brought before the custody officer as soon as practicable and a custody record must be opened in accordance with section 2 of Code C. The information given by the arresting officer on the circumstances and reason or reasons for arrest shall be recorded as part of the custody record. Alternatively, a copy of the record made by the officer in accordance with paragraph 4.1 above shall be attached as part of the custody record. See *paragraph 2.2* and *Code C paragraphs 3.4 and 10.3*.

4.4 The custody record will serve as a record of the arrest. Copies of the custody record will be provided in accordance with paragraphs 2.4 and 2.4A of Code C and access for inspection of the original record in accordance with paragraph 2.5 of Code C.

(b) Interviews and arrests

4.5 Records of interview, significant statements or silences will be treated in the same way as set out in sections 11 and 12 of Code C and in Codes E and F (audio and visual recording of interviews).

4.4.8 Arrest without Warrant—Arrest by Others

The Police and Criminal Evidence Act 1984 makes provision for the so-called citizen's arrest powers. Far narrower than the police powers, these powers of arrest are set out in s. 24A, which states:

(1) A person other than a constable may arrest without a warrant—
 (a) anyone who is in the act of committing an indictable offence;
 (b) anyone whom he has reasonable grounds for suspecting to be committing an indictable offence.
(2) Where an indictable offence has been committed, a person other than a constable may arrest without a warrant—
 (a) anyone who is guilty of the offence;
 (b) anyone whom he has reasonable grounds for suspecting to be guilty of it.
(3) But the power of summary arrest conferred by subsection (1) or (2) is exercisable only if—
 (a) the person making the arrest has reasonable grounds for believing that for any of the reasons mentioned in subsection (4) it is necessary to arrest the person in question; and
 (b) it appears to the person making the arrest that it is not reasonably practicable for a constable to make it instead.
(4) The reasons are to prevent the person in question:
 (a) causing physical injury to himself or any other person;
 (b) suffering physical injury;
 (c) causing loss of or damage to property; or
 (d) making off before a constable can assume responsibility for him.
(5) This section does not apply in relation to an offence under Part 3 or 3A of the Public Order Act 1986.

KEYNOTE

Unlike the powers of arrest available to police officers (which apply to any and every offence), the citizen's power of arrest only applies where the relevant offence is *indictable*. This power is available to police staff and others such as Police Community Support Officers.

Under s. 24A(2), an indictable offence must have been committed; it is not enough to suspect or even believe that such an offence has been committed, even if there are very good grounds for that suspicion or belief. This can cause difficulties for the person carrying out the arrest if the 'offender' is subsequently acquitted at court (*R* v *Self* [1992] 1 WLR 657).

'Summary arrest', in this context, means an arrest without warrant (regardless of whether the offence in question is a summary, either way or indictable only offence).

Racial and religious hatred offences provided by the Racial and Religious Hatred Act 2006 do not apply to this section (s. 24A(5)).

4.4.9 Arrest without Warrant—Other Powers of Arrest

Apart from the general power of arrest under s. 24 of the Police and Criminal Evidence Act 1984, several other powers of arrest exist.

4.4.9.1 Preserved Powers of Arrest

Section 26 of the Police and Criminal Evidence Act 1984 repealed all other powers of arrest without warrant which existed before the 1984 Act except those listed in sch. 2. This list has been further reduced by the provisions of the Serious Organised Crime and Police Act 2005.

The common law power of arrest for breach of the peace has been preserved by s. 26 of the 1984 Act (*DPP* v *Orum* [1989] 1 WLR 88).

4.4.9.2 Fingerprinting

The Police and Criminal Evidence Act 1984, s. 27 provides a power of arrest to take a person's fingerprints.

4.4.9.3 Failure to Answer Police Bail

Section 46A of the Police and Criminal Evidence Act 1984 provides a power of arrest when a person fails to answer police bail—this is discussed in detail in *Evidence and Procedure*, chapter 2.3.

4.4.9.4 Arrest to Take Samples

Section 63A of the Police and Criminal Evidence Act 1984 provides a power of arrest without warrant in respect of people:

- who have been charged with/reported for a recordable offence and who have not had a sample taken or the sample was unsuitable/insufficient for analysis;
- who have been convicted of a recordable offence and have not had a sample taken since conviction;
- who have been so convicted and have had a sample taken before or since conviction but the sample was unsuitable/insufficient for analysis.

This is simply a summary of s. 63A and reference should be made to the 1984 Act for the exact wording.

4.4.9.5 Cross-border Arrest without Warrant

The Criminal Justice and Public Order Act 1994 (ss. 136 to 140) makes provision for officers from one part of the United Kingdom to go into another part of the United Kingdom to arrest someone there in connection with an offence committed within their jurisdiction and gives them powers to search on arrest.

Under the 1994 Act an officer from a police service in England and Wales may arrest a person in Scotland where it appears to the officer that it would have been lawful for him/her to have exercised his/her powers had the suspected person been in England and Wales or where it would be impracticable to serve a summons for the same reasons which would justify an arrest in England and Wales.

A Scottish officer may arrest someone suspected of committing an offence in Scotland who is found in England, Wales or Northern Ireland if it would have been lawful to arrest that person had he/she been found in Scotland. In such a case the officer must take the person to a designated police station in Scotland or to the nearest designated police station in England or Wales (s. 137(7)).

The 1994 Act sets out where a person arrested outside the relevant country should be taken on arrest (s. 137(7)). The Act also provides wide powers of search in connection with arrests (s. 139).

4.4.10 Arrest under Warrant

Arrest warrants may be issued by magistrates (generally under s. 1 of the Magistrates' Courts Act 1980) and the Crown Court (under the Senior Courts Act 1981, s. 80(2)) where the statute in question, together with the powers of the court allow. Warrants of arrest may also be issued to secure the attendance of witnesses (s. 97 of the Magistrates' Courts Act 1980 and s. 4 of the Criminal Procedure (Attendance of Witnesses) Act 1965).

The police owe defendants a duty of care when drawing up and enforcing the contents of warrants. Therefore, where officers put the wrong date on an arrest warrant issued by a magistrates' court and, as a result, the defendant was not released by the Prison Service when he should have been, the police were liable in damages for the defendant's unlawful imprisonment (*Clarke* v *Chief Constable of Northamptonshire Police* (1999) *The Times*, 14 June). Though not employed by the police, civilian enforcement officers (CEOs) and approved enforcement agencies (AEAs) are nevertheless empowered to execute arrest warrants in certain circumstances. The details of these specific provisions are beyond the scope of this Manual.

Warrants issued in relation to an offence may be backed for bail, in which case the person is then granted bail in accordance with the conditions on the warrant. If not backed for bail, the warrant will specify where the person is to be brought (i.e. before the next sitting of the court).

Warrants issued in England, Wales, Scotland or Northern Ireland may be executed by officers from the country where they are issued or in the country where the person is arrested (s. 136 of the Criminal Justice and Public Order Act 1994).

Warrants from the Republic of Ireland (provided they are not issued for political offences) may be executed in England and Wales if so endorsed (s. 125 of the Magistrates' Courts Act 1980), as, indeed, may warrants issued in the Isle of Man or the Channel Islands if so endorsed (s. 13 of the Indictable Offences Act 1848).

Warrants issued in connection with 'an offence' do not need to be in the possession of the officer executing them at the time. The majority of warrants issued for the arrest of a person in England and Wales arise from matters such as failure to appear at court, breaching bail conditions or failing to pay fines. All of these were once a significant source of policing activity, but they are now enforceable by civilian enforcement officers and approved enforcement agencies.

The procedure dealing with European Arrest Warrants is outside the scope of this Manual.

4.4.11 Voluntary Attendance at a Police Station

There are a variety of situations where a person attends at a police station in a voluntary capacity. For example, where the person is a suspect, by pre-arrangement with the officers in the case or where the person learns that the police want to speak to him/her or perhaps where a person has elected to accompany a Police Community Support Officer to a police station rather than awaiting the arrival of a constable.

There is no distinction between a person being arrested at a police station after attending voluntarily, and a person arrested elsewhere, provided the arresting officers acted appropriately and reasonably (*Al Fayed*).

However, there are certain statutory provisions with regard to the entitlements and treatment of people who are 'voluntary attendees' and these are set out below.

The Police and Criminal Evidence Act 1984, s. 29 states:

Where for the purpose of assisting with an investigation a person attends voluntarily at a police station or at any other place where a constable is present or accompanies a constable to a police station or any such other place without having been arrested—
(a) he shall be entitled to leave at will unless he is placed under arrest;
(b) he shall be informed at once that he is under arrest if a decision is taken by a constable to prevent him from leaving at will.

KEYNOTE

The person's attendance at a police station or other place must be for the purpose of 'assisting with an investigation', which would, on a strict interpretation, encompass witnesses and victims. The principle behind s. 29 (and see also Code C, para. 3.2.1) is to avoid the situation where people find themselves at a police station (or any other place where there is a police officer present) and feel compelled to remain there but without the attendant procedural protection that follows a formal arrest. Section 29(b) is unusual in that it (along with s. 31 below) imposes an obligation on a police officer to make an arrest, an activity that is usually entirely within his/her discretion. The time when the need to arrest the person arises is when the officer takes the decision to prevent the person from leaving (e.g. the time when the officer decides him/herself). It is not the time when the person is actually prevented from leaving or even when he/she is told of the decision.

If such a person is cautioned (under PACE Code C, para. 10), he/she must also be told that he/she is free to leave the police station. Although not in police detention (s. 118), voluntary attendees should be given the opportunity to seek legal advice if they wish and should be given the appropriate notice (see Code C).

The Police and Criminal Evidence Act 1984, s. 31 states:

Where—
(a) a person—
    (i) has been arrested for an offence; and
    (ii) is at a police station in consequence of that arrest; and
(b) it appears to a constable that, if he were released from that arrest, he would be liable to arrest for some other offence, he shall be arrested for that other offence.

Like s. 29, this section also imposes an obligation to make an arrest under certain circumstances. The purpose of the s. 31 requirement is to prevent the release and immediate re-arrest of an offender. Therefore, s. 31 does not prevent any further arrest from being delayed until the release of the prisoner for the initial arrest is imminent (*R* v *Samuel* [1988] QB 615). It has been held that, where officers who had arrested a man for a breach of the peace failed to arrest him formally for the further offence of assault on the police, their omission did not impact on the magistrates' decision that there was a case to answer in respect of the assault charge (*Blench* v *DPP* [2004] EWHC 2717 (Admin)).

The power (though not, on the strict wording, the *obligation*) to arrest a person at a police station for a further offence under s. 31 is among those that can be conferred on an Investigating Officer designated under sch. 4 to the Police Reform Act 2002. Where this power is exercised by a designated Investigating Officer, the provisions of s. 36 of the Criminal Justice and Public Order Act 1994 (failing to account for objects etc.) will apply.

Where a person is re-arrested under this provision, the powers of search under s. 18 of the Police and Criminal Evidence Act 1984 apply (see para. 4.6.5.3).

4.4.12 After Arrest

The Police and Criminal Evidence Act 1984, s. 30 provides for the procedure to be adopted after a person has been arrested. Section 30 states:

(1) Subsection (1A) applies where a person is, at any place other than a police station—
    (a) arrested by a constable for an offence, or
    (b) taken into custody by a constable after being arrested for an offence by a person other than a constable.
(1A) The person must be taken by a constable to a police station as soon as practicable after the arrest.
(1B) Subsection (1A) has effect subject to section 30A (release on bail) and subsection (7) (release without bail).

(2) Subject to subsections (3) and (5) below, the police station to which an arrested person is taken under subsection (1A) above shall be a designated police station.

(3) A constable to whom this subsection applies may take an arrested person to any police station unless it appears to the constable that it may be necessary to keep the arrested person in police detention for more than six hours.

(4) Subsection (3) above applies—

    (a) to a constable who is working in a locality covered by a police station which is not a designated police station; and

    (b) to a constable belonging to a body of constables maintained by an authority other than a police authority.

(5) Any constable may take an arrested person to any police station if—

    (a) either of the following conditions is satisfied—

        (i) the constable has arrested him without the assistance of any other constable and no other constable is available to assist him;

        (ii) the constable has taken him into custody from a person other than a constable without the assistance of any other constable and no other constable is available to assist him; and

    (b) it appears to the constable that he will be unable to take the arrested person to a designated police station without the arrested person injuring himself, the constable or some other person.

(6) If the first police station to which an arrested person is taken after his arrest is not a designated police station, he shall be taken to a designated police station not more than six hours after his arrival at the first police station unless he is released previously.

(7) A person arrested by a constable at any place other than a police station must be released without bail if the condition in subsection (7A) is satisfied.

(7A) The condition is that, at any time before the person arrested reaches a police station, a constable is satisfied that there are no grounds for keeping him under arrest or releasing him on bail under section 30A.

KEYNOTE

When arrested at a place other than a police station, the person must be taken to a designated police station unless the conditions under s. 30(5) and (6) apply.

Under s. 30(7) and (7A), the officer *must* de-arrest a person if he/she is satisfied, before reaching the police station, that there are no grounds for detaining that person. This may happen where the person has been arrested under one of the general arrest conditions and the particular condition has ceased to apply (e.g. the person gives a suitable name and address having originally failed to do so). An officer who releases a prisoner under s. 30(7) and (7A) must record the fact that he/she has done so and must make that record as soon as practicable after the release (s. 30(8) and (9)).

Section 30(10) allows the officer to delay taking the arrested person to a police station where his/her presence elsewhere is *necessary in order to carry out such investigations as it is reasonable to carry out immediately*. Where there is such a delay, the reasons for it must be recorded when the person first arrives at the police station (s. 30(11)). The delay permitted under s. 30(10) and (11) will only apply if the matter requires *immediate* investigation; if it can wait, the exception will not apply and the person must be taken straight to a police station (*R* v *Kerawalla* [1991] Crim LR 451).

Taking an arrested person to check out an alibi before going to a police station may be justified in some circumstances (*Dallison* v *Caffery* [1965] 1 QB 348).

Escort Officers designated under sch. 4 to the Police Reform Act 2002 may be authorised to take people who have been arrested by a constable in the relevant police area to a police station under the provisions of s. 30(1). The provisions for taking a prisoner to a non-designated police station (s. 30(3) and 4(a)), and also the provisions allowing a delay in taking the prisoner to a police station (s. 30(10)) will also apply to any exercise of the powers by a designated Escort Officer (Police Reform Act 2002, sch. 4, part 4). Other exceptions in the application of s. 30(1) to terrorism and immigration are made by s. 30(12).

4.5 Stop and Search

PACE Code of Practice for the Exercise by Police Officers of Statutory Powers of Stop and Search; Police Officers and Police Staff of Requirements to Record Public Encounters (Code A)

A thick grey line down the margin denotes text that is an extract of the PACE Code itself (i.e. the actual wording of the legislation). This material is examinable for both Sergeants and Inspectors.

4.5.1 Introduction

Code A deals with the exercise by police officers of statutory powers of stop and search and has been incorporated into this chapter with the addition of keynotes in appropriate places. This permits additional useful and explanatory detail to be presented to candidates that would not ordinarily be mentioned in any standard version of the code.

The Best Use of Stop and Search Scheme is designed to enable forces to use stop and search strategically in an effort to improve confidence and trust. Forces are expected to adhere to the components of the scheme subject to exceptional circumstances. However, it is important to note that *nothing in the scheme is binding in law*; statute and case law on stop and search therefore *remain unaffected* by the scheme. While the Scheme *does not form part of the examination syllabus* officers wishing to be familiar with its contents as a matter of professional awareness should see <https://www.gov.uk/government/publications/best-use-of-stop-and-search-scheme> for further details.

4.5.2 PACE Code of Practice for the Exercise by Police Officers of Statutory Powers of Stop and Search; Police Officers and Police Staff of Requirements to Record Public Encounters (Code A)

This code applies to any search by a police officer and the requirement to record public encounters taking place after midnight on 19 March 2015.

1.0 General

1.01 This Code of Practice must be readily available at all police stations for consultation by police officers, police staff, detained persons and members of the public.

1.02 The notes for guidance (included within the keynotes of this chapter) are not provisions of this code, but are guidance to police officers and others about its application and interpretation. Provisions in the annexes to the code are provisions of this code.

1.03 This code governs the exercise by police officers of statutory powers to search a person or a vehicle without first making an arrest. The main stop and search powers to which this code applies are set out in Annex A, but that list should not be regarded as definitive. In addition, it covers requirements on police officers and police staff to record encounters not governed by statutory powers. This code does not apply to:

(a) the powers of stop and search under;

    (i) Aviation Security Act 1982, section 27(2);

    (ii) Police and Criminal Evidence Act 1984, section 6(1) (which relates specifically to powers of constables employed by statutory undertakers on the premises of the statutory undertakers).

(b) searches carried out for the purposes of examination under Schedule 7 to the Terrorism Act 2000 and to which the Code of Practice issued under paragraph 6 of Schedule 14 to the Terrorism Act 2000 applies.

(c) the powers to search persons and vehicles and to stop and search in specified locations to which the Code of Practice issued under section 47AB of the Terrorism Act 2000 applies.

4.5.3   1 Principles governing stop and search

1.1 Powers to stop and search must be used fairly, responsibly, with respect for people being searched and without unlawful discrimination. Under the Equality Act 2010, section 149, when police officers are carrying out their functions, they also have a duty to have due regard to the need to eliminate unlawful discrimination, harassment and victimisation, to advance equality of opportunity between people who share a relevant protected characteristic and people who do not share it, and to take steps to foster good relations between those persons. The Children Act 2004, section 11, also requires chief police officers and other specified persons and bodies to ensure that in the discharge of their functions they have regard to the need to safeguard and promote the welfare of all persons under the age of 18.

1.2 The intrusion on the liberty of the person stopped or searched must be brief and detention for the purposes of a search must take place at or near the location of the stop.

1.3 If these fundamental principles are not observed the use of powers to stop and search may be drawn into question. Failure to use the powers in the proper manner reduces their effectiveness. Stop and search can play an important role in the detection and prevention of crime, and using the powers fairly makes them more effective.

1.4 The primary purpose of stop and search powers is to enable officers to allay or confirm suspicions about individuals without exercising their power of arrest. Officers may be required to justify the use or authorisation of such powers, in relation both to individual searches and the overall pattern of their activity in this regard, to their supervisory officers or in court. Any misuse of the powers is likely to be harmful to policing and lead to mistrust of the police. Officers must also be able to explain their actions to the member of the public searched. The misuse of these powers can lead to disciplinary action.

1.5 An officer must not search a person, even with his or her consent, where no power to search is applicable. Even where a person is prepared to submit to a search voluntarily, the person must not be searched unless the necessary legal power exists, and the search must be in accordance with the relevant power and the provisions of this Code. The only exception, where an officer does not require a specific power, applies to searches of persons entering sports grounds or other premises carried out with their consent given as a condition of entry.

1.6 Evidence obtained from a search to which this Code applies may be open to challenge if the provisions of this Code are not observed.

2 Types of stop and search powers

2.1 This code applies, subject to paragraph 1.03, to powers of stop and search as follows:

    (a) powers which require reasonable grounds for suspicion, before they may be exercised; that articles unlawfully obtained or possessed are being carried such as section 1 of PACE for stolen and prohibited articles and section 23 of the Misuse of Drugs Act 1971 for controlled drugs;

    (b) authorised under section 60 of the Criminal Justice and Public Order Act 1994, based upon a reasonable belief that incidents involving serious violence may take place or that people are carrying dangerous instruments or offensive weapons within any locality in the police area or that it is expedient to use the powers to find such instruments or weapons that have been used in incidents of serious violence, and

    (c) *Not used.*

    (d) the powers in Schedule 5 to the Terrorism Prevention and Investigation Measures (TPIM) Act 2011 to search an individual who has not been arrested, conferred by:

        (i) paragraph 6(2)(a) at the time of serving a TPIM notice;

        (ii) paragraph 8(2)(a) under a search warrant for compliance purposes; and

        (iii) paragraph 10 for public safety purposes.

    See paragraph 2.18A.

    (e) powers to search a person who has not been arrested in the exercise of a power to search premises (see Code B paragraph 2.4).

KEYNOTE

This Code does not affect the ability of an officer to speak to or question a person in the ordinary course of the officer's duties without detaining the person or exercising any element of compulsion. It is not the purpose of the Code to prohibit such encounters between the police and the community with the cooperation of the person concerned and neither does it affect the principle that all citizens have a duty to help police officers to prevent crime and discover offenders. This is a civic rather than a legal duty; but when a police officer is trying to discover whether, or by whom, an offence has been committed he/she may question any person from whom useful information might be obtained, subject to the restrictions imposed by Code C. A person's unwillingness to reply does not alter this entitlement, but in the absence of a power to arrest, or to detain in order to search, the person is free to leave at will and cannot be compelled to remain with the officer.

The 'relevant protected characteristics' referred to in para. 1.1 include: age, disability, gender reassignment, pregnancy and maternity, race, religion or belief, sex and sexual orientation.

It is important to emphasise that Code A of the PACE Codes of Practice applies to any search by a police officer, i.e. the principles and processes created by Code A must be followed in *all* searches (there are exceptions for certain powers under the Aviation Security Act 1982 and those exercised by statutory undertakers).

Code A does not allow the routine searching of people with their consent and only permits very limited use of the power as a condition of entry (e.g. to a sports ground) (para. 1.5). This means the practice of conducting 'voluntary' searches in the street or other public places is not permitted.

There are many specific statutory authorities providing the police (and others) with powers to stop people and vehicles and search them (see Annex A of this Code at **appendix 4.3**). Perhaps the most important of these is the general power for police officers to stop and search people and vehicles under s. 1 of the Police and Criminal Evidence Act 1984 (PACE) referred to at para. 2.1(a).

A summary of s. 1 of the Police and Criminal Evidence Act 1984 is that it provides a constable with the power to stop, detain and search a person and/or a vehicle (or anything in or on a vehicle) for stolen articles, prohibited articles, bladed or sharply pointed articles and for fireworks. While such a summary is useful, a more detailed analysis of the power is required.

The Police and Criminal Evidence Act 1984, s. 1 states:

(1) A constable may exercise any power conferred by this section—

    (a) in any place to which at the time when he proposes to exercise the power the public or any section of the public has access, on payment or otherwise, as of right or by virtue of express or implied permission; or

(b) in any other place to which people have ready access at the time when he proposes to exercise the power but which is not a dwelling.

(2) Subject to subsection (3) to (5) below, a constable—

    (a) may search—

        (i) any person or vehicle;

        (ii) anything which is in or on a vehicle, for stolen or prohibited articles or any article to which subsection (8A) below applies or any firework to which subsection (8B) below applies; and

    (b) may detain a person or vehicle for the purpose of such a search.

(3) This section does not give a constable power to search a person or vehicle or anything in or on a vehicle unless he has reasonable grounds for suspecting that he will find stolen or prohibited articles or any article to which subsection (8A) below applies or any firework to which subsection (8B) below applies.

(4) If a person is in a garden or yard occupied with and used for the purposes of a dwelling or on other land so occupied and used, a constable may not search him in the exercise of the power conferred by this section unless the constable has reasonable grounds for believing—

    (a) that he does not reside in the dwelling; and

    (b) that he is not in the place in question with the express or implied permission of a person who resides in the dwelling.

(5) If a vehicle is in a garden or yard occupied with and used for the purposes of a dwelling or on other land so occupied and used, a constable may not search the vehicle or anything in or on it in the exercise of the power conferred by this section unless he has reasonable grounds for believing—

    (a) that the person in charge of the vehicle does not reside in the dwelling; and

    (b) that the vehicle is not in the place in question with the express or implied permission of a person who resides in the dwelling.

(6) If in the course of such a search a constable discovers an article which he has reasonable grounds for suspecting to be stolen or a prohibited article or an article to which subsection (8A) below applies or a firework to which subsection (8B) below applies, he may seize it.

(7) An article is prohibited for the purposes of this Part of this Act if it is—

    (a) an offensive weapon; or

    (b) an article—

        (i) made or adapted for use in the course of or in connection with an offence to which this sub-paragraph applies; or

        (ii) intended by the person having it with him for such use by him or by some other person.

(8) The offences to which subsection (7)(b)(i) above applies are—

    (a) burglary;

    (b) theft;

    (c) offences under section 12 of the Theft Act 1968 (taking motor vehicle or other conveyance without authority);

    (d) fraud (contrary to section 1 of the Fraud Act 2006); and

    (e) offences under section 1 of the Criminal Damage Act 1971 (destroying or damaging property).

(8A) This subsection applies to any article in relation to which a person has committed, or is committing or is going to commit an offence under section 139 of the Criminal Justice Act 1988.

(8B) This subsection applies to any firework which a person possesses in contravention of a prohibition imposed by fireworks regulations.

(8C) In this section—

    (a) 'firework' shall be construed in accordance with the definition of 'fireworks' in section 1(1) of the Fireworks Act 2003; and

    (b) 'fireworks regulations' has the same meaning as in that Act.

(9) In this Part of this Act 'offensive weapon' means any article—

    (a) made or adapted for use for causing injury to persons; or

    (b) intended by the person having it with him for such use by him or by some other person.

4.5.4.2

KEYNOTE

Search in a Garden, Yard or Land Connected to Dwelling

If the person to be searched is in a garden, yard or other land occupied with and used as part of a dwelling, the power to search *will not* apply unless the officer has 'reasonable grounds for *believing*' that the person does not live there and that he/she is not there with the permission (express or implied) of any person who does live there.

If the garden or yard is attached to a house that is not so 'occupied', the restriction at s. 1(4) would not appear to apply.

Similar restrictions are placed on the searching of vehicles found in such places by s. 1(5). For the meaning of 'in charge' of a vehicle, see *Road Policing*, chapter 3.1. For these purposes 'vehicle' includes vessels, aircraft and hovercraft (s. 2(10) of the 1984 Act).

4.5.4.3 **KEYNOTE**

Prohibited Articles

'Offensive weapon' is defined as any article made or adapted for use for causing injury to the person, or intended by the person having it with him for such use or by someone else. There are three categories of offensive weapons: those made for causing injury to the person; those adapted for such a purpose; and those not so made or adapted, but carried with the intention of causing injury to the person. A firearm, as defined by s. 57 of the Firearms Act 1968, would fall within the definition of offensive weapon if any of the criteria above apply.

The power under s. 1 of the Police and Criminal Evidence Act 1984 *does not* authorise an officer in plain clothes to stop a vehicle (s. 2(9)(b)).

The power is restricted to those places set out in s. 1(1)(a) or (b) of the 1984 Act. This does not mean that the search itself must be carried out there; in fact Code A, paras 3.6 and 3.7 require certain searches to be carried out away from public view (**see para. 4.5.5**).

The power under s. 1 of PACE applies where the officer has 'reasonable grounds for suspecting' that he/she will find stolen or prohibited articles or articles falling under s. 139 of the Criminal Justice Act 1988 (bladed or sharply pointed articles; **see chapter 4.13**) or any firework to which s.1(8B) of the 1984 Act applies.

The existence of reasonable grounds for suspicion is at the heart of the power under s. 1 and for that reason, Code A devotes considerable attention to the concept.

(a) Stop and search powers requiring reasonable grounds for suspicion— explanation

General

2.2 Reasonable grounds for suspicion is the legal test which a police officer must satisfy before they can stop and detain individuals or vehicles to search them under powers such as section 1 of PACE (to find stolen or prohibited articles) and section 23 of the Misuse of Drugs Act 1971 (to find controlled drugs). This test must be applied to the particular circumstances in each case and is in two parts:

(i) *Firstly,* the officer must have formed a *genuine suspicion* in their own mind that they will find the object for which the search power being exercised allows them to search (see Annex A, second column, for examples); and

(ii) *Secondly,* the suspicion that the object will be found must be *reasonable.* This means that there must be an *objective* basis for that suspicion based on facts, information and/ or intelligence which are relevant to the likelihood that the object in question will be found, so that a reasonable person would be entitled to reach the same conclusion based on the same facts and information and/or intelligence.

Officers must therefore be able to explain the basis for their suspicion by reference to intelligence or information about, or some specific behaviour by, the person concerned (see *paragraphs 3.8(d), 4.6* and *5.5*).

2.2A The exercise of these stop and search powers depends on the likelihood that the person searched is in possession of an item for which they may be searched; it does not depend on the person concerned being suspected of committing an offence in relation to the object of the search. A police officer who has reasonable grounds to suspect that a person is in *innocent possession* of a stolen or prohibited article, controlled drug or other item for which the officer is empowered to search, may stop and search the person even though there would be no power of arrest. This would apply when a child under the age of criminal responsibility (10 years) is suspected of carrying any such item, even if they knew they had it.

Personal factors can never support reasonable grounds for suspicion

2.2B Reasonable suspicion can never be supported on the basis of personal factors. This means that unless the police have information or intelligence which *provides a description* of a person suspected of carrying an article for which there is a power to stop and search, the following *cannot be used*, alone or in combination with each other, or in combination with any other factor, as the reason for stopping and searching any individual, including any vehicle which they are driving or are being carried in:

(a) A person's physical appearance with regard, for example, to any of the 'relevant protected characteristics' set out in the Equality Act 2010, section 149, which are age, disability, gender reassignment, pregnancy and maternity, race, religion or belief, sex and sexual orientation (see *paragraph 1.1*), or the fact that the person is known to have a previous conviction; and

(b) Generalisations or stereotypical images that certain groups or categories of people are more likely to be involved in criminal activity.

2.3 *Not used.*

Reasonable grounds for suspicion based on information and/or intelligence

2.4 Reasonable grounds for suspicion should normally be linked to accurate and current intelligence or information, relating to articles for which there is a power to stop and search, being carried by individuals or being in vehicles in any locality. This would include reports from members of the public or other officers describing:
- a person who has been seen carrying such an article or a vehicle in which such an article has been seen.
- crimes committed in relation to which such an article would constitute relevant evidence, for example, property stolen in a theft or burglary, an offensive weapon or bladed or sharply pointed article used to assault or threaten someone or an article used to cause criminal damage to property.

2.4A Searches based on accurate and current intelligence or information are more likely to be effective. Targeting searches in a particular area at specified crime problems not only increases their effectiveness but also minimises inconvenience to law-abiding members of the public. It also helps in justifying the use of searches both to those who are searched and to the public. This does not, however, prevent stop and search powers being exercised in other locations where such powers may be exercised and reasonable suspicion exists.

2.5 *Not used.*

Reasonable grounds for suspicion and searching groups

2.6 Where there is reliable information or intelligence that members of a group or gang habitually carry knives unlawfully or weapons or controlled drugs, and wear a distinctive item of clothing or other means of identification in order to identify themselves as members of that group or gang, that distinctive item of clothing or other means of identification may provide reasonable grounds to stop and search any person believed to be a member of that group or gang.

2.6A A similar approach would apply to particular organised protest groups where there is reliable information or intelligence:

    (a) that the group in question arranges meetings and marches to which one or more members bring articles intended to be used to cause criminal damage and/or injury to others in support of the group's aims;

    (b) that at one or more *previous* meetings or marches arranged by that group, such articles have been used and resulted in damage and/or injury; and

    (c) that on the subsequent occasion in question, one or more members of the group have brought with them such articles with similar intentions.

These circumstances may provide reasonable grounds to stop and search any members of the group to find such articles. See also *paragraphs 2.12* to *2.18*, '*Searches authorised under section 60 of the Criminal Justice and Public Order Act 1994*', when serious violence is anticipated at meetings and marches.

Reasonable grounds for suspicion based on behaviour, time and location

2.6B Reasonable suspicion may also exist without specific information or intelligence and on the basis of the behaviour of a person. For example, if an officer encounters someone on the street at night who is obviously trying to hide something, the officer may (depending on the other surrounding circumstances) base such suspicion on the fact that this kind of behaviour is often linked to stolen or prohibited articles being carried. An officer who forms the opinion that a person is acting suspiciously or that they appear to be nervous must be able to explain, with reference to specific aspects of the person's behaviour or conduct which they have observed, why they formed that opinion (see *paragraphs 3.8(d)* and *5.5*). A hunch or instinct which cannot be explained or justified to an objective observer can never amount to reasonable grounds.

2.7 *Not used.*

2.8 *Not used.*

Securing public confidence and promoting community relations

2.8A All police officers must recognise that searches are more likely to be effective, legitimate and secure public confidence when their reasonable grounds for suspicion are based on a range of objective factors. The overall use of these powers is more likely to be effective when up-to-date and accurate intelligence or information is communicated to officers and they are well-informed about local crime patterns. Local senior officers have a duty to ensure that those under their command who exercise stop and search powers have access to such information, and the officers exercising the powers have a duty to acquaint themselves with that information (see *paragraphs 5.1* to *5.6*).

Questioning to decide whether to carry out a search

2.9 An officer who has reasonable grounds for suspicion may detain the person concerned in order to carry out a search. Before carrying out the search the officer may ask questions about the person's behaviour or presence in circumstances which gave rise to the suspicion. As a result of questioning the detained person, the reasonable grounds for suspicion necessary to detain that person may be confirmed or, because of a satisfactory explanation, be dispelled. Questioning may also reveal reasonable grounds to suspect the possession of a different kind of unlawful article from that originally suspected. Reasonable grounds for suspicion however cannot be provided retrospectively by such questioning during a person's detention or by refusal to answer any questions asked.

2.10 If, as a result of questioning before a search, or other circumstances which come to the attention of the officer, there cease to be reasonable grounds for suspecting that an article of a kind for which there is a power to stop and search is being carried, no search may take place. In the absence of any other lawful power to detain, the person is free to leave at will and must be so informed.

2.11 There is no power to stop or detain a person in order to find grounds for a search. Police officers have many encounters with members of the public which do not involve detaining people against their will and do not require any statutory power for an officer to speak to a person (see *paragraph 4.12*). However, if reasonable grounds for suspicion emerge during such an encounter, the officer may detain the person to search them, even though no grounds existed when the encounter began. As soon as detention begins, and before searching, the officer must inform the person that they are being detained for the purpose of a search and take action in accordance with *paragraphs 3.8* to *3.11 under 'Steps to be taken prior to a search'*.

4.5.4.4

KEYNOTE

Reasonable Grounds for Suspicion

Innocent possession (mentioned at para. 2.2A) means that the person does have the guilty knowledge that they are carrying an unlawful item which is required before an arrest on suspicion that the person has committed an offence in respect of the item sought (if arrest is necessary—see PACE Code G) and/or a criminal prosecution can be considered. It is not uncommon for children under the age of criminal responsibility to be used by older children and adults to carry stolen property, drugs and weapons and, in some cases, firearms, for the criminal benefit of others, either:

- in the hope that police may not suspect they are being used for carrying the items; or
- knowing that if they are suspected of being couriers and are stopped and searched, they cannot be arrested or prosecuted for any criminal offence.

Stop and search powers therefore allow the police to intervene effectively to break up criminal gangs and groups that use young children to further their criminal activities.

Whenever a child under 10 is suspected of carrying unlawful items for someone else, or is found in circumstances which suggest that their welfare and safety may be at risk, the facts should be reported and actioned in accordance with established force safeguarding procedures. This will be in addition to treating the child as a potentially vulnerable or intimidated witness in respect of their status as a witness to the serious criminal offence(s) committed by those using them as couriers. Safeguarding considerations will also apply to other persons aged under 18 who are stopped and searched under any of the powers to which this Code applies. See para. 1.1 with regard to the requirement under the Children Act 2004, s. 11, for chief police officers and other specified persons and bodies to ensure that in the discharge of their functions they have regard to the need to safeguard and promote the welfare of all persons under the age of 18.

In some circumstances preparatory questioning may be unnecessary, but in general a brief conversation or exchange will be desirable not only as a means of avoiding unsuccessful searches, but to explain the grounds for the stop/search, to gain cooperation and reduce any tension there might be surrounding the stop/search process.

Where a person is lawfully detained for the purpose of a search, but no search in the event takes place, the detention will not thereby have been rendered unlawful.

The issue of when an officer has reasonable grounds for suspicion has been developed by the courts for many years. This common law development is supported by the inclusion of specific guidance on search powers that require reasonable grounds for suspicion.

'Suspicion' requires a lower degree of certainty than 'belief'. A statutory requirement for 'belief' imposes a greater degree of certainty on the officers concerned (*Baker* v *Oxford* [1980] RTR 315). Accordingly, police officers using powers that impose such an extra requirement must be prepared to justify their belief. Suspicion can be based on any evidence, even if the evidence itself would be inadmissible at trial (e.g. because it is hearsay). In fact Code A provides for occasions where a police officer has reasonable grounds to suspect that a person is in innocent possession of stolen or prohibited articles or other items which give rise to a power to search the person even though there would be no power of arrest, or no offence committed by that person.

The courts have accepted that reasonable grounds for suspicion can arise from information given to the officer by a colleague, an informant or even anonymously (*O'Hara* v *Chief Constable of the Royal Ulster Constabulary* [1997] AC 286).

The courts have held that it must be shown that any such grounds on which an officer acted would have been enough to give rise to that suspicion in a 'reasonable person' (*Nakkuda Ali* v *Jayaratne* [1951] AC 66).

However, the mere existence of such circumstances or evidence is not enough. The officer must actually have a 'reasonable suspicion' that the relevant articles will be found. If, in fact, the officer knows that there is little or no likelihood of finding the articles, the power could not be used (*R* v *Harrison* [1938] 3 All ER 134).

Paragraph 2.6 makes provision for the searching of members of gangs or groups who habitually carry knives unlawfully, weapons or drugs and wear a distinctive item of clothing or other means of identifying themselves with such a group, but only where there is reliable information or intelligence that members of the group or gang do so. Other means of identification might include jewellery, insignias, tattoos or other features which are known to identify members of the particular gang or group.

A decision to search individuals believed to be members of a particular group or gang must be judged on a case-by-case basis according to the circumstances applicable at the time of the proposed searches and in particular having regard to: (a) the number of items suspected of being carried; (b) the nature of those items and the risk they pose; and (c) the number of individuals to be searched. A group search will only be justified if it is a necessary and proportionate approach based on the facts and having regard to the nature of the suspicion in these cases. The extent and thoroughness of the searches must not be excessive. The size of the group and the number of individuals it is proposed to search will be a key factor and steps should be taken to identify those who are to be searched to avoid unnecessary inconvenience to unconnected members of the public who are also present. The onus is on the police to be satisfied and to demonstrate that their approach to the decision to search is in pursuit of a legitimate aim, necessary and proportionate.

Searches authorised under section 60 of the Criminal Justice and Public Order Act 1994

2.12   Authority for a constable in uniform to stop and search under section 60 of the Criminal Justice and Public Order Act 1994 may be given if the authorising officer reasonably believes:

(a)   that incidents involving serious violence may take place in any locality in the officer's police area, and it is expedient to use these powers to prevent their occurrence;

(b)   that persons are carrying dangerous instruments or offensive weapons without good reason in any locality in the officer's police area; or

(c)   that an incident involving serious violence has taken place in the officer's police area, a dangerous instrument or offensive weapon used in the incident is being carried by a person in any locality in that police area, and it is expedient to use these powers to find that instrument or weapon.

2.13   An authorisation under section 60 may only be given by an officer of the rank of inspector or above and in writing, or orally if paragraph 2.12(c) applies and it is not practicable to give the authorisation in writing. The authorisation (whether written or oral) must specify the grounds on which it was given, the locality in which the powers may be exercised and the period of time for which they are in force. The period authorised shall be no longer than appears reasonably necessary to prevent, or seek to prevent incidents of serious violence, or to deal with the problem of carrying dangerous instruments or offensive weapons or to find a dangerous instrument or offensive weapon that has been used. It may not exceed 24 hours. An oral authorisation given where paragraph 2.12(c) applies must be recorded in writing as soon as practicable.

2.14   An inspector who gives an authorisation must, as soon as practicable, inform an officer of or above the rank of superintendent. This officer may direct that the authorisation shall be extended for a further 24 hours, if violence or the carrying of dangerous instruments or offensive weapons has occurred, or is suspected to have occurred, and the continued use of the powers is considered necessary to prevent or deal with further such activity or to find a dangerous instrument or offensive weapon that has been used. That direction must be given in writing unless it is not practicable to do so, in which case it must be recorded in writing as soon as practicable afterwards.

2.14A   The selection of persons and vehicles under s. 60 to be stopped and, if appropriate searched should reflect an objective assessment of the nature of the incident or weapon in question and the individuals and vehicles thought likely to be associated with that incident or those weapons. The powers must not be used to stop and search persons and vehicles for reasons unconnected with the purpose of the authorisation. When selecting persons and vehicles to be stopped in response to a specific threat or incident, officers must take care not to discriminate unlawfully against anyone on the grounds of any of the protected characteristics set out in the Equality Act 2010 (see paragraph 1.1).

2.14B   The driver of a vehicle which is stopped under section 60 and any person who is searched under section 60 are entitled to a written statement to that effect if they apply within twelve months from the day the vehicle was stopped or the person was searched. This statement is a record which states that the vehicle was stopped or (as the case may be) that the person was searched under s. 60 and it may form part of the search record or be supplied as a separate record.

4.5.4.5   **KEYNOTE**

Section 60 of the Criminal Justice and Public Order Act 1994

Section 60 of the 1994 Act states:

(1)   If a police officer of or above the rank of inspector reasonably believes—
    (a) that incidents involving serious violence may take place in any locality in his police area, and that it is expedient to give an authorisation under this section to prevent their occurrence,
    (aa) that—
        (i)   an incident involving serious violence has taken place in England and Wales in his police area;
        (ii) a dangerous instrument or offensive weapon used in the incident is being carried in any locality in his police area by a person; and
        (iii) it is expedient to give an authorisation under this section to find the instrument or weapon; or
    (b) that persons are carrying dangerous instruments or offensive weapons in any locality in his police area without good reason, he may give an authorisation that the powers conferred by this section are to be exercisable at any place within that locality for a specified period not exceeding 24 hours.

(2)   (repealed)

(3)   ...

(3A) ...

(4)   This section confers on any constable in uniform power—
    (a) to stop any pedestrian and search him or anything carried by him for offensive weapons or dangerous instruments;
    (b) to stop any vehicle and search the vehicle, its driver and any passenger for offensive weapons or dangerous instruments.

The powers under s. 60 are *separate from* and *additional to* the normal stop and search powers which require reasonable grounds to suspect an individual of carrying an offensive weapon (or other article). Their overall purpose is to prevent serious violence and the widespread carrying of weapons which might lead to persons being seriously injured by disarming potential offenders or finding weapons that have been used in circumstances where other powers would not be sufficient. They should not therefore be used to replace or circumvent the normal powers for dealing with routine crime problems. A particular example might be an authorisation to prevent serious violence or the carrying of offensive weapons at a sports event by rival team supporters when the expected general appearance and age range of those likely to be responsible, alone, would not be sufficiently distinctive to support reasonable suspicion (see Code A, para. 2.6).

4.5.4.6

KEYNOTE

Authorisation

The *reasonable belief* on the part of the officer authorising the use of the power under s. 60 must have an objective basis, for example: intelligence or relevant information such as a history of antagonism and violence between particular groups; previous incidents of violence at, or connected with, particular events or locations; a significant increase in knife-point robberies in a limited area; reports that individuals are regularly carrying weapons in a particular locality or information following an incident in which weapons were used about where the weapons might be found.

Although the word 'necessary' does not appear in s. 60(1), the effect of Article 8 of the European Convention on Human Rights is that necessity remains relevant to each decision as to whether an authorisation is justified. Any authorisation made under s. 60 must be made only when the officer believes it is necessary. In practice, in addition to expediency, which is explicit in the 1994 Act, the authorising officer must also have considered the authorisation necessary to prevent serious violence or to find dangerous instruments or weapons after an incident involving serious violence, or to apprehend persons carrying weapons.

It is for the authorising officer to determine the period of time during which the power may be exercised and in any event must not exceed 24 hours. The officer should set the minimum period he/she considers necessary to deal with the risk of violence, the carrying of knives or offensive weapons or to find dangerous instruments or weapons that have been used. A direction to extend the period authorised under the power may be given only once (by a superintendent or above for a further period not exceeding 24 hours). So the maximum period a s. 60 authorisation could last for would be 48 hours—thereafter further use of the powers requires a new authorisation.

It is for the authorising officer to determine the geographical area in which the use of the powers is to be authorised. In doing so the officer may wish to take into account factors such as the nature and venue of the anticipated incident or the incident which has taken place, the number of people who may be in the immediate area of that incident, their access to surrounding areas and the anticipated level of violence. The officer should not set a geographical area which is wider than he/she believes necessary for the purpose of preventing anticipated violence, the carrying of knives or offensive weapons or for finding a dangerous instrument or weapon that has been used. It is particularly important to ensure that constables exercising such powers are fully aware of where they may be used. If the area specified is smaller than the whole force area, the officer giving the authorisation should specify either the streets which form the boundary of the area or a divisional boundary within the force area. If the power is to be used in response to a threat or incident that straddles police force areas, an officer from each of the forces concerned will need to give an authorisation.

If it appears to an officer of or above the rank of superintendent that:

- having regard to offences that have been, or are reasonably suspected to have been, committed
- in connection with any activity falling within the authorisation, and
- it is expedient to do so

he/she may authorise the continuation of the authority to exercise the powers under s. 60(1) for a further period of 24 hours (s. 60(3) and Code A, para. 2.14).

This authorisation must be in writing, signed by the officer giving it, and must specify:

- the grounds on which it is given
- the locality in which it is to operate, and
- the period during which the powers are exercisable

and any direction for the authorisation to continue must also be given in writing at the time or reduced into writing as soon as it is practicable to do so (s. 60(9)).

4.5.4.7   KEYNOTE

Interpretation

'Serious violence' is not defined in the 1994 Act but, although violence could relate to property, the whole tenor of the section suggests that it is aimed at tackling violence against people. 'Dangerous instruments' are bladed or sharply pointed instruments, while offensive weapons have the same meaning as that under s. 1(9) of the Police and Criminal Evidence Act 1984. For the purposes of s. 60, 'carrying' will mean 'having in your possession' (s. 60(11A)), a much wider meaning than carrying usually conveys.

4.5.4.8   KEYNOTE

Powers, Offences and Entitlements

A significant difference between this power and the general powers of stop and search (which are not affected by the granting of this power (s. 60(12))), is that it does not require any grounds at all for the officer to suspect that the person/vehicle is carrying offensive weapons or dangerous instruments (s. 60(5)). However, para. 2.14A is clear in that it states that the stopping of people and/or vehicles should reflect the purpose of the authorisation and should be capable of 'objective assessment'. A further difference is that the power under s. 60 authorises *officers in uniform* to stop vehicles in order to search them and their occupants.

The power allows the stopping and searching of pedestrians, vehicles (including caravans, aircraft, vessels and hovercraft) and passengers. If a dangerous instrument or anything reasonably suspected to be an 'offensive weapon' is found during the search, the officer may seize it (s. 60(6)).

The general requirements governing searches imposed by Code A apply to this power.

Failing to stop (or to stop a vehicle) when required to do so under this power is a summary offence punishable with one month's imprisonment and/or a fine (s. 60(8)(a)).

Powers to require removal of face coverings

2.15   Section 60AA of the Criminal Justice and Public Order Act 1994 also provides a power to demand the removal of disguises. The officer exercising the power must reasonably believe that someone is wearing an item wholly or mainly for the purpose of concealing identity. There is also a power to seize such items where the officer believes that a person intends to wear them for this purpose. There is no power to stop and search for disguises. An officer may seize any such item which is discovered when exercising a power of search for something else, or which is being carried, and which the officer reasonably believes is intended to be used for concealing anyone's identity. This power can only be used if an authorisation under section 60 or an authorisation under section 60AA is in force.

2.16   Authority for a constable in uniform to require the removal of disguises and to seize them under section 60AA may be given if the authorising officer reasonably believes that activities may take place in any locality in the officer's police area that are likely to involve the commission of offences and it is expedient to use these powers to prevent or control these activities.

2.17   An authorisation under section 60AA may only be given by an officer of the rank of inspector or above, in writing, specifying the grounds on which it was given, the locality in which the powers may be exercised and the period of time for which they are in force. The period authorised shall be no longer than appears reasonably necessary to prevent, or seek to prevent the commission of offences. It may not exceed 24 hours.

2.18   If an inspector gives an authorisation, he or she must, as soon as practicable, inform an officer of or above the rank of superintendent. This officer may direct that the authorisation shall be extended for a further 24 hours, if crimes have been committed, or is suspected to have been committed, and the continued use of the powers is considered necessary to prevent or deal with further such activity. This direction must also be given in writing at the time or as soon as practicable afterwards.

4.5.4.9

KEYNOTE

Section 60AA of the Criminal Justice and Public Order Act 1994

The Criminal Justice and Public Order Act 1994, s. 60AA states:

(1) Where—
   (a) an authorisation under section 60 is for the time being in force in relation to any locality for any period, or
   (b) an authorisation under subsection (3) that the powers conferred by subsection (2) shall be exercisable at any place in a locality is in force for any period,
   those powers shall be exercisable at any place in that locality at any time in that period.
(2) This subsection confers power on any constable in uniform—
   (a) to require any person to remove any item which the constable reasonably believes that person is wearing wholly or mainly for the purpose of concealing his identity;
   (b) to seize any item which the constable reasonably believes any person intends to wear wholly or mainly for that purpose.
(3) If a police officer of or above the rank of inspector reasonably believes—
   (a) that activities may take place in any locality in his police area that are likely (if they take place) to involve the commission of offences, and
   (b) that it is expedient, in order to prevent or control the activities, to give an authorization under this subsection,

he may give an authorisation that the powers conferred by this section shall be exercisable at any place within that locality for a specified period not exceeding twenty-four hours.

The purpose of the powers under s. 60AA is to prevent those involved in intimidatory or violent protests using face coverings to conceal identity.

These provisions are wider than those under s. 60 in that they are not restricted to anticipated outbreaks of serious violence. This is not simply a preventive power and can be used where the 'activities' are already under way.

4.5.4.10

KEYNOTE

Authorisation

The authorisation process closely follows that of an authorisation under s. 60 of the Act, i.e. the authorising officer reasonably believes that activities may take place in any locality in his/her police area that are likely (if they take place) to involve the commission of offences. This reasonable belief must have an objective basis, for example where the authorising officer is aware of previous incidents of crimes being committed while wearing face coverings to conceal identity. The requirements in relation to the further authority of a superintendent (or above) and the manner and form in which any authority is to be given are broadly similar to those set out in s. 60.

An authorisation (whether to grant the use of the power or to extend it) shall be in writing unless it is not practicable to do so. An oral authorisation will state the matters which would otherwise have been specified in a written authorisation (grounds for the search, locality and time period) and be recorded in writing as soon as it is practicable to do so.

The limitations and requirements as to the time and geographical extent of any authorisation are the same (see para. 4.5.4.9).

4.5.4.11

KEYNOTE

Interpretation

Any officer exercising these powers must reasonably *believe* that the person wearing the item is doing so *wholly or mainly for the purpose of concealing his/her identity or he/she intends to wear it wholly or mainly for that purpose.* Therefore if the person is a cyclist wearing a face mask to prevent the inhalation of traffic fumes, or a motorcyclist wearing a crash helmet, the fact that its *effect* is to conceal his/her identity will not be enough—concealing his/her identity has to be the purpose/main purpose of the wearer.

The expression 'item' is wide and would include balaclavas, scarves and crash helmets (if the officer believes that such items are being worn wholly or mainly to conceal identity). It is not specifically restricted to face coverings and extends to anything that could be worn wholly or mainly for the purpose of concealing identity (e.g. where offenders swap clothing after an offence). The purpose of the legislation is primarily to ensure that people are not allowed to commit offences anonymously in situations of public disorder.

4.5.4.12

KEYNOTE

Religious Sensitivities

Specific guidance in relation to religious sensitivities is provided by Code A. Many people customarily cover their heads or faces for religious reasons, e.g. Muslim women, Sikh men, Sikh or Hindu women or Rastafarian men or women. A police officer cannot order the removal of a head or face covering except where there is reason to believe that the item is being worn by the individual wholly or mainly for the purpose of disguising identity, not simply because it disguises identity. Where there may be religious sensitivities about ordering the removal of such an item, the officer should permit the item to be removed out of public view (perhaps in a police van or a police station if there is one nearby). Where practicable, the item should be removed in the presence of an officer of the same sex as the person and out of sight of anyone of the opposite sex.

4.5.4.13

KEYNOTE

Powers and Offences

Unlike s. 60, there is no specific power under this section to stop vehicles but, given that this is a power for police officers in uniform, the general power under s. 163 of the Road Traffic Act 1988 could be used.

There is no power to search for face coverings etc. under this power. The Divisional Court has held that the predecessor to this power (the old s. 60(4A)) neither involved nor required a 'search' and that therefore the provisions of s. 2 of the Police and Criminal Evidence Act 1984 did not apply (*DPP* v *Avery* [2001] EWHC Admin 748). The court went on to hold that, although the power amounted to a significant interference with a person's liberty, it was justified by the type of situation envisaged by the legislators whereby the police may need to call upon the law. Clearly if an item is found during a lawful search for other articles (say under s. 60(4)) which does not require any 'reasonable belief' by the officer, face coverings and masks could then be seized under subsection (b). The procedure to be followed in relation to the retention and disposal of items seized under s. 60 is set out in the Police (Retention and Disposal of Items Seized) Regulations 2002 (SI 2002/1372).

4.5.4.14

KEYNOTE

OFFENCE: **FAILING TO COMPLY WITH REQUIREMENT TO REMOVE ITEMS—*Criminal Justice and Public Order Act 1994, s. 60AA(7)***
- Triable summarily • One month's imprisonment and/or a fine

The Criminal Justice and Public Order Act 1994, s. 60AA states:

(7) A person who fails to remove an item worn by him when required to do so by a constable in the exercise of his power under this section shall be liable.

The wording of this offence is absolute. There is no requirement that the person failed without reasonable excuse or without good reason etc.; simply that he/she failed to remove an item worn by him/her. However, it must be shown that:

- the requirement was made (and presumably understood)
- it was made by a police officer in uniform
- in the exercise of powers authorised under s. 60

in the reasonable belief that the person was wearing the item wholly or mainly for the purpose of concealing his/her identity.

Searches under Schedule 5 to the Terrorism Prevention and Investigation Measures Act 2011

2.18A   Paragraph 3 of Schedule 5 to the TPIM Act 2011 allows a constable to detain an individual to be searched under the following powers:

   (i) paragraph 6(2)(a) when a TPIM notice is being, or has just been, served on the individual for the purpose of ascertaining whether there is anything on the individual that contravenes measures specified in the notice;

   (ii) paragraph 8(2)(a) in accordance with a warrant to search the individual issued by a justice of the peace in England and Wales, a sheriff in Scotland or a lay magistrate in Northern Ireland who is satisfied that a search is necessary for the purpose of determining whether an individual in respect of whom a TPIM notice is in force is complying with measures specified in the notice (see *paragraph 2.20*); and

   (iii) paragraph 10 to ascertain whether an individual in respect of whom a TPIM notice is in force is in possession of anything that could be used to threaten or harm any person. See *paragraph 2.1(e)*.

2.19   The exercise of the powers mentioned in paragraph 2.18A does not require the constable to have reasonable grounds to suspect that the individual:

   (a) has been, or is, contravening any of the measures specified in the TPIM notice; or

   (b) has on them anything which:

      - in the case of the power in sub-paragraph (i), contravenes measures specified in the TPIM notice;
      - in the case of the power in sub-paragraph (ii) is not complying with measures specified in the TPIM notice; or
      - in the case of the power in sub-paragraph (iii), could be used to threaten or harm any person.

2.20   A search of an individual on warrant under the power mentioned in paragraph 2.18A(ii) must carried out within 28 days of the issue of the warrant and:

      - the individual may be searched on one occasion only within that period;
      - the search must take place at a reasonable hour unless it appears that this would frustrate the purposes of the search.

2.21   *Not used.*

2.22   *Not used.*

2.23   *Not used.*

2.24   *Not used.*

2.24A   *Not used.*

2.25   *Not used.*

2.26 The powers under Schedule 5 only allow a constable to conduct a search of an individual only for specified purposes relating to a TPIM notice as set out above. However, anything found may be seized and retained if there are reasonable grounds for believing that it is or it contains evidence of any offence for use at a trial for that offence or to prevent it being concealed, lost, damaged, altered, or destroyed. However, this would not prevent a search being carried out under other search powers if, in the course of exercising these powers, the officer formed reasonable grounds for suspicion.

3 Conduct of searches

4.5.5

3.1 All stops and searches must be carried out with courtesy, consideration and respect for the person concerned. This has a significant impact on public confidence in the police. Every reasonable effort must be made to minimise the embarrassment that a person being searched may experience.

3.2 The cooperation of the person to be searched must be sought in every case, even if the person initially objects to the search. A forcible search may be made only if it has been established that the person is unwilling to co-operate or resists. Reasonable force may be used as a last resort if necessary to conduct a search or to detain a person or vehicle for the purposes of a search.

3.3 The length of time for which a person or vehicle may be detained must be reasonable and kept to a minimum. Where the exercise of the power requires reasonable suspicion, the thoroughness and extent of a search must depend on what is suspected of being carried, and by whom. If the suspicion relates to a particular article which is seen to be slipped into a person's pocket, then, in the absence of other grounds for suspicion or an opportunity for the article to be moved elsewhere, the search must be confined to that pocket. In the case of a small article which can readily be concealed, such as a drug, and which might be concealed anywhere on the person, a more extensive search may be necessary. In the case of searches mentioned in paragraph 2.1(b) and (d), which do not require reasonable grounds for suspicion, officers may make any reasonable search to look for items for which they are empowered to search.

3.4 The search must be carried out at or near the place where the person or vehicle was first detained.

3.5 There is no power to require a person to remove any clothing in public other than an outer coat, jacket or gloves except under section 60AA of the Criminal Justice and Public Order Act 1994 (which empowers a constable to require a person to remove any item worn to conceal identity). A search in public of a person's clothing which has not been removed must be restricted to superficial examination of outer garments. This does not, however, prevent an officer from placing his or her hand inside the pockets of the outer clothing, or feeling round the inside of collars, socks and shoes if this is reasonably necessary in the circumstances to look for the object of the search or to remove and examine any item reasonably suspected to be the object of the search. For the same reasons, subject to the restrictions on the removal of headgear, a person's hair may also be searched in public (see paragraphs 3.1 and 3.3).

3.6 Where on reasonable grounds it is considered necessary to conduct a more thorough search (e.g. by requiring a person to take off a T-shirt), this must be done out of public view, for example, in a police van unless paragraph 3.7 applies, or police station if there is one nearby. Any search involving the removal of more than an outer coat, jacket, gloves, headgear or footwear, or any other item concealing identity, may only be made by an officer of the same sex as the person searched and may not be made in the presence of anyone of the opposite sex unless the person being searched specifically requests it (see Code C, Annex L).

3.7 Searches involving exposure of intimate parts of the body must not be conducted as a routine extension of a less thorough search, simply because nothing is found in the course of the initial search. Searches involving exposure of intimate parts of the body may be carried out only at a nearby police station or other nearby location which is out of public view (but not a police vehicle). These searches must be conducted in accordance with paragraph 11 of Annex A to Code C except that an intimate search mentioned in paragraph 11(f) of Annex A to Code C may not be authorised or carried out under any stop and search powers. The other provisions of Code C do not apply to the conduct and recording of searches of persons detained at police stations in the exercise of stop and search powers.

4.5.5.1

KEYNOTE

A search of a person should be completed as soon as possible.

A person may be detained under a stop and search power at a place other than where the person was first detained only if that place, be it a police station or elsewhere, is nearby. Such a place should be located within a reasonable travelling distance using whatever mode of travel (on foot or by car) is appropriate. This applies to all searches under stop and search powers, whether or not they involve the removal of clothing or exposure of intimate parts of the body (see Code A, paras 3.6 and 3.7) or take place in or out of public view. It means, for example, that a search under the stop and search power in s. 23 of the Misuse of Drugs Act 1971 which involves the compulsory removal of more than a person's outer coat, jacket or gloves cannot be carried out unless a place which is both nearby the place he/she was first detained and out of public view, is available. If a search involves exposure of intimate parts of the body and a police station is not nearby, particular care must be taken to ensure that the location is suitable in that it enables the search to be conducted in accordance with the requirements of para. 11 of Annex A to Code C.

A search in the street itself should be regarded as being in public for the purposes of paras 3.6 and 3.7, even though it may be empty at the time a search begins.

Although there is no power to require a person to do so, there is nothing to prevent an officer from asking a person *voluntarily to remove* more than an outer coat, jacket or gloves.

Steps to be taken prior to a search

3.8   Before any search of a detained person or attended vehicle takes place the officer must take reasonable steps, if not in uniform (see paragraph 3.9), to show their warrant card to the person to be searched or in charge of the vehicle to be searched and whether or not in uniform, to give that person the following information:

(a) that they are being detained for the purposes of a search;

(b) the officer's name (except in the case of enquiries linked to the investigation of terrorism, or otherwise where the officer reasonably believes that giving their name might put him or her in danger, in which case a warrant or other identification number shall be given) and the name of the police station to which the officer is attached;

(c) the legal search power which is being exercised; and

(d) a clear explanation of:

(i) the object of the search in terms of the articles or articles for which there is a power to search; and

(ii) in the case of

• the power under section 60 of the Criminal Justice and Public Order Act 1994 (see paragraph 2.1(b)), the nature of the power, the authorisation and the fact that it has been given;

• the powers under Schedule 5 to the Terrorism Prevention and Investigation Measures Act 2011 (see *paragraph 2.1(e)* and *2.18A*):

~ the fact that a TPIM notice is in force or, (in the case of paragraph 6(2)(a)) that a TPIM notice is being served;

~ the nature of the power being exercised.

For a search under paragraph 8 of Schedule 5, the warrant must be produced and the person be provided with a copy of it.

- all other powers requiring reasonable suspicion (see paragraph 2.1(a)), the grounds for that suspicion. This means explaining the basis for the suspicion by reference to information and/or intelligence about, or some specific behaviour by, the person concerned (see *paragraph 2.2*).

(e) that they are entitled to a copy of the record of the search if one is made (see section 4 below) if they ask within 3 months from the date of the search and:

(i) if they are not arrested and taken to a police station as a result of the search and it is practicable to make a record on the spot, that immediately after the search is completed they will be given, if they request, either:
- a copy of the record, or
- a receipt which explains how they can obtain a copy of the full record or access to an electronic copy of the record, or

(ii) if they are arrested and taken to a police station as a result of the search, that the record will be made at the station as part of their custody record and they will be given, if they request, a copy of their custody record which includes a record of the search as soon as practicable whilst they are at the station.

3.9 Stops and searches under the power mentioned in paragraph 2.1(b) may be undertaken only by a constable in uniform.

3.10 The person should also be given information about police powers to stop and search and the individual's rights in these circumstances.

3.11 If the person to be searched, or in charge of a vehicle to be searched, does not appear to understand what is being said, or there is any doubt about the person's ability to understand English, the officer must take reasonable steps to bring information regarding the person's rights and any relevant provisions of this Code to his or her attention. If the person is deaf or cannot understand English and is accompanied by someone, then the officer must try to establish whether that person can interpret or otherwise help the officer to give the required information.

4.5.5.2

KEYNOTE

This Code A requirement is mirrored by the specific requirements of s. 2 of the Police and Criminal Evidence Act 1984.

The Police and Criminal Evidence Act 1984, s. 2 states:

(1) A constable who detains a person or vehicle in the exercise—
(a) of the power conferred by section 1 above; or
(b) of any other power—
(i) to search a person without first arresting him; or
(ii) to search a vehicle without making an arrest,
need not conduct a search if it appears to him subsequently—
(i) that no search is required; or
(ii) that a search is impracticable.

(2) If a constable contemplates a search, other than a search of an unattended vehicle, in the exercise—
(a) of the power conferred by section 1 above; or
(b) of any other power, except the power conferred by section 6 below and the power conferred by section 27(2) of the Aviation Security Act 1982—
(i) to search a person without first arresting him; or
(ii) to search a vehicle without making an arrest,
it shall be his duty, subject to subsection (4) below, to take reasonable steps before he commences the search to bring to the attention of the appropriate person—
(i) if the constable is not in uniform, documentary evidence that he is a constable; and
(ii) whether he is in uniform or not, the matters specified in subsection (3) below; and the constable shall not commence the search until he has performed that duty.

(3) The matters referred to in subsection (2)(ii) above are—
(a) the constable's name and the name of the police station to which he is attached;
(b) the object of the proposed search;

(c) the constable's grounds for proposing to make it; and

(d) the effect of section 3(7) or (8) below, as may be appropriate.

Having stopped a person for the purposes of searching him/her, there is no requirement for the officer to conduct the search if it appears that to do so is not necessary or that it is impracticable.

The officer carrying out the search must take reasonable steps to bring the matters at s. 2(3)(a)–(d) to the person's attention before starting the search. This information must be given whether it is requested or not. Whether reasonable steps have been taken to communicate information will ultimately be a question of fact for the court to decide and what is 'reasonable' will vary with the particular circumstances of each search (e.g. what is reasonable outside a busy city centre nightclub may well be different from that which is required on a rural public footpath). The courts have taken a firm position in interpreting and applying these requirements. For example, the requirements for officers to provide details of their names and police stations still apply even though that information is discernible from the officers' uniform; failure to provide the information in such circumstances will make any subsequent search unlawful and will mean that the person being searched may use reasonable force to resist it (*Osman* v *DPP* (1999) 163 JP 725). The requirement to provide the name of the officer concerned applies even if the officer conducting the search and the person who is subject to the search are well known to each other (*R (Michaels)* v *Highbury Corner Magistrates' Court* (2009) EWHC 2928 (Admin)). In a further case, the Divisional Court held that the officers conducting the stop and search had not informed the suspect of their intention to search him at an early enough stage before laying their hands on him. The suspect, who was standing with his hands in his pockets and who was suspected of drugs offences, had struggled with the officers when they took hold of him and had been arrested. The magistrates' court held that, where it was obvious that the people apprehending a suspect were police officers and where an officer was genuinely concerned for the safety of a fellow officer, it was not essential to comply with all the requirements of s. 2(3). However, the Divisional Court disagreed, quashing the conviction and holding that, where police officers contemplated a statutory search, they were required (by s. 2(2)) to comply with s. 2(3) before commencing the search (*Bonner* v *DPP* [2004] EWHC 2415 (Admin)).

The 'effect of section 3(7) or (8)' referred to in s. 2(3)(d) means the person's entitlement to a copy of any search record made.

The 'appropriate person' is the person to be searched or the person in charge of the vehicle to be searched (s. 2(5)).

4 Recording requirements

(a) Searches which do not result in an arrest

4.1 When an officer carries out a search in the exercise of any power to which this Code applies, and the search does not result in the person searched or person in charge of the vehicle searched being arrested and taken to a police station, a record must be made of it, electronically or on paper, unless there are exceptional circumstances which make this wholly impracticable (e.g. in situations involving public disorder or where the recording officer's presence is urgently required elsewhere). If a record is to be made, the officer carrying out the search must make the record on the spot unless this is not practicable, in which case, the officer must make the record as soon as practicable after the search is completed.

4.2 If the record is made at the time, the person who has been searched or who is in charge of the vehicle that has been searched must be asked if they want a copy and if they do, they must be given immediately, either:

- a copy of the record, or
- a receipt which explains how they can obtain a copy of the full record or access to an electronic copy of the record.

4.2A An officer is not required to provide a copy of the full record or a receipt at the time if they are called to an incident of higher priority.

(b) Searches which result in an arrest

4.2B If a search in the exercise of any power to which this Code applies results in a person being arrested and taken to a police station, the officer carrying out the search is responsible for ensuring that a record of the search is made as a part of their custody record. The custody officer must then ensure that the person is asked if they want a copy of the record and if they do, that they are given a copy as soon as practicable.

4.5.6.1

KEYNOTE

When the search results in the person searched or in charge of a vehicle which is searched being arrested, the requirement to make the record of search part of the person's custody record does not apply if the person is granted 'street bail' after arrest (s. 30A of the Police and Criminal Evidence Act 1984) to attend a police station and is not taken in custody to the police station. An arrested person's entitlement to a copy of the search record which is made as part of his/her custody record does not affect his/her entitlement to a copy of his/her custody record or any other provisions of PACE Code C, section 2 (Custody Records).

(c) Record of search

4.3 The record of a search must always include the following information:
   (a) A note of the self-defined ethnicity, and if different, the ethnicity as perceived by the officer making the search, of the person searched or of the person in charge of the vehicle (as the case may be);
   (b) The date, time and place the person or vehicle was searched;
   (c) The object of the search in terms of the article or articles for which there is a power to search;
   (d) In the case of:
      • the power under section 60 of the Criminal Justice and Public Order Act 1994 (see paragraph 2.1(b)), the nature of the power, the authorisation and the fact that it has been given;
      • the powers under Schedule 5 to the Terrorism Prevention and Investigation Measures Act 2011 (see paragraphs 2.1(e) and 2.18A):
         ~ the fact that a TPIM notice is in force or, (in the case of paragraph 6(2)(a)), that a TPIM notice is being served;
         ~ the nature of the power, and
         ~ for a search under paragraph 8, the date the search warrant was issued, the fact that the warrant was produced and a copy of it provided and the warrant must also be endorsed by the constable executing it to state whether anything was found and whether anything was seized, and
      • all other powers requiring reasonable suspicion (see paragraph 2.1(a)), the grounds for that suspicion.
   (e) subject to paragraph 3.8(b), the identity of the officer carrying out the search.
4.3A For the purposes of completing the search record, there is no requirement to record the name, address and date of birth of the person searched or the person in charge of a vehicle which is searched and the person is under no obligation to provide this information.
4.4 Nothing in paragraph 4.3 requires the names of police officers to be shown on the search record or any other record required to be made under this code in the case of enquiries linked to the investigation of terrorism or otherwise where an officer reasonably believes that recording names might endanger the officers. In such cases the record must show the officers' warrant or other identification number and duty station.

4.5   A record is required for each person and each vehicle searched. However, if a person is in a vehicle and both are searched, and the object and grounds of the search are the same, only one record need be completed. If more than one person in a vehicle is searched, separate records for each search of a person must be made. If only a vehicle is searched, the self-defined ethnic background of the person in charge of the vehicle must be recorded, unless the vehicle is unattended.

4.6   The record of the grounds for making a search must, briefly but informatively, explain the reason for suspecting the person concerned, by reference to information and/or intelligence about, or some specific behaviour by, the person concerned (see *paragraph 2.2*).

4.7   Where officers detain an individual with a view to performing a search, but the need to search is eliminated as a result of questioning the person detained, a search should not be carried out and a record is not required. [See paragraph 2.10]

4.8   After searching an unattended vehicle, or anything in or on it, an officer must leave a notice in it (or on it, if things on it have been searched without opening it) recording the fact that it has been searched.

4.9   The notice must include the name of the police station to which the officer concerned is attached and state where a copy of the record of the search may be obtained and how (if applicable) an electronic copy may be accessed and where any application for compensation should be directed.

4.10   The vehicle must if practicable be left secure.

4.10A   *Not used.*

4.10B   *Not used.*

4.5.6.2   **KEYNOTE**

Once again, Code A is mirrored by the requirements of s. 3 of the Police and Criminal Evidence Act 1984. The Police and Criminal Evidence Act 1984, s. 3 states:

(6)   The record of a search of a person or a vehicle—
    (a)   shall state—
        (i)   the object of the search;
        (ii)   the grounds for making it;
        (iii)   the date and time when it was made;
        (iv)   the place where it was made;
        (v)   except in the case of a search of an unattended vehicle, the ethnic origins of the person searched or the person in charge of the vehicle searched (as the case may be); and
    (b)   shall identify the constable who carried out the search.
(6A)   The requirement in subsection (6)(a)(v) above, for a record to state a person's ethnic origins is a requirement to state –
    (a)   the ethnic origins of the person as described by the person, and
    (b)   if different, the ethnic origins of the person as perceived by the constable.

Officers should record the self-defined ethnicity of every person stopped according to the categories used in the 2001 census question listed in Annex B. The person should be asked to select one of the five main categories representing broad ethnic groups and then a more specific cultural background from within this group. The ethnic classification should be coded for recording purposes using the coding system in Annex B. An additional 'Not stated' box is available but should not be offered to respondents explicitly. Officers should be aware and explain to members of the public, especially where concerns are raised, that this information is required to obtain a true picture of stop and search activity and to help improve ethnic monitoring, tackle discriminatory practice, and promote effective use of the powers. If the person gives what appears to the officer to be an 'incorrect' answer (e.g. a person who appears to be white states that he/she is black), the officer should record the response that has been given and then record his/her own perception of the ethnic background by using the PNC classification system. If the 'Not stated' category is used the reason for this must be recorded on the form.

It is important for monitoring purposes to specify if the authority for exercising a stop and search power was given under s. 60 of the Criminal Justice and Public Order Act 1994.

Where a person is lawfully detained for the purpose of a search, but no search in the event takes place, the detention will not thereby have been rendered unlawful.

The requirements of s. 3 will apply to the searches of vehicles, vessels, aircraft and hovercraft (s. 3(10)).

It has been held that a failure to make a record of a search does not thereby render the search unlawful (*Basher* v *DPP* [1993] COD 372). However, it is not only the lawfulness of a search that is of concern to police officers and the general principles set out in Code A should be borne in mind at all times.

In situations where it is not practicable to provide a written copy of the record or immediate access to an electronic copy of the record or a receipt of the search at the time (see para. 4.2A), the officer should consider providing the person with details of the station at which the person may attend for a record. A receipt may take the form of a simple business card which includes sufficient information to locate the record should the person ask for the copy, e.g. the date and place of the search, a reference number or the name of the officer who carried out the search (unless para. 4.4 applies).

Where a stop and search is conducted by more than one officer the identity of all the officers engaged in the search must be recorded on the record. Nothing prevents an officer who is present but not directly involved in searching from completing the record during the course of the encounter.

In the case of unattended vehicles, s. 2 of the Police and Criminal Evidence Act 1984 states:

(6) On completing a search of an unattended vehicle or anything in or on such a vehicle in the exercise of any such power as is mentioned in subsection (2) above a constable shall leave a notice—
    (a) stating that he has searched it;
    (b) giving the name of the police station to which he is attached;
    (c) stating that an application for compensation for any damage caused by the search may be made to that police station; and
    (d) stating the effect of section 3(8) below.
(7) The constable shall leave the notice inside the vehicle unless it is not reasonably practicable to do so without damaging the vehicle.

Recording of encounters not governed by Statutory Powers

4.11   *Not used.*
4.12   There is no national requirement for an officer who requests a person in a public place to account for themselves, i.e. their actions, behaviour, presence in an area or possession of anything, to make a record of the encounter or to give the person a receipt (see paragraph 2.11).
4.12A *Not used.*
4.13   *Not used.*
4.14   *Not used.*
4.15   *Not used.*
4.16   *Not used.*
4.17   *Not used.*
4.18   *Not used.*
4.19   *Not used.*
4.20   *Not used.*

4.5.6.3   **KEYNOTE**

Where there are concerns which make it necessary to monitor any local disproportionality, forces have discretion to direct officers to record the self-defined ethnicity of persons they request to account for themselves in a public place or who they detain with a view to searching but do not search. Guidance should be provided locally and efforts made to minimise the bureaucracy involved. Records should be closely monitored and supervised in line with paras 5.1 to 5.4 and forces can suspend or reinstate recording of these encounters as appropriate.

A person who is asked to account for him/herself should, if he/she requests, be given information about how to report his/her dissatisfaction about how he/she has been treated.

5 Monitoring and supervising the use of stop and search powers

General

5.1 Any misuse of stop and search powers is likely to be harmful to policing and lead to mistrust of the police by the local community and by the public in general. Supervising officers must monitor the use of stop and search powers and should consider in particular whether there is any evidence that they are being exercised on the basis of stereotyped images or inappropriate generalisations. Supervising officers must satisfy themselves that the practice of officers under their supervision in stopping, searching and recording is fully in accordance with this Code. Supervisors must also examine whether the records reveal any trends or patterns which give cause for concern and, if so, take appropriate action to address this. (See *paragraph 2.8A*.)

5.2 Senior officers with area or force-wide responsibilities must also monitor the broader use of stop and search powers and, where necessary, take action at the relevant level.

5.3 Supervision and monitoring must be supported by the compilation of comprehensive statistical records of stops and searches at force, area and local level. Any apparently disproportionate use of the powers by particular officers or groups of officers or in relation to specific sections of the community should be identified and investigated.

5.4 In order to promote public confidence in the use of the powers, forces in consultation with police and crime commissioners must make arrangements for the records to be scrutinised by representatives of the community, and to explain the use of the powers at a local level.

Suspected misuse of powers by individual officers

5.5 Police supervisors must monitor the use of stop and search powers by individual officers to ensure that they are being applied appropriately and lawfully. Monitoring takes many forms, such as direct supervision of the exercise of the powers, examining stop and search records (particularly examining the officer's documented reasonable grounds for suspicion) and asking the officer to account for the way in which they conducted and recorded particular searches or through complaints about a stop and search that an officer has carried out.

5.6 Where a supervisor identifies issues with the way that an officer has used a stop and search power, the facts of the case will determine whether the standards of professional behaviour as set out in the Code of Ethics [<http://www.college.police.uk/What-we-do/Ethics/Pages/Code-of-Ethics.aspx>] have been breached and which formal action is pursued. Improper use might be a result of poor performance or a conduct matter, which will require the supervisor to take appropriate action such as performance or misconduct procedures. It is imperative that supervisors take both timely and appropriate action to deal with all such cases that come to their notice.

4.5.7.1

KEYNOTE

Arrangements for public scrutiny of records should take account of the right to confidentiality of those stopped and searched. Anonymised forms and/or statistics generated from records should be the focus of the examinations by members of the public.

4.6 | Entry, Search and Seizure

PACE Code of Practice for Searches of Premises by Police Officers and the Seizure of Property found by Police Officers on Persons or Premises (Code B)

> A thick grey line down the margin denotes text that is an extract of the PACE Code itself (i.e. the actual wording of the legislation). This material is examinable for both Sergeants and Inspectors.

4.6.1 Introduction

The main police powers dealing with entry to premises, searching them and seizing evidence from them, are contained within the Police and Criminal Evidence Act 1984; Code B of the Codes of Practice provides detailed guidance in relation to these features.

There are many other statutes that allow such processes to take place. However, only one common law power of entry without warrant exists—to deal with a breach of the peace (**see chapter 4.11**).

A general point worth remembering is that where police officers enter premises *lawfully* (including where they are there by invitation), they are on the premises for *all* lawful purposes (*Foster* v *Attard* [1986] Crim LR 627). This means that they can carry out any lawful functions while on the premises, even if that was not the original purpose for entry. For instance, if officers entered under a lawful power provided by the Misuse of Drugs Act 1971, they may carry out other lawful functions such as enforcing the provisions of the Gaming Act 1968. If officers are invited onto premises by someone entitled to do so, they are lawfully there unless and until that invitation is withdrawn. Once the invitation is withdrawn, the officers will become trespassers unless they have a power to be there, and the person may remove them by force (*Robson* v *Hallett* [1967] 2 QB 939). If that invitation is terminated, the person needs to communicate that clearly to the officer; merely telling officers to 'fuck off' is not necessarily sufficient (*Snook* v *Mannion* [1982] RTR 321).

The above issues are of significance to police officers but the features of the Police and Criminal Evidence Act 1984 and Code B remain the most important for the purposes of operational policing and that is the focus of this chapter.

4.6.2 PACE Code of Practice for Searches of Premises by Police Officers and the Seizure of Property found by Police Officers on Persons or Premises (Code B)

This Code applies to applications for warrants made after midnight 6 March 2011 and to searches and seizures taking place after midnight on 27 October 2013.

1 Introduction

1.1 This Code of Practice deals with police powers to:
- search premises
- seize and retain property found on premises and persons

1.1A These powers may be used to find:
- property and material relating to a crime
- wanted persons
- children who abscond from local authority accommodation where they have been remanded or committed by a court

1.2 A justice of the peace may issue a search warrant granting powers of entry, search and seizure, e.g. warrants to search for stolen property, drugs, firearms and evidence of serious offences. Police also have powers without a search warrant. The main ones provided by the Police and Criminal Evidence Act 1984 (PACE) include powers to search premises:
- to make an arrest
- after an arrest

1.3 The right to privacy and respect for personal property are key principles of the Human Rights Act 1998. Powers of entry, search and seizure should be fully and clearly justified before use because they may significantly interfere with the occupier's privacy. Officers should consider if the necessary objectives can be met by less intrusive means.

1.3A Powers to search and seize must be used fairly, responsibly, with respect for people who occupy premises being searched or are in charge of property being seized and without unlawful discrimination. Under the Equality Act 2010, section 149, when police officers are carrying out their functions, they also have a duty to have due regard to the need to eliminate unlawful discrimination, harassment and victimisation, to advance equality of opportunity between people who share a relevant protected characteristic and people who do not share it, and to take steps to foster good relations.

1.4 In all cases, police should therefore:
- exercise their powers courteously and with respect for persons and property
- only use reasonable force when this is considered necessary and proportionate to the circumstances.

1.5 If the provisions of PACE and this Code are not observed, evidence obtained from a search may be open to question.

KEYNOTE

In para. 1.3A, 'relevant protected characteristic' includes: age, disability, gender reassignment, pregnancy and maternity, race, religion or belief, sex and sexual orientation.

---

2 General

2.1 This Code must be readily available at all police stations for consultation by:
- police officers
- police staff
- detained persons
- members of the public

2.2 The *Notes for Guidance* (incorporated within Keynotes of this Manual) are not provisions of this Code.

2.3 This Code applies to searches of premises:
  (a) by police for the purposes of an investigation into an alleged offence, with the occupier's consent, other than:

- routine scene of crime searches;
- calls to a fire or burglary made by or on behalf of an occupier or searches following the activation of fire or burglar alarms or discovery of insecure premises;
- searches when *paragraph 5.4* applies;
- bomb threat calls;

(b) under powers conferred on police officers by PACE, sections 17, 18 and 32;

(c) undertaken in pursuance of search warrants issued to and executed by constables in accordance with PACE, sections 15 and 16;

(d) subject to *paragraph 2.6*, under any other power given to police to enter premises with or without a search warrant for any purpose connected with the investigation into an alleged or suspected offence.

For the purposes of this Code, 'premises' as defined in PACE, section 23, includes any place, vehicle, vessel, aircraft, hovercraft, tent or movable structure and any offshore installation as defined in the Mineral Workings (Offshore Installations) Act 1971, section 1.

2.4   A person who has not been arrested but is searched during a search of premises should be searched in accordance with Code A.

2.5   This Code does not apply to the exercise of a statutory power to enter premises or to inspect goods, equipment or procedures if the exercise of that power is not dependent on the existence of grounds for suspecting that an offence may have been committed and the person exercising the power has no reasonable grounds for such suspicion.

2.6   This Code does not affect any directions or requirements of a search warrant, order or other power to search and seize lawfully exercised in England or Wales that any item or evidence seized under that warrant, order or power be handed over to a police force, court, tribunal, or other authority outside England or Wales. For example, warrants and orders issued in Scotland or Northern Ireland, and search warrants and powers provided for in sections 14 to 17 of the Crime (International Co-operation) Act 2003.

2.7   When this Code requires the prior authority or agreement of an officer of at least inspector or superintendent rank, that authority may be given by a sergeant or chief inspector authorised to perform the functions of the higher rank under PACE, section 107.

2.8   Written records required under this Code not made in the search record shall, unless otherwise specified, be made:
- in the recording officer's pocket book ('pocket book' includes any official report book issued to police officers) or
- on forms provided for the purpose.

2.9   Nothing in this Code requires the identity of officers, or anyone accompanying them during a search of premises, to be recorded or disclosed:

(a) in the case of enquiries linked to the investigation of terrorism; or

(b) if officers reasonably believe recording or disclosing their names might put them in danger.

In these cases officers should use warrant or other identification numbers and the name of their police station. Police staff should use any identification number provided to them by the police force.

2.10 The 'officer in charge of the search' means the officer assigned specific duties and responsibilities under this Code. Whenever there is a search of premises to which this Code applies one officer must act as the officer in charge of the search.

2.11 In this Code:

(a) 'designated person' means a person other than a police officer, designated under the Police Reform Act 2002, Part 4 who has specified powers and duties of police officers conferred or imposed on them;

(b) any reference to a police officer includes a designated person acting in the exercise or performance of the powers and duties conferred or imposed on them by their designation;

(c) a person authorised to accompany police officers or designated persons in the execution of a warrant has the same powers as a constable in the execution of the warrant and the search and seizure of anything related to the warrant. These powers must be exercised in the company and under the supervision of a police officer.

2.12 If a power conferred on a designated person:

(a) allows reasonable force to be used when exercised by a police officer, a designated person exercising that power has the same entitlement to use force;

(b) includes power to use force to enter any premises, that power is not exercisable by that designated person except:

(i) in the company and under the supervision of a police officer; or

(ii) for the purpose of:
- saving life or limb; or
- preventing serious damage to property.

2.13 Designated persons must have regard to any relevant provisions of the Codes of Practice.

4.6.3.1 KEYNOTE

The purpose of para. 2.9(b) of Code B is to protect those involved in serious organised crime investigations or arrests of particularly violent suspects when there is reliable information that those arrested or their associates may threaten or cause harm to the officers or anyone accompanying them during a search of premises. In cases of doubt, an officer of inspector rank or above should be consulted.

For the purposes of para. 2.10, the officer in charge of the search should normally be the most senior officer present. Some exceptions are:

(a) a supervising officer who attends or assists at the scene of a premises search may appoint an officer of lower rank as officer in charge of the search if that officer is:
- more conversant with the facts;
- a more appropriate officer to be in charge of the search;

(b) when all officers in a premises search are the same rank. The supervising officer if available must make sure one of them is appointed officer in charge of the search, otherwise the officers themselves must nominate one of their number as the officer in charge;

(c) a senior officer assisting in a specialist role. This officer need not be regarded as having a general supervisory role over the conduct of the search or be appointed or expected to act as the officer in charge of the search.

Except in (c), nothing in this keynote diminishes the role and responsibilities of a supervisory officer who is present at the search or knows of a search taking place.

An officer of the rank of inspector or above may direct a designated investigating officer not to wear a uniform for the purposes of a specific operation.

4.6.3.2 KEYNOTE

Application for Warrant—s. 15 PACE

The Police and Criminal Evidence Act 1984, s. 15 states:

(1) This section and section 16 below have effect in relation to the issue to constables under any enactment, including an enactment contained in an Act passed after this Act, of warrants to enter and search premises; and an entry on or search of premises under a warrant is unlawful unless it complies with this section and section 16 below.

(2) Where a constable applies for any such warrant, it shall be his duty—

(a) to state—

(i) the ground on which he makes the application;

(ii) the enactment under which the warrant would be issued; and

(iii) if the application is for a warrant authorising entry and search on more than one occasion, the ground on which he applies for such a warrant, and whether he seeks a warrant authorising an unlimited number of entries, or (if not) the maximum number of entries desired;

(b) to specify the matters set out in subsection (2A) below; and

(c) to identify, so far as is practicable, the articles or persons to be sought.

(2A) The matters which must be specified pursuant to subsection (2)(b) above are—

(a) if the application relates to one or more sets of premises specified in the application each set of premises which it is desired to enter and search; and

(b) if the application relates to any premises occupied or controlled by a person specified in the application—

    (i) as many sets of premises which it is desired to enter and search as it is reasonably practicable to specify;

    (ii) the person who is in occupation or control of those premises and any others which it is desired to enter and search;

    (iii) why it is necessary to search more premises than those specified under sub-paragraph (i); and

    (iv) why it is not reasonably practicable to specify all the premises which it is desired to enter and search.

(3) An application for such a warrant shall be made ex parte and supported by information in writing.

(4) The constable shall answer on oath any question that the justice of the peace or judge hearing the application asks him.

(5) A warrant shall authorise an entry on one occasion only unless it specifies that it authorises multiple entries.

(5A) If it specifies that it authorises multiple entries, it must also specify whether the number of entries authorised is unlimited, or limited to a specified maximum.

(6) A warrant—

  (a) shall specify—

    (i) the name of the person who applies for it;

    (ii) the date on which it is issued;

    (iii) the enactment under which it is issued;

    (iv) each set of premises to be searched, or (in the case of an all premises warrant) the person who is in occupation or control of premises to be searched, together with any premises under his occupation or control which can be specified and which are to be searched; and

  (b) shall identify, so far as is practicable, the articles or persons to be sought.

(7) Two copies shall be made of a warrant (see section 8(1A)(a) above) which specifies only one set of premises and does not authorise multiple entries; and as many copies as are reasonably required may be made of any other kind of warrant.

(8) The copies shall be clearly certified as copies.

4.6.3.3   KEYNOTE

Execution of a Warrant—s. 16 PACE

The Police and Criminal Evidence Act 1984, s. 16 states:

(1) A warrant to enter and search premises may be executed by any constable.

(2) Such a warrant may authorise persons to accompany any constable who is executing it.

(2A) A person so authorised has the same powers as the constable whom he accompanies in respect of—

  (a) the execution of the warrant, and

  (b) the seizure of anything to which the warrant relates.

(2B) But he may exercise those powers only in the company, and under the supervision, of a constable.

(3) Entry and search under a warrant must be within three months from the date of its issue.

(3A) If the warrant is an all premises warrant, no premises which are not specified in it may be entered or searched unless a police officer of at least the rank of inspector has in writing authorised them to be entered.

(3B) No premises may be entered or searched for the second or any subsequent time under a warrant which authorises multiple entries unless a police officer of at least the rank of inspector has in writing authorised that entry to those premises.

(4) Entry and search under a warrant must be at a reasonable hour unless it appears to the constable executing it that the purpose of a search may be frustrated on an entry at a reasonable hour.

(5) Where the occupier of premises which are to be entered and searched is present at the time when a constable seeks to execute a warrant to enter and search them, the constable—

  (a) shall identify himself to the occupier and, if not in uniform, shall produce to him documentary evidence that he is a constable;

  (b) shall produce the warrant to him; and

  (c) shall supply him with a copy of it.

(6) Where—

  (a) the occupier of such premises is not present at the time when a constable seeks to execute such a warrant; but

  (b) some other person who appears to the constable to be in charge of the premises is present, Subsection (5) above shall have effect as if any reference to the occupier were a reference to that other person.

(7) If there is no person present who appears to the constable to be in charge of the premises, he shall leave a copy of the warrant in a prominent place on the premises.

(8) A search under a warrant may only be a search to the extent required for the purpose for which the warrant was issued.

(9) A constable executing the warrant shall make an endorsement on it stating—

  (a) whether the articles or persons sought were found; and

(b) whether any articles were seized, other than articles which were sought; and

unless the warrant is a warrant specifying one set of premises only, he shall do so separately in respect of each set of premises entered and searched, which he shall in each case state in the endorsement.

(10) A warrant shall be returned to the appropriate person mentioned in subsection (10A) below—

(a) when it has been executed; or

(b) in the case of a specific premises warrant which has not been executed, or an all premises warrant, or any warrant authorising multiple entries, upon the expiry of the period of three months referred to in subsection (3) above or sooner.

(10A) The appropriate person is—

(a) if the warrant was issued by a justice of the peace, the designated officer for the local justice area in which the justice was acting when he issued the warrant;

(b) if it was issued by a judge, the appropriate officer of the court from which he issued it.

(11) A warrant which is returned under subsection (10) above shall be retained for 12 months from its return—

(a) by the designated officer for the local justice area, if it was returned under paragraph (i) of that subsection; and

(b) by the appropriate officer, if it was returned under paragraph (ii).

(12) If during the period for which a warrant is to be retained the occupier of premises to which it relates asks to inspect it, he shall be allowed to do so.

4.6.3.4

KEYNOTE

General Points

If an application for a warrant is refused, no further application can be made unless it is supported by additional grounds.

'Premises' include any place, and in particular, (a) any vehicle, vessel, aircraft or hovercraft; (b) any offshore installation; (c) any renewable energy installation; (d) any tent or moveable structure (s. 23 of the 1984 Act).

The details of the extent of the proposed search should be made clear in the application and the officer swearing the warrant out must be prepared to answer *any* questions put to him/her on oath under s. 15(4). Courts will go into background detail about the particular premises, or part of the premises, and who is likely to be present on the premises at the time the warrant is executed (e.g. children).

4.6.3.5

KEYNOTE

Examples

Sections 15 and 16 of the 1984 Act apply to all search warrants issued to and executed by constables under any enactment, e.g. search warrants issued by:

(a) a justice of the peace under:
- Theft Act 1968, s. 26—stolen property;
- Misuse of Drugs Act 1971, s. 23—controlled drugs;
- PACE, s. 8—evidence of an indictable offence;
- Terrorism Act 2000, sch. 5, para. 1;
- Terrorism Prevention and Investigation Measures Act 2011, sch. 5, para. 8(2)(b)—search of premises for compliance purposes.

(b) a Circuit judge under:
- PACE, sch. 1;
- Terrorism Act 2000, sch. 5, para. 11.

Examples of the other powers in para. 2.3(d) include:

(a) Road Traffic Act 1988, s. 6E(1) giving police power to enter premises under s. 6E(1) to:
- require a person to provide a specimen of breath; or
- arrest a person following
  — a positive breath test;
  — failure to provide a specimen of breath;

(b) Transport and Works Act 1992, s. 30(4) giving police powers to enter premises mirroring the powers in (a) in relation to specified persons working on transport systems to which the Act applies;

(c) Criminal Justice Act 1988, s. 139B giving police power to enter and search school premises for offensive weapons, bladed or pointed articles;

(d) Terrorism Act 2000, sch. 5, paras 3 and 15 empowering a superintendent in urgent cases to give written authority for police to enter and search premises for the purposes of a terrorist investigation;

(e) Explosives Act 1875, s. 73(b) empowering a superintendent to give written authority for police to enter premises, examine and search them for explosives;

(f) search warrants and production orders or the equivalent issued in Scotland or Northern Ireland endorsed under the Summary Jurisdiction (Process) Act 1881 or the Petty Sessions (Ireland) Act 1851 respectively for execution in England and Wales.

(g) Terrorism Prevention and Investigation Measures Act 2011, sch. 5, paras 5(1), 6(2)(b) and 7(2), searches relating to TPIM notices (see para. 10.1).

Searching Persons

The Criminal Justice Act 1988, s. 139B provides that a constable who has reasonable grounds for suspecting that an offence under the Criminal Justice Act 1988, s. 139A or 139AA has been or is being committed may enter school premises and search the premises and any persons on the premises for any bladed or pointed article or offensive weapon. Persons may be searched under a warrant issued under the Misuse of Drugs Act 1971, s. 23(3) to search premises for drugs or documents only if the warrant specifically authorises the search of persons on the premises. Powers to search premises under certain terrorism provisions also authorise the search of persons on the premises, e.g. under paras 1, 2, 11 and 15 of sch. 5 to the Terrorism Act 2000 and s. 52 of the Anti-terrorism, Crime and Security Act 2001.

Immigration Act 1971

The Immigration Act 1971, part III and sch. 2 gives immigration officers powers to enter and search premises, seize and retain property, with and without a search warrant. These are similar to the powers available to police under search warrants issued by a justice of the peace and without a warrant under ss. 17, 18, 19 and 32 of the 1984 Act except they only apply to specified offences under the Immigration Act 1971 and immigration control powers. For certain types of investigations and enquiries these powers avoid the need for the Immigration Service to rely on police officers becoming directly involved. When exercising these powers, immigration officers are required by the Immigration and Asylum Act 1999, s. 145 to have regard to this Code's corresponding provisions. When immigration officers are dealing with persons or property at police stations, police officers should give appropriate assistance to help them discharge their specific duties and responsibilities.

4.6.3.6   **KEYNOTE**

Exclusion of Evidence

If the provisions of these sections are not fully complied with, any entry and search made under a warrant will be unlawful. Although the officers executing the warrant may have some protection from personal liability where there has been a defect in the *procedure* by which the warrant was issued, failure to follow the requirements of ss. 15 and 16 may result in the exclusion of any evidence obtained under the warrant. Therefore, where officers failed to provide the occupier of the searched premises with a copy of the warrant (under s.16(5)(c)), they were obliged to return the property seized during the search (*R* v *Chief Constable of Lancashire, ex parte Parker* [1993] QB 577).

If a warrant itself is invalid for some reason, any entry and subsequent seizure made under it are unlawful (*R* v *Central Criminal Court and British Railways Board, ex parte AJD Holdings Ltd* [1992] Crim LR 669). After a warrant has been executed, or if it has not been used within three months (or sooner) from its date of issue, it must be returned to the designated officer for the local justice area in which the justice of the peace issued the warrant, or where it was issued by a judge to the appropriate officer of the court from which it was issued (s. 16(10) and (10A)).

Very minor departures from the letter of the warrant, however, will not render any search unlawful (*Attorney-General of Jamaica* v *Williams* [1998] AC 351).

KEYNOTE

Search Warrants for Indictable Offences—s. 8 PACE

The Police and Criminal Evidence Act 1984, s. 8 states:

(1) If on an application made by a constable a justice of the peace is satisfied that there are reasonable grounds for believing—

(a) that an indictable offence has been committed; and

(b) that there is material on premises mentioned in subsection (1A) below which is likely to be of substantial value (whether by itself or together with other material) to the investigation of the offence; and

(c) that the material is likely to be relevant evidence; and

(d) that it does not consist of or include items subject to legal privilege, excluded material or special procedure material; and

(e) that any of the conditions specified in subsection (3) below applies in relation to each set of premises specified in the application

he may issue a warrant authorising a constable to enter and search the premises.

(1A) The premises referred to in subsection (1)(b) above are—

(a) one or more sets of premises specified in the application (in which case the application is for a 'specific premises warrant'); or

(b) any premises occupied or controlled by a person specified in the application, including such sets of premises as are so specified (in which case the application is for an 'all premises warrant').

(1B) If the application is for an all premises warrant, the justice of the peace must also be satisfied—

(a) that because of the particulars of the offence referred to in paragraph (a) of subsection (1) above, there are reasonable grounds for believing that it is necessary to search premises occupied or controlled by the person in question which are not specified in the application in order to find the material referred to in paragraph (b) of that subsection; and

(b) that it is not reasonably practicable to specify in the application all the premises which he occupies or controls and which might need to be searched.

(1C) The warrant may authorise entry to and search of premises on more than one occasion if, on the application, the justice of the peace is satisfied that it is necessary to authorise multiple entries in order to achieve the purpose for which he issues the warrant.

(1D) If it authorises multiple entries, the number of entries authorised may be unlimited, or limited to a maximum.

(2) A constable may seize and retain anything for which a search has been authorised under subsection (1) above.

(3) The conditions mentioned in subsection (1)(e) above are—

(a) that it is not practicable to communicate with any person entitled to grant entry to the premises;

(b) that it is practicable to communicate with a person entitled to grant entry to the premises but it is not practicable to communicate with any person entitled to grant access to the evidence;

(c) that entry to the premises will not be granted unless a warrant is produced;

(d) that the purpose of a search may be frustrated or seriously prejudiced unless a constable arriving at the premises can secure immediate entry to them.

(4) In this Act 'relevant evidence', in relation to an offence, means anything that would be admissible in evidence at a trial for the offence.

(5) The power to issue a warrant conferred by this section is in addition to any such power otherwise conferred.

This section provides that a constable can apply for two different types of search warrant: a 'specific premises warrant' for the search of one set of premises; and an 'all premises warrant' when it is necessary to search all premises occupied or controlled by an individual, but where it is not reasonably practicable to specify all such premises at the time of applying for the warrant. The warrant allows access to all premises occupied or controlled by that person, both those which are specified on the application, and those which are not. Note that s. 8(1C) and (1D) provide that a warrant (either an 'all premises warrant' or a 'specific premises warrant') may authorise access on more than one occasion, and if multiple entries are authorised these may be unlimited or limited to a maximum.

The officer applying for a warrant under s. 8 must have reasonable grounds for believing that material which is likely *to be of substantial value to the investigation of the offence* is on the premises specified. Therefore, when executing such a warrant, the officer must be able to show that any material seized thereunder fell within that description (*R* v *Chief Constable of the Warwickshire Constabulary, ex parte Fitzpatrick* [1999] 1 WLR 564). Possession of a warrant under s. 8 does not authorise police officers to seize all material found on the relevant premises to be taken away and 'sifted' somewhere else (*R* v *Chesterfield Justices, ex parte Bramley* [2000] QB 576) (see s. 50 of the Criminal Justice and Police Act 2001 for the power to 'seize and sift').

This means that material which is solely of value for *intelligence* purposes may not be seized under a s. 8 warrant.

The power to apply for and execute a warrant under s. 8 and to carry out the actions under s. 8(2) are among those powers that can be conferred on a person designated as an Investigating Officer under sch. 4 to the Police Reform Act 2002.

The conditions set out under s. 8(1)(e) are part of the *application* process, not part of the general execution process (which is set out at s. 16 above). Therefore the officer swearing out a s. 8 warrant will have to satisfy the court that any of those conditions apply.

4.6.3.8

KEYNOTE

Legally Privileged Material

Material which falls within the definition in s. 10 of the 1984 Act is subject to legal privilege which means that it cannot be searched for or seized.

The Police and Criminal Evidence Act 1984, s. 10 states:

(1) Subject to subsection (2) below, in this Act 'items subject to legal privilege' means—
   (a) communications between a professional legal adviser and his client or any person representing his client made in connection with the giving of legal advice to the client;
   (b) communications between a professional legal adviser and his client or any person representing his client or between such an adviser or his client or any such representative and any other person made in connection with or in contemplation of legal proceedings and for the purposes of such proceedings; and
   (c) items enclosed with or referred to in such communications and made—
      (i) in connection with the giving of legal advice; or
      (ii) in connection with or in contemplation of legal proceedings and for the purposes of such proceedings,

when they are in the possession of a person who is entitled to possession of them.

Items held with the intention of furthering a criminal purpose are not subject to this privilege (s. 10(2)). When making an application for a warrant to search for and seize such material the procedure under sch. 1 should be used. Occasions where this will happen are rare and would include instances where a solicitor's firm is the subject of a criminal investigation (*R* v *Leeds Crown Court, ex parte Switalski* [1991] Crim LR 559). However, it may be possible during a search to ascertain which material is subject to legal privilege and which might be lawfully seized under the warrant being executed. Therefore, although a warrant cannot authorise a search for legally privileged material, the fact that such material is inadvertently seized in the course of a search authorised by a proper warrant does not render the search unlawful (*R* v *HM Customs and Excise, ex parte Popely* [2000] Crim LR 388).

4.6.3.9

KEYNOTE

Excluded Material

Access to 'excluded material' can generally only be gained by applying to a judge for a production order under the procedure set out in s. 9 of, and sch. 1 to, the 1984 Act and PACE Code B. That strict statutory procedure also applies to the application for and execution of warrants by Investigating Officers designated under sch. 4 to the Police Reform Act 2002.

The Police and Criminal Evidence Act 1984, s. 11 states:

(1) Subject to the following provisions of this section, in this Act 'excluded material' means—
   (a) personal records which a person has acquired or created in the course of any trade, business, profession or other occupation or for the purposes of any paid or unpaid office and which he holds in confidence;
   (b) human tissue or tissue fluid which has been taken for the purposes of diagnosis or medical treatment and which a person holds in confidence;
   (c) journalistic material which a person holds in confidence and which consists—

(i) of documents; or

(ii) of records other than documents.

(2) A person holds material other than journalistic material in confidence for the purposes of this section if he holds it subject—

(a) to an express or implied undertaking to hold it in confidence; or

(b) to a restriction on disclosure or an obligation of secrecy contained in any enactment, including an enactment contained in an Act passed after this Act.

(3) A person holds journalistic material in confidence for the purposes of this section if—

(a) he holds it subject to such an undertaking, restriction or obligation; and

(b) it has been continuously held (by one or more persons) subject to such an undertaking, restriction or obligation since it was first acquired or created for the purposes of journalism.

Medical records and dental records would fall into this category, as might records made by priests or religious advisers.

'Personal records' are defined under s. 12 of the 1984 Act and include records relating to the physical or mental health, counselling or assistance given to an individual who can be identified by those records.

'Journalistic material' is defined under s. 13 as material acquired or created for the purposes of journalism.

4.6.3.10

KEYNOTE

Special Procedure Material

Special procedure material can be gained by applying for a search warrant or a production order under sch. 1 to the 1984 Act.

The Police and Criminal Evidence Act 1984, s. 14 states:

(1) In this Act 'special procedure material' means—

(a) material to which subsection (2) below applies; and

(b) journalistic material, other than excluded material.

(2) Subject to the following provisions of this section, this subsection applies to material, other than items subject to legal privilege and excluded material, in the possession of a person who—

(a) acquired or created it in the course of any trade, business, profession or other occupation or for the purpose of any paid or unpaid office; and

(b) holds it subject—

(i) to an express or implied undertaking to hold it in confidence; or

(ii) to a restriction or obligation such as is mentioned in section 11(2)(b) above.

For items subject to 'legal privilege' and 'excluded material', see para. 4.6.3.8.

The person believed to be in possession of the material must have come by it under the circumstances set out at s. 14(2)(a) *and* must hold it under the undertakings or obligations set out at s. 14(2)(b).

4.6.4

3 Search warrants and production orders

(a) Before making an application

3.1 When information appears to justify an application, the officer must take reasonable steps to check the information is accurate, recent and not provided maliciously or irresponsibly. An application may not be made on the basis of information from an anonymous source if corroboration has not been sought.

3.2 The officer shall ascertain as specifically as possible the nature of the articles concerned and their location.

3.3 The officer shall make reasonable enquiries to:

(i) establish if:

- anything is known about the likely occupier of the premises and the nature of the premises themselves;
- the premises have been searched previously and how recently;

(ii) obtain any other relevant information.

3.4 An application:

(a) to a justice of the peace for a search warrant or to a Circuit judge for a search warrant or production order under PACE, Schedule 1 must be supported by a signed written authority from an officer of inspector rank or above:

Note: If the case is an urgent application to a justice of the peace and an inspector or above is not readily available, the next most senior officer on duty can give the written authority.

(b) to a circuit judge under the Terrorism Act 2000, Schedule 5 for

- a production order;
- search warrant; or
- an order requiring an explanation of material seized or produced under such a warrant or production order

must be supported by a signed written authority from an officer of superintendent rank or above.

3.5 Except in a case of urgency, if there is reason to believe a search might have an adverse effect on relations between the police and the community, the officer in charge shall consult the local police/community liaison officer:

- before the search; or
- in urgent cases, as soon as practicable after the search.

(b) Making an application

3.6 A search warrant application must be supported in writing, specifying:

(a) the enactment under which the application is made;

(b)

(i) whether the warrant is to authorise entry and search of:
- one set of premises; or
- if the application is under PACE section 8, or Schedule 1, paragraph 12, more than one set of specified premises or all premises occupied or controlled by a specified person; and

(ii) the premises to be searched;

(c) the object of the search;

(d) the grounds for the application, including, when the purpose of the proposed search is to find evidence of an alleged offence, an indication of how the evidence relates to the investigation;

(da) where the application is under PACE section 8, or Schedule 1, paragraph 12 for a single warrant to enter and search:

(i) more than one set of specified premises, the officer must specify each set of premises which it is desired to enter and search

(ii) all premises occupied or controlled by a specified person, the officer must specify:
- as many sets of premises which it is desired to enter and search as it is reasonably practicable to specify;
- the person who is in occupation or control of those premises and any others which it is desired to search;
- why it is necessary to search more premises than those which can be specified;
- why it is not reasonably practicable to specify all the premises which it is desired to enter and search;

(db) whether an application under PACE section 8 is for a warrant authorising entry and search on more than one occasion, and if so, the officer must state the grounds for this and whether the desired number of entries authorised is unlimited or a specified maximum;

(e) there are no reasonable grounds to believe the material to be sought, when making application to a:

   (i) justice of the peace or a Circuit judge consists of or includes items subject to legal privilege;

   (ii) justice of the peace, consists of or includes excluded material or special procedure material;

Note: this does not affect the additional powers of seizure in the Criminal Justice and Police Act 2001, Part 2 covered in paragraph 7.7;

   (f) if applicable, a request for the warrant to authorise a person or persons to accompany the officer who executes the warrant.

3.7 A search warrant application under PACE, Schedule 1, paragraph 12(a), shall if appropriate indicate why it is believed service of notice of an application for a production order may seriously prejudice the investigation. Applications for search warrants under the Terrorism Act 2000, Schedule 5, paragraph 11 must indicate why a production order would not be appropriate.

3.8 If a search warrant application is refused, a further application may not be made for those premises unless supported by additional grounds.

4.6.4.1

KEYNOTE

The identity of an informant need not be disclosed when making an application, but the officer should be prepared to answer any questions the magistrate or judge may have about:

- the accuracy of previous information from that source
- any other related matters.

Under s. 16(2) of the 1984 Act, a search warrant may authorise persons other than police officers to accompany the constable who executes the warrant. This includes, for example, any suitably qualified or skilled person or an expert in a particular field whose presence is needed to help accurately identify the material sought or to advise where certain evidence is most likely to be found and how it should be dealt with. It does not give them any right to force entry, but it gives them the right to be on the premises during the search and to search for or seize property without the occupier's permission.

   The information supporting a search warrant application should be as specific as possible, particularly in relation to the articles or persons being sought and where in the premises it is suspected they may be found. The meaning of 'items subject to legal privilege', 'excluded material' and 'special procedure material' are defined by ss. 10, 11 and 14 of the 1984 Act respectively.

4.6.5

4 Entry without warrant—particular powers

(a) Making an arrest etc

4.1 The conditions under which an officer may enter and search premises without a warrant are set out in PACE, section 17. It should be noted that this section does not create or confer any powers of arrest.

4.6.5.1

KEYNOTE

Power of Entry—s.17 PACE

The Police and Criminal Evidence Act 1984, s. 17 states:

(1) Subject to the following provisions of this section, and without prejudice to any other enactment, a constable may enter and search any premises for the purpose—

(a) of executing—

    (i) a warrant of arrest issued in connection with or arising out of criminal proceedings; or

    (ii) a warrant of commitment issued under section 76 of the Magistrates' Courts Act 1980;

(b) of arresting a person for an indictable offence;

(c) of arresting a person for an offence under—

    (i) section 1 (prohibition of uniforms in connection with political objectives) of the Public Order Act 1936;

    (ii) any enactment contained in sections 6 to 8 or 10 of the Criminal Law Act 1977 (offences relating to entering and remaining on property);

    (iii) section 4 of the Public Order Act 1986 (fear or provocation of violence);

    (iiia) section 4 (driving etc when under influence of drink or drugs) or 163 (failure to stop when required to do so by constable in uniform) of the Road Traffic Act 1988;

    (iiib) section 27 of the Transport and Works Act 1992 (which relates to offences involving drink or drugs);

    (iv) section 76 of the Criminal Justice and Public Order Act 1994 (failure to comply with interim possession order);

    (v) any of sections 4, 5, 6(1) and (2), 7 and 8(1) and (2) of the Animal Welfare Act 2006 (offences relating to the prevention of harm to animals);

    (vi) section 144 of the Legal Aid, Sentencing and Punishment of Offenders Act 2012 (squatting in a residential building);

(ca) of arresting, in pursuance of section 32(1A) of the Children and Young Persons Act 1969, any child or young person who has been remanded or committed to local authority accommodation or youth detention accommodation under section 91 of the Legal Aid, Sentencing and Punishment of Offenders Act 2012;

(caa) of arresting a person for an offence to which section 61 of the Animal Health Act 1981 applies;

(cab) of arresting a person under any of the following provisions—

    (i) section 30D(1) or (2A);

    (ii) section 46A(1) or (1A);

    (iii) section 5B(7) of the Bail Act 1976 (arrest where a person fails to surrender to custody in accordance with a court order);

    (iv) section 7(3) of the Bail Act 1976 (arrest where a person is not likely to surrender to custody etc);

    (v) section 97(1) of the Legal Aid, Sentencing and Punishment of Offenders Act 2012 (arrest where a child is suspected of breaking conditions of remand);

(cb) of recapturing any person who is, or is deemed for any purpose to be, unlawfully at large while liable to be detained—

    (i) in a prison, remand centre, young offender institution or secure training centre, or

    (ii) in pursuance of section 92 of the Powers of Criminal Courts (Sentencing) Act 2000 (dealing with children and young persons guilty of grave crimes), in any other place;

(d) of recapturing any person whatever who is unlawfully at large and whom he is pursuing; or

(e) of saving life or limb or preventing serious damage to property.

(2) Except for the purpose specified in paragraph (e) of subsection (1) above, the powers of entry and search conferred by this section—

(a) are only exercisable if the constable has reasonable grounds for believing that the person whom he is seeking is on the premises; and

(b) are limited, in relation to premises consisting of two or more separate dwellings, to powers to enter and search—

    (i) any parts of the premises which the occupiers of any dwelling comprised in the premises use in common with the occupiers of any other such dwelling; and

    (ii) any such dwelling in which the constable has reasonable grounds for believing that the person whom he is seeking may be.

(3) The powers of entry and search conferred by this section are only exercisable for the purposes specified in subsection (1)(c)(ii) or (iv) above by a constable in uniform.

(4) The power of search conferred by this section is only a power to search to the extent that is reasonably required for the purpose for which the power of entry is exercised.

(5) Subject to subsection (6) below, all the rules of common law under which a constable has power to enter premises without a warrant are hereby abolished.

(6) Nothing in subsection (5) above affects any power of entry to deal with or prevent a breach of the peace.

Force may be used in exercising the power of entry where it is necessary to do so. Generally, the officer should first attempt to communicate with the occupier of the premises, explaining by what authority and for what purpose entry is to be made, before making a forcible entry. Clearly though, there will be occasions where such communication is impossible, impracticable or unnecessary; in those cases there is no need for the officer to enter into such an explanation (*O'Loughlin* v *Chief Constable of Essex* [1998] 1 WLR 374).

In a case where police had been called to an address by an abandoned 999 call, the officers had to move a man away from the front door in order to gain entry under s. 17. It was held that the officers had the power to use reasonable force in order to do so under s. 117 of the Police and Criminal Evidence Act 1984 (*Smith (Peter John)* v *DPP* [2001] EWHC Admin 55).

'Unlawfully at large' does not have a particular statutory meaning and can apply to someone who is subject to an order under the Mental Health Act 1983 or someone who has escaped from custody. The pursuit of the person who is unlawfully at large must be 'fresh', that is, the power will only be available while the officer is actually 'pursuing' the person concerned (*D'Souza* v *DPP* [1992] 1 WLR 1073).

The power of a constable under s. 17(1)(d) to enter and search premises to recapture a person who is unlawfully at large and whom he/she is pursuing extends to entry to retake a mentally ill patient unlawfully at large provided that such a patient is liable to be retaken and returned to hospital and provided that the pursuit of such a person is almost contemporaneous with the entry to the premises, a term which is somewhat wider than 'hot pursuit'.

The officer must have reasonable grounds to *believe* that the person is on the premises in all cases except saving life and limb at s. 17(1)(e).

Note the requirement for an officer to be in uniform for the purposes of s. 17(1)(c)(ii) and (iv), and the restrictions on the power of search under s. 17(4) (i.e. that any such search is limited to the extent that is reasonably required for the purpose for which you entered the premises in the first place).

The power to enter and search any premises in the relevant police area for the purpose of saving life or limb or preventing serious damage to property above is among those that can be conferred on a designated person under sch. 4 to the Police Reform Act 2002.

(b) Search of premises where arrest takes place or the arrested person was immediately before arrest

4.2   When a person has been arrested for an indictable offence, a police officer has power under PACE, section 32 to search the premises where the person was arrested or where the person was immediately before being arrested.

4.6.5.2

KEYNOTE

Power to Search after Arrest—s. 32 PACE

The Police and Criminal Evidence Act 1984, s. 32 states:

(1)   A constable may search an arrested person, in any case where the person to be searched has been arrested at a place other than a police station, if the constable has reasonable grounds for believing that the arrested person may present a danger to himself or others.

(2)   Subject to subsections (3) to (5) below, a constable shall also have power in any such case—
   (a) to search the arrested person for anything—
      (i)   which he might use to assist him to escape from lawful custody; or
      (ii) which might be evidence relating to an offence; and
   (b) if the offence for which he has been arrested is an indictable offence, to enter and search any premises in which he was when arrested or immediately before he was arrested for evidence relating to the offence.

(3)   The power to search conferred by subsection (2) above is only a power to search to the extent that is reasonably required for the purpose of discovering any such thing or any such evidence.

(4)   The powers conferred by this section to search a person are not to be construed as authorising a constable to require a person to remove any of his clothing in public other than an outer coat, jacket or gloves but they do authorise a search of a person's mouth.

(5)   A constable may not search a person in the exercise of the power conferred by subsection (2)(a) above unless he has reasonable grounds for believing that the person to be searched may have concealed on him anything for which a search is permitted under that paragraph.

The power to search the arrested person under s. 32(1) is a general one relating to safety.

The House of Lords have confirmed that the police have a common law power to search for and seize property after a lawful arrest (*R* v *Governor of Pentonville Prison, ex parte Osman* [1990] 1 WLR 277). This decision was confirmed by the House of Lords in *R (On the Application of Rottman)* v *Commissioner of Police of the*

Metropolis [2002] UKHL 20. In *Rottman* it was held that it was a well-established principle of the common law that an arresting officer had the power to search a room in which a person had been arrested (per *Ghani v Jones* [1970] 1 QB 693). This extended power is not limited to purely 'domestic' offences, but also applies to cases involving extradition offences.

Section 32 also states:

(6) A constable may not search premises in the exercise of the power conferred by subsection (2)(b) above unless he has reasonable grounds for believing that there is evidence for which a search is permitted under that paragraph on the premises.

(7) In so far as the power of search conferred by subsection (2)(b) above relates to premises consisting of two or more separate dwellings, it is limited to a power to search—

   (a) any dwelling in which the arrest took place or in which the person arrested was immediately before his arrest; and

   (b) any parts of the premises which the occupier of any such dwelling uses in common with the occupiers of any other dwellings comprised in the premises.

(8) A constable searching a person in the exercise of the power conferred by subsection (1) above may seize and retain anything he finds, if he has reasonable grounds for believing that the person searched might use it to cause physical injury to himself or to any other person.

(9) A constable searching a person in the exercise of the power conferred by subsection (2)(a) above may seize and retain anything he finds, other than an item subject to legal privilege, if he has reasonable grounds for believing—

   (a) that he might use it to assist him to escape from lawful custody; or

   (b) that it is evidence of an offence or has been obtained in consequence of the commission of an offence.

(10) Nothing in this section shall be taken to affect the power conferred by section 43 of the Terrorism Act 2000.

Both 'reasonable grounds' and 'immediately' are questions of fact for a court to determine. It has been held that the power under s. 32(2)(b) is one for use at the time of arrest and should not be used to return to the relevant premises some time after the arrest in the way that s. 18 of the 1984 Act may be used (*R v Badham* [1987] Crim LR 202).

Officers exercising their power to enter and search under s. 32 must have a *genuine belief* that there is evidence on the premises; it is not a licence for a general fishing expedition (*R v Beckford* [1992] 94 Cr App R 43).

The Divisional Court has refused to allow s. 32 to be used in a situation where the arrested person had not been in the relevant premises (where he did not live) for a period of over two hours preceding his arrest and where there were no reasonable grounds for believing that he presented a danger to himself or others (*Hewitson* v *Chief Constable of Dorset Police* [2003] EWHC 3296 (QB)).

(c) Search of premises occupied or controlled by the arrested person

4.3 The specific powers to search premises which <u>are</u> occupied or controlled by a person arrested for an indictable offence are set out in PACE, section 18. They may not be exercised, except if section 18(5) applies, unless an officer of inspector rank or above has given written authority. That authority should only be given when the authorising officer is satisfied that the premises <u>are</u> occupied or controlled by the arrested person and that the necessary grounds exist. If possible the authorising officer should record the authority on the Notice of Powers and Rights and, subject to *paragraph 2.9*, sign the Notice. The record of the grounds for the search and the nature of the evidence sought as required by section 18(7) of the Act should be made in:

• the custody record if there is one, otherwise

• the officer's pocket book, or

• the search record.

Power to Search after Arrest for Indictable Offence—s.18 PACE

The Police and Criminal Evidence Act 1984, s. 18 states:

(1) Subject to the following provisions of this section, a constable may enter and search any premises occupied or controlled by a person who is under arrest for an indictable offence, if he has reasonable grounds for suspecting that there is on the premises evidence, other than items subject to legal privilege, that relates—

(a) to that offence; or

(b) to some other indictable offence which is connected with or similar to that offence.

(2) A constable may seize and retain anything for which he may search under subsection (1) above.

(3) The power to search conferred by subsection (1) above is only a power to search to the extent that is reasonably required for the purpose of discovering such evidence.

(4) Subject to subsection (5) below, the powers conferred by this section may not be exercised unless an officer of the rank of inspector or above has authorised them in writing.

(5) A constable may conduct a search under subsection (1)—

(a) before the person is taken to a police station or released on bail under section 30A, and

(b) without obtaining an authorisation under subsection (4), if the condition in subsection (5A) is satisfied.

(5A) The condition is that the presence of the person at a place (other than a police station) is necessary for the effective investigation of the offence.

(6) If a constable conducts a search by virtue of subsection (5) above, he shall inform an officer of the rank of inspector or above that he has made the search as soon as practicable after he has made it.

(7) An officer who—

(a) authorises a search; or

(b) is informed of a search under subsection (6) above, shall make a record in writing—

(i) of the grounds for the search; and

(ii) of the nature of the evidence that was sought.

(8) If the person who was in occupation or control of the premises at the time of the search is in police detention at the time the record is to be made, the officer shall make the record as part of his custody record.

The power under s. 18 only applies to premises which <u>are</u> occupied and controlled by a person under arrest for an indictable offence; reasonable *suspicion* that the person occupies or controls the premises *is not sufficient*. A short stay may be sufficient to amount to 'occupation', but it must be such as to support the belief that it will have caused or contributed to the evidence sought being on the premises (*R (AB and CD)* v *Huddersfield Magistrates' Court and Chief Constable of West Yorkshire Police* [2014] 2 Cr App R 409 (25)).

The search is limited to evidence relating to the indictable offence for which the person has been arrested or another indictable offence which is similar or connected; it does not authorise a general search for anything that might be of use for other purposes (e.g. for intelligence reports). The extent of the search is limited by s. 18(3). If you are looking for a stolen fridge-freezer, you would not be empowered to search through drawers or small cupboards. You would be able to, however, if you were looking for packaging, receipts or other documents relating to the fridge-freezer.

That authority is for a search which is lawful *in all other respects*, that is, the other conditions imposed by s. 18 must be met. An inspector cannot make an otherwise unlawful entry and search lawful simply by authorising it (*Krohn* v *DPP* [1997] COD 345).

Where officers carry out a search under s. 18 they must, so far as is possible in the circumstances, explain to the occupier(s) the reason for it. If officers attempt to carry out an authorised search under s. 18 without attempting to explain to an occupier the reason, it may mean that the officers are not acting in the execution of their duty and their entry may be lawfully resisted (*Lineham* v *DPP* [2000] Crim LR 861).

The provision under s. 18(5) relates to cases where the presence of the person *is in fact necessary* for the effective investigation of the offence. If such a search is made, the searching officer must inform an inspector (or above) as soon as practicable after the search.

If the person is in police detention after the arrest, the facts concerning the search must be recorded in the custody record. Where a person is re-arrested under s. 31 of the 1984 Act for an indictable offence, the powers to search under s. 18 begin again, that is, a new power to search is created in respect of each indictable offence.

5 Search with consent

5.1 Subject to *paragraph 5.4*, if it is proposed to search premises with the consent of a person entitled to grant entry the consent must, if practicable, be given in writing on the Notice of Powers and Rights before the search. The officer must make any necessary enquiries to be satisfied the person is in a position to give such consent.

5.2 Before seeking consent the officer in charge of the search shall state the purpose of the proposed search and its extent. This information must be as specific as possible, particularly regarding the articles or persons being sought and the parts of the premises to be searched. The person concerned must be clearly informed they are not obliged to consent, that any consent can be withdrawn at any time, including before the search starts or while it is under-way and anything seized may be produced in evidence. If at the time the person is not sus-pected of an offence, the officer shall say this when stating the purpose of the search.

5.3 An officer cannot enter and search or continue to search premises under *paragraph 5.1* if consent is given under duress or withdrawn before the search is completed.

5.4 It is unnecessary to seek consent under *paragraphs 5.1* and *5.2* if this would cause dispropor-tionate inconvenience to the person concerned.

KEYNOTE

In a lodging house or similar accommodation, every reasonable effort should be made to obtain the consent of the tenant, lodger or occupier. A search should not be made solely on the basis of the landlord's consent.

If the intention is to search premises under the authority of a warrant or a power of entry and search without warrant, and the occupier of the premises cooperates in accordance with para. 6.4, there is no need to obtain written consent.

Paragraph 5.4 is intended to apply when it is reasonable to assume innocent occupiers would agree to, and expect, police to take the proposed action, e.g. if:

- a suspect has fled the scene of a crime or to evade arrest and it is necessary quickly to check surrounding gardens and readily accessible places to see if the suspect is hiding or;
- police have arrested someone in the night after a pursuit and it is necessary to make a brief check of gar-dens along the pursuit route to see if stolen or incriminating articles have been discarded.

6 Searching premises—general considerations

(a) Time of searches

6.1 Searches made under warrant must be made within three calendar months of the date of the warrant is issued or within the period specified in the enactment under which the warrant is issued if this is shorter.

6.2 Searches must be made at a reasonable hour unless this might frustrate the purpose of the search.

6.3 When the extent or complexity of a search mean it is likely to take a long time, the officer in charge of the search may consider using the seize and sift powers referred to in *section 7*.

6.3A A warrant under PACE, section 8 may authorise entry to and search of premises on more than one occasion if, on the application, the justice of the peace is satisfied that it is necessary to authorise multiple entries in order to achieve the purpose for which the warrant is issued. No premises may be entered or searched on any subsequent occasions without the prior written authority of an officer of the rank of inspector who is not involved in the investigation. All other warrants authorise entry on one occasion only.

6.3B Where a warrant under PACE section 8, or Schedule 1, paragraph 12 authorises entry to and search of all premises occupied or controlled by a specified person, no premises which are not specified in the warrant may be entered and searched without the prior written authority of an officer of the rank of inspector who is not involved in the investigation.

(b) Entry other than with consent

6.4 The officer in charge of the search shall first try to communicate with the occupier, or any other person entitled to grant access to the premises, explain the authority under which entry is sought and ask the occupier to allow entry, unless:
   (i) the search premises are unoccupied;
   (ii) the occupier and any other person entitled to grant access are absent;
   (iii) there are reasonable grounds for believing that alerting the occupier or any other person entitled to grant access would frustrate the object of the search or endanger officers or other people.

6.5 Unless sub-paragraph 6.4(iii) applies, if the premises are occupied the officer, subject to paragraph 2.9, shall, before the search begins:
   (i) identify him or herself, show their warrant card (if not in uniform) and state the purpose of, and grounds for, the search, and
   (ii) identify and introduce any person accompanying the officer on the search (such persons should carry identification for production on request) and briefly describe that person's role in the process.

6.6 Reasonable and proportionate force may be used if necessary to enter premises if the officer in charge of the search is satisfied the premises are those specified in any warrant, or in exercise of the powers described in *paragraphs 4.1* to *4.3*, and if:
   (i) the occupier or any other person entitled to grant access has refused entry;
   (ii) it is impossible to communicate with the occupier or any other person entitled to grant access; or
   (iii) any of the provisions of *paragraph 6.4* apply.

(c) Notice of Powers and Rights

6.7 If an officer conducts a search to which this Code applies the officer shall, unless it is impracticable to do so, provide the occupier with a copy of a Notice in a standard format:
   (i) specifying if the search is made under warrant, with consent, or in the exercise of the powers described in *paragraphs 4.1* to *4.3*. Note: the notice format shall provide for authority or consent to be indicated, see *paragraphs 4.3* and *5.1*;
   (ii) summarising the extent of the powers of search and seizure conferred by PACE and other relevant legislation as appropriate;
   (iii) explaining the rights of the occupier, and the owner of the property seized;
   (iv) explaining compensation may be payable in appropriate cases for damages caused entering and searching premises, and giving the address to send a compensation application, and
   (v) stating this Code is available at any police station.

6.8 If the occupier is:
   • present, copies of the Notice and warrant shall, if practicable, be given to them before the search begins, unless the officer in charge of the search reasonably believes this would frustrate the object of the search or endanger officers or other people
   • not present, copies of the Notice and warrant shall be left in a prominent place on the premises or appropriate part of the premises and endorsed, subject to *paragraph 2.9* with the name of the officer in charge of the search, the date and time of the search
   the warrant shall be endorsed to show this has been done.

(d) Conduct of searches

6.9 Premises may be searched only to the extent necessary to achieve the object of the search, having regard to the size and nature of whatever is sought.

6.9A A search may not continue under:
- a warrant's authority once all the things specified in that warrant have been found
- any other power once the object of that search has been achieved.

6.9B No search may continue once the officer in charge of the search is satisfied whatever is being sought is not on the premises. This does not prevent a further search of the same premises if additional grounds come to light supporting a further application for a search warrant or exercise or further exercise of another power. For example, when, as a result of new information, it is believed articles previously not found or additional articles are on the premises.

6.10 Searches must be conducted with due consideration for the property and privacy of the occupier and with no more disturbance than necessary. Reasonable force may be used only when necessary and proportionate because the cooperation of the occupier cannot be obtained or is insufficient for the purpose.

6.11 A friend, neighbour or other person must be allowed to witness the search if the occupier wishes unless the officer in charge of the search has reasonable grounds for believing the presence of the person asked for would seriously hinder the investigation or endanger officers or other people. A search need not be unreasonably delayed for this purpose. A record of the action taken should be made on the premises search record including the grounds for refusing the occupier's request.

6.12 A person is not required to be cautioned prior to being asked questions that are solely necessary for the purpose of furthering the proper and effective conduct of a search, see Code C, *paragraph 10.1(c)*. For example, questions to discover the occupier of specified premises, to find a key to open a locked drawer or cupboard or to otherwise seek cooperation during the search or to determine if a particular item is liable to be seized.

6.12A If questioning goes beyond what is necessary for the purpose of the exemption in Code C, the exchange is likely to constitute an interview as defined by Code C, *paragraph 11.1A* and would require the associated safeguards included in Code C, *section 10*.

(e) Leaving premises

6.13 If premises have been entered by force, before leaving the officer in charge of the search must make sure they are secure by:
- arranging for the occupier or their agent to be present
- any other appropriate means.

(f) Searches under PACE Schedule 1 or the Terrorism Act 2000, Schedule 5

6.14 An officer shall be appointed as the officer in charge of the search, see *paragraph 2.10*, in respect of any search made under a warrant issued under PACE Act 1984, Schedule 1 or the Terrorism Act 2000, Schedule 5. They are responsible for making sure the search is conducted with discretion and in a manner that causes the least possible disruption to any business or other activities carried out on the premises.

6.15 Once the officer in charge of the search is satisfied material may not be taken from the premises without their knowledge, they shall ask for the documents or other records concerned. The officer in charge of the search may also ask to see the index to files held on the premises, and the officers conducting the search may inspect any files which, according to the index, appear to contain the material sought. A more extensive search of the premises may be made only if:

- the person responsible for them refuses to:
  - produce the material sought, or
  - allow access to the index
- it appears the index is:
  - inaccurate, or
  - incomplete
  - for any other reason the officer in charge of the search has reasonable grounds for believing such a search is necessary in order to find the material sought.

4.6.7.1

KEYNOTE

Whether compensation is appropriate depends on the circumstances in each case. Compensation for damage caused when effecting entry is unlikely to be appropriate if the search was lawful, and the force used can be shown to be reasonable, proportionate and necessary to effect entry. If the wrong premises are searched by mistake everything possible should be done at the earliest opportunity to allay any sense of grievance and there should normally be a strong presumption in favour of paying compensation.

It is important that, when possible, all those involved in a search are fully briefed about any powers to be exercised and the extent and limits within which it should be conducted.

In all cases the number of officers and other persons involved in executing the warrant should be determined by what is reasonable and necessary according to the particular circumstances.

4.6.8

7 Seizure and retention of property

(a) Seizure

7.1 Subject to *paragraph 7.2*, an officer who is searching any person or premises under any statutory power or with the consent of the occupier may seize anything:

(a) covered by a warrant

(b) the officer has reasonable grounds for believing is evidence of an offence or has been obtained in consequence of the commission of an offence but only if seizure is necessary to prevent the items being concealed, lost, disposed of, altered, damaged, destroyed or tampered with

(c) covered by the powers in the Criminal Justice and Police Act 2001, Part 2 allowing an officer to seize property from persons or premises and retain it for sifting or examination elsewhere.

7.2 No item may be seized which an officer has reasonable grounds for believing to be subject to legal privilege, as defined in PACE, section 10, other than under the Criminal Justice and Police Act 2001, Part 2.

7.3 Officers must be aware of the provisions in the Criminal Justice and Police Act 2001, section 59, allowing for applications to a judicial authority for the return of property seized and the subsequent duty to secure in section 60, see *paragraph 7.12(iii)*.

7.4 An officer may decide it is not appropriate to seize property because of an explanation from the person holding it but may nevertheless have reasonable grounds for believing it was obtained in consequence of an offence by some person. In these circumstances, the officer should identify the property to the holder, inform the holder of their suspicions and explain the holder may be liable to civil or criminal proceedings if they dispose of, alter or destroy the property.

7.5 An officer may arrange to photograph, image or copy, any document or other article they have the power to seize in accordance with *paragraph 7.1*. This is subject to specific restrictions on the examination, imaging or copying of certain property seized under the Criminal Justice and Police Act 2001, Part 2. An officer must have regard to their statutory obligation to retain an original document or other article only when a photograph or copy is not sufficient.

7.6   If an officer considers information stored in any electronic form and accessible from the premises could be used in evidence, they may require the information to be produced in a form:

- which can be taken away and in which it is visible and legible; or
- from which it can readily be produced in a visible and legible form.

4.6.8.1

KEYNOTE

General Powers of Seizure—s.19 PACE

The Police and Criminal Evidence Act 1984, s. 19 states:

(1) The powers conferred by subsections (2), (3) and (4) below are exercisable by a constable who is lawfully on any premises.

(2) The constable may seize anything which is on the premises if he has reasonable grounds for believing—
  (a) that it has been obtained in consequence of the commission of an offence; and
  (b) that it is necessary to seize it in order to prevent it being concealed, lost, damaged, altered or destroyed.

(3) The constable may seize anything which is on the premises if he has reasonable grounds for believing—
  (a) that it is evidence in relation to an offence which he is investigating or any other offence; and
  (b) that it is necessary to seize it in order to prevent the evidence being concealed, lost, altered or destroyed.

(4) The constable may require any information which is stored in any electronic form and is accessible from the premises to be produced in a form in which it can be taken away and in which it is visible and legible or from which it can readily be produced in a visible and legible form if he has reasonable grounds for believing—
  (a) that—
    (i) it is evidence in relation to an offence which he is investigating or any other offence; or
    (ii) it has been obtained in consequence of the commission of an offence; and
  (b) that it is necessary to do so in order to prevent it being concealed, lost, or destroyed.

(5) The powers conferred by this section are in addition to any power otherwise conferred.

(6) No power of seizure conferred on a constable under any enactment (including an enactment contained in an Act passed after this Act) is to be taken to authorise the seizure of an item which the constable exercising the power has reasonable grounds for believing to be subject to legal privilege.

For this power to apply, the officers concerned must be on the premises lawfully. If the officers are on the premises only with the consent of the occupier, they become trespassers once that consent has been withdrawn. Once the officers are told to leave, they are no longer 'lawfully' on the premises. They must be given a reasonable opportunity to leave and cannot then seize any property that they may find. For this reason, it is far safer to exercise a power where one exists, albeit that the *cooperation* of the relevant person should be sought.

Where the 'premises' searched is a vehicle (s. 23), the vehicle (the 'premises') can itself be seized (*Cowan* v *Commissioner of Police for the Metropolis* [2000] 1 WLR 254). In *Cowan* it was held that the power to seize 'premises', where it was appropriate and practical to do so, was embodied in both ss. 18 and 19 and also at common law. Therefore, the powers of seizure conferred by ss. 18(2) and 19(3) of the Police and Criminal Evidence Act 1984 extend to the seizure of the whole premises when it is physically possible to seize and retain the premises in their totality and practical considerations make seizure desirable. The police may remove premises such as tents, vehicles or caravans to a police station for the purpose of preserving evidence. However, it does not extend to seizing things that are not on the premises, such as a car parked in a car park adjacent to the premises (*Wood* v *North Avon Magistrates' Court* [2009] EWHC 3614 (Admin)).

Unless the elements above are satisfied, the power under s. 19 will not apply. Therefore, the power does not authorise the seizure of property purely for intelligence purposes.

Section 19(5) expressly preserves any common law power of search and seizure; however, in *R (On the Application of Rottman)* v *Commissioner of Police for the Metropolis* [2002] UKHL 20, it was held that s. 19 was confined to 'domestic' offences (and did not extend to extradition offences). The same applies to powers under s. 18 of the Police and Criminal Evidence Act 1984.

If the warrant under which entry or seizure was made is invalid, the officers will not be on the premises lawfully.

The power of seizure under s. 19(1), along with the power to require information stored in any electronic form to be made accessible under s. 19(4), are among those that can be conferred on an Investigating Officer designated under sch. 4 to the Police Reform Act 2002. The safeguards provided by s. 19(6) in relation to privileged material also apply to the exercise of these powers by designated Investigating Officers.

4.6.8.2 KEYNOTE

Powers of Seizure and Information in Electronic Form

The Police and Criminal Evidence Act 1984, s. 20 states:

(1) Every power of seizure which is conferred by an enactment to which this section applies on a constable who has entered premises in the exercise of a power conferred by an enactment shall be construed as including a power to require any information stored in any electronic form and accessible from the premises to be produced in a form in which it can be taken away and in which it is visible and legible or from which it can readily be produced in a visible and legible form.

(2) This section applies—

(a) to any enactment contained in an Act passed before this Act;

(b) to sections 8 and 18 above;

(c) to paragraph 13 of Schedule 1 to this Act; and

(d) to any enactment contained in an Act passed after this Act.

This provision applies to:

- powers conferred under pre-PACE statutes;
- powers exercised under a s. 8 warrant (for 'indictable offences');
- powers exercised under s. 18 (following arrest for an indictable offence);
- powers under sch. 1 ('excluded' or 'special procedure material');
- powers exercised under s. 19 (officers lawfully on premises);
- powers of seizure exercised by Investigating Officers designated under sch. 4 to the Police Reform Act 2002.

4.6.8.3 KEYNOTE

Supply of Copies of Seized Material

Section 21 of the 1984 Act makes provision for the supplying of copies of records of seizure to certain people after property has been seized. If requested by the person who had custody or control of the seized property immediately before it was seized, the officer in charge of the investigation must allow that person access to it under police supervision. The officer must also make provisions to allow for the property to be photographed or copied by that person or to supply the person with photographs/copies of it within a reasonable time. Such a request need not be complied with if there are reasonable grounds to believe that to do so would prejudice any related investigation or criminal proceedings (s. 21(8)).

4.6.8.4 KEYNOTE

Retention of Seized Material

The provisions for accessing and copying of seized material as set out in ss. 21 and 22 of the Police and Criminal Evidence Act 1984 also apply to powers of seizure exercised by Investigating Officers designated under sch. 4 to the Police Reform Act 2002.

Section 22 of the 1984 Act makes provision for the retention of seized property. Section 22(1) provides that anything seized may be retained for as long as necessary in all the circumstances. However, s. 22(2) allows for property to be retained for use as evidence in a trial, forensic examination or further investigation *unless a photograph or copy would suffice*. Seized property may be retained in order to establish its lawful owner (s. 22(2)(b)). Once this power to retain property is exhausted, a person claiming it can rely on his/her right to possession at the time the property was seized as giving sufficient title to recover the property from the police.

This situation was confirmed by the Court of Appeal in a case where the purchaser of a stolen car was allowed to rely upon his possession of the car at the time it was seized. As it could not be established that anyone else was entitled to the vehicle, the court allowed the claimant's action for return of the car to him (*Costello* v *Chief Constable of Derbyshire Constabulary* [2001] EWCA Civ 381). Clearly any claim based on previous possession where it would be unlawful for the police to return the property (e.g. a controlled drug) could not be enforced. Provisions amending this area of legislation are now contained in the Criminal Justice and Police Act 2001. There is no specific provision under s. 22 for the retention of property for purely intelligence purposes.

The importance of police officers being able to point clearly to the need for retaining property either in order to establish its owner or as a necessary part of the investigative or law enforcement process when relying on the above powers, was highlighted by the Court of Appeal in *Gough* v *Chief Constable of the West Midlands Police* [2004] EWCA Civ 206. In that case it was clear that neither of these purposes was being served and therefore the officers could not rely on the statutory power for retaining the property.

Property seized simply to prevent an arrested person from using it to escape or to cause injury, damage etc. cannot be retained for those purposes once the person has been released (s. 22(3)). This includes car keys belonging to someone who is released from police detention having been detained under the relevant drink driving legislation.

4.6.8.5

KEYNOTE

Prohibitions on Re-use of Information Seized

Information gained as a result of a lawful search may be passed on to other individuals and organisations for purposes of investigation and prosecution. It must not be used for private purposes (*Marcel* v *Commissioner of Police for the Metropolis* [1992] Ch 225).

4.6.8.6

KEYNOTE

Disposal of Property in Police Possession

Any person claiming property seized by the police may apply to a magistrates' court under the Police (Property) Act 1897 for its possession and should, if appropriate, be advised of this procedure.

(b) Criminal Justice and Police Act 2001: Specific procedures for seize and sift powers

7.7 The Criminal Justice and Police Act 2001, Part 2 gives officers limited powers to seize property from premises or persons so they can sift or examine it elsewhere. Officers must be careful they only exercise these powers when it is essential and they do not remove any more material than necessary. The removal of large volumes of material, much of which may not ultimately be retainable, may have serious implications for the owners, particularly when they are involved in business or activities such as journalism or the provision of medical services. Officers must carefully consider if removing copies or images of relevant material or data would be a satisfactory alternative to removing originals. When originals are taken, officers must be prepared to facilitate the provision of copies or images for the owners when reasonably practicable.

7.8 Property seized under the Criminal Justice and Police Act 2001, sections 50 or 51 must be kept securely and separately from any material seized under other powers. An examination under section 53 to determine which elements may be retained must be carried out at the earliest practicable time, having due regard to the desirability of allowing the person from whom the property was seized, or a person with an interest in the property, an opportunity of being present or represented at the examination.

7.8A   All reasonable steps should be taken to accommodate an interested person's request to be present, provided the request is reasonable and subject to the need to prevent harm to, interference with, or unreasonable delay to the investigatory process. If an examination proceeds in the absence of an interested person who asked to attend or their representative, the officer who exercised the relevant seizure power must give that person a written notice of why the examination was carried out in those circumstances. If it is necessary for security reasons or to maintain confidentiality officers may exclude interested persons from decryption or other processes which facilitate the examination but do not form part of it.

7.9   It is the responsibility of the officer in charge of the investigation to make sure property is returned in accordance with sections 53 to 55. Material which there is no power to retain must be:

- separated from the rest of the seized property
- returned as soon as reasonably practicable after examination of all the seized property.

7.9A   Delay is only warranted if very clear and compelling reasons exist, e.g. the:

- unavailability of the person to whom the material is to be returned
- need to agree a convenient time to return a large volume of material.

7.9B   Legally privileged, excluded or special procedure material which cannot be retained must be returned:

- as soon as reasonably practicable
- without waiting for the whole examination.

7.9C   As set out in section 58, material must be returned to the person from whom it was seized, except when it is clear some other person has a better right to it.

7.10   When an officer involved in the investigation has reasonable grounds to believe a person with a relevant interest in property seized under section 50 or 51 intends to make an application under section 59 for the return of any legally privileged, special procedure or excluded material, the officer in charge of the investigation should be informed as soon as practicable and the material seized should be kept secure in accordance with section 61.

7.11   The officer in charge of the investigation is responsible for making sure property is properly secured. Securing involves making sure the property is not examined, copied, imaged or put to any other use except at the request, or with the consent, of the applicant or in accordance with the directions of the appropriate judicial authority. Any request, consent or directions must be recorded in writing and signed by both the initiator and the officer in charge of the investigation.

7.12   When an officer exercises a power of seizure conferred by sections 50 or 51 they shall provide the occupier of the premises or the person from whom the property is being seized with a written notice:

(i) specifying what has been seized under the powers conferred by that section;

(ii) specifying the grounds for those powers;

(iii) setting out the effect of sections 59 to 61 covering the grounds for a person with a relevant interest in seized property to apply to a judicial authority for its return and the duty of officers to secure property in certain circumstances when an application is made;

(iv) specifying the name and address of the person to whom:

- notice of an application to the appropriate judicial authority in respect of any of the seized property must be given;
- an application may be made to allow attendance at the initial examination of the property.

7.13   If the occupier is not present but there is someone in charge of the premises, the notice shall be given to them. If no suitable person is available, so the notice will easily be found it should either be:

- left in a prominent place on the premises
- attached to the exterior of the premises.

KEYNOTE

Seize and Sift Powers

The Criminal Justice and Police Act 2001 powers allow officers to remove materials from the premises being searched where there are real practical difficulties in not doing so.

These seize and sift powers only extend the scope of *some other existing power*. They do not provide free-standing powers to seize property—rather, they supplement other powers of search and seizure where the relevant conditions and circumstances apply. The full list of these powers is set out in sch. 1 to the Act and includes all the relevant powers under the Police and Criminal Evidence Act 1984, along with those under other key statutes such as the Firearms Act 1968 and the Misuse of Drugs Act 1971. If there is no existing power of seizure other than the Criminal Justice and Police Act 2001, then there is no power.

Section 50 of the 2001 Act provides the extended powers to seize material where it is not reasonably practicable to sort through it at the scene of the search. The factors that can be taken into account in considering whether or not it is reasonably practicable for something to be determined, or for relevant material to be separated from other materials, are set out in s. 50(3); these include the length of time and number of people that would be required to carry out the determination or separation on those premises within a reasonable period, whether that would involve damage to property, any apparatus or equipment that would be needed and (in the case of separation of materials) whether the separation would be likely to prejudice the use of some or all of the separated seizable property. Section 50 also allows for the seizure of material that is reasonably believed to be legally privileged where it is not reasonably practicable to separate it. In some cases, the power to 'seize' will be read as a power to take copies (s. 63).

Section 51 provides for extended seizure of materials in the same vein as above but where the material is found on people who are being lawfully searched.

Initial Examination

Where any property has been seized under ss. 50 or 51, the officer in possession of it is under a duty to make sure that a number of things are done (s. 53). These include ensuring that an initial examination of the property is carried out *as soon as reasonably practicable* after the seizure. In determining the earliest practicable time to carry out an initial examination of the seized property, due regard must be had to the desirability of allowing the person from whom it was seized (or a person with an interest in it) an opportunity of being present, or of being represented, at the examination (s. 53(4)). Officers should consider reaching agreement with owners and/or other interested parties on the procedures for examining a specific set of property, rather than awaiting the judicial authority's determination. Agreement can sometimes give a quicker and more satisfactory route for all concerned and minimise costs and legal complexities. What constitutes a relevant interest in specific material may depend on the nature of that material and the circumstances in which it is seized. Anyone with a reasonable claim to ownership of the material and anyone entrusted with its safe keeping by the owner should be considered.

The officer must also ensure that any such examination is confined to whatever is *necessary* for determining how much of the property:

- is property for which the person seizing it had power to search when making the seizure but is not property that has to be returned (by s. 54—see Protected Material, below);
- is property authorised to be retained (by s. 56—**see para. 4.6.8.9**); or
- is something which, in all the circumstances, it will not be reasonably practicable, following the examination, to separate from the property above (see generally s. 53(3)).

The officer must ensure that anything found not to fall within the categories above is separated from the rest of the seized property and *is returned as soon as reasonably practicable* after the examination of all the seized property. That officer is also under a duty to ensure that, until the initial examination of all the seized property has been completed and anything which does not fall within the categories above has been returned, the seized property is kept separate from anything seized under any other power. There are special provisions where the property is inextricably linked to relevant material (e.g. where the 'innocent' material is completely mixed up with or inseparable from the material that is properly the subject of the investigation). However, those provisions place very strict limits on what use can be made of this inextricably linked material (s. 62).

Protected Material

If, at any time, after a seizure of anything has been made in exercise of *any statutory power of seizure*, it appears that the property is subject to legal privilege (or it has such an item comprised in it), s. 54 imposes a general duty on the officer in possession of the property to ensure that the item is returned as soon as reasonably practicable after the seizure. This general duty is subject to some exceptions (e.g. where in all the circumstances it is not reasonably practicable for that item to be separated from the rest of that property without prejudicing the use of the rest of that property—see s. 54(2)) but is otherwise very wide-ranging and absolutely clear. A similar duty is generally imposed in relation to property that appears to be excluded material or special procedure material (s. 55).

4.6.8.8

(c) Retention

7.14 Subject to *paragraph 7.15*, anything seized in accordance with the above provisions may be retained only for as long as is necessary. It may be retained, among other purposes:
   (i) for use as evidence at a trial for an offence;
   (ii) to facilitate the use in any investigation or proceedings of anything to which it is inextricably linked;
   (iii) for forensic examination or other investigation in connection with an offence;
   (iv) in order to establish its lawful owner when there are reasonable grounds for believing it has been stolen or obtained by the commission of an offence.
7.15 Property shall not be retained under *paragraph 7.14(i)*, *(ii)* or *(iii)* if a copy or image would be sufficient.

4.6.8.9

KEYNOTE

Retention of Property

The Act authorises the retention of certain seized property by the police. In order to be retained, the property must have been seized on any premises by a constable who was lawfully on the premises, by a person authorised under a relevant statute (s. 56(5)) who was on the premises accompanied by a constable, or by a constable carrying out a lawful search of any person (s. 56). Generally property so seized will fall within these categories if there are reasonable grounds for believing:

- that it is property obtained in consequence of the commission of an offence; or
- that it is evidence in relation to any offence; *and* (in either case)
- that it is necessary for it to be retained in order to prevent its being concealed, lost, altered or destroyed

(for full details see s. 56(2) and (3)). Note, so far as s. 56(2) is concerned, property may be retained if it is necessary to prevent it being 'damaged', in addition to the other factors listed.

   These are fairly wide provisions and, if the property fits the above description, it may be retained even if it was not being searched for. Section 57 goes on to make certain provisions for the retention of property under other statutes such as s. 5(4) of the Knives Act 1997, para. 7(2) of sch. 9 to the Data Protection Act 1998, and sch. 5 to the Human Tissue Act 2004.

4.6.8.10

(d) Rights of owners etc

7.16 If property is retained, the person who had custody or control of it immediately before seizure must, on request, be provided with a list or description of the property within a reasonable time.
7.17 That person or their representative must be allowed supervised access to the property to examine it or have it photographed or copied, or must be provided with a photograph or copy, in either case within a reasonable time of any request and at their own expense, unless the officer in charge of an investigation has reasonable grounds for believing this would:

(i) prejudice the investigation of any offence or criminal proceedings; or

(ii) lead to the commission of an offence by providing access to unlawful material such as pornography.

A record of the grounds shall be made when access is denied.

4.6.8.11

KEYNOTE

Paragraph 7.14(ii) applies if inextricably linked material is seized under the Criminal Justice and Police Act 2001, ss. 50 or 51. Inextricably linked material is material it is not reasonably practicable to separate from other linked material without prejudicing the use of that other material in any investigation or proceedings. For example, it may not be possible to separate items of data held on computer disk without damaging their evidential integrity. Inextricably linked material must not be examined, imaged, copied or used for any purpose other than for proving the source and/or integrity of the linked material.

Notice

Where a person exercises a power of seizure conferred by ss. 50 or 51, that person will be under a duty, on doing so, to give the occupier or person from whom property is seized a written notice (s. 52). That notice will specify:

- what has been seized and the grounds on which the powers have been exercised;
- the effect of the safeguards and rights to apply to a judicial authority for the return of the property (see Return of Property Seized, below);
- the name and address of the person to whom notice of an application to a judge and an application to be allowed to attend the initial examination should be sent.

Where it appears to the officer exercising a power of seizure under s. 50 that the occupier of the premises is not present at the time of the exercise of the power, but there is some other person present who is in charge of the premises, the officer may give the notice to that other person (s. 52(2)). Where it appears that there is no one present on the premises to whom a notice can be given, the officer must, before leaving the premises, attach a notice in a prominent place to the premises (s. 52(3)).

Return of Property Seized

There are specific obligations on the police to return property seized under these powers—particularly where the property includes legally privileged, excluded or special procedure material. The general rule is that any extraneous property initially seized under these provisions must be returned—usually—to the person from whom it was seized unless the investigating officer considers that someone else has a better claim to it (ss. 53 to 58).

Any person with a relevant interest in the seized property may apply to the appropriate judicial authority, on one or more of the grounds in s. 59(3) for the return of the whole or a part of the seized property. Generally those grounds are that there was no power to make the seizure or that the seized property did not fall into one of the permitted categories (s. 59). Where a person makes such an application, the police must secure the property in accordance with s. 61 (e.g. in a way that prevents investigators from looking at or copying it until the matter has been considered by a judge). There are other occasions where protected material is involved that will also give rise to the duty to secure the property under s. 61. The mechanics of securing property vary according to the circumstances; 'bagging up', i.e. placing material in sealed bags or containers and strict subsequent control of access, is the appropriate procedure in many cases. The 'judicial authority' (at least a Crown Court judge) will be able to make a number of wide-ranging orders in relation to the treatment of the seized property, including its return or examination by a third party. Failure to comply with any such order will amount to a contempt of court (s. 59(9)). Requirements to secure and return property apply equally to all copies, images or other material created because of seizure of the original property.

When material is seized under the powers of seizure conferred by the Police and Criminal Evidence Act 1984, the duty to retain it under the Code of Practice issued under the Criminal Procedure and Investigations Act 1996 is subject to the provisions on retention of seized material in s. 22 of the 1984 Act.

8 Action after searches

8.1 If premises are searched in circumstances where this Code applies, unless the exceptions in *paragraph 2.3(a)* apply, on arrival at a police station the officer in charge of the search shall make or have made a record of the search, to include:

   (i) the address of the searched premises;

   (ii) the date, time and duration of the search;

   (iii) the authority used for the search:

   - if the search was made in exercise of a statutory power to search premises without warrant, the power which was used for the search:

   - if the search was made under a warrant or with written consent;

     - a copy of the warrant and the written authority to apply for it, see paragraph 3.4; or

     - the written consent;

shall be appended to the record or the record shall show the location of the copy warrant or consent.

   (iv) subject to paragraph 2.9, the names of:

   - the officer(s) in charge of the search;

   - all other officers and any authorised persons who conducted the search;

   (v) the names of any people on the premises if they are known;

   (vi) any grounds for refusing the occupier's request to have someone present during the search, see *paragraph 6.11*;

   (vii) a list of any articles seized or the location of a list and, if not covered by a warrant, the grounds for their seizure;

   (viii) whether force was used, and the reason;

   (ix) details of any damage caused during the search, and the circumstances;

   (x) if applicable, the reason it was not practicable:

   (a) to give the occupier a copy of the Notice of Powers and Rights, see *paragraph 6.7*;

   (b) before the search to give the occupier a copy of the Notice, see *paragraph 6.8*;

   (xi) when the occupier was not present, the place where copies of the Notice of Powers and Rights and search warrant were left on the premises, *see paragraph 6.8*.

8.2 On each occasion when premises are searched under warrant, the warrant authorising the search on that occasion shall be endorsed to show:

   (i) if any articles specified in the warrant were found and the address where found;

   (ii) if any other articles were seized;

   (iii) the date and time it was executed and if present, the name of the occupier or if the occupier is not present the name of the person in charge of the premises;

   (iv) subject to paragraph 2.9, the names of the officers who executed it and any authorised persons who accompanied them;

   (v) if a copy, together with a copy of the Notice of Powers and Rights was:

   - handed to the occupier; or

   - endorsed as required by paragraph 6.8; and left on the premises and where.

8.3 Any warrant shall be returned within three calendar months of its issue or sooner on completion of the search(es) authorised by that warrant, if it was issued by a:

   - justice of the peace, to the designated officer for the local justice area in which the justice was acting when issuing the warrant; or

   - judge, to the appropriate officer of the court concerned.

9 Search registers

9.1 A search register will be maintained at each sub-divisional or equivalent police station. All search records required under *paragraph 8.1* shall be made, copied, or referred to in the register.

KEYNOTE

Paragraph 9.1 also applies to search records made by immigration officers. In these cases, a search register must also be maintained at an immigration office.

10 Searches under Schedule 5 to the Terrorism Prevention and Investigation Measures Act 2011

10.1 This Code applies to the powers of constables under Schedule 5 to the Terrorism Prevention and Investigation Measures Act 2011 relating to TPIM notices to enter and search premises subject to the modifications in the following paragraphs.

10.2 In paragraph 2.3(d), the reference to the investigation into an alleged or suspected offence include the enforcement of terrorism prevention and investigation measures which may be imposed on an individual by a TPIM notice in accordance with the Terrorism Prevention and Investigation Measures Act 2011.

10.3 References to the purpose and object of the entry and search of premises, the nature of articles sought and what may be seized and retained include (as appropriate):

(a) in relation to the power to search *without a search warrant in paragraph 5* (for purposes of serving TPIM notice), finding the individual on whom the notice is to be served.

(b) in relation to the power to search *without a search warrant in paragraph 6* (at time of serving TPIM notice), ascertaining whether there is anything in the premises, that contravenes measures specified in the notice.

(c) in relation to the power to search *without a search warrant under paragraph 7* (suspected absconding), ascertaining whether a person has absconded or if there is anything on the premises which will assist in the pursuit or arrest of an individual in respect of whom a TPIM notice is in force who is reasonably suspected of having absconded.

(d) in relation to the power to search *under a search warrant* issued under *paragraph 8* (for compliance purposes), determining whether an individual in respect of whom a TPIM notice is in force is complying with measures specified in the notice.

KEYNOTE

Searches of individuals under sch. 5, paras 6(2)(a) (at time of serving TPIM notice) and 8(2)(a) (for compliance purposes) must be conducted and recorded in accordance with Code A. See Code A, para. 2.18A for details.

PART TWO

Community Safety

4.7 | Hatred and Harassment Offences

4.7.1 Introduction

The law in relation to offences involving hatred and harassment has been subject to considerable development in recent times. The result is a wide-ranging set of offences and powers that enable appropriate action to be taken in relation to such activity and, in certain circumstances, to protect against such activity occurring in the first place.

4.7.2 Offences Involving Racial, Religious or Sexual Orientation Hatred

Offences involving racial, religious or sexual orientation hatred are dealt with by the Public Order Act 1986. This section provides a summary of these offences which are aimed at addressing incidents specifically motivated by racial hatred, religious hatred or hatred on the grounds of sexual orientation.

For the purposes of the offences contrary to ss. 18 to 23 of the 1986 Act, 'racial hatred' means hatred against a group of persons defined by reference to colour, race, nationality (including citizenship) or ethnic or national origins (s. 17).

For the purposes of offences contrary to ss. 29B to 29G of the 1986 Act, 'religious hatred' means hatred against a group of persons defined by reference to religious belief or lack of religious belief (s. 29A).

Section 29AB of the 1986 Act defines 'hatred on the grounds of sexual orientation'. The definition covers hatred against a group of persons defined by reference to their sexual orientation, be they heterosexual, homosexual or bi-sexual.

4.7.2.1 Use of Words, Behaviour or Display of Written Material

OFFENCE: **Use of Words or Behaviour or Display of Written Material—*Public Order Act 1986, s. 18***
- Triable either way • Seven years' imprisonment and/or a fine on indictment
- Six months' imprisonment and/or a fine summarily

The Public Order Act 1986, s. 18 states:

(1) A person who uses threatening, abusive or insulting words or behaviour, or displays any written material which is threatening, abusive or insulting, is guilty of an offence if—
  (a) he intends thereby to stir up racial hatred, or
  (b) having regard to all the circumstances racial hatred is likely to be stirred up thereby.
(2) An offence under this section may be committed in a public or a private place, except that no offence is committed where the words or behaviour are used, or the written material is displayed, by a person inside a dwelling and are not heard or seen except by other persons in that or another dwelling.

4.7.2.2 Defence

The Public Order Act 1986, s. 18 states:

(4) In proceedings for an offence under this section it is a defence for the accused to prove that he was inside a dwelling and had no reason to believe that the words or behaviour used, or the written material displayed, would be heard or seen by a person outside that or any other dwelling.

4.7.2.3 Publishing or Distributing Written Material

OFFENCE: **Publishing or Distributing Written Material—*Public Order Act 1986, s. 19***
- Triable either way • Seven years' imprisonment and/or a fine on indictment
- Six months' imprisonment and/or a fine summarily

The Public Order Act 1986, s. 19 states:

(1) A person who publishes or distributes written material which is threatening, abusive or insulting is guilty of an offence if—
    (a) he intends thereby to stir up racial hatred, or
    (b) having regard to all the circumstances racial hatred is likely to be stirred up thereby.
(2) ...
(3) References in this Part to the publication or distribution of written material are to its publication or distribution to the public or a section of the public.

4.7.2.4 Defence

The Public Order Act 1986, s. 19 states:

(2) In proceedings for an offence under this section it is a defence for an accused who is not shown to have intended to stir up racial hatred to prove that he was not aware of the content of the material and did not suspect, and had no reason to suspect, that it was threatening, abusive or insulting.

4.7.2.5 Use of Words, Behaviour or Display of Written Material

OFFENCE: **Use of Words or Behaviour or Display of Written Material—*Public Order Act 1986, s. 29B***
- Triable either way • Not exceeding seven years' imprisonment and/or a fine on indictment • Not exceeding six months' imprisonment and/or a fine summarily

The Public Order Act 1986, s. 29B states:

(1) A person who uses threatening words or behaviour, or displays any written material which is threatening, is guilty of an offence if he intends thereby to stir up religious hatred or hatred on the grounds of sexual orientation.

(2) An offence under this section is committed in a public or private place, except that no offence is committed where the words or behaviour are used, or the written material is displayed, by a person inside a dwelling and are not heard or seen except by other persons in that or another dwelling.

KEYNOTE

This differs from the other sections under the 1986 Act which have no specific power of arrest since the provisions of the Serious Organised Crime and Police Act 2005 were introduced.

The defences available to the offence under s. 18 apply to this particular section (no reason to believe the words or behaviour, etc., would be heard or seen outside the dwelling (s. 29B(4)), or where used solely for the purpose of being included in a programming service (s. 29D(5)).

Section 29J of the Act provides that the offences of stirring up religious hatred are not intended to limit or restrict discussion, criticism or expressions of antipathy, dislike, ridicule or insult or abuse of particular religions or belief systems or lack of religion or of the beliefs and practices of those who hold such beliefs or to apply to persons newly converted to a religious faith, evangelism or the seeking to convert people to a particular belief or to cease holding a belief.

In relation to the sexual orientation element of these offences the relevant act (namely, words, behaviour, written material or recordings or programme) must be threatening, and the offender must intend thereby to stir up hatred on the grounds of sexual orientation.

4.7.2.6   Publishing or Distributing Material

OFFENCE: **Publishing or Distributing Written Material—*Public Order Act 1986, s. 29C***

> • Triable either way • Not exceeding seven years' imprisonment and/or a fine on indictment • Not exceeding six months' imprisonment and/or a fine summarily

The Public Order Act 1986, s. 29C states:

(1) A person who publishes or distributes written material which is threatening is guilty of an offence if he intends thereby to stir up religious hatred or hatred on the grounds of sexual orientation.

(2) References in this Part to the publication or distribution of written material are to its publication or distribution to the public or a section of the public.

KEYNOTE

The offences under ss. 29B and 29C differ from the offences of stirring up racial hatred in part 3 of the 1986 Act, in two respects. First, the offences apply only to 'threatening' words or behaviour, rather than 'threatening, abusive or insulting' words or behaviour. Secondly, the offences apply only to words or behaviour if the accused 'intends' to stir up religious hatred or hatred on grounds of sexual orientation, rather than if hatred is either intentional or 'likely' to be stirred up.

4.7.3   Harassment and Stalking

There is a significant amount of material to examine in relation to the offences associated with harassment and stalking under the Protection from Harassment Act 1997. To aid understanding, the offences have been broken down into their component parts and follow the below order:

- Harassment contrary to ss. 1 and 2 of the Act (**see para. 4.7.4**). This section includes the law in relation to injunctions and restraining orders
- Putting people in fear of violence contrary to s. 4 of the Act (**see para. 4.7.5**)
- Stalking contrary to s. 2A of the Act and stalking involving fear of violence etc. contrary to s. 4A of the Act (**see para. 4.7.6**).

4.7.4　The Harassment Offences

OFFENCE: **Harassment—*Protection from Harassment Act 1997, ss. 1 and 2***
- Triable summarily • Six months' imprisonment and/or a fine

OFFENCE: **Racially or Religiously Aggravated Harassment—*Crime and Disorder Act 1998, s. 32(1)(a)***
- Triable either way • Two years' imprisonment and/or a fine on indictment
- Six months' imprisonment and/or a fine summarily

The Protection from Harassment Act 1997, ss. 1 and 2 state:

1.—(1) A person must not pursue a course of conduct—
   (a) which amounts to harassment of another, and
   (b) which he knows or ought to know amounts to harassment of the other.
(1A) A person must not pursue a course of conduct—
   (a) which involves harassment of two or more persons, and
   (b) which he knows or ought to know involves harassment of those persons, and
   (c) by which he intends to persuade any person (whether or not one of those mentioned above)—
      (i) not to do something that he is entitled or required to do, or
      (ii) to do something that he is not under any obligation to do.
   ...
2.—(1) A person who pursues a course of conduct in breach of section 1(1) or (1A) is guilty of an offence.

4.7.4.1　'Person' and Companies

'Person' here does not include companies or corporate bodies and therefore they cannot be the victim of harassment or apply for injunctions under this part of the legislation. However, an individual employee or a clearly defined group of individuals could be such a victim (*DPP* v *Dziurzynski* [2002] EWHC 1380 (Admin)) and as such they can apply for injunctions (*Daiichi UK Ltd* v *(1) Stop Huntingdon Cruelty, and (2) Animal Liberation Front* [2003] EWHC 2337 (QB)). For injunctions relating to companies **see para. 4.7.4.10**.

In *Majrowski* v *Guy's and St Thomas' NHS Trust* [2005] EWCA Civ 251, the Court of Appeal held that a company could be a 'person' capable of harassing 'another' within the meaning of the Act. This ruling could therefore have implications in relation to the self-employed, customers and suppliers of businesses and members of the public in general. Where it can be shown that the conduct was carried out in the course of employment the employer could be held to be vicariously liable for that conduct.

4.7.4.2　'Course of Conduct'

The 'course of conduct' by a person is defined under s. 7 of the Act which states:

(3) A 'course of conduct' must involve—
   (a) in the case of conduct in relation to a single person (see s. 1(1)), conduct on at least two occasions in relation to that person, or

(b) in the case of conduct in relation to two or more persons (see s. 1(1A)), conduct on at least one occasion in relation to each of those persons.

(3A) A person's conduct on any occasion shall be taken, if aided, abetted, counselled or procured by another—

(a) to be conduct on that occasion of the other (as well as conduct of the person whose conduct it is); and

(b) to be conduct in relation to which the other's knowledge and purpose, and what he ought to have known, are the same as they were in relation to what was contemplated or reasonably foreseeable at the time of the aiding, abetting, counselling or procuring.

(4) 'Conduct' includes speech.

(5) References to a person, in the context of the harassment of a person, are references to a person who is an individual.

> **KEYNOTE**
>
> The definition of a 'course of conduct' in s. 7 is an inclusive but not exhaustive list.
>
> It appears that doing something remotely which has the desired effect on the victim, such as deliberately making a dog bark at someone, could form part of a 'course of conduct' for the purposes of an offence under the 1997 Act (*R (On the Application of Taffurelli)* v *DPP* [2004] EWHC 2791 (Admin)). However, simply *failing* to stop a dog barking is a different matter and one that the Divisional Court in *Taffurelli* did not resolve.

4.7.4.3 'Harassment'

'Harassment' includes alarming the person or causing him/her distress (s. 7(2) of the 1997 Act). The inclusion of harm and distress is significant as it has been held that a person, in this case a police officer, can be alarmed for the safety of another (*Lodge* v *DPP* [1989] COD 179). Although the words used in s. 7 are 'alarm *and* distress', the Divisional Court has held that they should be taken disjunctively and not conjunctively, that is, the court need only be satisfied that the behaviour involved one or the other; alarm *or* distress (*DPP* v *Ramsdale* [2001] EWHC Admin 106).

4.7.4.4 The s. 1(1A) Offence

The s. 1(1A) offence was introduced specifically to protect employees working for certain companies from harassment by animal rights protestors. Because of the courts' strict interpretation of the elements of the s. 1 offence (as discussed above) it was unclear how far such employees could be protected by this provision when they had not previously been harassed *individually* even where fellow employees had been. Section 1(1A) makes it an offence for a person to pursue a course of conduct involving the harassment of two or more people on separate occasions which the defendant knows or ought to know involves harassment. The purpose of such harassment is to persuade *any person* (not necessarily one of the people being harassed) not to do something he/she is entitled to do (such as going to work) or to do something he/she is not under any obligation to do (such as releasing animals or passing on confidential information).

The sort of behaviour envisaged by the offence would be the making of threats and intimidation which forces an individual or individuals to stop doing lawful business with another company or with another person. The subsection is not intended to outlaw peaceful protesting or lobbying. For instance, a person simply distributing leaflets outside a shop would not commit this offence unless they threatened or intimidated the people to whom they were handing their leaflets and that person felt harassed, alarmed or distressed. There would also need to be at least two separate incidents amounting to 'a course of conduct'.

4.7.4.5 General Points

Not all courses of conduct will satisfy the offence of harassment. *Lau* v *DPP* [2000] 1 FLR 799 involved a battery (slapping across the face) against the complainant on one occasion, followed sometime later by a threat being made to the complainant's boyfriend in her presence. The court held that the evidence of a 'course of conduct' by the defendant was insufficient to convict. It stated that regard should be had to the number of incidents and the relative times when they took place; the fewer the incidents and the further apart in time that they took place, the less likely it was that a court would find that harassment had taken place.

There are some incidents that do not amount to harassment. Where a defendant approached the victim to strike up conversations and had sent her a gift, this was insufficient to constitute harassment. However, such incidents could provide a background to later behaviour that included covertly filming the victim and rummaging through her rubbish (*King* v *DPP* [2001] ACD 7).

On occasions the courts have accepted that two instances of behaviour by the defendant several months apart will suffice. Where a defendant wrote two threatening letters to a member of the Benefits Agency staff, he was convicted of harassment even though there had been four and a half months' interval between the two letters (*Baron* v *CPS* (2000) 13 June, unreported). The opposite course of conduct was found to amount to harassment where a defendant made several calls to the victim's mobile phone in the space of five minutes. In this case several abusive and threatening messages were left on the victim's voicemail facility and later replayed one after the other (*Kelly* v *DPP* [2002] EWHC 1428 (Admin)). The court held that it was enough that the victim was alarmed or distressed by the course of conduct as a whole rather than by each act making up the course of conduct. This is a different requirement from the more serious offence under s. 4 where the victim must be caused to fear violence on at least two occasions. In relation to that more serious offence, a magistrates' court has been allowed to regard a defendant's conduct on the second occasion as almost retrospectively affecting previous conduct on the first occasion.

There is no specific requirement that the activity making up the course of conduct be of the same nature. Therefore two distinctly different types of behaviour by the defendant (e.g. making a telephone call on one occasion and damaging the victim's property on another) may suffice. In a case involving the racially or religiously aggravated offence, the aggravating element will need to be proved in relation to both instances of the defendant's conduct.

Some behaviour will be sufficiently disturbing or alarming for two instances alone to suffice (e.g. the making of overt threats). Other behaviour, however, may not be sufficient to establish 'harassment' after only two occasions (e.g. the sending of flowers and gifts) and may require more than the bare statutory minimum of two occasions.

Although it may be helpful in terms of proving the occurrence of two or more acts amounting to 'a course of conduct', the practice in some police areas of issuing warnings and maintaining a register of the same (particularly in relation to their own officers) is not a specific requirement of the Act and may raise some issues of procedural fairness.

The repeated commission of other offences (say, public order offences or offences against property) involving the same victim may also amount to harassment. In such cases the advice of the CPS should be sought as to which charge(s) to prefer.

To recap the s. 1 offence, you must prove that:

• the 'person' pursued a 'course of conduct' and
• the 'course of conduct' amounted to 'harassment'.

The final element required to prove the offence is that the defendant knew, or ought to have known, that his/her conduct amounted to harassment.

To avoid the practical difficulties of proving the subjective intention of the defendant, the offence focuses on an *objective test*.

4.7.4.6 What a Reasonable Person Would Think Amounts to Harassment

In addition, s. 1 of the 1997 Act states:

> (2) For the purposes of this section, the person whose course of conduct is in question ought to know that it amounts to or involves harassment of another if a reasonable person in possession of the same information would think the course of conduct amounted to or involved harassment of the other.

KEYNOTE

Section 1(2) requires the jury/court to consider whether the defendant ought to have known that his/her conduct amounted to or involved harassment by the *objective* test of what a 'reasonable person' would think. Section 1(3)(c) also imposes an *objective* test as to whether that conduct was reasonable in the judgment of the jury/court. As a result, the Court of Appeal has held that no characteristics of the defendant can be attached to the word 'reasonable' (*R v Colohan* [2001] EWCA Crim 1251).

Although the defendant's mental illness may be relevant to sentence, the protective and preventive nature of the Act together with the objective nature of the tests above means that such illness does not provide a defence.

4.7.4.7 Aiding and Abetting

If someone aids, abets, counsels or procures another to commit an offence under the 1997 Act, the conduct of the 'primary' defendant will be taken to be the conduct of the aider, abettor, counsellor or procurer of the offence. This does not prevent the primary defendant's conduct from being relevant; what it does is to make the aider, abettor, etc. of the offence liable for the conduct which he/she has facilitated. The Act also makes provision for determining the knowledge and intention of aiders, abettors, etc. and although this is referred to as 'collective harassment', it overlaps with the concept of incomplete offences (**see *Crime*, chapter 1.3**) and the advice of the CPS should be sought in formulating appropriate charges.

4.7.4.8 Defences

If the person concerned in the course of conduct can show that he/she did so:

• for the purpose of preventing or detecting crime, or
• under any enactment or rule of law to comply with a particular condition or requirement, or
• in circumstances whereby the course of conduct was reasonable

the offence under s. 1(1) and (1A) will not apply (s. 1(3)).

The burden of proving any of these features or circumstances lies with the defendant (on the balance of probabilities). Examples might be police or DSS surveillance teams, or court officers serving summonses.

Whether a course of conduct is 'reasonable' will be a question of fact for a court to decide in the light of all the circumstances. The wording of s. 1(2) suggests that such a test is an *objective* one (i.e. as a reasonable bystander) and not one based upon the particular belief or perception of the defendant, otherwise the main effect of the 1997 Act would be considerably diluted.

KEYNOTE

In *KD* v *Chief Constable of Hampshire* [2005] EWHC 2550 (QB) a police officer obtained from a female interviewee, over the course of several visits to her home, detailed explicit information about her sexual conduct. The interviewee was the mother of a complainant who had been allegedly raped and assaulted. The court held that the information obtained was not for the purpose of preventing or detecting crime under s. 1(3)(a) but to satisfy the officer's lewd interest.

4.7.4.9 Injunctions and Restraining Orders

The courts have two significant sources of power available to them to deal with harassment under the 1997 Act. These are injunctions and restraining orders. Injunctions are issued in the ordinary way of any civil injunction whereas restraining orders follow a *conviction* for an offence under ss. 2 or 4 (**see para 4.7.5**) of the Act.

4.7.4.10 Injunctions

Under ss. 3 and 3A of the Protection from Harassment Act 1997, the High Court or a county court may issue an injunction in respect of civil proceedings brought in respect of an actual or apprehended breach of s. 1(1) and (1A). The effect of this is that a defendant may be made the subject of an injunction even though his/her behaviour has not amounted to an offence under the 1997 Act.

Section 3 also states:

(3) Where—
  (a) in such proceedings the High Court or a county court grants an injunction for the purpose of restraining the defendant from pursuing any conduct which amounts to harassment, and
  (b) the plaintiff considers that the defendant has done anything which he is prohibited from doing by the injunction,
  the plaintiff may apply for the issue of a warrant for the arrest of the defendant.

The person who is the victim of the offence under s. 1(1A) or any person at whom the persuasion is aimed, may apply for an injunction. Therefore, where people who work for a life science or fur company are being harassed in order to persuade them not to work for that company, or in order to persuade the company not to supply another company, either the employees themselves or the company in question could apply for an injunction.

Section 3A states:

(1) This section applies where there is an actual or apprehended breach of section 1(1A) by any person ('the relevant person').
(2) In such a case—
  (a) any person who is or may be a victim of the course of conduct in question, or
  (b) any person who is or may be a person falling within section 1(1A)(c),
  may apply to the High Court or the county court for an injunction restraining the relevant person from pursuing any conduct which amounts to harassment in relation to any person or persons mentioned or described in the injunction.

(3) Sections 3(3) to (9) apply in relation to an injunction granted under subsection (2) above as they apply in relation to an injunction granted as mentioned in section 3(3)(a).

KEYNOTE

Anyone arrested under a warrant issued under s. 3(3)(b) may be dealt with by the court at the time of his/her appearance. Alternatively, the court may adjourn the proceedings and release the defendant, dealing with him/her within 14 days of his/her arrest provided the defendant is given not less than two days' notice of the adjourned hearing (Rules of the Supreme Court (Amendment) 1998 (SI 1998/1898) and the County Court (Amendment) Rules 1998 (SI 1998/1899)).

In a case involving an injunction restraining the actions of an anti-vivisection group, the Divisional Court held that the 1997 Act was not a means of preventing individuals from exercising their right to protest over issues of public interest. Such an extension of the law had clearly not been Parliament's intention and the courts would resist any attempts to interpret the Act widely (*Huntingdon Life Sciences Ltd* v *Curtin* (1997) *The Times*, 11 December).

The application for an injunction is essentially a private matter being pursued by an individual. The point at which the matter becomes of concern to policing is where the injunction is breached without reasonable excuse. The civil standard of proof (balance of probabilities) will apply to injunction applications (*Hipgrave* v *Jones* [2004] EWHC 2901 (QB)).

In harassment cases the High Court can grant a provisional injunction under s. 37(1) of the Senior Courts Act 1981. This injunction can restrain conduct which is not in itself tortious or unlawful but is reasonably necessary to protect the legitimate interests of others. This includes the power to impose an exclusion zone when granting a non-molestation injunction (*Burris* v *Azadani* [1995] 1 WLR 1372). However in *Hall* v *Save Newchurch Guinea Pigs (Campaign)* [2005] EWHC 372 (QB), the court held that a 200 km^2 exclusion zone was not reasonably necessary for the protection of the protected person's rights.

4.7.4.11 Breach of Injunctions

OFFENCE: **Breach of Injunction—*Protection from Harassment Act 1997, s. 3(6)***
- Triable either way • Five years' imprisonment and/or a fine on indictment
- Six months' imprisonment and/or a fine summarily

The Protection from Harassment Act 1997, s. 3 states:

(6) Where—
  (a) the High Court or a county court grants an injunction for the purpose mentioned in subsection (3)(a), and
  (b) without reasonable ...
  he is guilty of an offence.

KEYNOTE

Civil injunctions generally will only involve the police where a power of an arrest has been attached (e.g. under s. 3(3) above). In these cases the role of the police will be to bring the defendant before the court in order that he/she can explain his/her behaviour. There is therefore no investigative or prosecuting function on the part of the officers. Section 3(6), however, creates a specific offence of breaching the terms of an injunction.

If a defendant breaches an injunction and commits the offence under s. 3(6), he/she will be dealt with in the way of any other prisoner brought into police detention and will face a prison sentence of five years.

4.7.4.12 Civil Claims for Harassment

Under s. 3(1) conduct or apprehended conduct falling within s. 1(1) and (1A) may be the subject of a civil claim by the victim/intended victim. This creates a 'statutory tort' of harassment in addition to the criminal offence.

4.7.4.13 Restraining Orders

The Protection from Harassment Act 1997, s. 5 states:

(2) The order may, for the purpose of protecting the victim or victims of the offence, or any other person mentioned in the order, from conduct which—
(a) amounts to harassment, or
(b) will cause a fear of violence,
prohibit the defendant from doing anything described in the order.

Section 5A of the Act enables the courts in England and Wales to impose a restraining order, when sentencing for any offence, for the purpose of protecting a person from conduct which amounts to harassment or will cause a fear of violence (**see para. 4.7.5**) by the defendant. The court will be able to make a restraining order on acquittal for any offence where it considers it necessary to protect a person from harassment. Any person mentioned in the restraining order has the right to make a representation if an application is made to vary or discharge the restraining order (equivalent powers are available in respect of Northern Ireland).

KEYNOTE

Unlike the injunction under s. 3(3), restraining orders can be made in a criminal court.

The order may be made for the protection of the victim or anyone else mentioned and it may run for a specified period or until a further order. Any order must identify by name the parties it is intended to protect (*R* v *Mann* (2000) 97(14) LSG 41).

In a case arising out of protests against fur retailers, the Divisional Court held that restraining orders under the 1997 Act did not generally breach the right to freedom of speech and association as protected by Articles 10 and 11 of the European Convention on Human Rights (*Silverton* v *Gravett* (2001) LTL 31 October).

The prosecutor, the defendant or anyone else mentioned in the order may apply to the court that made it to have the order varied or discharged (s. 5(4)). The courts have the power to vary an order made for a specified period of time so as to extend the expiry date of the order (*DPP* v *Hall* [2005] EWHC 2612 (Admin)). In *R* v *Debnath* [2005] EWCA Crim 3472 an order prohibiting an offender from publishing information indefinitely was held to be lawful and not in breach of Article 10 (Freedom of Expression) of the European Convention on Human Rights.

An example of how restraining orders can operate can be seen in *R* v *Evans (Dorothy)* [2004] EWCA 3102. In that case the appellant had been convicted of harassing her neighbours and a restraining order under s. 5(5) had been made by the court. Among other things, the order prohibited the appellant from 'using abusive words or actions' towards her neighbours. Some time into the life of the order, the neighbour called a plumber out to their house and he parked his van in the street. It was alleged that the appellant then moved her own car, which was also parked in the street, into such a position that it effectively blocked the plumber's van. The appellant was convicted of the offence of breaching the order and appealed, partly on the basis that her conduct could not properly be said to have amounted to 'abusive action'. The Court of Appeal held that such matters should be approached in the same way as specific legislation which outlaws abusive conduct, and that a jury was entitled to conclude that, as she had been motivated by spite, the appellant's actions could be 'abusive' for this purpose.

4.7.4.14 Breach of Restraining Order

OFFENCE: **Breach of Restraining Order—*Protection from Harassment Act 1997, s. 5(5)***

- Triable either way • Five years' imprisonment and/or a fine on indictment
- Six months' imprisonment and/or a fine summarily

The Protection from Harassment Act 1997, s. 5 states:

(5) If without reasonable excuse the defendant does anything which he is prohibited from doing by an order under this section, he is guilty of an offence.

KEYNOTE

The above offence is one of strict liability and therefore whether the defendant believed that the order was no longer in force is only relevant to the extent that he/she may have a reasonable excuse (*Barber* v *CPS* [2004] EWHC 2605 (Admin)). The prosecution needs simply to prove the existence and terms of the order (which it can do by an admission from the defendant in interview) and the doing of anything prohibited by it. Once that is done the offence is complete.

In the case of *R* v *Evans (Dorothy)* [2004] EWCA Crim 3102, the Court of Appeal held that harassment takes many forms and therefore the courts need to be able to prohibit conduct in fairly wide terms (e.g. in the wording of the order). It is, however, unclear just how far the defendant's subjective understanding of the terms of the order will be relevant. If a defendant honestly believed that his/her conduct did not breach the terms of the order, this would certainly be relevant when considering whether or not he/she had a 'reasonable excuse'.

Substituting or failing to include a charge under ss. 2 or 4 removes the court's powers to make a restraining order which may be the main remedy sought by a victim. In any cases of doubt the guidance of the CPS should be sought.

4.7.5 Putting People in Fear of Violence

OFFENCE: **Putting People in Fear of Violence—*Protection from Harassment Act 1997, s. 4***
- Triable either way • Five years' imprisonment and/or a fine on indictment
- Six months' imprisonment and/or a fine summarily

OFFENCE: **Racially or Religiously Aggravated—*Crime and Disorder Act 1998, s. 32(1)(b)***
- Triable either way • Seven years' imprisonment and/or a fine on indictment
- Six months' imprisonment and/or a fine summarily

The Protection from Harassment Act 1997, s. 4 states:

(1) A person whose course of conduct causes another to fear, on at least two occasions, that violence will be used against him is guilty of an offence if he knows or ought to know that his course of conduct will cause the other so to fear on each of those occasions.

KEYNOTE

'Course of conduct' is discussed above.

The defendant's course of conduct must cause the victim to fear that violence *will* (rather than might) be used against *him or her* (rather than someone else) so:

- showing that the conduct caused the victim to be seriously frightened of what *might happen* in the future is not enough (*R* v *Henley* [2000] Crim LR 582);
- causing a person to fear, on at least two occasions, that violence would be used against a member of their family is not enough (*Mohammed Ali Caurti* v *DPP* [2001] EWHC Admin 867).

The defendant must know, or ought to know that their conduct will cause the other person to fear violence. This may be shown by any previous conversations or communications between the defendant and the victim, together with the victim's response to the defendant's earlier behaviour (e.g. running away, calling the police, etc.).

The fear of violence being used against the victim must be present on both occasions. If it is present on one occasion but not the other, the offence under s. 2 above may be appropriate. This is not necessarily as straightforward

---

as it may seem. What if the defendant's conduct on the first occasion (e.g. a threat to burn the victim's house down) did not cause the victim undue concern, but a second threat some time later to do the same thing *did* put the victim in fear of violence, partly because this was the second time the threat had been made? These were the circumstances in *R (On the Application of A)* v *DPP* [2004] EWHC 2454 (Admin), where the defendant argued that the victim had only been put in fear of violence by his threats to burn her house down on the second occasion and that therefore the offence had not been made out. The Divisional Court disagreed and held that the magistrates were entitled to find as a matter of fact that the two incidents had put the victim in fear of violence, notwithstanding her admission that, on the first occasion, she had not been too concerned.

Unlike some of the other racially or religiously aggravated offences, provisions are specifically made for alternative verdicts in relation to harassment (s. 32(6) of the Crime and Disorder Act 1998). Where the racially or religiously aggravated form of the offence is charged, the aggravating element of the defendant's conduct must be shown in relation to both instances.

As with the s. 2 offence, a single instance of behaviour may be enough to support a charge for another offence.

This offence is not one of *intent* but one which is subject to a test of reasonableness against the standard of an ordinary person in possession of the same information as the defendant.

For the powers of a court to issue a restraining order in relation to this offence, **see para. 4.7.4.13**.

The Protection from Harassment Act 1997, s. 4 goes on to state:

> (2) For the purposes of this section, the person whose course of conduct is in question ought to know that it will cause another to fear that violence will be used against him on any occasion if a reasonable person in possession of the same information would think the course of conduct would cause the other so to fear on that occasion.

4.7.5.1 Defence

The Protection from Harassment Act 1997, s. 4 states:

> (3) It is a defence for a person charged with an offence under this section to show that—
>   (a) his course of conduct was pursued for the purpose of preventing or detecting crime,
>   (b) his course of conduct was pursued under any enactment or rule of law or to comply with any condition or requirement imposed by any person under any enactment, or
>   (c) the pursuit of his course of conduct was reasonable for the protection of himself or another or for the protection of his or another's property.

KEYNOTE

There is a slight difference in the wording of the defence when compared with that under s. 1(3) above. There, the defendant may show that his/her conduct was reasonable in the particular circumstances. In relation to the offence under s. 4, the defendant must show that his/her conduct was reasonable *for the protection of him/herself, another person or his/her own/another's property*. These are the only grounds on which the defendant may argue reasonableness in answer to a charge under s. 4. He/she could not therefore argue, say, that the pursuit of the course of conduct was 'reasonable' in order to enforce a debt or to communicate with the victim.

In addition, s. 12 allows for the Secretary of State to certify that the conduct was carried out by a 'specified person' on a 'specified occasion' related to:

- national security,
- the economic well-being of the United Kingdom, or
- the prevention or detection of serious crime

on behalf of the Crown. If such a certification is made, the conduct of the specified person will not be an offence under the 1997 Act.

4.7.6　The Stalking Offences

The Protection of Freedoms Act 2012 created the specific offence of 'stalking' and inserted the below offences into the Protection from Harassment Act 1997.

4.7.6.1　The Offence of Stalking

OFFENCE: **Stalking—*Protection from Harassment Act 1997, s. 2A***
- Triable summarily • Six months' imprisonment and/or a fine

OFFENCE: **Racially or Religiously Aggravated Stalking—*Crime and Disorder Act 1998, s. 32(1)(a)***
- Triable either way • Two years' imprisonment and/or a fine on indictment
- Six months' imprisonment and/or a fine summarily

The Protection from Harassment Act 1997, s. 2A states:

(1) A person is guilty of an offence if—
   (a) the person pursues a course of conduct in breach of s. 1(1), and
   (b) the course of conduct amounts to stalking.

For the purposes of the offence under s. 2A (and also the following offence under s. 4A below), a course of conduct amounts to stalking of another person if:

- it amounts to harassment of that person (under s. 7(2) of the Protection from Harassment Act 1997, references to harassing a person include alarming the person or causing the person distress);
- the acts or omissions involved are ones associated with stalking; and
- the person whose course of conduct it is knows or ought to know that the course of conduct amounts to harassment of the other person.

KEYNOTE

What is 'Stalking'?

Section 2A(3) lists examples of behaviours associated with stalking. The list is not exhaustive but gives an indication of the types of behaviour that may be displayed in a stalking offence. The listed behaviours are:

- following a person;
- contacting, or attempting to contact, a person by any means;
- publishing any statement or other material (i) relating or purporting to relate to a person, or (ii) purporting to originate from a person;
- monitoring the use by a person of the internet, email or any other form of electronic communication;
- loitering in any place (whether public or private);
- interfering with any property in the possession of a person;
- watching or spying on a person.

Section 2A does not include a specific defence for stalking. However, because an offence of stalking can only be established where an offence of harassment has occurred, a person charged with an offence under s. 2A could rely on the defence to harassment under s. 1(3) (**see para. 4.7.4.8**).

Under s. 2B of the Act the police have a power of entry in relation to the s. 2A stalking offence. A constable can apply to a justice of the peace, who may issue a warrant authorising entry and search of premises providing there are reasonable grounds to believe the conditions in s. 2B are met. A constable may seize and retain anything for which a search was authorised, and may use reasonable force, if necessary, in the exercise of any power conferred by s. 2B.

4.7.6.2 Stalking Involving Fear of Violence or Serious Alarm or Distress

OFFENCE: **Stalking Involving Fear of Violence or Serious Alarm or Distress—** *Protection from Harassment Act 1997, s. 4A*
   • Triable either way • Seven years' imprisonment and/or an unlimited fine on indictment • Six months' imprisonment and/or a fine summarily

OFFENCE: **Racially or Religiously Aggravated Stalking Involving Fear of Violence or Serious Alarm or Distress—*Crime and Disorder Act 1998, s. 32(1)(b)***
   • Triable either way • Two years' imprisonment and/or a fine on indictment
   • Six months' imprisonment and/or a fine summarily

The Protection from Harassment Act 1997, s. 4A states:

(1) A person ('A') whose course of conduct—
   (a) amounts to stalking, and
   (b) either—
      (i) causes another ('B') to fear, on at least two occasions, that violence will be used against B, or
      (ii) causes B serious alarm or distress which has a substantial adverse effect on B's usual day-to-day activities,
   is guilty of an offence if A knows or ought to know that A's conduct will cause B so to fear on each of those occasions or (as the case may be) will cause such alarm or distress.

KEYNOTE

For the purposes of s. 4A(1)(b)(i) a person (A) ought to know that A's course of conduct will cause another (B) to fear that violence will be used against B on any occasion if a reasonable person in possession of the same information would think the course of conduct would cause B so to fear on that occasion.

The second arm of the offence prohibits a course of conduct which causes 'serious alarm or distress' which has a 'substantial adverse effect on the day-to-day activities of the victim'. It is designed to recognise the serious impact that stalking may have on victims, even where an explicit fear of violence is not created by each incident of stalking behaviour.

The phrase 'substantial adverse effect on the usual day-to-day activities' is not defined in s. 4A, and thus its construction will be a matter for the courts via judicial interpretation. However, the Home Office considers that evidence of a substantial adverse effect caused by the stalker may include:

• victims changing their routes to work, work patterns or employment;
• victims arranging for friends or family to pick up children from school (to avoid contact with the stalker);
• victims putting in place additional security measures in their home;
• victims moving home;
• physical or mental ill-health;
• victims' deterioration in performance at work due to stress;
• victims stopping or changing the way they socialise.

Although some victims try to continue their existing routines in defiance of a stalker, they may still be able to evidence substantial impact on their usual day-to-day activities, depending on the individual case.

For the purposes of s. 4A(1)(b)(ii), A ought to know that A's course of conduct will cause B serious alarm or distress which has a substantial adverse effect on B's usual day-to-day activities if a reasonable person in possession of the same information would think the course of conduct would cause B such alarm or distress.

Under s. 4A(4), there is a defence to the offence of stalking involving fear of violence or serious alarm or distress which is a mirror image of the defence to the offence under s.4 (**see para. 4.7.5.1**).

4.7.7 Police Direction to Prevent Intimidation or Harassment

In response to a number of campaigns against individuals believed to be involved in animal experiments, the Criminal Justice and Police Act 2001 gives the police specific powers to prevent the intimidation or harassment of people in their own or others' homes. Situations envisaged by the legislation typically arise where protestors gather outside a house where a particular individual is believed to be. Under such circumstances s. 42 provides the most senior ranking police officer at the scene with discretionary powers to give directions to people in the vicinity. The power arises where:

- the person is outside (or in the vicinity of) any premises that are used by any individual as his/her dwelling, and
- the constable *believes*, on reasonable grounds, that the person is there for the purpose of representing or persuading the resident (or anyone else)
- that he/she should not do something he/she is entitled or required to do or
- that he/she should do something that he/she is under no obligation to do, and
- the constable also believes, on reasonable grounds, that the person's presence amounts to, or is likely to result in, the harassment of the resident or is likely to cause alarm or distress to the resident.

Although the premises involved may be in use by any 'individual' (e.g. *not* a company) and the purpose may be to persuade that or any other 'individual', the officer must believe that the ultimate effect will be harassment, alarm or distress of the *resident*. The requirement for reasonable grounds means that their existence or otherwise will be judged objectively and not simply from the personal standpoint of the officer using the power. Nevertheless, the officer is given a great deal of individual discretion in using this power.

A direction given under s. 42 requires the person(s) to do all such things as the officer specifies as being *necessary* to prevent the harassment, alarm or distress of the resident, including:

- a requirement to leave the vicinity of the premises in question, and
- a requirement to leave that vicinity and not to return to it within such period as the constable may specify, not being longer than three months;

and (in either case) the requirement to leave the vicinity may be to do so immediately or after a specified period of time (s. 42(4)).

The direction may be given orally and, where appropriate, may be given to a group of people together (s. 42(3)). There is no requirement that the officer giving the direction be in uniform.

The power under s. 42 cannot be used to direct someone to refrain from conduct made lawful under s. 220 of the Trade Union and Labour Relations (Consolidation) Act 1992 (Peaceful picketing; **see chapter 4.14**).

4.7.7.1 Contravening a s. 42 Direction

OFFENCE: **Knowingly Contravening a s. 42 Direction—*Criminal Justice and Police Act 2001, s. 42(7)***
- Triable summarily • Three months' imprisonment and/or a fine

The Criminal Justice and Police Act 2001, s. 42 states:

(7) Any person who knowingly fails to comply with a requirement in a direction given to him under this section (other than a requirement under subsection (4)(b)) shall be guilty of an offence.

OFFENCE: **Unlawfully Returning to Vicinity—*Criminal Justice and Police Act 2001, s. 42(7A)***

- Triable summarily - Imprisonment for a term not exceeding six months and/or a fine

The Criminal Justice and Police Act 2001, s. 42 states:

(7A) Any person to whom a constable has given a direction including a requirement under subsection (4)(b) commits an offence if he—
   (a) returns to the vicinity of the premises in question within the period specified in the direction beginning with the date on which the direction is given; and
   (b) does so for the purpose described in subsection (1)(b).

4.7.7.2 Harassment etc. of Person in their Home

OFFENCE: **Harassment of a Person in their Home—*Criminal Justice and Police Act 2001, s. 42A***

- Triable summarily - Imprisonment for a term not exceeding six months and/or a fine

The Criminal Justice and Police Act 2001, s. 42A states:

(1) A person commits an offence if—
   (a) that person is present outside or in the vicinity of any premises that are used by any individual ('the resident') as his dwelling;
   (b) that person is present there for the purpose (by his presence or otherwise) of representing to the resident or another individual (whether or not one who uses the premises as his dwelling), or of persuading the resident or such another individual—
      (i) that he should not do something that he is entitled or required to do; or
      (ii) that he should do something that he is not under any obligation to do;
   (c) that person—
      (i) intends his presence to amount to the harassment of, or to cause alarm or distress to, the resident; or

(ii) knows or ought to know that his presence is likely to result in the harassment of, or to cause alarm or distress to, the resident; and

(d) the presence of that person—

(i) amounts to the harassment of, or causes alarm or distress to, any person falling within subsection (2); or

(ii) is likely to result in the harassment of, or to cause alarm or distress to, any such person.

(2) A person falls within this subsection if he is—

(a) the resident,

(b) a person in the resident's dwelling, or

(c) a person in another dwelling in the vicinity of the resident's dwelling.

KEYNOTE

This offence has a number of elements, each of which must be proved if a successful prosecution is to be brought. The ingredients include:

- **Place**—the defendant must be shown to have been in the relevant place (outside or in the vicinity of a 'dwelling'). 'Dwelling' means any structure or part of a structure occupied as a person's home or as other living accommodation (whether the occupation is separate or shared with others) but does not include any part not so occupied (s. 42A(7)).

- **Purpose**—the defendant's purpose in being there must be to represent to, or persuade the resident/another individual that he/she should not do something he/she is entitled/required to do or that he/she should do something that he/she is not under any obligation to do.

- **Intention/knowledge**—you must prove that the defendant intended his/her presence to amount to harassment of, or to cause alarm or distress to, the resident or that he/she knew/ought to have known that his/her presence was likely to have that result.

- **Consequences**—you must show that the defendant's presence amounted to/was likely to result in the harassment of, or causing alarm or distress to, any resident, person in the resident's dwelling, or person in another dwelling in the vicinity of the resident's dwelling.

References in s. 42A(1)(c) and (d) to a person's presence are references either to his/her presence alone or together with that of any other people who are also present (s. 42A(3)).

For the purposes of this section a person ought to know that his/her presence is likely to result in the harassment of, or to cause alarm or distress to, a resident if a reasonable person in possession of the same information would think that it was likely to have that effect (s. 42A(4)).

4.8 | Anti-social Behaviour

4.8.1 Introduction

The term 'anti-social behaviour' (ASB) describes the everyday nuisance, disorder and crime that impact on victims' quality of life. In the year ending June 2016, 1.8 million incidents of anti-social behaviour (ASB) were recorded by the police (including the British Transport Police) in England and Wales. However, many incidents are not reported at all, or are reported to other agencies such as local councils or social landlords, and some will also be categorised as crime.

The Crime and Disorder Act 1998 introduced the Anti-social Behaviour Order (ASBO) to deal with such incidents. However, while a total of 24,427 ASBOs were issued between April 1999 and December 2013, they were breached on numerous occasions. Over time this undermined the effectiveness and confidence in ASBOs as a tool for effectively dealing with anti-social behaviour. Consequently, the ASBO has been replaced by new provisions in the Anti-social Behaviour, Crime and Policing Act 2014.

The 2014 Act aims to simplify and improve the powers available to deal with ASB. The previous set of 19 measures has been reduced to six, a number of which give new powers to the police and are described in detail below.

4.8.2 Injunctions under the Anti-social Behaviour, Crime and Policing Act 2014

Part 1 of the 2014 Act introduces the new regime of injunctions for dealing with anti-social behaviour. Section 1 of the 2014 Act deals with the power to grant injunctions detailed in subsections (1) to (7) below:

(1) A court may grant an injunction under this section against a person aged 10 or over ('the respondent') if two conditions are met.

(2) The first condition is that the court is satisfied, on the balance of probabilities, that the respondent has engaged or threatens to engage in anti-social behaviour.

(3) The second condition is that the court considers it just and convenient to grant the injunction for the purpose of preventing the respondent from engaging in anti-social behaviour.

(4) An injunction under this section may for the purpose of preventing the respondent from engaging in anti-social behaviour—

    (a) prohibit the respondent from doing anything described in the injunction;

    (b) require the respondent to do anything described in the injunction.

(5) Prohibitions and requirements in an injunction under this section must, so far as practicable, be such as to avoid—

    (a) any interference with the times, if any, at which the respondent normally works or attends school or any other educational establishment;

    (b) any conflict with the requirements of any other court order or injunction to which the respondent may be subject.

(6) An injunction under this section must—

    (a) specify the period for which it has effect, or

    (b) state that it has effect until further order.

    In the case of an injunction granted before the respondent has reached the age of 18, a period must be specified and it must be no more than 12 months.

(7) An injunction under this section may specify periods for which particular prohibitions or requirements have effect.

4.8.2.1 The Injunction

The injunction is a purely civil injunction available in the county court for adults and in the youth court for those under the age of 18. The injunction replaces a range of current tools including the anti-social behaviour order (ASBO) on application, the anti-social behaviour injunction (ASBI), the drinking banning order on application, intervention orders and individual support orders and can be used to tackle a wide range of anti-social behaviour problems.

Section 1 sets out a two-part test for granting an injunction. An injunction may be made against a person aged 10 or over if the court is satisfied, on the balance of probabilities (the civil standard of proof), that the person has engaged in, or is threatening to engage in, anti-social behaviour and that it is just and convenient to grant the injunction.

4.8.2.2 Anti-social Behaviour

Section 2(1) defines 'anti-social behaviour' for this purpose:

> (1) In this Part 'anti-social behaviour' means—
>   (a) conduct that has caused, or is likely to cause, harassment, alarm or distress to any person,
>   (b) conduct capable of causing nuisance or annoyance to a person in relation to that person's occupation of residential premises, or
>   (c) conduct capable of causing housing-related nuisance or annoyance to any person.

4.8.2.3 Prohibitions or Requirements

The injunction could include prohibitions or requirements that assist in the prevention of future anti-social behaviour (s. 1(3)). Such prohibitions may include, for example, not being in possession of a can of spray paint in a public place, not entering a particular area, or not being drunk in a public place. Requirements would be designed to deal with the underlying causes of an individual's anti-social behaviour and could include, for example, attendance at an alcohol or drugs misuse course or dog training in the case of irresponsible dog owners.

Where an injunction imposes requirements on the respondent, it must specify the person (an individual or an organisation) who is responsible for supervising compliance (s. 3). The court must receive evidence on the suitability and enforceability of a requirement from this person. Such individuals or organisations could include the local authority, youth offending teams, recognised providers of substance misuse recovery or dog training providers for irresponsible dog owners.

4.8.2.4 Time Limits

There is no minimum or maximum term for the injunction for adults, so the court may decide that the injunction should be for a specified period or an indefinite period. However, in the case of injunctions against under-18s, the maximum term is 12 months (s. 1(6)). The duration of any prohibitions or requirements may be shorter than the duration of the injunction itself.

4.8.2.5 Power of Arrest

Section 4 provides officers with a power of arrest in certain circumstances:

> (1) A court granting an injunction under section 1 may attach a power of arrest to a prohibition or requirement of the injunction if the court thinks that—
>   (a) the anti-social behaviour in which the respondent has engaged or threatens to engage consists of or includes the use or threatened use of violence against other persons, or
>   (b) there is a significant risk of harm to other persons from the respondent.
>   'Requirement' here does not include one that has the effect of requiring the respondent to participate in particular activities.
> (2) If the court attaches a power of arrest, the injunction may specify a period for which the power is to have effect which is shorter than that of the prohibition or requirement to which it relates.

A power of arrest attached to an injunction allows a police officer to arrest the respondent without a warrant if the respondent breached a condition in the injunction, that is, a prohibition or a requirement (s. 9). Where no power of arrest is attached to the injunction, the applicant may apply to the court to issue a warrant of arrest of a respondent if the applicant thinks that the respondent has breached the injunction (s. 10). Section 11 and sch. 1 make provision for the remand, whether on bail or in custody, of a person arrested for breach of an injunction.

4.8.2.6 Applying for an Injunction

There is a formal requirement for the applicant to consult with the local youth offending team (YOT) before making an application, if an injunction is against someone under the age of 18. The consultation requirement does not give a veto power to the local YOT. The applicant must also inform any other body or individual about the application that they think appropriate (s. 14), again before making an application. This could include a social landlord (when an application is made by another body against one of their tenants) or mental health team.

Applications for an injunction would normally be made to the county court or High Court where the respondent is an adult, or to the youth court where the respondent is under 18. However, s. 18(2) makes provision for cases involving multiple respondents where one (or more) of them is aged 18 or over and one (or more) is under that age. In such a case, an applicant may apply at the time of the application to the youth court for permission for the application in respect of the adult(s) to be heard in that court. The youth court would be able to grant the application if it was in the interest of justice. Sections 8(2)(b), 9(3)(b) and 10(2)(b) ensure that while an application in respect of an under-18 will be heard by the youth court, subsequent proceedings against a defendant who has attained the age of 18 since the injunction was made would take place in the appropriate adult court.

Injunction applications would normally be made following the giving of notice to the respondent; however, s. 6 allows an application for an injunction to be made without notice. Without notice applications would, in practice, only be made in exceptional or urgent circumstances and the applicant would need to produce evidence to the court as to why a without notice hearing was necessary. Where a without notice application is made, the court would be able to grant an interim injunction pending a full hearing following the giving of notice to the respondent (ss. 6 and 7). The consultation requirements in s. 14 do not apply to without notice applications.

4.8.2.7 Breaching an Injunction

Breach of an injunction by an adult will be contempt of court, punishable in the usual way by the county court by a term of imprisonment of up to two years or an unlimited fine. Breach of an injunction by someone aged under 18 could result in the youth court imposing a supervision order or a detention order. A detention order can be made for breaching the injunction or for breaching a supervision order that was imposed for breaching the injunction. The court may revoke the supervision order and impose a new one or it may revoke the supervision order and make a detention order. The court can only impose a detention order where it considers that the severity or extent of the behaviour warrants it and that no other sanction available to it is appropriate. The court must be satisfied beyond reasonable doubt that the under-18 has, without reasonable excuse, breached the injunction or breached a supervision order that was imposed for breaching the injunction before it can make the detention order. The court must also consider any representations from the YOT specified in the supervision order before imposing a detention order. The maximum duration of a detention order is three months and it cannot be imposed on under-14s (s. 12 and sch. 2). A supervision order may contain one or more of the following requirements: a supervision requirement, an activity requirement or a curfew requirement. An electronic monitoring requirement may be attached to a curfew requirement in order to monitor compliance.

4.8.2.8 Special Measures

Section 16 enables the court to give a special measures direction to protect vulnerable or intimidated witnesses in injunction proceedings. Such measures may include giving evidence behind a screen or by video link or in private.

4.8.3 Criminal Behaviour Orders

Part 2 of the Anti-social Behaviour, Crime and Policing Act 2014 creates the Criminal Behaviour Order (CBO).

4.8.3.1 The Order

An order may only be made against an offender when he/she has been sentenced for the offence or given a conditional discharge (s. 22(6)). No order may be made where the offender has been given an absolute discharge or has only been bound over to keep the peace. The order is aimed at tackling the most serious and persistent offenders where their behaviour has brought them before a criminal court. The CBO replaces the ASBO on conviction and the drinking banning order on conviction. A court will be able to make a CBO against an offender only if the prosecutor applies for it, on the advice of the police or the local authority.

4.8.3.2 Granting an Order

Section 22 sets out a two-part test for granting an order. An order may be made against a person over the age of 10 if the court is satisfied that the offender has engaged in behaviour that caused, or was likely to cause, harassment, alarm or distress to any person; and the court considers that making the order will assist in preventing the offender from engaging in such behaviour. The standard of proof would be the criminal standard, that is, 'beyond reasonable doubt' (s. 22(3)).

4.8.3.3 Prohibitions and/or Requirements

The order could include prohibitions and/or positive requirements that assist in preventing the offender from engaging in behaviour that could cause harassment, alarm or distress in the future (s. 22(5)). Such prohibitions are similar to those mentioned in relation to injunctions (**see para. 4.8.2.3**), for example, they could include not being in possession of a can of spray paint in a public place, not entering a particular area, or not being drunk in a public place. The requirements in an order could include attendance at a course to educate offenders on alcohol and its effects.

4.8.3.4 Consultation Requirements

The only formal consultation requirement applies where an offender is under 18 years of age. In those cases, the prosecution must find out the views of the local YOT before applying for the CBO. The views of the YOT must be included in the file of evidence forwarded to the prosecution. In practice, the consultation with the YOT must be carried out by the organisation preparing the application for the CBO, namely the council or police force.

The legislation has deliberately kept formal consultation requirements to a minimum, to enable agencies to act quickly where needed to protect victims and communities. However, in most cases it is likely there would be a number of agencies the police or local council would wish to consult with. This could include local organisations that have come into contact with the individual, such as schools and colleges of further education, providers of probation services, social services, mental health services, housing providers or others.

4.8.3.5 Time Limits and Reviews

The terms of the CBO must include the duration of the order. For adults this is a minimum of two years up to an indefinite period. For under-18s the order must be between one and three years. Reviews must be held every 12 months for offenders under the age of 18 (s. 28). The 12 month period starts from the date the order was made, or from the date it was subsequently varied. The review must consider the offender's compliance with the order and the support provided to help him or her comply with it, and give consideration to whether an application should be made to vary or discharge the order. The review should be carried out by the police with the local authority and any other relevant person or body (s. 29).

4.8.3.6 Special Measures

In any proceedings in relation to a CBO it is open to the court to make a special measures direction in relation to vulnerable and intimidated witnesses. Such measures may include the physical screening of a witness, enabling evidence to be given in private or the use of a video-recorded interview.

4.8.3.7 Offences and Penalties

It is a criminal offence if an offender fails to comply, without reasonable excuse, with either the requirements or prohibitions in the CBO. Failure to comply with a prohibition or requirement should be notified to the police. The court has the power to impose serious penalties on conviction, including:

- on summary conviction in the magistrates' court: a maximum of six months in prison or a fine or both;
- on conviction on indictment in the Crown Court: a maximum of five years in prison or a fine or both.

Hearings for those under 18 will take place in the youth court where the maximum sentence is a two year detention and training order.

4.8.3.8 Publicising a CBO

Making the public aware of the offender and the terms of the order can be an important part of the process in dealing with anti-social behaviour. It can provide reassurance to communities that action is being taken when they report anti-social behaviour. It will also provide the information local people need to identify and report breaches. The decision to publicise a CBO will be taken by the police or council unless the court has made a s. 39 order (Children and Young Persons Act 1933) prohibiting publication. When deciding whether to publicise a CBO, public authorities (including the courts) must consider that it is necessary and proportionate to interfere with the young person's right to privacy, and the likely impact on a young person's behaviour. This will need to be balanced against the need to provide reassurance to the victims and the wider community as well as providing them with information so that they can report any breaches. Each case should be decided carefully on its own facts.

4.8.4 Dispersal Powers

Part 3 of the Anti-social Behaviour, Crime and Policing Act 2014 establishes a new dispersal power that will enable officers (constables in uniform and police community support officers (PCSOs)) to direct a person who has committed, or is likely to commit, anti-social behaviour to leave a specified area and not return for a specified period of up to 48 hours.

The test would be that the officer is satisfied on reasonable grounds that the person's behaviour is contributing, or is likely to contribute to anti-social behaviour or crime or disorder in the area and that the direction is necessary to prevent the same (s. 35(2) and (3)). Police officers would have access to all elements of the power, and PCSOs could have access to some or all elements of the power at the discretion of the chief constable (s. 40).

4.8.4.1 Authoring the Power

The dispersal power can only be used where an officer of at least the rank of inspector has authorised its use in a specified locality (s. 34(1)). The authorisation can last a maximum of 48 hours. That authorisation can only be given where the police officer of or above the rank of inspector reasonably believes that, in respect of any locality within their police area, the exercise of the dispersal powers in part 3 of the Act may be required in order to remove or reduce the likelihood of the anti-social behaviour occurring. For instance, the inspector may have intelligence to indicate that there is likely to be anti-social behaviour on a particular housing estate during the weekend and authorise the use of the dispersal for 48 hours. Alternatively, in a situation where an officer needs to use the dispersal power in an area that has not been authorised, the officer can contact an inspector for an authorisation and describe the circumstances to him or her.

Before authorising the use of the dispersal power in a specified area, the authorising police officer must have particular regard to the rights of freedom of expression and freedom of assembly and association (s. 34(3)). A similar duty is placed on a constable before issuing a dispersal direction (s. 36(5)).

The direction would in most instances be given in writing to ensure that those individuals being dispersed are clear where they are being dispersed from. Where this is not reasonably practicable, the direction could be given orally (s. 35(5)(a)) and the officer would keep a written record of the direction (s. 38). Any constable can vary or withdraw a direction and must do this in writing to the person originally issued with the order unless not reasonably practicable (s. 35(8) and (9)).

4.8.4.2 Powers and Offences

The officer must specify the area from which the person is excluded, and may specify when and by which route they must leave the area (s. 35(5)(b) and (c)). Where the officer believes an individual is under the age of 16, an officer can remove that individual to a place where he or she lives or to a place of safety (s. 35(7)).

Failure to comply with the direction would be a criminal offence and would carry a maximum penalty of a level 4 fine (currently £2,500) and/or three months imprisonment (s. 39).

An officer would also be able to require an individual to hand over items causing, or likely to cause, anti-social behaviour—for instance, alcohol or a can of spray paint (s. 37). Failure to comply with the requirement is a criminal offence, the maximum penalty for which is a level 2 fine (currently £500) (s. 39(4)). These sanctions are in line with current equivalent powers, and are designed to ensure there is an appropriately serious consequence to failing to comply.

However, the officer does not have power under this provision to retain any seized item indefinitely. The officer must give the person information in writing about how and when they can recover the item, which must not be returned before the exclusion period is over. If the person is under 16 the officer can require that person to be accompanied by an adult when collecting the item.

4.8.5 Community Protection Notices and Closure of Premises Associated with Nuisance or Disorder

Part 4 of the Anti-social, Crime and Policing Act 2014 deals with the newly introduced Community Protection Notice (CPN). The notice is intended to deal with unreasonable, ongoing problems or nuisances which negatively affect the community's quality of life by targeting the person responsible (s. 43(1)). The notice can direct any individual over the age of 16, business or organisation responsible to stop causing the problem and it could also require the person responsible to take reasonable steps to ensure that it does not occur again (s. 43(3)).

4.8.5.1 Issuing a CPN

The test is designed to be broad and focus on the impact anti-social behaviour is having on victims and communities. A CPN can be issued if on reasonable grounds the issuer is satisfied that the conduct of the individual, business or organisation:

- is having a detrimental effect on the quality of life of those in the locality;
- is persistent or continuing in nature; and
- is unreasonable.

In many areas, councils already take the lead in dealing with these kinds of issues and they will continue to be able to issue the new notice. However, the power to issue a notice will also be available to the police and PCSOs, if designated by the chief constable (s. 53(5); under s. 53(6) a PCSO will also be able to issue a fixed penalty notice for the offence of breaching a community protection notice, if designated for that).

The notice should be issued to someone who can be held responsible for the anti-social behaviour (s. 44). For instance, if a small shop were allowing litter to be deposited outside the property and not dealing with the issue, a notice could be issued to the business owner, whereas if a large national supermarket were to cause a similar issue, the company itself or the store manager could be issued with a notice.

CPNs replace measures such as litter clearing notices, defacement removal notices and street litter control notices. They are not meant to replace the statutory nuisance regime, although there is no legal bar to it being used where behaviour is such as to amount to a statutory nuisance under s. 79 of the Environmental Protection Act 1990. For example, a local authority could issue a CPN to address anti-social behaviour while investigating whether it constitutes statutory nuisance. Part 3 of the Environmental Protection Act 1990 places a duty on a local authority to investigate complaints of statutory nuisance from people living within its area. Issue of a CPN does not relieve the local authority of its obligation under part 3 of the Environmental Protection Act 1990 to serve an abatement notice where the relevant test is met.

Before issuing a notice, an authorised person is required to inform whatever agencies or persons he/she considered appropriate (e.g. the landlord of the person in question, or the local authority), partly in order to avoid duplication (s. 43(6)). The person would also have to have issued a written warning in advance and allowed an appropriate amount of time to pass (s. 43(5)). This is to ensure that the perpetrator is aware of their behaviour and allows them time to rectify the situation. It will be for the person issuing the written warning to decide how long is appropriate before serving a notice. In the example where a dog owner's fence needs to be fixed, this could be days or weeks, in order to allow the individual to address the problem. However, it could be minutes or hours in a case where, for example, someone was persistently playing loud music in a park.

Wherever possible, the notice should be issued in person. However, where this is not possible, it can be posted or left at the proper address (s. 55(1)). In the case of the latter when it relates to a business, the address may be different from the location of the anti-social behaviour.

4.8.5.2 Consultation and Communication

Before issuing the notice, the police or local authority must consult any person or agency they consider appropriate, and must also make reasonable efforts to inform the owner, landlord, licensee and anyone who appears to be residing in the premise (s. 76(6) and (7)). The police or local authority must also take into account any special considerations arising from the presence, or likely presence, of any children or vulnerable adults on the premises. Authorised persons will have a power of entry to the premises, using reasonable force if necessary, to secure the notice to the premises (s. 79(4)). The service of the notice on relevant people is required of the constable or local authority (or contractor employed by the local authority) if possible to do so (s. 79(2)). If a closure notice is no longer required the police or local authority that issued the notice must cancel the closure notice with a cancellation notice (s. 78(2)).

4.8.5.3 Closure Notices and Orders

When a closure notice is issued, the police or local authority must apply to the magistrates' court for a closure order (s. 80(1)). The magistrates' court must hear the application for the closure order within 48 hours of the closure notice being issued (excluding Christmas Day) unless the closure notice has been cancelled by a cancellation notice (s. 80(3)). The court can make a closure order for a maximum period of three months (s. 80(6)) if it is satisfied that: a person has engaged in disorder, anti-social or criminal behaviour on the premises (or that such behaviour is likely if the order is not made) or the use of the premises is associated with the occurrence of disorder or serious nuisance to members of the public (or that such disorder or serious nuisance is likely if the order is not made); and that the order is necessary to prevent the continuation or occurrence or reoccurrence of such disorder or behaviour (s. 80(5)). Unlike the closure notice, a closure order can prohibit access to anyone, including the landlord, owner or habitual residents (s. 80(7)).

4.8.5.4 Breaching the Notice

Breach of any requirement in the notice, without reasonable excuse, would be a criminal offence, subject to a fixed penalty notice (which attracts a penalty of £100) (s. 52) or prosecution. On summary conviction an individual would be liable to a level 4 fine (currently up to £2,500). An organisation such as a company is liable to a fine not exceeding £20,000. On conviction, the magistrates' court would have the power to order forfeiture and destruction of any item used in the commission of the offence—for instance, noise equipment (s. 50). Where necessary, the court can also issue a warrant allowing a constable or local authority to seize such items (s. 51).

A remedial order may also require the defendant to carry out specified work (this could set out the original CPN requirements); or to allow work to be carried out by, or on behalf of, a specified local authority.

Breach of the notice or the order, without reasonable excuse, would be a criminal offence (s. 86). On summary conviction, a person would be liable to an unlimited fine and/or up to three months' imprisonment if in breach of a notice and up to six months' imprisonment if in breach of an order (or 51 weeks following the commencement of s. 281(5) of the Criminal Justice Act 2003). Organisations and businesses would be subject to an unlimited fine. A person guilty of obstructing an officer in the process of closing a property also commits an offence and is liable to a fine and/or up to three months' imprisonment.

4.8.6 Nuisance

There are many forms of behaviour which are a source of annoyance or disquiet to the community. Some of these activities are usefully classified as 'nuisances', while others come under 'environmental' legislation. What follows is a brief summary of some of the main areas covered by both types of legislation.

4.8.6.1 Public Nuisance

There is a specific offence of creating or being responsible for a public nuisance, an offence that overlaps with some other aspects of criminal behaviour.

The common law concept of nuisance is separated into public and private nuisance. Private nuisance is dealt with under civil law as a *tort* ('wrong'). Public nuisance, however, can also be dealt with under criminal law.

A public nuisance is an unlawful act or an omission to discharge a duty which, in either case, obstructs or causes inconvenience or damage to the public in the exercise of their common rights (*Attorney-General* v *PYA Quarries Ltd (No. 1)* [1957] 2 QB 169).

Although there is no 'magic number' of people who must suffer from the annoyance or obstruction in order for it to amount to a *public nuisance*, you must show that the act or omission affected the public in general as opposed to a small group of people (such as the employees of a firm). Therefore, in *R* v *Madden* [1975] 1 WLR 1379, where a person made a hoax bomb call to an organisation, it was held that such behaviour could in theory amount to a public nuisance, although in *Madden* it did not as the annoyance/obstruction was limited in its effect.

People who entered school premises for the purpose of glue sniffing were held to have committed a public nuisance by unduly interfering with the comfortable and convenient enjoyment of the land, even though the school was empty (*Sykes* v *Holmes* [1985] Crim LR 791).

Given that the courts have unlimited sentencing power in relation to this offence, there may well be advantages in considering its application to cases where the only other offences disclosed would be summary offences. An example is the case of *R* v *Johnson* [1997] 1 WLR 367 where the defendant made several hundred obscene telephone calls to women across a county over a period of five years.

4.8.6.2 Offence of Public Nuisance

OFFENCE: **Public Nuisance—*Common Law***
- Triable either way • Unlimited powers of sentence on indictment
- Statutory maxima apply summarily

It is an offence at common law for a person to cause a public nuisance.

KEYNOTE

As this offence is a common law 'misdemeanour', a court may pass sentence at its discretion on indictment, that is, its sentencing powers are unlimited.

Although the typical and obvious causes of public nuisance are now the subject of express statutory prohibition, the common law offence still exists and is not in breach of Article 7 (No Punishment without Crime) of the European Convention on Human Rights (*R* v *Rimmington; R* v *Goldstein* [2005] UKHL 63).

The behaviour of the defendant must interfere with the material rights enjoyed by a class of Her Majesty's subjects (*R* v *Johnson* [1997] 1 WLR 367).

In *Attorney-General* v *PYA Quarries Ltd (No. 2)* [1961] 2 QB 169, it was said that a nuisance would need to be 'so widespread in its range or so indiscriminate in its effect' that it would not be reasonable to expect one person to bring proceedings on his/her own to put a stop to it. However, it is not necessary to prove that every

---

member within a class of people in the community has been affected by the defendant's behaviour; simply that a representative cross-section has been so affected. Such a cross-section might include members of a housing estate or users of a public transport facility such as a main-line railway station.

There is no need to show that the defendant intended his/her actions or omission to cause a public nuisance and it will be enough that he/she knew or ought to have known that the conduct would bring about a public nuisance (*R* v *Shorrock* [1994] QB 279).

An example of how the law of public nuisance can be used in a policing context can be seen in *R* v *Harvey* [2003] EWCA Crim 112. In that case the defendant was convicted of causing a public nuisance after following different groups of children in his car, sounding the horn and smiling at them. Evidence was adduced to show that he presented a real threat to children with the possibility of his luring them into his car for unlawful purposes. Although the defendant was originally sentenced to life imprisonment, that was later reduced in the absence of features of sex or violence, to three years.

Other examples of criminal public nuisances have included:

- allowing a rave to take place in a field (*R* v *Shorrock* [1994] QB 279)
- making hundreds of nuisance telephone calls to at least 13 women (*R* v *Johnson* [1997] 1 WLR 367)
- contaminating 30 houses with dust and noise from a quarry (*PYA* above)
- selling meat which was unfit for consumption (*R* v *Stephens* (1866) LR 1 QB 702).

In addition, s. 79 of the Environmental Protection Act 1990 sets out a list of 'statutory nuisances', any of which would potentially be capable of amounting to a criminal offence if it met the relevant conditions.

4.8.6.3 Defence

Statutory authorisation for a person's conduct (e.g. building a road or a railway) will be a defence provided the behaviour is specifically permitted by that statute (*Hammersmith and City Railway Co.* v *Brand and Louisa* (1869–70) LR 4 HL 171).

4.8.6.4 Enforcement

In addition to providing powers of arrest and sentencing for tackling public nuisance through the criminal process, there is always the preventive measure of a court injunction available. Historically, the Attorney-General has sought injunctions on behalf of the public at large. However, local authorities have the power to apply for a public nuisance injunction under the Local Government Act 1972 (*Stoke-on-Trent City Council* v *B & Q (Retail) Ltd* [1984] AC 754) and there appears to be no reason why chief officers should not do the same.

4.8.7 Fireworks

The Fireworks Act 2003 regulates the sale and use of fireworks under certain circumstances and makes provision for further regulations by the Secretary of State. The principal regulations in this regard are the Fireworks Regulations 2004 (SI 2004/1836). The relevant aspects of this legislation affecting practical policing are summarised below.

4.8.7.1 Controls on Supplying Fireworks

Sections 2 and 3 of the Fireworks Act 2003 allow for regulations to ensure that there is no risk that the use of fireworks will lead to death, injury, or distress to people and animals or the destruction of, or damage to, property.

Generally 'fireworks' mean fireworks for the purposes of the British Standard Specification published on 30 November 1988 (BS 7114) or any British Standard Specification replacing it. The regulations go on to categorise specific types of firework according to the danger they present. These range from caps and party poppers to the elaborate pyrotechnic devices as used in public displays.

4.8.7.2 Possession of Fireworks

OFFENCE: **Possession of Fireworks—*Fireworks Regulations 2004, regs 4 and 5***
- Triable summarily • Six months' imprisonment and/or a fine

Regulations 4 and 5 state:

> 4.—(1) Subject to regulation 6 below, no person under the age of eighteen years shall possess an adult firework in a public place.
>
> ...
>
> 5. Subject to regulation 6 below, no person shall possess a category 4 firework.

KEYNOTE

'Public place' has the usual meaning of any place to which at the material time the public have or are permitted access, whether on payment or otherwise (reg. 4(2)). An 'adult firework' is broadly any firework which does not comply with the relevant requirements of part 2 of BS 7114 (except for a cap, cracker snap, novelty match, party popper, serpent, sparkler or throwdown). A category 4 firework is one specified as such in BS 7114.

The exemptions in reg. 6 generally cover people who have such fireworks in the course of their work or business or who are properly authorised to conduct displays.

Fireworks, as defined in s. 1(1) of the Fireworks Act 2003 and in the Regulations, are 'prohibited articles' for the purposes of s. 1 of the Police and Criminal Evidence Act 1984 (general stop and search powers; see chapter 4.5).

4.8.7.3 Prohibition of Use of Certain Fireworks at Night

Regulation 7 states:

> (1) Subject to paragraph (2) below, no person shall use an adult firework during night hours.

KEYNOTE

For the general definition of an 'adult firework' see para. 4.8.7.2.

'Night hours' are the period beginning at 11 pm and ending at 7 am the following day (reg. 7(3)).

The exception referred to in reg. 7(2) deals with three main types of firework display, namely, a 'permitted fireworks night', a firework display by a local authority, and a national public celebration or a national commemorative event.

Taking the first exception, the above restriction on using adult fireworks will not apply to use during permitted fireworks nights—an exception that has been built into the legislation to take account of the various festivals and celebrations that traditionally involve fireworks. The expression 'permitted fireworks night' means a period:

- beginning at 11 pm on the first day of the Chinese New Year and ending at 1 am the following day;
- beginning at 11 pm and ending at midnight on 5 November;
- beginning at 11 pm on the day of Diwali and ending at 1 am the following day; or
- beginning at 11 pm on 31 December and ending at 1 am the following day.

(See reg. 7(3).)

The other two exceptions—a firework display by a local authority or a national public celebration/commemorative event—*only* apply to a person who is employed by a local authority.

As with the regulations governing possession, breach of this regulation will be an offence under s. 11 of the 2003 Act (see para. 4.8.7.5).

4.8.7.4 Other Fireworks Regulations

Sections 4 and 5 of the Act allow for regulations to prohibit the supply of fireworks in certain circumstances or the supply of certain types of firework (such as excessively loud fireworks which are defined and regulated by reg. 8 of the 2004 Regulations). In addition, reg. 9 imposes a general requirement for anyone supplying adult fireworks (or exposing them for supply) to be licensed. However, this requirement does *not* apply:

- on the first day of the Chinese New Year or on the day of Diwali and the three days immediately preceding it;
- during the period beginning on 15 October and ending on 10 November; or
- during the period beginning on 26 December and ending on 31 December.

These exemptions are designed to work in conjunction with 'permitted fireworks nights'.

'Supplying' includes selling, exchanging and giving fireworks (even as prizes) but does not include supplying otherwise than in the course of business (s. 1(3)). People licensed by the local authority to supply adult fireworks have to comply with certain conditions. Where the supply or exposure for supply takes place on premises, the person must display in a prominent position a notice of the prescribed size stating that it is illegal to sell adult fireworks to anyone under the age of 18 and that it is illegal for anyone under the age of 18 to possess adult fireworks in a public place (reg. 10). There are also further requirements under reg. 10 for suppliers to provide full details as to their own suppliers and customers in cases of larger transactions of *any* fireworks (not just adult fireworks) and an absolute restriction on importing *any* fireworks unless certain information has been given to the Commissioners of Her Majesty's Revenue and Customs (reg. 11).

The Act goes on to make provision for the regulation of public fireworks displays, the requirement of suppliers to attend training courses, the licensing of suppliers and the provision of information about fireworks generally.

4.8.7.5 Breach of Fireworks Regulations

OFFENCE: **Breach of Regulations—*Fireworks Act 2003, s. 11***
- Triable summarily • Six months' imprisonment and/or a fine

The Fireworks Act 2003, s. 11 states:

(1) Any person who contravenes a prohibition imposed by fireworks regulations is guilty of an offence.
(2) Any person who fails to comply with a requirement imposed by or under fireworks regulations to give or not to give information is guilty of an offence.
(3) Where a requirement to give information is imposed by or under fireworks regulations, a person is guilty of an offence if, in giving the information, he—
    (a) makes a statement which he knows is false in a material particular; or
    (b) recklessly makes a statement which is false in a material particular.

KEYNOTE

There is some overlap between regulations made under the Consumer Protection Act 1987 and this offence and both pieces of legislation should be checked.

In particular, the general defence of due diligence (under s. 39 of that Act) will apply to offences at s. 11(1) and (2) above.

The regulations are amended regularly and reference should be made to the latest version when considering the enforcement of their provisions. Many of the regulations are concerned with the way in which fireworks are advertised, displayed and sold.

In relation to the supply of, offer or agreement to supply fireworks to a child or young person, s. 11(8) creates a defence for the defendant to show that he/she had no reason to suspect that the person was under the relevant age.

The sections of the Consumer Protection Act 1987 allowing for enforcement measures such as test purchases and powers of search, generally apply to the above offences.

OFFENCE: **Throwing Fireworks into Highway or Street—*Explosives Act 1875, s. 80***

- Triable summarily   • Fine

The Explosives Act 1875, s. 80 states:

> If any person throw, cast, or fire any fireworks in or into any highway, street, thoroughfare, or public place, he shall be guilty of an offence and liable.

KEYNOTE

This offence is a 'penalty offence' for the purposes of s. 1 of the Criminal Justice and Police Act 2001.

4.8.8   Noise

The creation of noise is environmental issue that can severely affect quality of life in the community. There are several statutory provisions allowing the relevant agencies to address problems associated with noise and its sources.

Under the Anti-social Behaviour Act 2003 the chief executive of a relevant local authority can apply to a court for an order to close licensed premises in certain circumstances involving noise **(see chapter 4.17)**.

In addition to the above legislation, the Noise Act 1996 provides powers to allow local authorities to tackle the problems of noise within their community. For instance, ss. 2 and 3 of the 1996 Act allow for the serving of warning notices in relation to 'excessive noise' emanating from one house which can be heard in another at night. Night is defined as being between 11 pm and 7 am (s. 2(6)). The Clean Neighbourhoods and Environment Act 2005 has extended s. 2 to include noise emitted from any premises in respect of which a premises licence (Licensing Act 2003—**see para. 4.17.4.1**), or a temporary event notice (Licensing Act 2003—**see para. 4.17.4.4**) has been issued, that can be heard in a dwelling (s. 2(2)(b) of the 1996 Act). The noise level must be measured using an 'approved device' (s. 6). Any warning must be served on the person who appears to be responsible for the noise or by leaving the warning notice at the 'offending premises' (s. 3(3)). (Note that under the Environmental Protection Act 1990 there is no requirement for evidence of acoustic measurements and a court may convict on other evidence (e.g. evidence from an environmental enforcement officer of excessively loud music being played (*Lewisham Borough Council* v *Hall* [2002] EWHC 960 (Admin)).

OFFENCE: **Where Noise from a Dwelling Exceeds Permitted Level after Service of Notices—*Noise Act 1996, s. 4(1)***

- Triable summarily   • Fine

The Noise Act 1996, s. 4 states:

> (1) If a warning notice has been served in respect of noise emitted from a dwelling, any person who is responsible for noise which—
>   (a) is emitted from the dwelling in the period specified in the notice, and
>   (b) exceeds the permitted level, as measured from within the complainant's dwelling, is guilty of an offence.
> (2) It is a defence for a person charged with an offence under this section to show that there was a reasonable excuse for the act, default or sufferance in question.

OFFENCE: **Where Noise from Other Premises Exceeds Permitted Level after Service of Notice—*Noise Act 1996, s. 4A(1)***

- Triable summarily   • Fine

The Noise Act 1996, s. 4A states:

(1) If—

    (a) a warning notice has been served under section 3 in respect of noise emitted from premises,

    (b) noise is emitted from the premises in the period specified in the notice, and

    (c) the noise exceeds the permitted level, as measured from within the complainant's dwelling, the person responsible in relation to the offending premises at the time at which the noise referred to in paragraph (c) is emitted is guilty of an offence.

KEYNOTE

The 'permitted level' may be set or varied under regulations made by the Secretary of State (s. 5).

Sections 8 and 9 provide for the local authority to implement a 'fixed penalty procedure' whereby liability to prosecution under s. 4 above can be avoided by paying the fee (currently £100) within the prescribed period. Under s. 4A the current fee is £500.

Section 10 provides powers of entry to local authority officers where a warning notice has been served in respect of the offending premises and excessive noise is still measured as having come therefrom. There is also a power to seize any sound equipment involved, together with a power to apply for a warrant for local authority officers to enter premises.

Obstruction of anyone exercising these powers is a summary offence (s. 10(8)) and the provisions for the seizure and disposal of any equipment are set out in the schedule to the 1996 Act.

4.8.9 Litter

The law regulating the roles of local authorities in controlling litter can be found in the Litter Act 1983. The 1983 Act makes allowances for actions by 'litter authorities' (i.e. local councils, see s. 10) to discourage the dropping of litter and for the provision of litter bins.

Removing or interfering with local authority litter bins or litter notices is a summary offence under s. 5(9).

The remainder of the provisions regulating the dropping of litter are in the Environmental Protection Act 1990.

OFFENCE: **Leaving Litter—*Environmental Protection Act 1990, s. 87(1)***
- Triable summarily • Fine

The Environmental Protection Act 1990, s. 87 states:

(1) A person is guilty of an offence if he throws down, drops or otherwise deposits any litter in any place to which this section applies and leaves it.

KEYNOTE

This section applies to *any place* in the area of a principal litter authority which is open to the air (i.e. a local council etc.), other than a place to which the public does not have access (with or without payment) (s. 87(3)).

This offence applies equally to the depositing of litter on land or in water (s. 87(4)).

No offence is committed under s. 87(1) where the depositing of the litter is authorised by law or done by or with the consent of the owner, occupier or other person having control of the place where it is deposited (s. 87(4A)).

A telephone kiosk enclosed on all sides with a six inch gap around the bottom was held not to be a 'public open place' in *Felix* v *DPP* [1998] Crim LR 657.

'Litter' can include animal droppings for this purpose (Litter (Animal Droppings) Order 1991 (SI 1991/961)).

Similarly, s. 88 of the Environmental Protection Act 1990 makes provision for the issuing of fixed penalty notices in respect of the general litter offence above. Section 88 provides that, where a notice setting out the prescribed details is given to an offender, by an authorised officer of a litter authority, no proceedings can be

---

instituted against that person for 14 days. Payment of the fixed penalty will prevent the person's prosecution for that offence. Where the offender pays by posting the required amount properly to the relevant address, payment will be regarded as having been made at the time of the expected *delivery* (not the time the letter is posted) in the normal course of post (s. 88(4)).

The power to issue fixed penalty notices in relation to the Clean Neighbourhoods and Environment Act 2005 and the Environmental Protection Act 1990 are among those that can be conferred on a Community Support Officer designated under sch. 4 to the Police Reform Act 2002 and a person accredited under sch. 5 to that Act, along with the relevant power to require the person to give their name and address.

The Clean Neighbourhoods and Environment Act 2005 clarifies that 'litter', for the purposes of part 4 of the Environmental Protection Act 1990, specifically includes cigarettes, cigars and like products and discarded chewing gum (including bubble gum).

Under s. 91 of the 1990 Act, a magistrates' court may act on a complaint of anyone who is aggrieved by the defacement by litter or refuse of any relevant road, highway or land occupied by relevant statutory undertakers or educational institutions. Before doing so, the court must notify the occupier of the complaint. The court may then issue a litter abatement order requiring the relevant person to remedy the situation and failure to comply with such an order is a summary offence under s. 91(9).

Section 99 of and sch. 4 to the 1990 Act give local authorities powers to deal with problems involving the abandonment of shopping trolleys and luggage trolleys. Schedule 4 allows local authorities (after abiding by the procedure in s. 99) to seize, retain and ultimately dispose of such trolleys. The Clean Neighbourhoods and Environment Act 2005 has extended the powers of local authorities and they can now charge the person believed to be the owner of an abandoned shopping or luggage trolley for its removal, storage and disposal.

Section 87 also states:

(4A) No offence is committed under subsection (1) above where the depositing of the litter is—
   (a) authorised by law; or
   (b) done by or with the consent of the owner, occupier or other person having control of the place where it is deposited.

4.8.10 Begging

Section 3 of the Vagrancy Act 1824 creates the offence of begging or gathering alms in streets and public places. This summary offence is still relevant today. It has been held that the mischief to which the 1824 Act was directed was conduct that forces passers-by to deal with the defendant's activities (*Mathers* v *Penfold* [1915] 1 KB 514) and there is authority to suggest that a single act of approaching one person and asking for money is not, without more, enough to raise a *prima facie* case of begging (*R* v *Dalton* [1982] Crim LR 375). Where the person seeking money is doing something in exchange, such as singing as a busker, it has been held that this conduct does not amount to begging (*Gray* v *Chief Constable of Greater Manchester Police* [1983] Crim LR 45).

There is a further summary offence of 'persistent' begging, and both offences (s. 3 and s. 4) are 'trigger offences' for the purposes of the Criminal Justice and Court Services Act 2000. This has a number of consequences for those charged with such an offence. The principal consequence is that he/she will come within the provisions of s. 63B of the Police and Criminal Evidence Act 1984. This effectively allows (in certain circumstances) for a sample of urine or a non-intimate sample to be taken for the purpose of ascertaining the presence of any specified Class A drug in his/her body.

4.9 | Offences Involving Communications

4.9.1 Introduction

The continual and substantial terrorist threat posed to society makes the offences contained in this chapter exceptionally relevant to day-to-day policing. This chapter details specific offences that deal with the making of general threats and other communications which are intended to cause alarm or anxiety among people receiving them. Such offences are frequently carried out using platforms such as Facebook and Twitter to send malicious messages or make threats, such as in the case of *Chambers v DPP* [2012] EWHC 2157 (Admin) which examined a message interpreted as a bomb hoax at an airport.

4.9.2 Placing or Sending Material

OFFENCE: **Placing or Sending Substances—*Anti-terrorism, Crime and Security Act 2001, s. 114***

- Triable either way • Seven years' imprisonment on indictment
- Six months' imprisonment and/or a fine summarily

The Anti-terrorism, Crime and Security Act 2001, s. 114 states:

(1) A person is guilty of an offence if he—
   (a) places any substance or other thing in any place; or
   (b) sends any substance or other thing from one place to another (by post, rail or any other means whatever);
   with the intention of inducing in a person anywhere in the world a belief that it is likely to be (or contain) a noxious substance or other noxious thing and thereby endanger human life or create a serious risk to human health.

OFFENCE: **Placing or Sending Articles—*Criminal Law Act 1977, s. 51(1)***

- Triable either way • Seven years' imprisonment on indictment
- Six months' imprisonment and/or a fine summarily

The Criminal Law Act 1977, s. 51 states:

(1) A person who—
   (a) places any article in any place whatever; or
   (b) dispatches any article by post, rail or any other means whatever of sending things from one place to another,
   with the intention (in either case) of inducing in some other person a belief that it is likely to explode or ignite and thereby cause personal injury or damage to property is guilty of an offence.

In this subsection 'article' includes substance.

KEYNOTE

These definitions are very wide. The Criminal Law Act 1977 offence relates specifically to bomb threats while the 2001 offence (which is modelled on the earlier offence) relates to 'substances' (which includes any biological agent and any other natural or artificial substance whatever its form, origin or method of production (s. 115(1))).

The offence under the Anti-terrorism, Crime and Security Act 2001 was intended to 'plug the gap' left by the Criminal Law Act 1977 insofar as 'substances' were not catered for in the 1977 Act. Section 114 is far broader: a person is guilty of an offence if he communicates any information which he knows or believes to be false with the intention of inducing in a person anywhere in the world a belief that a noxious substance is likely to be present (whether at the time the information is communicated or later) in any place and thereby endanger human life or create a serious risk to human health. While this is not specifically stated in the 1977 Act, it would therefore appear that the offence under s. 51(1) would take the same approach.

The 'article' concerned in s. 51(1) can also be anything at all.

It is the inducing of a relevant belief in someone else that is the key element to the first offence, not any actual endangering of life or risk to human health. You do not have to show that the defendant had any particular person in mind in whom he/she intended to induce the belief in question (Anti-terrorism, Crime and Security Act 2001, s. 115(2) and Criminal Law Act 1977, s. 51(3)).

The Home Office guidance to the Anti-terrorism, Crime and Security Act 2001 offence gives examples of acts which, though at one time would not have been seen as threatening, would now amount to an offence under this section, for example, scattering white powder in a public place or spraying water droplets around in an underground train, in each case with the requisite intent.

4.9.3   Threats and Communication of False Information

OFFENCE: **Communicating False Information—*Criminal Law Act 1977, s. 51(2)***
- Triable either way • Seven years' imprisonment on indictment
- Six months' imprisonment and/or a fine summarily

The Criminal Law Act 1977, s. 51 states:

(2) A person who communicates any information which he knows or believes to be false to another person with the intention of inducing in him or any other person a false belief that a bomb or other thing liable to explode or ignite is present in any place or location whatever is guilty of an offence.

OFFENCE: **Threats Involving Noxious Substances or Things—*Anti-terrorism, Crime and Security Act 2001, s. 114***
- Triable either way • Seven years' imprisonment on indictment
- Six months' imprisonment and/or a fine summarily

The Anti-terrorism, Crime and Security Act 2001, s. 114 states:

(2) A person is guilty of an offence if he communicates any information which he knows or believes to be false with the intention of inducing in a person anywhere in the world a belief that a noxious substance or other noxious thing is likely to be present (whether at the time the information is communicated or later) in any place and thereby endanger human life or create a serious risk to human health.

KEYNOTE

The essence of these offences is the communication of information which the defendant knows or believes to be false. Again, the 1977 Act offence relates specifically to bomb hoaxes while the 2001 Act offence relates to 'substances'.

The meaning of 'substance' for the 2001 Act offence is the same as in **para. 4.9.2**, Keynote and in neither case is there a need to show that the defendant had any particular person in mind.

Under the Criminal Law Act 1977 it has been held that while the information communicated need not be specific, a message saying that there is a bomb somewhere has been held to be enough, even though no location was given (*R* v *Webb* (1995) 92(27) LSG 31).

The wording of the 1977 Act offence is in the *present* tense which suggests that a message threatening to place a bomb etc. sometime in the *future* would not suffice, while the 2001 Act specifically allows for such a situation.

The use of some form of code word is not a prerequisite of the offence but it does go towards proving the defendant's intention that the threat etc. be taken seriously; it may also be taken into account when passing sentence.

The 'communication' can be in any form (including the Internet) and can be direct (e.g. to a railway station or department store where the bomb or device is alleged to be) or indirect (e.g. to a radio station switchboard).

There is no need for the person making the communication to have any particular person in mind at the time (s. 51(3)).

4.9.4 Misuse and Obstruction of Postal Services

OFFENCE: **Interfering with Mail—*Postal Services Act 2000, s. 84***

- Triable summarily • Six months' imprisonment and/or a fine

The Postal Services Act 2000, s. 84 states:

(1) A person commits an offence if, without reasonable excuse, he—
   (a) intentionally delays or opens a postal packet in the course of its transmission by post, or
   (b) intentionally opens a mail-bag
(2) ...
(3) A person commits an offence if, intending to act to a person's detriment and without reasonable excuse, he opens a postal packet which he knows or reasonably suspects has been incorrectly delivered to him.

KEYNOTE

The Postal Services Act 2000 creates two offences in relation to interfering with the mail, along with a further offence of opening someone else's mail that has been incorrectly delivered.

The first general offence, under s. 84(1), applies to anyone. You must show that the defendant acted without any reasonable excuse and that he/she also acted intentionally. The offence does not apply where the actions were carried out under a lawful warrant or statutory provision (e.g. the Regulation of Investigatory Powers Act 2000). Similarly, any action carried out in accordance with the terms and conditions of postage will not attract criminal liability here. Delays (but not the opening of mail) caused by industrial action also fall outside this offence.

The offence under s. 84(3) requires proof of a number of elements. First, it must be shown that the defendant opened a postal packet (as opposed to delaying it under s. 84(1)). It must also be shown that he/she did so intending 'to act to another person's detriment'; this can be any other person's detriment, not simply the addressee, but it is nevertheless a key feature of the offence. It must also be shown that the defendant knew or reasonably suspected that the postal packet had been incorrectly delivered to him/her. This means that the packet must have been 'delivered'; it would be difficult to show that someone reasonably suspected a packet that is still in transit to have been 'incorrectly delivered' to him/her. As with the general offence under s. 84(1), any opening of postal packets that is done properly in pursuance of a warrant, statutory authority or under the conditions of postage will not be an offence under s. 84(3).

There is a second offence (under s. 83) which specifically applies to postal workers and which is triable either way, carrying a maximum of two years' imprisonment. Under the second, more specific, offence, you have to prove the same elements as the offence under s. 84(1) but also need to show that the person was engaged in the business of a postal operator and that he/she was acting contrary to his/her duty.

4.9.4.1 Sending Prohibited Article by Post

OFFENCE: **Sending Prohibited Article by Post**—*Postal Services Act 2000, s. 85*
- Triable either way • 12 months' imprisonment on indictment
- Fine summarily

The Postal Services Act 2000, s. 85 states:

(1) A person commits an offence if he sends by post a postal packet which encloses any creature, article or thing of any kind which is likely to injure other postal packets in course of their transmission by post or any person engaged in the business of a postal operator.

(2) Subsection (1) does not apply to postal packets which enclose anything permitted (whether generally or specifically) by the postal operator concerned.

(3) A person commits an offence if he sends by post a postal packet which encloses—
  (a) any indecent or obscene print, painting, photograph, lithograph, engraving, cinematograph film or other record of a picture or pictures, book, card or written communication, or
  (b) any other indecent or obscene article (whether or not of a similar kind to those mentioned in paragraph (a)).

(4) A person commits an offence if he sends by post a postal packet which has on the packet, or on the cover of the packet, any words, marks or designs which are of an indecent or obscene character.

KEYNOTE

The first offence addresses the sending of things that are likely to harm either other postal packets or postal workers. Evidence that any article is in the course of transmission by post, or has been accepted by a postal operator for transmission by post, will be enough to prove that it is in fact a 'postal packet' (s. 109). This offence will not apply to the sending of things that are permitted by the relevant postal operator.

The other offences under s. 85 apply irrespective of whether the offending packets are permitted by the postal operator and include indecent or obscene contents or packaging.

Whether an article is obscene etc. is a question of fact for the court to determine in each case. That test will not look at the particular views or frailties of the recipient but will be an objective test based on a reasonable bystander (*Kosmos Publications Ltd* v *DPP* [1975] Crim LR 345).

4.9.4.2 Obstruction of Postal Service

OFFENCE: **Obstruction**—*Postal Services Act 2000, s. 88*
- Triable summarily • Fine

The Postal Services Act 2000, s. 88 states:

(1) A person commits an offence if, without reasonable excuse, he—
  (a) obstructs a person engaged in the business of a universal service provider in the execution of his duty in connection with the provision of a universal postal service, or
  (b) obstructs, while in any universal postal service post office or related premises, the course of business of a universal service provider.

(2) ...

(3) A person commits an offence if without reasonable excuse, he fails to leave a universal postal service post office or related premises when required to do so by a person who—
  (a) is engaged in the business of a universal service provider, and
  (b) reasonably suspects him of committing an offence under subsection (1).

(4) A person who commits an offence under subsection (3)—
  (a) ...
  (b) may be removed by any person engaged in the business of a universal service provider.

4.9.5   Malicious Communications

OFFENCE: **Malicious Communications—*Malicious Communications Act 1988, s. 1(1)***
   • Triable summarily • Six months' imprisonment and/or a fine

The Malicious Communications Act 1988, s. 1 states:

(1) Any person who sends to another person—
   (a) a letter, electronic communication or article of any description which conveys—
      (i)   a message which is indecent or grossly offensive;
      (ii) a threat; or
      (iii) information which is false and known or believed to be false by the sender; or
   (b) any article or electronic communication which is, in whole or part, of an indecent or grossly offensive nature,
   is guilty of an offence if his purpose, or one of his purposes, in sending it is that it should, so far as falling within paragraph (a) or (b) above, cause distress or anxiety to the recipient or to any other person to whom he intends that it or its contents or nature should be communicated.

4.9.5.1 Defence Regarding Malicious Communications

Section 1 of the 1988 Act goes on to state:

> (2) A person is not guilty of an offence by virtue of subsection (1)(a)(ii) above if he shows—
>   (a) that the threat was used to reinforce a demand *made by him on reasonable grounds*; and
>   (b) that he believed, *and had reasonable grounds for believing*, that the use of the threat was a proper means of reinforcing the demand.

KEYNOTE

The italicised words in the offence (author's emphasis) make the relevant test *objective*. It will not be enough that the person claiming the defence under s. 1(2) *subjectively* believed that he/she had reasonable grounds; the defendant will have to show:

- that there were *in fact* reasonable grounds for making the demand;
- that he/she believed that the accompanying threat was a proper means of enforcing the demand; and
- that *reasonable grounds existed* for that belief.

Given the decisions of the courts in similarly worded defences under the Theft Act 1968 (e.g. blackmail; see *Crime*, chapter 1.14), it is unlikely that any demand could be reasonable where agreement to it would amount to a crime.

The defence is intended to cover financial institutions and other commercial concerns which often need to send forceful letters to customers.

4.9.6 Public Communications

OFFENCE: **Improper Use of Public Electronic Communications Network— *Communications Act 2003, s.127***

- Triable summarily • Six months' imprisonment and/or a fine

The Communications Act 2003, s. 127 states:

> (1) A person is guilty of an offence if he—
>   (a) sends by means of a public electronic communications network a message or other matter that is grossly offensive or of an indecent, obscene or menacing character; or
>   (b) causes any such message or matter to be so sent.
> (2) A person is guilty of an offence if, for the purpose of causing annoyance, inconvenience or needless anxiety to another, he—
>   (a) sends by means of a public electronic communications network, a message that he knows to be false;
>   (b) causes such a message to be sent; or
>   (c) persistently makes use of a public electronic communications network.

KEYNOTE

These offences are designed to deal with 'nuisance' calls. They only apply to 'public' electronic communications networks. These are defined as an electronic communications network provided wholly or mainly for the purpose of making electronic communications services available to members of the public (s. 151) and would therefore not generally include internal calls in a workplace.

The wording would apply to the sending of messages via the Internet (provided the system used comes within the definition under s. 151). They also take in public social media systems such as Twitter, as the case of *Chambers* v *DPP* [2012] EWHC 2157 (Admin) has held. This involved a man posting a joke on his Twitter account about a bomb hoax at an airport. He was arrested and charged under s. 127.

There is no need to show a particular 'purpose' (intention) on the part of the defendant for the first offence under s. 127(1) and that offence is complete if the message is, as a matter of fact, grossly offensive, indecent, obscene or menacing.

The offence also covers actions which cause others to send such a message.

Unlike the offence under s. 51(2) of the Criminal Law Act 1977 (see para. 4.9.3), there is no need for any information passed to be 'false'. In determining whether a message is 'grossly offensive', it is the message and not the content that is the basic ingredient of the offence. What constitutes 'grossly offensive' has to be judged by considering the reaction of reasonable people and the standards of an open and just multiracial society (*DPP* v *Collins* [2005] EWHC 1308 (Admin)).

The second offence, under s. 127(2), requires that you show the defendant acted with the purpose of causing annoyance, inconvenience or needless anxiety.

A person is to be treated as 'persistently misusing' a network or service in any case in which his/her misuse is repeated on a sufficient number of occasions for it to be clear that the misuse represents a pattern of behaviour or practice, or recklessness as to whether persons suffer annoyance, inconvenience or anxiety (s. 128(6)).

In assessing these points it is immaterial that the misuse was in relation to a 'network' on some occasions and in relation to a communications 'service' on others, that different networks or services were involved on different occasions or that the people likely to suffer annoyance, inconvenience or anxiety were different on different occasions (s. 128(7)).

This second offence is a 'penalty offence' for the purposes of s. 1 of the Criminal Justice and Police Act 2001.

Where a number of calls have been made to several different people within the community, the offence of public nuisance may also be considered.

4.9.6.1 False Alarms of Fire

OFFENCE: **Making False Alarm of Fire—*Fire and Rescue Services Act 2004, s. 49***
- Triable summarily • Imprisonment for a term not exceeding 51 weeks and/or a fine (In relation to an offence committed before the commencement of s. 281(5) of the Criminal Justice Act 2003, the reference to 51 weeks is to be read as a reference to three months)

The Fire and Rescue Services Act 2004, s. 49 states:

(1) A person commits an offence if he knowingly gives or causes to be given a false alarm of fire to a person acting on behalf of a fire and rescue authority.

KEYNOTE

The offence requires proof that the defendant acted 'knowingly' (as opposed to e.g. mistakenly). The offence clearly applies where someone makes a malicious call to a fire and rescue authority. However, the wording 'causes to be given' potentially covers the making of a false report to a body other than a fire and rescue authority, e.g. the police, if the person knew that this would result in the police passing that call to the relevant fire and rescue authority.

This offence is a 'penalty offence' for the purposes of s. 1 of the Criminal Justice and Police Act 2001.

Terrorism and Associated Offences

4.10.1 Introduction

The law on terrorism contained in this chapter relates to the Terrorism Act 2000, Anti-terrorism, Crime and Security Act 2001, Terrorism Act 2006, Counter-Terrorism Act 2008, Terrorism Prevention and Investigation Measures Act 2011 and the Counter-Terrorism and Security Act 2015.

4.10.2 Terrorism Defined

Terrorism is defined in the Terrorism Act 2000, s. 1 as:

(1) ... the use or threat of action where—
   (a) the action falls within subsection (2),
   (b) the use or threat is designed to influence the government or an international governmental organisation, or to intimidate the public or a section of the public, and
   (c) the use or threat is made for the purpose of advancing a political, religious, ideological or racial cause.
(2) Action falls within this subsection if it—
   (a) involves serious violence against a person,
   (b) involves serious damage to property,
   (c) endangers a person's life, other than that of the person committing the action,
   (d) creates a serious risk to the health or safety of the public or a section of the public, or
   (e) is designed seriously to interfere with or seriously to disrupt an electronic system.
(3) The use or threat of action falling within subsection (2) which involves the use of firearms or explosives is terrorism whether or not subsection (1)(b) is satisfied.

KEYNOTE

This definition includes domestic terrorism, and should be considered when dealing with other, more familiar offences such as blackmail, contamination of goods and threats to kill.

The definition recognises that terrorist activity may be motivated by religious, racial or fundamental reasons rather than simply political ones. It also encompasses broad activities (including threats) which, though potentially devastating in their impact on society, may not be overtly violent. Examples of such activity might be interference with domestic water and power supplies or serious disruption of computer networks.

The provision at s. 1(3) means that, where the relevant criminal activity involves the use of firearms or explosives, there is no further need to show that the behaviour was designed to influence the government or to intimidate the public or a section of the public. An example of such activity might be the shooting of a senior military or political figure. A 'firearm' for this purpose includes air weapons (s. 121); it is not clear whether the definition includes imitation firearms.

The reference to 'action' here includes action outside the United Kingdom. Similarly, references to people, property, the public and governments apply to all those features whether in the United Kingdom or elsewhere (s. 1(4)).

4.10.2.1 Membership of a Proscribed Organisation

OFFENCE: **Membership of a Proscribed Organisation—*Terrorism Act 2000, s. 11***
- Triable either way • 10 years' imprisonment and/or a fine on indictment
- Six months' imprisonment and/or a fine summarily

The Terrorism Act 2000, s. 11 states:

(1) A person commits an offence if he belongs or professes to belong to a proscribed organisation.

(2) It is a defence for a person charged with an offence under subsection (1) to prove—

(a) that the organisation was not proscribed on the last (or only) occasion on which he became a member or began to profess to be a member, and

(b) that he has not taken part in the activities of the organisation at any time while it was proscribed.

KEYNOTE

Specific organisations are proscribed by the Secretary of State and include some of the most active and widely known terrorist groups across the world, including Al-Qa'ida (sch. 2 to the Act). What amounts to membership is likely to depend on the nature of an organisation, e.g. membership of a loose and unstructured organisation may not need any formal steps or express process by which a person becomes a member (*R* v *Ahmed* [2011] EWCA Crim 184).

The reverse burden of proof contained in s. 11(2) has been held as imposing an evidential, as opposed to a persuasive, burden of proof (*Attorney-General's Reference* (*No. 4 of 2002*), *Sheldrake* v *DPP* [2004] UKHL 43).

Other offences relating to proscribed organisations are provided by s. 12 and include: inviting support; arranging or managing (or assisting in doing so) a meeting of three or more people in public or private, to support, further the activities or be addressed by a person belonging to a proscribed organisation; or addressing a meeting to encourage support or further the activities of the organisation.

The Act also created a summary offence of wearing an item of clothing, or wearing, carrying or displaying an article in such a way or in such circumstances as to arouse reasonable suspicion that the defendant is a member or supporter of a proscribed organisation (s. 13).

4.10.3 Terrorism Act 2000: Financial Measures

The main financial measures under the Terrorism Act 2000 relate to terrorist fundraising, possession of property and funding arrangements, and include:

- *inviting* another to provide money or other property (s. 15(1));
- *providing* money or other property (s. 15(3));
- *receiving* money or other property (s. 15(2));
- *possessing* money or other property (s. 16(2));
- *arranging* for money or other property to be made available (s. 17);

in each case intending that, or having reasonable cause to suspect that, it may be used for the purposes of terrorism (ss. 15, 16(2) and 17);

- *using* money or other property for the purposes of terrorism (s. 16(1));
- *concealing, moving or transferring* any terrorist property (s. 18).

Each of these offences is punishable by a maximum of 14 years' imprisonment on indictment (s. 22).

4.10.4 Terrorism Act 2000: Duty of Disclosure and Tipping Off

The 2000 Act creates a number of offences in relation to the unlawful disclosure of information and provides where disclosure is permissible.

4.10.4.1 Disclosure of Information

OFFENCE: **Disclosure of Information—*Terrorism Act 2000, s. 19***
- • Triable either way • Five years' imprisonment and/or a fine on indictment
- • Six months' imprisonment and/or a fine summarily

The Terrorism Act 2000, s. 19 states:

(1) This section applies where a person—
  (a) believes or suspects that another person has committed an offence under any of sections 15 to 18, and
  (b) bases his belief or suspicion on information which comes to his attention—
    (i) in the course of a trade, profession or business, or
    (ii) in the course of his employment (whether or not in the course of a trade, profession or business).
(1A) But this section does not apply if the information came to the person in the course of a business in the regulated sector.
(2) The person commits an offence if he does not disclose to a constable as soon as is reasonably practicable—
  (a) his belief or suspicion, and
  (b) the information on which it is based.

KEYNOTE

In relation to s. 19(2), a constable includes an authorised member of staff of the National Crime Agency (s. 19(7B)).

This section requires banks and other businesses to report any suspicions they may have that someone is laundering terrorist money or committing any of the other terrorist property offences in ss. 15 to 18. Section 19(1)(b) ensures the offence is focused on suspicions which arise at work.

'Employment' means any employment (paid or unpaid) including work under a contract for services or as an office holder, work experience provided pursuant to a training course or programme or in the course of training for employment, and voluntary work (s. 22A).

It is a defence for a person to prove that he/she had a reasonable excuse for not making the disclosure (s. 19(3)), or that the matters specified were disclosed in accordance with an established procedure for the making of disclosures (s. 19(4)). Disclosure by a professional legal adviser is not required if the information was obtained in privileged circumstances (s. 19(5)).

The Act also provides for offences of failure to disclose information in the 'regulated sector', i.e. accountancy firms, investment companies, etc. (s. 21A) and tipping-off in the regulated sector (s. 21D).

4.10.4.2 Disclosure of Information: Permission

The Terrorism Act 2000, s. 20 states:

(1) A person may disclose to a constable—
  (a) a suspicion or belief that any money or other property is terrorist property or is derived from terrorist property;
  (b) any matter on which the suspicion or belief is based.
(2) A person may make a disclosure to a constable in the circumstances mentioned in section 19(1) and (2).
(3) Subsections (1) and (2) shall have effect notwithstanding any restriction on the disclosure of information imposed by statute or otherwise.
(4) Where—
  (a) a person is in employment, and

(b) his employer has established a procedure for the making of disclosures of the kinds mentioned in subsection (1) and section 19(2),

subsections (1) and (2) shall have effect in relation to that person as if any reference to disclosure to a constable included a reference to disclosure in accordance with the procedure.

KEYNOTE

Section 20 ensures that businesses can disclose information to the police without fear of breaching legal restrictions.

4.10.4.3 Information about Acts of Terrorism

OFFENCE: **Information about Acts of Terrorism—*Terrorism Act 2000, s. 38B***
- Triable either way • Five years' imprisonment and/or a fine on indictment
- Six months' imprisonment and/or a fine summarily

The Terrorism Act 2000, s. 38B states:

(1) This section applies where a person has information which he knows or believes might be of material assistance—
   (a) in preventing the commission by another person of an act of terrorism, or
   (b) in securing the apprehension, prosecution or conviction of another person, in the United Kingdom, for an offence involving the commission, preparation or instigation of an act of terrorism.
(2) The person commits an offence if he does not disclose the information as soon as reasonably practicable in accordance with subsection (3).
(3) Disclosure is in accordance with this subsection if it is made—
   (a) in England and Wales, to a constable …

KEYNOTE

This offence relates to any person who has information that he/she knows or believes might help prevent an act of terrorism or help bring terrorists to justice.

A person resident in the United Kingdom could be charged with this offence notwithstanding that he/she was outside the country when he/she became aware of the information (s. 38B(6)).

It is a defence for a person charged to prove that he/she had a reasonable excuse for not making the disclosure (s. 38B(4)).

4.10.4.4 Disclosure of and Interference with Information Offences

OFFENCE: **Disclosure of Information etc.—*Terrorism Act 2000, s. 39***
- Triable either way • Five years' imprisonment and/or a fine on indictment
- Six months' imprisonment and/or a fine summarily

The Terrorism Act 2000, s. 39 states:

(1) Subsection (2) applies where a person knows or has reasonable cause to suspect that a constable is conducting or proposes to conduct a terrorist investigation.
(2) The person commits an offence if he—
   (a) discloses to another anything which is likely to prejudice the investigation, or
   (b) interferes with material which is likely to be relevant to the investigation.
(3) Subsection (4) applies where a person knows or has reasonable cause to suspect that a disclosure has been or will be made under any of sections 19 to 21B or 38B.
(4) The person commits an offence if he—
   (a) discloses to another anything which is likely to prejudice an investigation resulting from the disclosure under that section, or
   (b) interferes with material which is likely to be relevant to an investigation resulting from the disclosure under that section.

4.10.5 Terrorism Act 2000: Other Offences

The Terrorism Act 2000 also creates a number of other offences in relation to terrorism. In summary, the key offences are:

- *Directing* the activities of an organisation which is concerned in the commission of acts of terrorism (s. 56). This offence (which is often easier to prove than some of the better known offences) carries a maximum sentence of life imprisonment.

- *Providing or receiving instruction or training* in the making or use of firearms or explosives or radioactive material or weapons designed or adapted for the discharge of any radioactive material, or chemical, biological or nuclear weapons (s. 54).

- *Possessing articles* in circumstances which give rise to a reasonable suspicion that the possession is for a purpose connected with the commission, preparation or instigation of an act of terrorism (s. 57). It must be shown that the defendant(s) possessed extremist material for use in the future to incite the commission of terrorist acts (*R v Zafar* [2008] EWCA Crim 184). See also *R v G*; *R v J* [2009] UKHL 13.

- *Collecting or making a record* of information (including photographs and electronic records) of a kind likely to be useful to a person committing or preparing an act of terrorism, or possessing a document or record containing information of that kind (s. 58). The document, etc. concerned must be of a kind that is likely to provide practical assistance to a person, rather than simply encouraging the commission of terrorist acts (*R v K* [2008] EWCA Crim 185) and *R v Muhammed* [2010] EWCA Crim 227. The prosecution only has to prove that the material could be useful to a terrorist. It does not have to prove the information is true as it is possible to prove that something is likely to be useful even though not true (*R v Amjad* [2016] EWCA Crim 1618). In *R v Brown* [2011] EWCA Crim 2751, it was held that s. 58 did not infringe the appellant's right to free speech under Article 10 of the European Convention on Human Rights, insofar as it penalised the collection and distribution of materials and advice (*The Anarchist Cookbook*) on bomb-making, poisoning and other such activities. This ruling also applies to s. 2 of the Terrorism Act 2006.

- *Eliciting or attempting to elicit* information about a member of the armed forces or the intelligence services or a constable, which is likely to be useful to a person committing or preparing an act of terrorism, or publishing or communicating information of that kind (s. 58A).

- *Inciting* another person to commit an act of terrorism wholly or partly outside the United Kingdom (s. 59).

- *Terrorist bombing and financing terrorists* outside the United Kingdom (ss. 62 and 63).

- *Extended jurisdiction for offences committed abroad for terrorist purposes* (ss. 63A to 63E). These provisions extend the jurisdiction of the UK courts to deal with offences outside it by or against persons associated with the United Kingdom, e.g. UK nationals and UK residents.

4.10.6 Terrorism Act 2006: Offences

For the purposes of the 2006 Act the offences are grouped into three specific areas; encouragement etc. of terrorism; preparation of terrorist acts and terrorist training; offences involving radioactive devices and materials and nuclear facilities and sites.

4.10.6.1 Encouragement etc. of Terrorism

The offences within this group are:

- publishes a statement to encourage the commission, preparation or instigation of acts of terrorism or Convention offences (s. 1(2));
- engages in the dissemination of terrorist publications (s. 2(1)).

For the purposes of both these sections it is necessary to prove that they glorify the act of terrorism and that members of the public could reasonably be expected to infer that what is being glorified is being glorified as conduct that should be copied by them in existing circumstances. 'Glorification' includes any form of praise or celebration, and similar expressions are to be construed accordingly (s. 20(2)). The 'Convention offences' mentioned in s. 1(2) are those offences listed in sch. 1 to the Act and include offences in relation to explosives, biological weapons, chemical weapons, nuclear weapons, hostage-taking, hijacking, terrorist funds, etc.

In relation to an offence under s. 2 of the Act it was held that videos uploaded onto the Internet of scenes showing attacks on soldiers of the Coalition forces in Iraq and Afghanistan by insurgents were depicting scenes of terrorism within the definition of s. 1 of the 2000 Act (*R* v *Gul* [2013] UKSC 64). Under this section, although the accused is free to argue that the prosecution constituted an unacceptable interference with the applicant's right to freedom of speech at common law, this defence is always a matter to be determined by the jury (*R* v *Brown* [2011] EWCA Crim 2751). In *Faraz* v *R* [2012] EWCA Crim 2820, it was held that evidence of possession of a publication cannot prove by itself that a person was encouraged by it to commit or instigate terrorist offences.

Section 3(1) provides that the offences under ss. 1 and 2 can be committed by publishing a statement electronically, i.e. via the Internet. In *Iqbal* v *R* [2014] EWCA Crim 2650 the defendant posted and shared videos, articles and lectures that amounted to the glorification or encouragement of terrorism. 'Statement' includes a communication of any description, including a communication without words consisting of sounds or images or both (s. 20(6)). Section 3(3) provides for a notice to be served by a constable on the person electronically publishing the statement declaring that it is, in the constable's opinion, unlawfully terrorism-related and requiring its removal or modification (s. 3(3)). The methods for giving such a notice are provided in s. 4 of the Act. The offences under ss. 1 and 2 are punishable on indictment by a term of imprisonment not exceeding seven years or a fine or both, and summarily by a term of imprisonment not exceeding six months or a fine or both.

4.10.6.2 Preparation of Terrorist Acts and Terrorist Training

The offences within this group are:

- preparation for terrorist acts (s. 5(1));
- providing instruction or training in any of the skills mentioned for the commission or preparation of acts of terrorism or Convention offences (s. 6(1));
- receiving instruction or training in any of the skills mentioned for the commission or preparation of acts of terrorism or Convention offences (s. 6(2));
- attendance at a place used for terrorist training s. 8(1)).

For an offence under s. 5(1) it is irrelevant whether the intention and preparations relate to one or more particular acts of terrorism, acts of terrorism of a particular description or acts of terrorism generally (s. 5(2) (*R* v *Roddis* [2009] EWCA Crim 585; *R* v *Khan* [2013] EWCA Crim 468). The punishment for an offence under this section is imprisonment for life.

In relation to the offences of providing or receiving instruction or training under s. 6, the skills mentioned include: the making, handling or use of a noxious substance; the use of any method or technique for doing anything capable of being done for the purposes of terrorism; and the design or adaptation for the purposes of terrorism of any method or technique for doing anything. In *R* v *Da Costa* [2009] EWCA Crim 482, it was held that the person delivering the training had to know that one or more of those receiving it intended to use it for a terrorist purpose.

The offence under s. 8(1) may be committed either in the United Kingdom or elsewhere. It must be shown that the person either knew or believed that the instruction or training was wholly or partly for purposes connected with the commission or preparation of acts of terrorism, or that the person could not reasonably have failed to understand the purpose of such instruction or training (s. 8(2)).

The punishment for offences under s. 6(1), 6(2) and 8(1) is on indictment a term of imprisonment not exceeding 10 years and/or a fine, and on summary conviction imprisonment for a term not exceeding six months and/or a fine.

4.10.6.3 Radioactive Devices, Materials and Nuclear Facilities

The offences within this group are:

- making and possession of devices or materials (s. 9(1) of the 2006 Act);
- misuse of devices or material and misuse and damage of facilities (s. 10 of the 2006 Act);
- terrorist threats relating to devices, materials or facilities (s. 11 of the 2006 Act);
- use or threat of use of noxious substance or things to cause harm or intimidate (s. 113 of the Anti-terrorism, Crime and Security Act 2001);
- hoaxes involving noxious substances or things (s. 114 of the 2001 Act).

For offences under the 2006 Act the punishment is imprisonment for life, and for the two offences under the Anti-terrorism, Crime and Security Act 2001 the punishment is imprisonment up to 14 years and/or a fine.

In addition to the above offences, there is also an offence of trespassing on a nuclear site contained in s. 128(1) of the Serious Organised Crime and Police Act 2005 (**see para. 4.16.7**).

There are other legislative provisions relating to biological, chemical and nuclear weapons contained in the Biological Weapons Act 1974, the Chemical Weapons Act 1996 and the Nuclear Material (Offences) Act 1983. However, there is no requirement to prove actions were for terrorist purposes for offences under these statutes.

4.10.7 Terrorism Act 2000: Police Powers

The Terrorism Act 2000 provides the police with many wide-ranging powers which exist *in addition* to any more general powers that the police may have. They include powers of arrest, search of persons and vehicles, authorisations of stop and search in specified locations, and the power to set up cordons.

4.10.7.1 Arrest without Warrant

The Terrorism Act 2000, s. 41 states:

(1) A constable may arrest without a warrant a person whom he reasonably suspects to be a terrorist.

4.10.7.2 Search of Persons

The Terrorism Act 2000, s. 43 states:

(1) A constable may stop and search a person whom he reasonably suspects to be a terrorist to discover whether he has in his possession anything which may constitute evidence that he is a terrorist.

(2) A constable may search a person arrested under section 41 to discover whether he has in his possession anything which may constitute evidence that he is a terrorist.

(3) ...

(4) A constable may seize and retain anything which he discovers in the course of a search of a person under subsection (1) or (2) and which he reasonably suspects may constitute evidence that the person is a terrorist.

(4A) Subsection (4B) applies if a constable, in exercising the power under subsection (1) to stop a person whom the constable reasonably suspects to be a terrorist, stops a vehicle (see section 116(2)).

4.10.7.3 Search of Vehicles

The Terrorism Act 2000, s. 43A states:

(1) Subsection (2) applies if a constable reasonably suspects that a vehicle is being used for the purposes of terrorism.

(2) The constable may stop and search—

(a) the vehicle;

(b) the driver of the vehicle;

(c) a passenger in the vehicle;

(d) anything in or on the vehicle or carried by the driver or a passenger;

to discover whether there is anything which may constitute evidence that the vehicle is being used for the purposes of terrorism.

'Driver' in relation to an aircraft, hovercraft or vessel, means the captain, pilot or other person with control of the aircraft, hovercraft or vessel or any member of its crew and, in relation to a train, includes any member of its crew (s. 43A(5)).

The Terrorism Act 2000 (Codes of Practice for the Exercise of Stop and Search Powers) Order 2012 (SI 2012/1794) provided Codes of Practice for the exercise of stop and search powers under ss. 43 and 43A of the Terrorism Act 2000, and the authorisation and exercise of stop and search powers relating to s. 47A of, and sch. 6B to, the Terrorism Act 2000.

4.10.7.4 Stop and Search in Specified Locations

The Terrorism Act 2000, s. 47A states:

(1) A senior police officer may give an authorisation under subsection (2) or (3) in relation to a specified area or place if the officer—
    (a) reasonably suspects that an act of terrorism will take place; and
    (b) reasonably considers that—
        (i) the authorisation is necessary to prevent such an act;
        (ii) the specified area or place is no greater than is necessary to prevent such an act; and
        (iii) the duration of the authorisation is no longer than is necessary to prevent such an act.
(2) An authorisation under this subsection authorises any constable in uniform to stop a vehicle in the specified area or place and to search—
    (a) the vehicle;
    (b) the driver of the vehicle;
    (c) a passenger in the vehicle;
    (d) anything in or on the vehicle or carried by the driver or a passenger.
(3) An authorisation under this subsection authorises any constable in uniform to stop a pedestrian in the specified area or place and to search—
    (a) the pedestrian;
    (b) anything carried by the pedestrian.

KEYNOTE

A constable in uniform may exercise the power conferred by an authorisation only for the purpose of discovering whether there is anything which may constitute evidence that the vehicle concerned is being used for the purposes of terrorism or (as the case may be) that the person concerned is a terrorist within the meaning of s. 40 (s. 47A(4)). However, the power conferred by such an authorisation may be exercised whether or not the constable reasonably suspects that there is such evidence (s. 47A(5)).

A constable may seize and retain anything which the constable discovers in the course of a search if he/she reasonably suspects that it may constitute evidence that the vehicle concerned is being used for the purposes of terrorism or (as the case may be) that the person is a terrorist (s. 47A(6)).

A 'senior police officer' who may give an authorisation is a police officer for the area who is of at least the rank of assistant chief constable (or commander) (sch. 6B).

4.10.7.5 Designated Cordoned Areas

The Terrorism Act 2000, s. 33 states:

(1) An area is a cordoned area for the purposes of this Act if it is designated under this section.
(2) A designation may be made only if the person making it considers it expedient for the purposes of a terrorist investigation.
(3) If a designation is made orally, the person making it shall confirm it in writing as soon as is reasonably practicable.

4.10.7.6 Power to Designate

The Terrorism Act 2000, s. 34 states:

(1) Subject to subsections (1A), (1B) and (2), a designation under section 33 may only be made—
   (a) where the area is outside Northern Ireland and is wholly or partly within a police area, by an officer for the police area who is of at least the rank of superintendent, and
   (b) ...

(1A) ...

(1B) ...

(1C) ...

(2) A constable who is not of the rank required by subsection (1) may make a designation if he considers it necessary by reason of urgency.

(3) Where a constable makes a designation in reliance on subsection (2) he shall as soon as is reasonably practicable—
   (a) make a written record of the time at which the designation was made, and
   (b) ensure that a police officer of at least the rank of superintendent is informed.

(4) An officer who is informed of a designation in accordance with subsection (3)(b)—
   (a) shall confirm the designation or cancel it with effect from such time as he may direct, and
   (b) shall, if he cancels the designation, make a written record of the cancellation and the reason for it.

4.10.7.7 Cordons and Police Powers

The Terrorism Act 2000, s. 36 states:

(1) A constable in uniform may—
   (a) order a person in a cordoned area to leave it immediately,
   (b) order a person immediately to leave premises which are wholly or partly in or adjacent to a cordoned area,

(c) order the driver or person in charge of a vehicle in a cordoned area to move it from the area immediately,

(d) arrange for the removal of a vehicle from a cordoned area,

(e) arrange for the movement of a vehicle within a cordoned area,

(f) prohibit or restrict access to a cordoned area by pedestrians or vehicles.

KEYNOTE

The officer giving the order or making the arrangements and prohibitions set out here must be in uniform. Therefore detectives or other plain clothes officers involved in the terrorist investigation will not have these powers available to them.

The powers under s. 36 are among those that can be conferred on a Police Community Support Officer designated under sch. 4 to the Police Reform Act 2002.

Failing to comply with an order, prohibition or restriction under this section is a summary offence punishable by three months' imprisonment and/or a fine (s. 36(2) and (4)).

This wording will presumably cover refusal. There is a defence if the person can show that he/she had a reasonable excuse for the failure.

A superintendent or above may request passenger, service and crew information from an owner or agent of a ship or aircraft which is arriving, or expected to arrive, at any place in the United Kingdom or is leaving, or expected to leave, from any place in the United Kingdom (Immigration, Asylum and Nationality Act 2006, s. 32(2)). There is a similar power to request freight information from the owners or agents of a ship or aircraft, and in the case of a vehicle, the owner or hirer (s. 33(2) and (3)).

It is an offence if without reasonable excuse a person fails to comply with a requirement imposed under ss. 32(2) or 33(2). The request must be for a police purpose, i.e. the prevention, detection, investigation or prosecution of criminal offences; safeguarding national security; and such other purposes as may be specified (s. 33(5)).

4.10.8   Terrorism Prevention and Investigation Measures

Terrorism Prevention and Investigation Measures (TPIMs), created by the Terrorism Prevention and Investigation Measures Act 2011, are a civil preventative measure intended to protect the public from the risk posed by suspected terrorists who can be neither prosecuted nor, in the case of foreign nationals, deported, by the Secretary of State imposing restrictions intended to prevent or disrupt their engagement in terrorism-related activity.

KEYNOTE

The measures that may be imposed by the Secretary of State are set out in sch. 1 to the 2011 Act and have a time limit of two years. They may regulate a person's overnight place of residence, restrict travel outside the area of residence, prevent contact with particular individuals, prohibit possession of firearms, offensive weapons and explosives, and require daily reporting to a police station.

It is an offence for a person to contravene, without reasonable excuse, any measure specified in a TPIM (s. 23(1)). The offence is triable either way and is punishable on summary conviction with up to six months' imprisonment and/or a fine, and on indictment with up to five years' imprisonment and/or a fine.

4.10.8.1   Terrorism Prevention and Investigation Measures: Police Powers

The Terrorism Prevention and Investigation Measures Act 2011, sch. 5 states:

1 This Schedule confers powers of entry, search, seizure and retention on constables in connection with the imposition of measures on individuals.

2 A power conferred on a constable by virtue of this Schedule—

(a) is additional to powers which the constable has at common law or by virtue of any other enactment, and

(b) is not to be taken as affecting those powers.

3 A constable may detain an individual for the purpose of carrying out a search of that individual under a power conferred by virtue of this Schedule.

4 A constable may use reasonable force, if necessary, for the purpose of exercising a power conferred on the constable by virtue of this Schedule.

KEYNOTE

The PACE Code of Practice for the Exercise by Police Officers of Statutory Powers of Stop and Search (Code A) (2015) in relation to searches under sch. 5 of the 2011 Act is reproduced at **para. 4.5.4**.

4.10.9   Offences Involving Explosive Substances

OFFENCE: **Causing Explosion Likely to Endanger Life or Property—*Explosive Substances Act 1883, s. 2***

  • Triable on indictment • Life imprisonment

The Explosive Substances Act 1883, s. 2 states:

(1) A person who in the United Kingdom or (being a citizen of the United Kingdom and Colonies) in the Republic of Ireland unlawfully and maliciously causes by any explosive substance an explosion of a nature likely to endanger life or to cause serious injury to property shall, whether any injury to person or property has been actually caused or not, be guilty of an offence.

KEYNOTE

The consent of the Attorney-General (or Solicitor-General) is required before prosecuting this offence (s. 7(1) of the 1883 Act).

'Explosive substance' includes any materials for making any explosive substance; any implement or apparatus used, or intended or adapted to be used for causing or aiding any explosion (s. 9(1)).

The definition of 'explosive' under the Explosives Act 1875 also applies to this offence (*R* v *Wheatley* [1979] 1 WLR 144). Therefore fireworks and petrol bombs will be covered (*R* v *Bouch* [1983] QB 246).

Articles which have been held to amount to 'explosive substances' include:

• shotguns (*R* v *Downey* [1971] NI 224);

• electronic timers (*R* v *Berry (No. 3)* [1995] 1 WLR 7; *R* v *G* [2009] UKHL 13);

• gelignite with a fuse and detonator (*R* v *McCarthy* [1964] 1 WLR 196).

You must prove that the act was carried out 'maliciously'.

Sections 73 to 75 of the Explosives Act 1875 provide powers to search for explosives in connection with the offences under ss. 2, 3 and 4.

OFFENCE: **Attempting to Cause Explosion or Keeping Explosive with Intent— *Explosive Substances Act 1883, s. 3***

  • Triable on indictment • Life imprisonment

The Explosive Substances Act 1883, s. 3 states:

(1) A person who in the United Kingdom or a dependency or (being a citizen of the United Kingdom and Colonies) elsewhere unlawfully and maliciously—

(a) does any act with intent to cause, or conspires to cause, by an explosive substance an explosion of a nature likely to endanger life, or cause serious injury to property, whether in the United Kingdom or elsewhere, or

(b) makes or has in his possession or under his control an explosive substance with intent by means thereof to endanger life, or cause serious injury to property, whether in the United Kingdom or elsewhere, or to enable any other person so to do

shall, whether any explosion does or does not take place, and whether any injury to person or property is actually caused or not, be guilty of an offence ...

OFFENCE: **Making or Possessing Explosive under Suspicious Circumstances— *Explosive Substances Act 1883, s. 4***

  • Triable on indictment • 14 years' imprisonment

The Explosive Substances Act 1883, s. 4 states:

(1) Any person who makes or knowingly has in his possession or under his control any explosive substance under such circumstances as to give rise to a reasonable suspicion that he is not making it or does not have it in his possession or under his control for a lawful object, shall, unless he can show that he made it or had it in his possession or under his control for a lawful object, be guilty of [an offence] ...

KEYNOTE

The offence under s. 3 is one of specific intent.

Both of the offences under ss. 3 and 4 require the consent of the Attorney-General (or Solicitor-General) before a prosecution can be brought.

In cases of 'possession' the wording of these offences requires the prosecution to prove that a defendant *had* the relevant article in his/her possession and that he/she *knew* the nature of it (*R v Hallam* [1957] 1 QB 569). This should be contrasted with the usual approach to offences involving 'possession' where the second part (knowledge of the 'quality' of an item) does not need to be shown. However, the concept of 'in your possession' or 'under your control' is a wide one, as illustrated in a case where the defendant had moved out of his property and left homemade bombs and other articles in some boxes with a friend. New tenants in the property had discovered the boxes which later turned up on a rubbish tip. The defendant went to the police station after learning that he was a suspect and he claimed that he had collected the articles many years previously when he was too young to appreciate how dangerous they were. Although he had left the boxes with his friend he was nevertheless convicted of the offence under s. 4(1) as he still had the explosives under his control when he left the property (*R v Campbell* [2004] EWCA Crim 2309).

'Reasonable suspicion' in this case will be assessed *objectively*, that is, you must prove that the circumstances of the possession or making of the explosive substance would give rise to suspicion in a reasonable and objective bystander (*R v Fegan* (1971) 78 Cr App R 189; *R v G* [2009] UKHL 13).

Whether a person's purpose in having the items prohibited by these offences is a 'lawful object' will need to be determined in each case (*Fegan*). In *R v Riding* [2009] EWCA Crim 892, the defendant alleged he had made a pipe bomb out of mere curiosity, using explosives drained from a number of fireworks. The defence contended that 'lawful object' meant the absence of a criminal purpose rather than a positive object that was lawful. However, the court was satisfied it meant the latter and mere curiosity could not be a 'lawful object' in making a lethal pipe bomb.

There is no need to show any criminal intent or an unlawful purpose on the part of the defendant (see *Campbell*).

4.10.10 Offences Relating to Gunpowder

The Offences Against the Person Act 1981 creates further offences in relation to gunpowder:

• causing bodily injury by gunpowder or other explosive substance (s. 28);
• causing gunpowder or other explosive substance to explode, sending an explosive substance or throwing corrosive fluid with intent (s. 29);

- placing gunpowder or other explosive substance near a building, ship or vessel with intent to do bodily injury to any person (s. 30);
- making or having gunpowder, explosive substance, or any dangerous or noxious thing, or any machine, engine, instrument, or thing with intent to enable any person to commit any of the felonies in this Act (s. 64).

All offences are triable on indictment only. Section 28 and 29 offences have a maximum penalty of imprisonment for life; s. 30 offences imprisonment for up to 14 years; and s. 64 offences imprisonment for up to two years.

4.10.11   Animal Experiments and Vivisection

The activities of anti-vivisection campaigners and others opposed to the 'commercial exploitation' of animals have led to specific changes in legislation and also significant policing operations to protect individuals who work with animals in certain circumstances.

The Serious Organised Crime and Police Act 2005 provides two offences in relation to animal research organisations.

4.10.11.1   Interference with Contractual Relationship so as to Harm Animal Research Organisation

OFFENCE: **Interference with Contractual Relationships so as to Harm Animal Research Organisation—*Serious Organised Crime and Police Act 2005, s. 145(1)***
  - Triable either way • Five years' imprisonment and/or a fine on indictment
  - 12 months' imprisonment and/or a fine summarily

The Serious Organised Crime and Police Act 2005, s. 145 states:

(1) A person (A) commits an offence if, with the intention of harming an animal research organisation, he—
  (a) does a relevant act, or
  (b) threatens that he or somebody else will do a relevant act, in circumstances in which that act or threat is intended or likely to cause a second person (B) to take any of the steps in subsection (2).
(2) The steps are—
  (a) not to perform any contractual obligation owed by B to a third person (C) (whether or not such non-performance amounts to a breach of contract);
  (b) to terminate any contract B has with C;
  (c) not to enter into a contract with C.
(3) For the purposes of this section, a 'relevant act' is—
  (a) an act amounting to a criminal offence, or
  (b) a tortious act causing B to suffer loss or damage of any description;
  but paragraph (b) does not include an act which is actionable on the ground only that it induces another person to break a contract with B.

KEYNOTE

To commit this offence the defendant needs to do a relevant act. This means a criminal offence or a tortious act causing loss or damage or to threaten that he/she or another will commit a crime or such a tortious act. A tortious act is an act that is a civil wrong but is not a criminal offence. It then needs to be shown that the conduct of the defendant was likely or intended to cause the person against whom the crime/tortious act is committed (or threatened) to fail to perform a contractual obligation, to terminate a contract or to decide not to enter into a contract.

The intent to harm an animal research organisation needs to be proved. 'Animal research organisation' has two specific meanings for the purposes of ss. 145 and 146:

- A person or organisation who is the owner, lessee or licensee of premises constituting or including:
    + a place specified in a licence granted under ss. 4 or 5 of the Animals (Scientific Procedures) Act 1986,
    + a scientific procedure establishment designated under s. 6 of that Act, or
    + a breeding or supplying establishment designated under s. 7 of that Act. (s. 148(2)).
- A person or organisation employed or engaged under a contract for services, as:
    + the holder of a personal or project licence granted under the 1986 Act,
    + a person specified under ss. 6(5) or 7(5) of that Act

(s. 148(3)).

'Harming' an animal research organisation means to cause such an organisation loss or damage of any description, or to prevent or hinder such an organisation from carrying on any of its activities (s. 145(5)).

By virtue of s. 145(3)(b), no offence is committed if the only relevant tortious act is an inducement to break a contract. This means that no offence is committed by people peacefully arguing, or representing, that one person should cease doing business with another on the basis of the other's involvement with an animal research organisation.

Generally this section does not apply to any act done wholly or mainly in contemplation or furtherance of a trade dispute (s. 145(6)). However, there are some changes to the definition of such a dispute that need to be taken into account (s. 145(7)).

No proceedings for an offence under either of those sections may be instituted except by or with the consent of the DPP.

4.10.11.2   Intimidation of Persons Connected with Animal Research Organisation

OFFENCE: **Intimidation of Persons Connected with Animal Research Organisation—*Serious Organised Crime and Police Act 2005, s. 146(1)***
- Triable either way • Five years' imprisonment and/or a fine on indictment
- 12 months' imprisonment and/or a fine summarily

The Serious Organised Crime and Police Act 2005, s. 146 states:

(1) A person (A) commits an offence if, with the intention of causing a second person (B) to abstain from doing something which B is entitled to do (or to do something which B is entitled to abstain from doing)—

  (a) A threatens B that A or somebody else will do a relevant act, and

  (b) A does so wholly or mainly because B is a person falling within subsection (2).

KEYNOTE

In summary, a person falls within subsection (2) if he/she is:

- an employee or officer of an animal research organisation;
- a student at an educational establishment that is an animal research organisation;
- a lessor or licensor of any premises occupied by an animal research organisation;
- a person with a financial interest in, or who provides financial assistance to, an animal research organisation;
- a customer or supplier of an animal research organisation (s. 146(2)).

A person who is contemplating becoming someone within the categories covered by the third, fourth and fifth bullet points is covered, as is a person who is (or is contemplating becoming) a customer or supplier of such people/organisations.

Employees and employers of someone within these descriptions are covered, as are people with a financial interest in, or providing financial assistance to the above.

Subsection (2) also extends to spouses, civil partners, friends or relatives, or people known personally to someone within any of these descriptions.

As with the offence under s. 145, this section does not generally apply to any act done wholly or mainly in contemplation or furtherance of a trade dispute and no proceedings for an offence under either of those sections may be instituted except by or with the consent of the DPP.

4.11 Public Order, Processions and Assemblies

4.11.1 Introduction

The principal piece of legislation dealing with public order is the Public Order Act 1986. While this chapter examines some of the more well-known elements of this legislation it also looks at other laws (e.g. the Anti-social Behaviour Act 2003) that contain provisions in relation to the behaviour of citizens as well as the common law offence of breach of the peace. The European Convention on Human Rights will continue to have a significant impact on a number of the areas concerned within this chapter and especially Article 10 (Freedom of Expression) and Article 11 (Freedom of Assembly and Association). These two Articles are discussed in the following paragraphs.

4.11.1.1 Article 10—Freedom of Expression

Article 10 of the Convention states:

1. Everyone has the right to freedom of expression. This right shall include freedom to hold opinions and to receive and impart information and ideas without interference by public authority and regardless of frontiers. This Article shall not prevent States from requiring the licensing of broadcasting, television or cinema enterprises.
2. The exercise of these freedoms, since it carries with it duties and responsibilities, may be subject to such formalities, conditions, restrictions or penalties as are prescribed by law and are necessary in a democratic society, in the interests of national security, territorial integrity or public safety, for the prevention of disorder or crime, for the protection of health or morals, for the protection of the reputation or rights of others, for preventing the disclosure of information received in confidence, or for maintaining the authority and impartiality of the judiciary.

KEYNOTE

Article 10 protects the freedom:

- of expression,
- to hold opinions, and
- to receive and impart information and ideas

in each case without interference by a public authority.

'Expression' here includes the creation of pictures and images (*Stevens* v *United Kingdom* (1986) 46 DR 245).

Although not providing a general 'right to freedom of information', Article 10 has been used in a number of different settings including the protection of artistic, political and economic expression. It has been used to protect journalists' sources (*Goodwin* v *United Kingdom* (1996) 22 EHRR 123).

As the right to express freely has to be balanced against the rights of others and the needs of democratic society generally, this area of Convention rights has generated some considerable problems and is often intermingled with issues of freedom of thought, conscience and religion (under Article 9).

In a case where the defendant damaged the perimeter fence of a Trident defence base, the Divisional Court held that her acts could be characterised as an expression of her opinion under Article 10 but that the Convention required the expression of that opinion to be proportionate. There were other ways in which the

---

defendant could have expressed her opinion without committing a crime and therefore her conviction for criminal damage was upheld (*Hutchinson* v *DPP* (2000) *The Independent*, 20 November).

Article 10(1) is drafted to allow for State licensing of broadcasts, television and cinema performances but, as you might expect, the courts will be unlikely to tolerate interference with the freedom of expression without compelling reasons. Once again, the courts will look for a 'pressing social need' and, indeed, one of the main cases setting out the requirement for proportionality (*Handyside* v *United Kingdom* (1979–80) 1 EHRR 737) involved an action under Article 10.

Article 10(2) clearly allows for an individual's freedom of expression to be curtailed under a number of circumstances including the prevention of disorder or crime and the protection of morals. Balancing these competing needs is one area where the European Court of Human Rights has allowed a reasonable 'margin of appreciation'. Nevertheless, any restrictions on an individual's freedom of expression will be narrowly construed and closely scrutinised. It has been held that the exercise of the right to free speech could fall within the concept of harassment for the purposes of the Protection from Harassment Act 1997 where the ingredients for the offence were present (*Howlett* v *Harding* [2006] EWHC 41 (QB)).

4.11.1.2 Article 11—Freedom of Assembly and Association

Article 11 of the Convention states:

1. Everyone has the right to freedom of peaceful assembly and to freedom of association with others, including the right to form and to join trade unions for the protection of his interests.
2. No restrictions shall be placed on the exercise of these rights other than such as are prescribed by law and are necessary in a democratic society in the interests of national security or public safety, for the prevention of disorder or crime, for the protection of health or morals or for the protection of the rights and freedoms of others. This Article shall not prevent the imposition of lawful restrictions on the exercise of these rights by members of the armed forces, of the police or of the administration of the State.

KEYNOTE

Article 11 is closely related to Article 10 and is often raised in conjunction with it, particularly in situations involving the arrest of demonstrators and protestors. In addition to refraining from interference with the individual's right to peaceful assembly, the State is also under a positive duty to prevent others from doing so. The assembly must, however, be *peaceful* and any intention to use violence or to cause disorder may take the individual's actions outside the protection of Article 11.

As with Article 10, there are allowances for reducing rights of assembly etc. under certain conditions including the prevention of disorder and crime and the interests of national security and public safety.

The right to freedom of association and to join trade unions means, among other things, that trade unions may be victims for the purposes of bringing an action under this Article. The State can impose 'lawful restrictions' on the exercise of these rights.

4.11.2 Breach of the Peace

A breach of the peace is defined specifically in *R* v *Howell* [1982] QB 416. A breach of the peace generally occurs when an act is done, or threatened to be done:

- which harms a person or, in his/her presence, his/her property; or
- which is likely to cause such harm; or
- which puts someone in fear of such harm.

The common law provides a power of arrest and also the power to intervene and/or detain by force, in order to prevent any action likely to result in a breach of the peace in either public or private places.

Breach of the peace is dealt with by way of complaint and is not a criminal offence (*R v County of London Quarter Sessions Appeals Committee, ex parte Metropolitan Police Commissioner* [1948] 1 KB 670). Although not a criminal offence in domestic law, it may be treated as such for the purposes of the European Convention on Human Rights (*Steel v UK* (1999) 28 EHRR 603). In *Williamson v Chief Constable of West Midlands Police* [2003] EWCA Civ 337 the Court of Appeal held that a person arrested for a breach of the peace is not, strictly speaking, in police detention for the purposes of s. 118 of the Police and Criminal Evidence Act 1984 and the provisions in relation to bail do not apply. A person may be detained and placed before the next available court, or detained until there is no further likelihood of a reoccurrence of the breach of the peace. In *Williamson* it was considered good practice for people arrested and detained for breach of the peace to be treated in accordance with the provisions of PACE, and that they should also be cautioned.

4.11.2.1 Breach of the Peace on Private Premises

A breach of the peace may take place on private premises as well as in public places (*R v Chief Constable of Devon and Cornwall, ex parte Central Electricity Generating Board* [1982] QB 458). The police are entitled to enter premises to prevent a breach of the peace and to remain there in order to do so (*Thomas v Sawkins* [1935] 2 KB 249). This power has not been affected by the general powers of entry provided by the Police and Criminal Evidence Act 1984 (**see chapter 4.6** and s. 17(6) of the 1984 Act).

Where a breach of the peace takes place on private property, there is no requirement to show that the resulting disturbance affected members of the public outside that property—*McQuade v Chief Constable of Humberside Police* [2001] EWCA Civ 1330. The presence of a member (or members) of the public is, however, a highly relevant factor when dealing with a breach of the peace (*McConnell v Chief Constable of Greater Manchester Police* [1990] 1 WLR 364).

4.11.2.2 Police Powers are Discretionary

Although the police have a general duty to preserve the Queen's peace, and enjoy common law powers to carry out that duty, they also have a wide discretion as to how they go about that function. The common law powers of the police allow them, where appropriate, to prevent people from travelling to certain locations (e.g. striking miners heading for a working coalfield where their presence would give reasonable grounds to apprehend a breach of the peace (*Moss v McLachlan* [1985] IRLR 76)). Such an 'anticipatory' power is, however, exceptional (*Foulkes v Chief Constable of Merseyside Police* [1998] 3 All ER 705) and requires a balancing of the individual rights of the people involved against the wider interests of public safety, the maintenance of public order and the prevention of crime. Such exceptional powers to impose anticipatory restrictions on the movement of individuals, falling short of arrest, only arise if there is an imminent threat to public order.

The practicalities involved in this balancing exercise were considered in *R (On the Application of Laporte) v Chief Constable of Gloucestershire* [2006] UKHL 55. In *Laporte* a lawful assembly had been arranged under the provisions of ss. 12 and 14 of the Public Order Act 1986 in connection with protests against the war in Iraq. As the result of a stop and search order made under s. 60 of the Criminal Justice and Public Order Act 1994 (**see para. 4.5.4**) the police stopped a number of coaches en route to the lawful assembly at Fairford US Air Force base, and then escorted them back to London. Intelligence had been received that the passengers would cause disorder at the base. The House of Lords ruled that the police had acted unlawfully because a breach of the peace was not imminent when the coaches were stopped. This action interfered with the passengers' rights under Articles 10 and 11 of the European Convention on Human Rights and was disproportionate.

4.11.2.3   Which Parties are Likely to Present Actual Threat?

When exercising discretionary powers to prevent disorder, police officers will be expected to focus their attention on those who are likely to present the actual threat of violence or disorder. In *Redmond-Bate* v *DPP* [1999] Crim LR 998, people preaching on the steps of a church were warned by police that they were antagonising passers-by. Despite the warning, the preachers continued and, as there was an imminent likelihood of a recently gathered crowd attacking them, the preachers were arrested. The Divisional Court felt that the approach taken by the police was incompatible with Article 10 of the European Convention on Human Rights and that the officers' attention should have been directed at the crowd from whom the threat to the 'peace' was emanating. The individuals preaching were simply exercising their right to freedom of expression. It was the crowd who, in the court's view, ought to have received the warning and who should have been arrested in the event of their continuing to represent a threat to public order.

However, it will not always be practicable to separate those who are directly and individually presenting a threat to the peace and those who are part of a larger crowd. In *Austin* v *Commissioner of Police of the Metropolis* [2009] UKHL 5 it was held that in extreme and exceptional circumstances it would be lawful for the police to contain demonstrators and members of the public caught up in that demonstration, even though they themselves did not appear to be about to commit a breach of the peace. This would be the case where it was necessary to prevent an imminent breach of the peace by others, and no other means would achieve that. In *Austin* v *United Kingdom* (2012) 55 EHRR 14 the European Court of Human Rights decided, by a majority, that there had been no violation of Article 5 (right to liberty and security) of the European Convention on Human Rights. *Austin* [2009] was followed in *R (On the Application of Moos)* v *Commissioner of Police of the Metropolis* [2011] EWHC 957 (Admin) which related to a Climate Camp protest against the G20 Summit in London. It is only when the police reasonably believe that there is no other means whatsoever to prevent an imminent breach of the peace that they can as a matter of necessity curtail the lawful exercise of their rights of freedom of expression by third parties. The test of necessity is met only in truly extreme and exceptional circumstances. The action taken has to be both reasonably necessary and proportionate and taken in good faith. In *R (On the Application of McClure)* v *Commissioner of Police of the Metropolis* [2012] EWCA Civ 12, the Court of Appeal concluded that a decision to contain a substantial crowd of demonstrators whose behaviour, though at times unruly and somewhat violent, did not of itself justify containment was, however, justifiable on the ground that containment was the least drastic way of preventing what the police officer responsible for the decision reasonably apprehended would be imminent and serious breaches of the peace.

Where demonstrators were contained in a police pen, in a demonstration against Israel and its Head of State, it was held that the police may deploy reasonable force to prevent a breach of the peace that they reasonably apprehend as imminent (*Wright* v *Commissioner of Police for the Metropolis* [2013] EWHC 2739 (QB)).

Where officers were directed by senior officers to arrest persons for breach of the peace, it was held to be lawful where those senior officers had good reason to believe that had those persons been allowed to proceed to a nearby demonstration point there would have been a strong likelihood of a breach of the peace occurring (*R (On the Application of Hicks)* v *Commissioner of Police of the Metropolis* [2014] EWCA Civ 3).

Guidance on 'immediacy' in relation to conduct in a domestic setting is contained in *Wragg* v *DPP* [2005] EWHC 1389 (Admin). Police officers attending a domestic dispute found one of the parties, who had been in a heated argument with a relative also living in the house, to have consumed a large amount of alcohol. In relation to the immediacy or imminence test the police officers believed that a breach of the peace could take place in the house after they departed that night in so far as the other household member was at risk of immediate assault while the accused was still in drink. The arrest of the accused was held to be lawful. In *Demetriou* v *DPP* [2012] EWHC 2443 (Admin) it was also held that an arrest was lawful if a person willing to leave premises but who an officer believed would return to cause violence gave rise to a reasonable basis for fearing imminent violence.

4.11.2.4 Power of Arrest

A constable or any other person may arrest without warrant any person:

- who is committing a breach of the peace;
- whom he/she reasonably believes will commit a breach of the peace in the immediate future; or
- who has committed a breach of the peace, where it is reasonably believed that a recurrence of the breach of the peace is threatened.

There is an element of pre-emptive risk assessment involved in application of the test as to whether or not a breach of the peace is actually occurring even before moving on to consider whether such a breach, if not occurring, is imminent (*Laporte* v *Commissioner of Police of the Metropolis* [2014] EWHC 3574 (QB)).

This power of arrest may be exercised on private premises, even where there is no other member of the public present (*R* v *Howell* [1982] QB 416).

In *Bibby* v *Chief Constable of Essex Police* (2000) 164 JP 297, the Court of Appeal held that the power of arrest for breach of the peace was wholly exceptional and set out the conditions that must be met before this power should be used. These conditions are:

- there must be the clearest of circumstances and a real and present threat to the peace to justify the arrest
- the threat must be coming from the person who is ultimately arrested
- his/her conduct must be clearly interfering with the rights of another
- that conduct must be unreasonable.

Even if exercising the power under circumstances where a breach of the peace has not yet occurred, it is enough that a constable uses the wording 'I am arresting you for a breach of the peace' when arresting the person (*R* v *Howell* [1982] QB 416).

4.11.3 Riot

OFFENCE: **Riot—*Public Order Act 1986, s. 1***
- Triable on indictment • 10 years' imprisonment and/or a fine

The Public Order Act 1986, s. 1 states:

(1) Where 12 or more persons who are present together use or threaten unlawful violence for a common purpose and the conduct of them (taken together) is such as would cause a person of reasonable firmness present at the scene to fear for his personal safety, each of the persons using unlawful violence for the common purpose is guilty of riot.

(2) It is immaterial whether or not the 12 or more use or threaten unlawful violence simultaneously.

(3) The common purpose may be inferred from conduct.

(4) No person of reasonable firmness need actually be, or be likely to be, present at the scene.

(5) Riot may be committed in private as well as in public places.

This offence requires the consent of the DPP before a prosecution can be brought.

It is not necessary that all 12 people concerned use or threaten unlawful violence at the same time. However, the courts have held that each defendant must be shown to have *used* unlawful violence and not merely threatened to do so (*R* v *Jefferson* [1994] 1 All ER 270). A defendant must be shown to have *intended* to use/threaten violence or to have *been aware* that his/her conduct may have been violent (s. 6(1)).

Although there must be a common purpose, this need not be part of a pre-determined plan, nor be unlawful in itself. A common purpose to get into a rock concert or even the January sales at a high street store could therefore be enough, provided all other elements are present.

4.11.3.1 Unlawful Violence

The Public Order Act 1986, s. 8 states:

'violence' means any violent conduct, so that—

(a) except in the context of affray, it includes violent conduct towards property as well as violent conduct towards persons, and

(b) it is not restricted to conduct causing or intended to cause injury or damage but includes any other violent conduct (for example, throwing at or towards a person a missile of a kind capable of causing injury which does not hit or falls short).

The term 'unlawful' was included in the Act to allow for the general defences such as self-defence to be applicable (*R* v *Rothwell* [1993] Crim LR 626).

4.11.3.2 Drunkenness

Parliament has specifically catered for self-induced intoxication, not just for the offence of riot, but in relation to other offences under the 1986 Act, by s. 6 which states:

(5) For the purposes of this section a person whose awareness is impaired by intoxication shall be taken to be aware of that of which he would be aware if not intoxicated, unless he shows either that his intoxication was not self-induced or that it was caused solely by the taking or administration of a substance in the course of medical treatment.

(6) In subsection (5) 'intoxication' means any intoxication, whether caused by drink, drugs or other means, or by a combination of means.

4.11.4 Violent Disorder

OFFENCE: **Violent Disorder—*Public Order Act 1986, s. 2***
- Triable either way • Five years' imprisonment and/or a fine on indictment
- Six months' imprisonment and/or a fine summarily

The Public Order Act 1986, s. 2 states:

(1) Where 3 or more persons who are present together use or threaten unlawful violence and the conduct of them (taken together) is such as would cause a person of reasonable firmness present at the scene to fear for his personal safety, each of the persons using or threatening unlawful violence is guilty of violent disorder.

(2) It is immaterial whether or not the 3 or more use or threaten unlawful violence simultaneously.

(3) No person of reasonable firmness need actually be, or be likely to be, present at the scene.

(4) Violent disorder may be committed in private as well as in public places.

In order to convict a defendant of this offence, you must show that there were three or more people using or threatening unlawful violence. However, while three or more persons must have been present and used or threatened unlawful violence, it is not necessary that three or more persons should actually be charged or prosecuted with the offence. Further, where there are three defendants and two are acquitted of the charge, the remaining defendant can still be convicted of violent disorder (*R* v *Mahroof* (1989) 88 Cr App R 317) as long as *it can be proved that there were three or more people using or threatening violence* (perhaps from CCTV evidence of the incident). If it *cannot be proved* that there were three or more people using or threatening unlawful violence the court should acquit each defendant (*R* v *McGuigan* [1991] Crim LR 719).

In *R* v *NW* [2010] EWCA Crim 404, the circumstances of the case were that a person was violently resisting arrest by a police officer, during which time a crowd gathered and various members of the crowd used or threatened violence. The Court of Appeal held that for the purposes of this section it was not necessary for a person to act deliberately in combination with at least two other people present at the scene, but that it is sufficient that at least three people be present, each separately using or threatening unlawful violence. The court's view was that the phrase, 'where 3 or more persons who are present together use or threaten violence…' consists of ordinary words which must be given their ordinary meaning.

There is no requirement to prove a common purpose.

Again, a defendant must be shown to have *intended* to use/threaten violence or to have *been aware* that his/her conduct may have been violent (s. 6(2)). 'Violence' for these purposes can include violent conduct towards property (s. 8).

4.11.5 Affray

OFFENCE: **Affray—*Public Order Act 1986, s. 3***

- Triable either way • Three years' imprisonment and/or a fine on indictment
- Six months' imprisonment and/or a fine summarily

The Public Order Act 1986, s. 3 states:

(1) A person is guilty of affray if he uses or threatens unlawful violence towards another and his conduct is such as would cause a person of reasonable firmness present at the scene to fear for his personal safety.

(2) Where 2 or more persons use or threaten the unlawful violence, it is the conduct of them taken together that must be considered for the purposes of subsection (1).

(3) For the purposes of this section a threat cannot be made by the use of words alone.

(4) No person of reasonable firmness need actually be, or be likely to be, present at the scene.

(5) Affray may be committed in private as well as in public places.

The House of Lords held that, in order to prove the offence of affray, the threat of unlawful violence has to be towards a person(s) present at the scene (*I* v *DPP* [2001] UKHL 10). Once this element has been proved, it will be necessary to prove the second element, namely, whether the defendant's conduct would have caused a hypothetical person present at the scene to fear for his/her personal safety (*R* v *Sanchez* (1996) 160 JP 321 and *R* v *Carey* [2006] EWCA Crim 17). However, where the likelihood of a hypothetical person of reasonable firmness being present was low this element of the offence was not satisfied. In *R (On the Application of Leeson)* v *DPP* [2010] EWHC 994 (Admin) a woman had issued a drunken threat to kill her long-term partner while holding a knife, in a bathroom, in an otherwise unoccupied house. In these circumstances the court held that there was no possibility of hypothetical bystanders fearing for their safety.

The threat cannot be made by words alone (s. 3(3)), therefore there must be some action by the defendant—even if that 'action' consists of utilising something else such as a dog to threaten the violence (*R* v *Dixon* [1993] Crim LR 579).

The effect of s. 3(4) is that it is not necessary to show that the defendant's behaviour either was or could have been seen by someone at the time.

Although violence is 'not restricted to conduct causing or intended to cause injury or damage but includes any other violent conduct' (s. 8), the expression does not include conduct towards property as it does with the offences under ss. 1 and 2.

Once more, a defendant must be shown to have *intended* to use/threaten violence or to have *been aware* that his/her conduct may have been violent (s. 6(2)).

4.11.6   Fear or Provocation of Violence

OFFENCE: **Fear or Provocation of Violence—*Public Order Act 1986, s. 4***
- Triable summarily • Six months' imprisonment and/or a fine

OFFENCE: **Racially or Religiously Aggravated—*Crime and Disorder Act 1998, s. 31(1)(a)***
- Triable either way • Two years' imprisonment and/or a fine on indictment
- Six months' imprisonment and/or a fine summarily

The Public Order Act 1986, s. 4 states:

(1) A person is guilty of an offence if he—
   (a) uses towards another person threatening, abusive or insulting words or behaviour, or
   (b) distributes or displays to another person any writing, sign or other visible representation which is threatening, abusive or insulting,
   with intent to cause that person to believe that immediate unlawful violence will be used against him or another by any person, or to provoke the immediate use of unlawful violence by that person or another, or whereby that person is likely to believe that such violence will be used or it is likely that such violence will be provoked.
(2) An offence under this section may be committed in a public or a private place, except that no offence is committed where the words or behaviour are used, or the writing, sign or other visible representation is distributed or displayed, by a person inside a dwelling and the other person is also inside that or another dwelling.

KEYNOTE

Whether words or behaviour are threatening, abusive or insulting will be a question of fact for the magistrate(s) to decide in each case (*Brutus* v *Cozens* [1973] AC 854).

It is not enough that conduct is 'offensive' but it has been held that masturbation towards a police officer in a public lavatory is capable of being insulting (*Parkin* v *Norman* [1983] QB 92).

'Immediate' unlawful violence does not have to be instantaneous but it must be shown that the defendant's conduct was likely to lead to more than some form of violence at some later date. Therefore publication and sale of material by the author Salman Rushdie, however insulting it may have been to some people, was not enough on its facts to support a charge against the publishers under s. 4 (*R* v *Horseferry Road Metropolitan Stipendiary Magistrate, ex parte Siadatan* [1991] 1 QB 260). 'Immediate' here requires some close proximity between the acts of the defendant and the apprehended violence, with no intervening occurrence.

The prosecution must prove that the accused intended the victim to fear immediate unlawful violence. This is not possible where it was the intention of the accused to take the victim by surprise so that he/she did not know he/she would be assaulted until the act had occurred. The court considered that the accused should have been charged with assault (*Hughes* v *DPP* [2012] EWHC 606 (Admin)).

There are a number of ways in which this offence can be committed (see below). In all of these, however, there must be the use of threatening/abusive/insulting words or behaviour (or distribution/display of writing, signs, etc.). This must be carried out with the requisite state of mind set out at s. 6(3) which states:

(3) A person is guilty of an offence under section 4 only if he intends his words or behaviour, or the writing, sign or other visible representation, to be threatening, abusive or insulting, or is aware that it may be threatening, abusive or insulting.

In addition, it must be shown that the person further *intended* to bring about the consequences set out below (at (a) and (b)) or that the consequences (at (c) and (d)) were likely.

In relation to s. 4(1)(b), 'writing' includes typing, printing, lithography, photography and other modes of presenting or reproducing words in a visible form (Interpretation Act 1978, s. 5 and sch. 1).

The offence was broken down into four component parts in *Winn* v *DPP* (1992) 156 JP 881. For each of these parts it must be shown:

(a) that the defendant:
- intended the person against whom the conduct was directed
- to believe
- that immediate unlawful violence would be used
- either against him/her or against anyone else
- by the defendant or anyone else; *or*

(b) that he/she:
- intended to provoke the immediate use of unlawful violence
- by that person or anyone else; *or*

(c) that:
- the person against whom the words or behaviour (or distribution/display of writing etc.) were directed
- was likely to believe
- that immediate unlawful violence would be used; *or*

(d) that it was likely that immediate unlawful violence would be provoked.

In the case at (a) above, it does not have to be shown that the other person *actually believed* that immediate violence would be used; it has to be shown that the defendant *intended to cause* him/her to believe it (*Swanston* v *DPP* (1997) 161 JP 203).

The person in whom the defendant intends to create that belief must be the same person at whom the conduct is directed (*Loade* v *DPP* [1990] 1 QB 1052).

4.11.6.1 Definition of Dwelling

Under the Public Order Act 1986, s. 8, 'dwelling' is defined as:

> ...any structure or part of a structure occupied as a person's home or as other living accommodation (whether the occupation is separate or shared with others) but does not include any part not so occupied, and for this purpose 'structure' includes a tent, caravan, vehicle, vessel or other temporary or movable structure.

KEYNOTE

Given that the offence at s. 4 can be committed in private (under the restrictions in relation to dwellings by s. 4(2); see para. 4.11.6), it appears that the offence could be committed by a person sending out emails or other forms of communication from his/her house to other non-dwellings or from his/her place of work to people's houses.

Communal landings which form access routes to separate dwellings have been held not to constitute part of a dwelling even though they could only be entered by way of an entry phone system (*Rukwira* v *DPP* [1993] Crim LR 882). Similarly, in *Le Vine* v *DPP* [2010] EWHC 1128 (Admin) a laundry room, commonly used by tenants in sheltered housing, did not form part of a dwelling. Also a police cell has been held not to be living accommodation (*R* v *Francis* [2006] EWCA Crim 3323).

Intentional Harassment, Alarm or Distress

OFFENCE: **Intentionally Causing Harassment, Alarm or Distress—*Public Order Act 1986, s. 4A***

  • Triable summarily • Six months' imprisonment and/or a fine

OFFENCE: **Racially or Religiously Aggravated—*Crime and Disorder Act 1998, s. 31(1)(b)***

  • Triable either way • Two years' imprisonment and/or a fine on indictment
  • Six months' imprisonment and/or a fine summarily

The Public Order Act 1986, s. 4A states:

(1) A person is guilty of an offence if, with intent to cause a person harassment, alarm or distress, he—
    (a) uses threatening or abusive words or behaviour, or disorderly behaviour, or
    (b) displays any writing, sign or other visible representation which is threatening, abusive or insulting,
    thereby causing that or another person harassment, alarm or distress.

KEYNOTE

For the purpose of the racially or religiously aggravated form of causing fear or provocation of violence, any words used by the defendant have to be construed within the meaning that they are given in England and Wales. In construing those words, the courts should not have any regard to the *defendant's* own racial, national or ethnic origins—or presumably their religious beliefs or lack of such (*R* v *White* (*Anthony Delroy*) [2001] EWCA Crim 216).

In order to prove this offence you must show that the defendant *intended* to cause harassment, alarm or distress and, it seems, that by so doing, the defendant actually caused some harassment, alarm or distress. In *Steele* v *DPP* [2008] EWHC 438 (Admin) the defendant took a digital photograph of the complainant and posted it on the Internet with a speech bubble and text alleging the complainant had previous convictions for violence. It was several months later that the photograph was shown to the complainant by the police and the Divisional Court held that the time and the circumstances in which it had been brought fully to the attention of the complainant were immaterial.

Harassment, alarm or distress are not defined and it would appear that they are to be given their ordinary everyday meaning. A police officer can be caused such harassment, alarm or distress (*DPP* v *Orum* [1989] 1 WLR 88), and can also be the victim of the racially aggravated form of the offence (*R* v *Jacobs* [2001] 2 Cr App R(S) 38), and he/she can feel that harassment, alarm or distress for someone else present (e.g. a child (*Lodge* v *DPP* [1989] COD 179)). Police officers are expected to display a degree of fortitude and, for an officer to be caused harassment, alarm or distress, the conduct complained of must go beyond that which he/she would regularly come across in the ordinary course of police duties.

Whether the use of a particular phrase, in the context and circumstances in which it was used, was intended to cause harassment, alarm or distress for the offences above is a question of fact for the relevant magistrate/jury to decide (*DPP* v *Weeks* (2000) *The Independent*, 17 July). Consequently, in that case where the defendant was alleged to have called the victim a 'black bastard' during a heated argument over a business transaction, the magistrates were still entitled to find him not guilty of the aggravated s. 4A offence if they were satisfied that the relevant intention was not present.

Posting a threatening, abusive or insulting letter through someone's letter box is not an offence under this section (*Chappell* v *DPP* (1989) 89 Cr App R 82). It may, however, amount to an offence under the Malicious Communications Act 1988 (see para. 4.9.5).

As with the offence under s. 4, an offence under s. 4A can be committed in a public or private place, but no offence is committed where the words or behaviour are used, etc. by a person inside a dwelling and the person who is harassed, alarmed or distressed is also inside that or another dwelling (s. 4A(2)). For the definition of a 'dwelling' see para. 4.11.6.1.

4.11.7.1 Defences

The Public Order Act 1986, s. 4A states:

> (3) It is a defence for the accused to prove—
> (a) that he was inside a dwelling and had no reason to believe that the words or behaviour used, or the writing, sign or other visible representation displayed, would be heard or seen by a person outside that or any other dwelling, or
> (b) that his conduct was reasonable.

KEYNOTE

It is for the defendant to prove that one of the elements existed at the time of the offence. The standard of proof here will be that of the balance of probabilities, i.e. that it was more likely than not.

4.11.8 Harassment, Alarm or Distress

OFFENCE: **Harassment, Alarm or Distress—*Public Order Act 1986, s. 5***
- Triable summarily • Fine

OFFENCE: **Racially or Religiously Aggravated—*Crime and Disorder Act 1998, s. 31(1)(c)***
- Triable summarily • Fine

The Public Order Act 1986, s. 5 states:

> (1) A person is guilty of an offence if he—
> (a) uses threatening or abusive words or behaviour, or disorderly behaviour, or
> (b) displays any writing, sign or other visible representation which is threatening or abusive,
> within the hearing or sight of a person likely to be caused harassment, alarm or distress thereby.

KEYNOTE

Unlike the other racially or religiously aggravated forms of public order offences, the offence under s. 5 remains triable summarily, even if aggravated by the conditions set out in s. 28 of the Crime and Disorder Act 1998 (s. 31(5)).

In a case where the defendant used the words 'You're fucking Islam' in an aggressive manner towards a Sikh police officer of Asian appearance, the Divisional Court held that the expression itself was almost undeniably abusive if not insulting (*R (On the Application of DPP)* v *Humphrey* [2005] EWHC 822 (Admin)). In *Kendall* v *DPP* [2008] EWHC 1848 (Admin), British National Party posters showing a photograph of three black men with the caption 'Illegal Immigrant Murder Scum' were found to be threatening, abusive and insulting and racially aggravated.

The racially or religiously aggravated circumstances set out at s. 28(1)(a) of the Crime and Disorder Act 1998 deal with situations where the defendant demonstrates racial or religious hostility at the time of (or immediately before or after) committing the offence, towards the *victim*. To clarify such situations in relation to the racially or religiously aggravated form of the above offence, s. 31(7) provides that the person 'likely to be caused harassment, alarm or distress' will be treated as the 'victim'.

Note that 'disorderly' is not defined and ought to be given its ordinary everyday meaning. It need not be shown that the disorderly behaviour is itself threatening, abusive or insulting, nor that it brought about any feelings of apprehension in the person to whom it was directed (*Chambers and Edwards* v *DPP* [1995] Crim LR 896). The wording of s. 5 is not limited to rowdy behaviour and will extend to any behaviour that could be construed as threatening or abusive.

The discussion at **para. 4.11.7** in relation to intentional harassment, alarm or distress also applies to this offence, except here there needs to be a person within whose sight or hearing the conduct takes place. This

---

requirement was confirmed in *Taylor* v *DPP* [2006] EWHC 1202 (Admin) where it was held that there must be at least evidence that there was someone who could see, or could hear, at the material time, what the individual was doing. However, there was no requirement for the prosecution to call evidence that that someone did actually hear the words spoken or see the behaviour. In *Harvey* v *DPP* [2011] EWHC 3992 (Admin), the defendant had used bad language when detained by the police (saying, e.g. 'I told you you wouldn't find fuck all') and although this might have been considered abusive or insulting, there was no evidence that anyone involved, or any bystanders, had suffered or were likely to have been caused any harassment, alarm or distress. All those involved would have heard such language on many occasions and in consequence the Appeal Court quashed the conviction. In *R (On the Application of Reda)* v *DPP* [2011] EWHC 1550 (Admin), where an accused was acquitted of a s. 5 offence but found guilty of assaulting a police officer, the High Court upheld the assault police conviction as the arrest for the s. 5 offence had been made in good faith, i.e. there were reasonable grounds to suspect that an offence had been committed.

Abdul v DPP [2011] EWHC 247 (Admin) related to a parade to celebrate soldiers returning from Afghanistan and Iraq and a group of protesters who carried placards, chanted slogans such as 'British soldiers burn in hell', and called the soldiers murderers, rapists and baby-killers. The defence contended that the prosecution under this section was disproportionate bearing in mind the right to freedom of expression. The court held that in striking the right balance when determining whether speech was threatening, abusive or insulting, the focus on minority rights was not to result in overlooking the rights of the majority. Where the line between legitimate freedom of expression and a threat to public order was crossed, freedom of speech would not be impaired by 'ruling out' threatening, abusive or insulting speech; the prosecution was a proportionate response.

This offence is a 'penalty offence' for the purposes of s. 1 of the Criminal Justice and Police Act 2001.

As with the offence under s. 4, an offence under s. 5 can be committed in a public place or a private place, but no offence is committed where the words or behaviour are used, etc. by a person inside a dwelling and the other person is also inside that or another dwelling (s. 5(2)). For the definition of a 'dwelling' see para. 4.11.6.1.

4.11.8.1 State of Mind

The Public Order Act 1986, s. 6 states:

> (4) A person is guilty of an offence under section 5 only if he intends his words or behaviour, or the writing, sign or other visible representation, to be threatening or abusive, or is aware that it may be threatening or abusive or (as the case may be) he intends his behaviour to be or is aware that it may be disorderly.

4.11.8.2 Defences

The Public Order Act 1986, s. 5 states:

> (3) It is a defence for the accused to prove—
>   (a) that he had no reason to believe that there was any person within hearing or sight who was likely to be caused harassment, alarm or distress, or
>   (b) that he was inside a dwelling and had no reason to believe that the words or behaviour used, or the writing sign or other visible representation displayed, would be heard or seen by a person outside that or any other dwelling, or
>   (c) that his conduct was reasonable.

KEYNOTE

It is for the defendant to prove that one of the elements existed at the time of the offence. The standard of proof here will be that of the balance of probabilities, i.e. that it was more likely than not.

In deciding whether a defendant's conduct was reasonable under s. 5(3)(c) an objective test will be applied (*DPP* v *Clarke* (1992) 94 Cr App R 359).

The relationship between the Public Order Act 1986, s. 5(1), Article 10 of the European Convention on Human Rights and the supposed 'right' to go naked in public was considered in the 'naked rambler' case, *Gough* v *DPP* [2013] EWHC 3267 (Admin). It was held that the appellant foresaw the consequence of his voluntary decision to walk naked through a town centre and was at least aware that his behaviour may have been threatening, abusive, insulting or disorderly. Thus the intent required by the legislation was proved.

4.11.9 Causing Nuisance or Disturbance on NHS Premises

OFFENCE: **Causing a Nuisance or Disturbance on NHS Premises—*Criminal Justice and Immigration Act 2008, s. 119***

- Triable summarily

The Criminal Justice and Immigration Act 2008, s. 119 states:

(1) A person commits an offence if—
  (a) the person causes, without reasonable excuse and while on NHS premises, a nuisance or disturbance to an NHS staff member who is working there or otherwise there in connection with work,
  (b) the person refuses, without reasonable excuse, to leave the NHS premises when asked to do so by a constable or an NHS staff member, and
  (c) the person is not on the NHS premises for the purpose of obtaining medical advice, treatment or care for himself or herself.

KEYNOTE

A person ceases to be on NHS premises for the purpose of obtaining medical advice, treatment or care for him/herself once the person has received the advice, treatment or care. Also, a person is not on NHS premises for the purpose of obtaining medical advice, treatment or care for him/herself if the person has been refused the advice, treatment or care during the last eight hours (s. 119(3)).

If a constable reasonably suspects that a person is committing or has committed an offence under s. 119, the constable may remove the person from the NHS premises concerned (s. 120(1)).

If an authorised officer reasonably suspects that a person is committing or has committed an offence he/she may remove the person from the NHS premises concerned, or authorise an appropriate NHS staff member to do so (s. 120(2)).

Any person removing another person from NHS premises under this section may, if necessary, use reasonable force (s. 120(3)).

An authorised officer cannot remove the person or authorise another person to do so if it is reasonably believed he/she is in need of medical advice, etc. or that such removal would endanger his/her mental or physical health (s. 120(4)). An authorised officer is a duly authorised NHS staff member (s. 120(5)).

4.11.10 Public Processions and Assemblies

The law relating to public processions and assemblies is primarily provided by the Public Order Act 1986 and is discussed below.

4.11.10.1 Advance Notice of Public Processions

The Public Order Act 1986, s. 11 states:

(1) Written notice shall be given in accordance with this section of any proposal to hold a public procession intended—
  (a) to demonstrate support for or opposition to the views or actions of any person or body of persons,

(b) to publicise a cause or campaign, or

(c) to mark or commemorate an event,

unless it is not reasonably practicable to give any advance notice of the procession.

(2) Subsection (1) does not apply where the procession is one commonly or customarily held in the police area (or areas) in which it is proposed to be held or is a funeral procession organised by a funeral director acting in the normal course of his business.

(3) The notice must specify the date when it is intended to hold the procession, the time when it is intended to start it, its proposed route, and the name and address of the person (or of one of the persons) proposing to organise it.

(4) Notice must be delivered to a police station—

(a) in the police area in which it is proposed the procession will start, or

(b) where it is proposed the procession will start in Scotland and cross into England, in the first police area in England on the proposed route.

KEYNOTE

In relation to s. 11(2) it was held that an organised cycle ride that started at the same time and place on the last Friday of every month, even though there was no fixed, settled or predetermined route, end-time or destination, was a commonly or customarily held procession (*R (On the Application of Kay)* v *Commissioner of Police of the Metropolis* [2008] UKHL 69).

If the notice is delivered not less than six clear days before the date when the procession is intended to be held, the notice may be delivered by post by the recorded delivery service (s. 11(5)). Otherwise, the notice must be delivered by hand not less than six clear days before the date when the procession is intended to be held or, if that is not reasonably practicable, as soon as delivery is reasonably practicable (s. 11(6)).

Where a public procession is held, each of the persons organising it is guilty of an offence if the requirements of this section as to notice have not been satisfied, or the date when it is held, the time when it starts, or its route, differs from the date, time or route specified in the notice (s. 11(7)).

It is a defence for the accused to prove that he/she did not know of, and neither suspected nor had reason to suspect, the failure to satisfy the requirements or (as the case may be) the difference of date, time or route (s. 11(8)). To the extent that an alleged offence turns on a difference of date, time or route, it is a defence for the accused to prove that the difference arose from circumstances beyond his/her control or from something done with the agreement of a police officer or by the officer's direction (s. 11(9)).

4.11.10.2 Imposing Conditions on Public Processions

The Public Order Act 1986, s. 12 states:

(1) If the senior police officer, having regard to the time or place at which and the circumstances in which any public procession is being held or is intended to be held and to its route or proposed route, reasonably believes that—

(a) it may result in serious public disorder, serious damage to property or serious disruption to the life of the community, or

(b) the purpose of the persons organising it is the intimidation of others with a view to compelling them not to do an act they have a right to do, or to do an act they have a right not to do,

he may give directions imposing on the persons organising or taking part in the procession such conditions as appear to him necessary to prevent such disorder, damage, disruption or intimidation, including conditions as to the route of the procession or prohibiting it from entering any public place specified in the directions.

KEYNOTE

This section may also apply to a commonly or customarily held procession as described in s. 11(2) (see para. 4.11.10.1). It enables a senior police officer, who reasonably believes that a procession may result in serious disruption to the life of the community, to give such directions imposing conditions as to the route of the procession as appear to him necessary to prevent such disruption. This can be done days before the procession, or at the point of assembly or during the procession itself. The giving of directions is a preventive measure whenever given (*Powlesland* v *DPP* [2013] EWHC 3846 (Admin)).

In relation to a procession being held, or to a procession intended to be held in a case where persons are assembling with a view to taking part in it, the 'senior police officer' is the most senior in rank of the police officers present at the scene (s. 12(2)(a)). For any other intended procession it is the chief officer of police (s. 12(2)(b)), whose direction must be given in writing (s. 12(3)).

A person who organises a public procession and knowingly fails to comply with a condition imposed under this section is guilty of a summary offence, but it is a defence to prove that the failure arose from circumstances beyond his/her control (s. 12(4)).

A person who takes part in a public procession and knowingly fails to comply with a condition imposed under this section is guilty of a summary offence, but it is a defence to prove that the failure arose from circumstances beyond his/her control (s. 12(5)). Those participating in a public procession are entitled to leave it, but they are not entitled to move from the route of the procession while they remain as participants in it (*Jukes* v *DPP* [2013] EWHC 195 (Admin)).

A person who incites another to commit a summary offence under s. 12(5) is guilty of an offence (s. 12(6)).

4.11.10.3 Prohibiting Public Processions

The Public Order Act 1986, s. 13 states:

(1) If at any time the chief officer of police reasonably believes that, because of particular circumstances existing in any district or part of a district, the powers under section 12 will not be sufficient to prevent the holding of public processions in that district or part from resulting in serious public disorder, he shall apply to the council of the district for an order prohibiting for such period not exceeding 3 months as may be specified in the application the holding of all public processions (or of any class of public procession so specified) in the district or part concerned.

(2) On receiving such an application, a council may with the consent of the Secretary of State make an order either in the terms of the application or with such modifications as may be approved by the Secretary of State.

(3) Subsection (1) does not apply in the City of London or the metropolitan police district.

KEYNOTE

A person who organises a public procession the holding of which he/she knows is prohibited by virtue of an order under this section is guilty of a summary offence (s. 13(7)). A person who takes part in a public procession the holding of which he/she knows is prohibited by virtue of an order under this section is guilty of a summary offence (s. 13(8)), and a person who incites another to commit an offence under s. 13(8) is guilty of a summary offence (s. 13(9)).

4.11.10.4 Imposing Conditions on Public Assemblies

The Public Order Act 1986, s. 14 states:

(1) If the senior police officer, having regard to the time or place at which and the circumstances in which any public assembly is being held or is intended to be held, reasonably believes that—
   (a) it may result in serious public disorder, serious damage to property or serious disruption to the life of the community, or
   (b) the purpose of the persons organising it is the intimidation of others with a view to compelling them not to do an act they have a right to do, or to do an act they have a right not to do, he may give directions imposing on the persons organising or taking part in the assembly such conditions as to the place at which the assembly may be (or continue to be) held, its maximum duration, or the maximum number of persons who may constitute it, as appear to him necessary to prevent such disorder, damage, disruption or intimidation.

(2) In subsection (1) 'the senior police officer' means—

(a) in relation to an assembly being held, the most senior in rank of the police officers present at the scene, and

(b) in relation to an assembly intended to be held, the chief officer of police.

(3) A direction given by a chief officer of police by virtue of subsection (2)(b) shall be given in writing.

KEYNOTE

Where a chief officer gives a direction he/she must identify what limb of s. 14(1) was being relied upon and in sufficient detail to enable demonstrators to understand why the decision was made and for a court to understand if a decision was reasonable or not (*R (On the Application of Brehony)* v *Chief Constable of Greater Manchester Police* [2005] EWHC 640 (Admin)).

A direction under this section was lawful where a senior police officer imposed a condition that a Climate Camp protest against the G20 Summit in London must stop. The demonstration had lasted the best part of 12 hours—quite long enough for the protestors to take advantage of their human rights under Article 10 (Freedom of Expression) and Article 11 (Freedom of Assembly and Association)—and those wishing to remain were intent on continuing to block the highway, the main thoroughfare into and out of the City. There was no justification to prolong the demonstration and its continuation would cause serious disturbances and disruption to traffic and pedestrians wishing to use the highway. The police had a duty to clear the highway that could not be done without removing the protestors by force if necessary (*R (On the Application of Moos)* v *Commissioner of Police of the Metropolis* [2011] EWHC 957 (Admin)).

In *R* v *Lucas* (2014) 17 April, unreported, an assembly was already taking place and the notice under s. 14 was signed by a chief officer who was not present at the scene. It was held that the notice was invalid as the police officer giving it was not the authorised officer as required by s. 2(a).

The necessity for imposing a condition must genuinely appear to the relevant senior police officer and must be proportional to the circumstances in which the public assembly is being held (*James* v *DPP* [2015] EWHC 3296 (Admin)).

A person who organises a public assembly and knowingly fails to comply with a condition imposed under this section is guilty of a summary offence, but it is a defence to prove that the failure arose from circumstances beyond his/her control (s. 14(4)). A person who takes part in a public assembly and knowingly fails to comply with a condition imposed under this section is guilty of a summary offence, but it is a defence to prove that the failure arose from circumstances beyond his/her control (s. 14(5)). A person who incites another to commit an offence under s. 14(5) is guilty of a summary offence (s. 14(6)).

The distinction between this section and s. 12 concerns the conditions that may be imposed under each section. In *DPP* v *Jones* [2002] EWHC 110 (Admin) demonstrators against the Huntingdon Life Sciences Centre were prosecuted for failing to comply with a condition set out in a police notice issued under s. 14. It was held that some of the conditions imposed were more properly concerned with a public procession and therefore were beyond the police powers under s. 14. The offending parts of the police notice were 'severed' leaving the enforceable parts intact. However it may be safer for the police to issue two separate notices, in appropriate circumstances, one relating to the conditions to be observed by participants in the 'procession' element of an operation and the other imposing conditions on the 'assembly' element.

4.11.10.5   **Prohibiting Trespassory Assemblies**

The provisions of s. 14 (**see para. 4.11.10.4**) apply to public assemblies. However, occasions have arisen where the assembly has been *trespassory*, that is, on land which is either private or where there is only a limited right of public access and the permission of the relevant landowner has not been granted. In such instances, s. 14A of the Public Order Act 1986 provides the police with certain powers.

The Public Order Act, s. 14A states:

(1) If at any time the chief officer of police reasonably believes that an assembly is intended to be held in any district at a place on land to which the public has no right of access or only a limited right of access and that the assembly—

(a) is likely to be held without the permission of the occupier of the land or to conduct itself in such a way as to exceed the limits of any permission of his or the limits of the public's right of access, and

(b) may result—

  (i) in serious disruption to the life of the community, or

  (ii) where the land, or a building or monument on it, is of historical, architectural, archaeological or scientific importance, in significant damage to the land, building or monument,

he may apply to the council of the district for an order prohibiting for a specified period the holding of all trespassory assemblies in the district or a part of it, as specified.

KEYNOTE

An 'assembly' for the purpose of this section means 20 or more people, 'land' means land in the open air, and 'public' includes a section of the public (s. 14A(9)).

A classic example of a trespassory assembly might be found at sites such as Stonehenge.

On receiving an application from a chief officer the council may make an order either in the terms of the application, or with modifications, either of which must be approved by the Secretary of State (s. 14A(2)(a)), and the order must be in writing or reduced to writing as soon as practicable after being made (s. 14A(8)).

An order must not last for more than four days, nor must it apply to an area beyond a radius of five miles from a specified centre (s. 14A(6)).

A person who organises an assembly the holding of which he/she knows is prohibited by an order under s. 14A is guilty of a summary offence (s. 14B(1)). A person who takes part in an assembly which he/she knows is prohibited by an order under s. 14A is guilty of a summary offence (s. 14B(2)), and a person who incites another to commit an offence under s. 14B(2) is guilty of a summary offence (s. 14B(3)). Even where an order has been made, there will be a need to show that the assembly was obstructive of the highway or at least that it exceeded the public's general right of access (*DPP* v *Jones* [1999] 2 AC 240).

4.11.10.6 Trespassory Assemblies Police Powers

The Public Order Act 1986, s. 14C states:

(1) If a constable in uniform reasonably believes that a person is on his way to an assembly within the area to which an order under section 14A applies which the constable reasonably believes is likely to be an assembly which is prohibited by that order, he may, subject to subsection (2) below—

  (a) stop that person, and

  (b) direct him not to proceed in the direction of the assembly.

(2) The power conferred by subsection (1) may only be exercised within the area to which the order applies.

(3) A person who fails to comply with a direction under subsection (1) which he knows has been given to him is guilty of an offence.

KEYNOTE

This power allows officers to stop people, though not, it would seem, vehicles (in which case the general power under s. 163 of the Road Traffic Act 1988 must be used).

4.11.10.7 Public Meetings

It is an offence to attempt to break up a public meeting.

OFFENCE: **Trying to Break up a Public Meeting—*Public Meeting Act 1908, s. 1***

  • Triable summarily • Six months' imprisonment and/or a fine *(No specific power of arrest)*

The Public Meeting Act 1908, s. 1 states:

(1) Any person who at a lawful public meeting acts in a disorderly manner for the purpose of preventing the transaction of the business for which the meeting was called together shall be guilty of an offence and shall on summary conviction be liable to imprisonment for a term not exceeding six months or to a fine not exceeding £1,000 or to both...

(2) Any person who incites others to commit an offence under this section shall be guilty of a like offence.

KEYNOTE

'Public meeting' is not defined in the 1908 Act. There appears to be no requirement for the meeting to be lawfully assembled.

This offence does not apply to meetings held in relation to s. 97 of the Representation of the People Act 1983 (meetings concerned with public elections) (s. 1(4)). In the case of people acting or inciting others to act in a disorderly way at such meetings, there is a specific summary offence under s. 97(1) of the 1983 Act.

If a constable reasonably suspects any person of committing this offence, he/she may, *if requested by the person chairing the meeting*, require the offender to declare his/her name and address immediately. Failing to comply with such a request or giving false details is a summary offence (s. 1(3)).

4.11.11 Injunctions to Prevent Gang-related Violence and Drug Dealing Activity

The Policing and Crime Act 2009, as amended by the Serious Crime Act 2015, provides courts with the power to grant injunctions to prevent gang-related violence and drug dealing activity.

Section 34 of the 2009 Act, as amended, states:

(1) A court may grant an injunction under this section against a respondent aged 14 or over if the first and second conditions are met.

(2) The first condition is that the court is satisfied on the balance of probabilities that the respondent has engaged in or has encouraged or assisted—

 (a) gang-related violence, or

 (b) gang-related drug-dealing activity.

(3) The second condition is that the court thinks it is necessary to grant the injunction for either or both of the following purposes—

 (a) to prevent the respondent from engaging in, or encouraging or assisting, gang-related violence or gang-related drug-dealing activity;

 (b) to protect the respondent from gang-related violence or gang-related drug-dealing activity.

(4) An injunction under this section may (for either or both of those purposes)—

 (a) prohibit the respondent from doing anything described in the injunction;

 (b) require the respondent to do anything described in the injunction.

(5) For the purposes of this section, something is 'gang-related' if it occurs in the course of, or is otherwise related to, the activities of a group that—

 (a) consists of at least three people, and

 (b) has one or more characteristics that enable its members to be identified by others as a group.

(6) In this section 'violence' includes a threat of violence.

(7) In this Part 'drug-dealing activity' means the unlawful production, supply, importation or exportation of a controlled drug.

'Production', 'supply' and 'controlled drug' here have the meanings given by s. 37(1) of the Misuse of Drugs Act 1971.

KEYNOTE

These injunctions are a civil tool allowing the police or local authority to apply to the High Court, a county court or, in the case of juveniles, a youth court (sitting in a civil capacity), for an injunction against an individual who has been involved in gang-related violence or drug dealing activity. A range of prohibitions and requirements on the behaviour and activities of a person can be included in an injunction such as prohibiting someone from being in a particular place or requiring them to participate in rehabilitative activities (s. 35).

The court may attach a power of arrest in relation to (a) any prohibition in the injunction, or (b) any requirement in the injunction other than one which has the effect of requiring the respondent to participate in particular activities (s. 36). Where a power of arrest is attached to a provision a constable may arrest without warrant a person whom the constable has reasonable cause to suspect to be in breach of the provision. The constable must inform the person who applied for the injunction of the arrest, and the person arrested must be brought before a relevant judge within 24 hours of the arrest (s. 43).

Sporting Events

4.12.1 Introduction

There are several offences and statutory measures which are specifically aimed at tackling disorder and anti-social behaviour at sporting events.

4.12.2 Designated and Regulated Football Matches

Many of the offences and powers relating to football fixtures apply to 'designated' or 'regulated' football matches. In summary, the expressions generally have the following meaning:

- An association football match (in the United Kingdom) as described below will be a regulated football match for the purposes of part II of the Football Spectators Act 1989. The description will cover association football matches in which one or both of the participating teams represents a club which is, for the time being, a member (whether a full or associate member) of the Football League, the Football Association Premier League, the Football Conference or the Welsh Premier League, the Scottish Premier League, or the Scottish Professional Football League, or represents a country or territory.
- An association football match (outside the United Kingdom) as described below will also be a regulated football match for the purposes of part II of the 1989 Act. The description will cover an association football match involving:
  - ✦ a national team appointed by the Football Association to represent England or the Football Association of Wales to represent Wales; or
  - ✦ a team playing in the Football Association Cup (other than in a preliminary or qualifying round); or
  - ✦ a team representing a club which is, at the time the match is played, a member (whether a full or associate member) of the Football League, the Football Association Premier League, the Football Conference or the Welsh Premier League, the Scottish Premier League, or the Scottish Professional Football League; or
  - ✦ any match involving a country or territory whose football association is for the time being a member of Fédération Internationale de Football Association (FIFA), where the match is part of a competition or tournament organised by or under the authority of FIFA or the Union des Associations Européennes de Football (UEFA), and where the competition or tournament is one in which the England or Wales national team is eligible to participate or has participated;
  - ✦ any match involving a club whose national football association is a member of FIFA, where the match is part of a competition or tournament organised by or under the authority of FIFA or UEFA, and where the competition or tournament is one in which a club from the Football League, the Football Association Premier League, the Football Conference or the League of Wales is eligible to participate or has participated; or
  - ✦ any match involving a club whose home ground is outside England or Wales but they are playing within England or Wales.

4.12.3 The Football (Offences) Act 1991

OFFENCE: **Misbehaviour at Designated Football Match**—*Football (Offences) Act 1991, ss. 2, 3 and 4*

> • Triable summarily • Fine

The Football (Offences) Act 1991, ss. 2, 3 and 4 state:

2. It is an offence for a person at a designated football match to throw anything at or towards—
   (a) the playing area, or any area adjacent to the playing area to which spectators are not generally admitted, or
   (b) any area in which spectators or other persons are or may be present, without lawful authority or lawful excuse (which shall be for him to prove).

3. (1) It is an offence to engage or take part in chanting of an indecent or racialist nature at a designated football match.
   (2) For this purpose—
      (a) 'chanting' means the repeated uttering of any words or sounds (whether alone or in concert with one or more others); and
      (b) 'of a racialist' nature means consisting of or including matter which is threatening, abusive or insulting to a person by reason of his colour, race, nationality (including citizenship) or ethnic or national origins.

4. It is an offence for a person at a designated football match to go onto the playing area, or any area adjacent to the playing area to which spectators are not generally admitted, without lawful authority or lawful excuse (which shall be for him to prove).

KEYNOTE

Section 1(2) of the 1991 Act provides that references to things done at a 'designated football match' include anything done at the ground:

- within the period beginning two hours before the start of the match or (if earlier) two hours before the time at which it is advertised to start and ending one hour after the end of the match;
- where the match is advertised to start at a particular time on a particular day but does not take place, within the period beginning two hours before and ending one hour after the advertised starting time.

A 'designated' match for these purposes is the same as a 'regulated' match under the Football Spectators Act 1989 (see para. 4.12.2).

These offences can be separated into those affecting the playing area and adjacent parts of the ground (ss. 2 and 4) and the offence of indecent or racialist chanting (s. 3).

In the case of the first offence (s. 2), throwing anything at or towards the playing area etc., there is a defence of having lawful authority or lawful excuse (which presumably would cover returning the ball to the field of play). Generally there seem to be few occasions on which a defendant would have lawful authority/ reasonable excuse for the behaviour prohibited by s. 2.

Section 4 makes the same savings in relation to lawful authority/reasonable excuse and, in both cases, the burden of proof falls on the defendant. (The *standard* of proof will be that of the balance of probabilities.)

For the offence under s. 3, the defendant must be shown to have *repeated* the words or sounds before it can be classed as 'chanting'.

The wording of s. 3(2)(b) requires that the chanting *is*, rather than, *might be*, threatening, abusive or insulting. Although not expressly required, the best way to prove this element of the offence would be the evidence of a person who was threatened, abused or insulted. In relation to chants 'of a racialist' nature, shouting 'You're just a town full of Pakis' at supporters from Oldham fell squarely within the definition (*DPP v Stoke on Trent Magistrates' Court* [2003] EWHC 1593 (Admin)).

'Indecent' is not defined and will be a question of fact for the court to decide in all the circumstances.

4.12.4 Banning Orders and Detention

The Football Spectators Act 1989 contains the powers to impose banning orders that exclude offenders from attendance at regulated football matches in England, Wales, Scotland and Northern Ireland and international football matches.

There are two ways in which a banning order can be made, first where a person is convicted of a relevant offence (s. 14A), and secondly, by way of complaint by the relevant chief officer, or the DPP (s. 14B(1)).

4.12.4.1 Convicted of Relevant Offences

The relevant offences are set out in sch. 1 to the 1989 Act and include offences relating to drunkenness, violence or threats of violence, or public order offences committed at or in connection with a football match or when travelling to or from a football match (whether or not the match was actually attended by the offender). In *R v Elliott* [2007] EWCA Crim 1002, banning orders were quashed where it was found that violence involving a group of men in a public house was unrelated to the match. In making a banning order a court may take into account the potential deterrent effect of the order on persons other than the offender (*R v Curtis* [2010] EWCA Crim 123).

Rather than simply having the power to make such orders, courts are under a statutory duty to pass such orders if they are satisfied that there are reasonable grounds to believe that the orders would help prevent violence or disorder at or in connection with a 'regulated football match' (**see para. 4.12.2**). Violence here includes violence towards property, and disorder includes stirring up racial hatred (1989 Act, s. 14C). Where these criteria are established, there is no discretion not to make an order (*R v Allen* [2011] EWCA Crim 3076). In *Commissioner of Police of the Metropolis v Thorpe* [2015] EWHC 3339 (Admin) a banning order restricted to three named clubs was held to be lawful. Such an order enabled the subject to continue an interest in football other than at the three named clubs where a court had decided that his absence would be helpful in reducing violence and disorder at such events.

The court may adjourn any proceedings in relation to an order even after sentencing the offender and may remand the offender (s. 14A(4A) and (4BA)). Where the offender is remanded on bail he/she may be required not to leave England and Wales before appearing before the court and to surrender his/her passport to a constable (s. 14A(4BB)).

If a magistrates' court fails to make a banning order, the prosecution have a right of appeal to the Crown Court, or to the Court of Appeal where the Crown Court failed to make an order (s. 14A(5A)). If the offender does not appear for any adjourned proceedings, the court may further adjourn the proceedings, or it may issue a warrant for his/her arrest but only after it is satisfied that he/she has had adequate notice of the time and place of the adjourned proceedings (s. 14A(4B) and (4C)).

KEYNOTE

Banning orders made under s. 14A of the 1989 Act (on conviction of a relevant offence) in addition to an immediate sentence of imprisonment will have a minimum of six and a maximum of 10 years' duration (s. 14F(3)). Other banning orders made under s. 14A (i.e. where they do not accompany a sentence of immediate imprisonment) have a minimum of three and a maximum of five years' duration (s. 14F(4)).

4.12.4.2 Complaint by Chief Officer or DPP

On such an application a magistrates' court can make an order if the person has at any time caused or contributed to any violence or disorder in the United Kingdom or elsewhere. The court may impose conditions on banning orders and must require the surrender of the person's passport in connection with regulated football matches outside the United Kingdom

(s. 14E(3)). Where proceedings are adjourned, as with the first way of obtaining a banning order, the offender may be remanded and, where bailed, be required to surrender his/her passport (s. 14B(5)). Again, where the magistrates have failed to make a banning order, the prosecution have a right of appeal to the Crown Court (s. 14D(1A)).

The effect of a banning order, unless a person is detained in legal custody, is that he/she must initially report to a specified police station in England, Wales, Scotland or Northern Ireland, within five days of the order being made (s. 14E(2)). He/she must also notify the enforcing authority of specified changes to his/her personal circumstances within seven days of the occurrence of any such changes (s. 14E(2B) and (2C)).

KEYNOTE

Banning orders made under s. 14B (on complaint by a chief officer of police) have a minimum of three and a maximum of five years' duration (s. 14F(5)).

4.12.4.3   Banning Orders—General

If a banning order has been in effect for at least two-thirds of its period, the person subject to it can apply to the court which passed the order for its termination. The National Crime Agency (NCA) has responsibility for monitoring the movement of football spectators and collating relevant intelligence. The Football Banning Orders Authority is the 'designated authority' for the purposes of the 1989 Act. Under the Football Disorder Act 2000, the NCA is empowered to disclose information for the purposes of the 1989 Act.

International banning orders do not contravene either the general European law on the free movement of people within the European Union, or the European Convention on Human Rights (*Gough* v *Chief Constable of Derbyshire* [2002] EWCA Civ 351). In *Gough*, the Court of Appeal held that there was no absolute right to leave one's country. As banning orders were to be imposed only where there were strong grounds for concluding that the person had a propensity to take part in football hooliganism, the court held that it was appropriate that such people should be subject to a scheme that restricted their ability to indulge in that hooliganism. Banning orders are not criminal charges, nor are the proceedings in applying for them 'criminal' proceedings (*Gough*).

4.12.4.4   Failing to Comply with Banning Order

OFFENCE: **Failing to Comply with Banning Order—*Football Spectators Act 1989, s. 14J***
   • Triable summarily • Six months' imprisonment and/or a fine

The Football Spectators Act 1989, s. 14J states:

   (1) A person subject to a banning order who fails to comply with—
      (a) any requirement imposed by the order, or
      (b) any requirement imposed under section 19(2B) or (2C) below is guilty of an offence.

KEYNOTE

The reference to s. 19(2B) and (2C) is to the power for the enforcing authority to issue written notices requiring individuals to report to a police station in England, Wales, Scotland or Northern Ireland and, where relevant, to surrender their passports, in advance of certain matches.

A number of exemptions are provided for under s. 20. These allow, among other things, for the person on whom an order has been passed to apply for exemption from the duties of the order under special circumstances.

4.12.4.5   Power of Detention

The Football Spectators Act 1989, s. 21A states:

(1) This section and section 21B below apply during any control period in relation to a regu-
    lated football match outside the United Kingdom or an external tournament if a constable in
    uniform—
    (a) has reasonable grounds for suspecting that the condition in section 14B(2) above is met in
        the case of a person present before him, and
    (b) has reasonable grounds to believe that making a banning order in his case would help to pre-
        vent violence or disorder at or in connection with any regulated football matches.
(2) The constable may detain the person in his custody (whether there or elsewhere) until he has
    decided whether or not to issue a notice under section 21B below, and shall give the person his
    reasons for detaining him in writing.
    This is without prejudice to any power of the constable apart from this section to arrest the
    person.
(3) A person may not be detained under subsection (2) above for more than four hours or, with the
    authority of an officer of at least the rank of inspector, six hours.

KEYNOTE

'Control period' means, in relation to a regulated football match outside the United Kingdom, the period:

(a) beginning five days before the day of the match, and

(b) ending when the match is finished or cancelled

and in relation to an external tournament, means any period described in an order made by the Secretary of State:

(a) beginning five days before the day of the first football match outside the United Kingdom which is included
    in the tournament, and

(b) ending when the last football match outside the United Kingdom which is included in the tournament is
    finished or cancelled,

but, for the purposes of para. (a), any football match included in the qualifying or pre-qualifying stages of the
tournament is to be ignored (s. 14(5) and (6)). An example of a specified 'control period' was the Football
Spectators (2016 European Championship Control Period) Order 2016 (SI 2016/141), which commenced 10
days before the first match in the tournament, and ended when the last match in the tournament was finished
or cancelled.

The power under s. 21A requires the police officer to be in uniform and may be exercised only in relation to
a person who is a British citizen (see s. 21C(1)).

The initial period of detention allowed is a *maximum* of four hours, extendable to a further *maximum* of six hours
by an inspector. There is no requirement under this section that the inspector be either present or in uniform. The
purpose of the detention is for the officer to decide whether or not to issue a notice (**see para. 4.12.4.6**).

The condition under s. 14B(2) referred to is that the person has at any time caused or contributed to any
violence or disorder in the United Kingdom or elsewhere.

References to football matches include matches intended to be played (s. 14(7)). A person who has been
detained under s. 21A(2) may only be further detained under that subsection in the same control period in
reliance on information which was not available to the constable who previously detained him/her; and a
person on whom a notice has been served under s. 21B(2) may not be detained under s. 21A(2) in the same
control period (s. 21A(4)).

4.12.4.6   Service of Notice

The Football Spectators Act 1989, s. 21B states:

(1) A constable in uniform may exercise the power in subsection (2) below if authorised to do so by
    an officer of at least the rank of inspector.
(2) The constable may give the person a notice in writing requiring him—

(a) to appear before a magistrates' court at a time, or between the times, specified in the notice,

(b) not to leave England and Wales before that time (or the later of those times), and

(c) if the control period relates to a regulated football match outside the United Kingdom or to an external tournament which includes such matches, to surrender his passport to the constable and stating the grounds referred to in section 21A(1) above.

(3) The times for appearance before the magistrates' court must be within the period of 24 hours beginning with—

(a) the giving of the notice, or

(b) the person's detention under section 21A(2) above, whichever is the earlier.

KEYNOTE

The power applies during any control period in relation to a regulated football match outside England and Wales or an external tournament (as to which, see **para. 4.12.4.5**, Keynote).

A constable may arrest a person to whom he/she is giving a notice if he/she has reasonable grounds to believe that it is *necessary* to do so in order to ensure that the person complies with the notice (s. 21B(5)).

For the purposes of s. 14B, the notice is to be treated as an application for a banning order made by complaint (s. 21B(4)).

As with the provision for detention under s. 21A, the powers conferred by s. 21B may be exercised only in relation to a person who is a British citizen (s. 21C(1)).

4.12.4.7 Failure to Comply with Notice under Section 21B

OFFENCE: **Failing to Comply with Notice—*Football Spectators Act 1989, s. 21C***
  • Triable summarily • Six months' imprisonment and/or a fine

The Football Spectators Act 1989, s. 21C states:

(2) A person who fails to comply with a notice given to him under section 21B above is guilty of an offence …

KEYNOTE

The notice must have been lawfully given in order to attract liability for this offence. Where a person who has been given a notice appears before a magistrates' court as required by the notice (whether under arrest or not), the court may remand him/her and the court may require the person not to leave England and Wales as a condition of bail (s. 21C(3) and (4)). Also, if the control period relates to a regulated football match outside the United Kingdom or to an external tournament which includes such matches, the court can order the person to surrender his/her passport to a police constable, if he/she has not already done so.

4.12.5 The Sporting Events (Control of Alcohol etc.) Act 1985

OFFENCE: **Alcohol on Coaches and Trains—*Sporting Events (Control of Alcohol etc.) Act 1985, s. 1***
  • Triable summarily • Three months' imprisonment and/or a fine (s. 1(3))
  • Fine (s. 1(2) and (4))

The Sporting Events (Control of Alcohol etc.) Act 1985, s. 1 states:

(1) This section applies to a vehicle which—

(a) is a public service vehicle or railway passenger vehicle, and

(b) is being used for the principal purpose of carrying passengers for the whole or part of a journey to or from a designated sporting event.

(2) A person who knowingly causes or permits alcohol to be carried on a vehicle to which the section applies is guilty of an offence—
  (a) if the vehicle is a public service vehicle and he is the operator of the vehicle or the servant or agent of the operator, or
  (b) if the vehicle is a hired vehicle and he is the person to whom it is hired or the servant or agent of that person.
(3) A person who has alcohol in his possession while on a vehicle to which this section applies is guilty of an offence.
(4) A person who is drunk on a vehicle to which this section applies is guilty of an offence.

KEYNOTE

Section 1 creates a number of offences in relation to public service vehicles and trains being used principally (though not exclusively) to carry passengers for the whole or part of a journey, to or from a designated sporting event.

The offences can be committed by the vehicle operator/hirer or his/her servant or agent provided there is evidence of *knowingly* causing or permitting the carrying of alcohol.

The other offences are committed by people who have alcohol in their 'possession' and by people who are drunk on a relevant vehicle. Generally, any mature and competent witness may give evidence as to drunkenness.

Section 7(3) provides a power for a police officer to stop a public service vehicle in order to search it where he/she has reasonable grounds to suspect that an offence under this section *is being or has been committed* in respect of that vehicle. It also provides a power to search a railway carriage (though not to stop the train) under the same circumstances. The power to search people in those vehicles comes from s. 7(2). The PACE Code of Practice for the Exercise by Police Officers of Statutory Powers of Stop and Search (Code A) (2014) (see para. 4.5.4) applies to searches under s. 7, i.e. searches of persons, coaches and trains at designated sports grounds or coaches and trains travelling to or from a designated sporting event.

OFFENCE: **Alcohol on Other Vehicles—*Sporting Events (Control of Alcohol etc.) Act 1985, s. 1A***

- Triable summarily • Three months' imprisonment and/or a fine (s. 1A(3))
- Fine (s. 1A(2) and (4))

The Sporting Events (Control of Alcohol etc.) Act 1985, s. 1A states:

(1) This section applies to a motor vehicle which—
  (a) is not a public service vehicle but is adapted to carry more than 8 passengers, and
  (b) is being used for the principal purpose of carrying two or more passengers for the whole or part of a journey to or from a designated sporting event.
(2) A person who knowingly causes or permits alcohol to be carried on a motor vehicle to which this section applies is guilty of an offence—
  (a) if he is its driver, or
  (b) if he is not its driver but is its keeper, the servant or agent of its keeper, a person to whom it is made available (by hire, loan or otherwise) by its keeper or the keeper's servant or agent, or the servant or agent of a person to whom it is so made available.
(3) A person who has alcohol in his possession while on a motor vehicle to which this section applies is guilty of an offence.
(4) A person who is drunk on a motor vehicle to which this section applies is guilty of an offence.

KEYNOTE

This section creates similar offences to those set out under s. 1 but these relate to mechanically propelled vehicles that are intended or adapted for use on roads and that are adapted to carry more than eight passengers (not being PSVs).

For the purposes of the above offences, a vehicle's 'keeper' is the person having the duty to take out a vehicle excise licence for it (s. 1A(5)).

The power to stop and search vehicles and their occupants under s. 7(3) above also applies to an offence under this section.

4.12.6 Power to Prohibit Sale of Alcohol on Trains

The Licensing Act 2003, s. 157 states:

> (1) A magistrates' court acting for a petty sessions area may make an order prohibiting the sale of alcohol, during such period as may be specified, on any railway vehicle—
>   (a) at such station or stations as may be specified, being stations in that area, or
>   (b) travelling between such stations as may be specified, at least one of which is in that area.

KEYNOTE

Unlike some other aspects relating to the control of pre- and post-match events, there is no specific restriction on the period over which such an order may be made. However, the court cannot make such an order unless it is satisfied that the order is *necessary* to prevent disorder (s. 157(3)).

A court may only make an order under this section on the application of a senior police officer (s. 157(2)). 'Senior police officer' means a police officer of, or above, the rank of inspector (s. 157(7)).

Where an order is made, the police officer who applied for the order (or, if the chief officer of police of the force in question has designated another senior police officer for the purpose, that other officer) must immediately serve a copy of the order on the train operator (or each train operator) affected by the order (s. 157(4)).

OFFENCE: **Contravening Prohibition Order for Sale of Alcohol on Trains—*Licensing Act 2003, s. 157(5)***
   • Triable summarily • Three months' imprisonment and/or a fine not exceeding £20,000

The Licensing Act 2003, s. 157 states:

> (5) A person commits an offence if he knowingly—
>   (a) sells or attempts to sell alcohol in contravention of an order under this section, or
>   (b) allows the sale of alcohol in contravention of such an order.

KEYNOTE

The defendant must be shown to have acted *knowingly*, and proof that the order was properly made and in force so far as that date and location were concerned will be critical.

4.12.7 Designated Sports Grounds, Sporting Events and Related Offences

There are several offences associated with designated sports grounds and designated sporting events. Before examining these offences it is useful to examine what these terms mean.

4.12.7.1 Designated Sports Ground

Under s. 9 of the Sporting Events (Control of Alcohol etc.) Act 1985, a 'designated sports ground' means:

> (2) ...any place—
>   (a) used (wholly or partly) for sporting events where accommodation is provided for spectators, and
>   (b) for the time being designated, or of a class designated, by order made by the Secretary of State, and an order under this subsection may include provision for determining for the purposes of this Act the outer limit of any designated sports ground.

4.12.7.2 Designated Sporting Event

A 'designated sporting event' means an event or proposed event which has been designated or is part of a class designated by order made by the Secretary of State. It also includes events designated under comparable Scottish legislation. Events which are to be held outside Great Britain can also be designated (s. 9(3) of the 1985 Act).

4.12.7.3 Designated Sporting Event—Time Period

The period of a 'designated sporting event' is also covered by s. 9 of the Sporting Events (Control of Alcohol etc.) Act 1985:

> (4) The period of a designated sporting event is the period beginning two hours before the start of the event or (if earlier) two hours before the time at which it is advertised to start and ending one hour after the end of the event, but—
>
> (a) where an event advertised to start at a particular time on a particular day is postponed to a later day, the period includes the period in the day on which it is advertised to take place beginning two hours before and ending one hour after that time, and
>
> (b) where an event advertised to start at a particular time on a particular day does not take place, the period is the period referred to in paragraph (a) above.

KEYNOTE

The Sports Grounds and Sporting Events (Designation) Order 2005 (SI 2005/3204) provides for the classes of sporting events for the purposes of the 1985 Act. These differ slightly from those contained in the Football Spectators Act 1989 and include:

- Association football matches in which one or both of the participating teams represents a club which is for the time being a member (whether a full or associate member) of the Football League, the Football Association Premier League, the Football Conference National Division, the Scottish Professional Football League, or Welsh Premier League, or represents a country or territory.
- Association football matches in competition for the Football Association Cup (other than in a preliminary or qualifying round).
- Association football matches at a sports ground outside England and Wales in which one or both of the participating teams represents a club which is for the time being a member (whether a full or associate member) of the Football League, the Football Association Premier League, the Football Conference National Division, the Scottish Professional Football League, or Welsh Premier League, or represents the Football Association or the Football Association of Wales.

4.12.7.4 Alcohol, Containers etc. at Sports Grounds

> OFFENCE: **Alcohol at Sports Grounds—*Sporting Events (Control of Alcohol etc.) Act 1985, s. 2***
>
> - Triable summarily • Three months' imprisonment and /or a fine (s. 2(1))
> - Fine (s. 2(2))

The Sporting Events (Control of Alcohol etc.) Act 1985, s. 2 states:

> (1) A person who has alcohol or an article to which this section applies in his possession—
>
> (a) at any time during the period of a designated sporting event when he is in any area of a designated sports ground from which the event may be directly viewed, or
>
> (b) while entering or trying to enter a designated sports ground at any time during the period of a designated sporting event at that ground, is guilty of an offence.
>
> (2) A person who is drunk in a designated sports ground at any time during the period of a designated sporting event at that ground or is drunk while entering or trying to enter such a ground at any time during the period of a designated sporting event at that ground is guilty of an offence.

4.12.7.5   Fireworks, Flares and Similar Objects at Sports Grounds and Events

OFFENCE: **Having Fireworks, Flares etc.—*Sporting Events (Control of Alcohol etc.) Act 1985, s. 2A***

- Triable summarily • Three months' imprisonment and/or a fine

The Sporting Events (Control of Alcohol etc.) Act 1985, s. 2A states:

(1) A person is guilty of an offence if he has an article or substance to which this section applies in his possession—
   (a) at any time during the period of a designated sporting event when he is in any area of a designated sports ground from which the event may be directly viewed, or
   (b) while entering or trying to enter a designated sports ground at any time during the period of a designated sporting event at the ground.
(2) …
(3) This section applies to any article or substance whose main purpose is the emission of a flare for purposes of illuminating or signalling (as opposed to igniting or heating) or the emission of smoke or a visible gas; and in particular it applies to distress flares, fog signals, and pellets and capsules intended to be used as fumigators or for testing pipes, but not to matches, cigarette lighters or heaters.
(4) This section also applies to any article which is a firework.

4.12.8   Ticket Touts

OFFENCE: **Ticket Touts—*Criminal Justice and Public Order Act 1994, s. 166***
- Triable summarily • Fine

The Criminal Justice and Public Order Act 1994, s. 166 states:

(1) It is an offence for an unauthorised person to—
   (a) sell a ticket for a designated football match, or
   (b) otherwise to dispose of such a ticket to another person.

(2) For this purpose—
  (a) a person is 'unauthorised' unless he is authorised in writing to sell or otherwise dispose of tickets for the match by the organisers of the match;
  (aa) a reference to selling a ticket includes a reference to—
    (i) offering to sell a ticket;
    (ii) exposing a ticket for sale;
    (iii) making a ticket available for sale by another;
    (iv) advertising that a ticket is available for purchase; and
    (v) giving a ticket to a person who pays or agrees to pay for some other goods or services or offering to do so;
  (b) a 'ticket' means anything which purports to be a ticket; and
  (c) a 'designated football match' means a football match of a description, or a particular football match, for the time being designated for the purposes of this section by order made by the Secretary of State.

KEYNOTE

Section 32 of the Police and Criminal Evidence Act 1984 (search of persons and premises (including vehicles) upon arrest) shall have effect, in its application in relation to an offence under this section, as if the power conferred on a constable to enter and search any vehicle extended to any vehicle which the constable has reasonable grounds for believing was being used for any purpose connected with the offence (s. 166(5)).

Section 166A is designed to ensure that the offence in s. 166 is compatible with European Directive 2000/31/EC. It ensures that the provisions in s. 166 do not apply to internet service providers based outside the United Kingdom, but makes it an offence for an internet service provider established in the United Kingdom to sell or otherwise dispose of tickets for designated football matches regardless of where the sale etc., takes place.

For the purposes of s. 166(2)(c) a 'designated football match' is currently described in the Ticket Touting (Designation of Football Matches) Order 2007 (SI 2007/790). Article 2 of the Order designates association football matches in England and Wales in which one or both participating teams represent a club which is a member of the Football League, Football Association Premier League, Football Conference or League of Wales, or represents a country or territory. Article 2(3) designates association football matches outside England and Wales involving a national team of England or Wales, or a team representing a club which is a member of the Football League, Football Association Premier League, Football Conference or League of Wales, or matches in competitions or tournaments organised by or under the authority of FIFA (Fédération Internationale de Football Association) or UEFA (Union des Associations Européennes de Football), in which any of such English or Welsh domestic or national teams is eligible to participate or has participated.

4.13 | Weapons

4.13.1 Introduction

Offences involving weapons are an increasingly important consideration for police officers who will be well acquainted with the sometimes terrible consequences that the possession and use of such weapons can have. This chapter examines some of the legislation designed to deal with such behaviour.

4.13.2 Having Offensive Weapon in Public Place

OFFENCE: **Having Offensive Weapon in Public Place—*Prevention of Crime Act 1953, s. 1(1)***
   - Triable either way • Four years' imprisonment and/or a fine on indictment
   - Six months' imprisonment and/or a fine summarily

The Prevention of Crime Act 1953, s. 1 states:

> (1) Any person who without lawful authority or reasonable excuse, the proof whereof shall lie on him, has with him in any public place any offensive weapon shall be guilty of an offence.

4.13.2.1 Lawful Authority

'Lawful authority' means those occasions where people from time to time are required to carry weapons as a matter of duty, such as police officers or members of the armed forces (*Bryan* v *Mott* (1976) 62 Cr App R 71). Security guards carrying truncheons, even if required to do so by their contracts of employment, are not covered (*R* v *Spanner* [1973] Crim LR 704). If someone does not fall into this—very limited—group, he/she may still have a 'reasonable excuse' for having the weapon with him/her.

4.13.2.2 Reasonable Excuse

'Reasonable excuse' may arise from a number of circumstances. People having tools with them in the course of their trade (e.g. craft knives for fitting carpets or hammers for carpentry) may have a 'reasonable excuse' (*Ohlson* v *Hylton* [1975] 1 WLR 724). If a person passing the scene of a recent disturbance sees a weapon lying on the ground and he/she picks it up and puts it in his/her car intending to take it to the nearest police station, those circumstances would amount to a reasonable excuse for having the weapon with him/her.

The issues arising out of reasonable excuses under this offence overlap greatly with those of 'good reason' under the Criminal Justice Act 1988 offence below (**see para. 4.13.4.1**) and the two should be read together to assist understanding of this area of law. Magistrates retain a wide degree of discretion in what they accept as a 'reasonable excuse' and the cases below do *not* mean that this discretion is fettered and that the courts must follow this reasoning in every case (*DPP* v *Patterson* [2004] EWHC 2744 (Admin)) (magistrates' court finding that a defendant in possession of a butterfly knife in a shopping centre because 'he needed it for feeding and stabling horses' and had meant to deposit it in a safe place that day but had not had the chance to do so, had a 'reasonable excuse'). Against that background, however, the following situations have been considered and pronounced upon by the courts:

- Not being aware that you have an offensive weapon with you is *not* a reasonable excuse in itself (*R* v *Densu* [1998] 1 Cr App R 400).
- Neither is forgetting that you have a weapon with you (*R* v *Lorimer* [2003] EWCA Crim 721) generally, or forgetting that there is one in the car you are driving (*R* v *McCalla* (1988) 87 Cr App R 372).
- However, where a taxi driver was found with a piece of wood and a cosh in the back of his cab where they had been left by passengers earlier in the week, the Court of Appeal held that his forgetting to remove the weapons might have been accepted as a reasonable excuse and the question should have been left for the jury (*R* v *Glidewell* (1999) 163 JP 557).
- Under the Criminal Justice Act offence below (**see para. 4.13.4.1**), however, there can be circumstances where forgetfulness could be relevant to the defence of 'good reason' (e.g. where it results from illness or medication) (*Bayliss* v *DPP* [2003] EWHC 245 (Admin)).

It is not reasonable to have a weapon with you as *a general precaution* in case you are attacked (*Evans* v *Hughes* [1972] 1 WLR 1452). It may be reasonable to have a weapon if you have good grounds to anticipate an unprovoked or unlawful attack (e.g. for a person guarding cash transits (*Malnik* v *DPP* [1989] Crim LR 451)). However, in *N* v *DPP* [2011] EWHC 1807 (Admin), the defence of reasonable excuse was not made out where a person picked up a metal bar for protection having been threatened five minutes earlier by a group of young men in a car who were found to have no weapons. Even if the defendant did believe that he was at risk of an imminent attack, his belief was not a reasonable one in the circumstances.

Having a weapon for some other reason may amount to a reasonable excuse and whether or not it does so is a matter of fact for the court/jury to decide For example, in *Houghton* v *Chief Constable of Greater Manchester Police* (1987) 84 Cr App R 319 where the defendant was in 'fancy dress' costume as a police officer and had a truncheon with him as part of the costume this was held to amount to 'reasonable excuse'.

The defendant's state of mind when deciding whether the defence of 'good reason' was made out, for example, whether they had an angry and/or intoxicated and/or traumatised state of mind, is a matter that should be left to a jury (*R* v *Clancy* [2012] EWCA Crim 8).

The burden of proving the reasonable excuse or lawful authority rests with the defendant, but only when the prosecution have established that the defendant had an offensive weapon with him/her at the time. That burden of proof will be judged against the balance of probabilities.

4.13.2.3 Has With Him

This expression shows that the offence is designed to prevent the carrying of weapons; it is not an offence of *intention* and the reported decisions of the courts have consistently reflected that fact. The reasonable excuse must relate to the *carrying* of the weapon or article and not the *intention* of the person carrying it (*R* v *Jura* [1954] 1 QB 503).

This is most apparent where an 'innocent' article is used offensively. In *Ohlson* v *Hylton* [1975] 1 WLR 724 the defendant had a bag of tools with him in the course of his trade. He produced a hammer from the bag and used it to hit someone. The court held that, as he had formed the intention to use the hammer *after* it came into his possession, the offence was not made out. Although the court accepted that there might be times where a later intention to use an innocent article offensively would amount to an offence under the 1953 Act, the main purpose of the law was to prevent people from arming themselves with weapons. Similar decisions have been reached in relation to picking up a discarded knife during a fight (*Bates* v *Bulman* [1979] 1 WLR 1190), brandishing a jack taken from a car (*R* v *Dayle* [1974] 1 WLR 181) and using a penknife, which the defendant happened to be carrying, to stab someone who attacked him (*R* v *Humphreys* [1977] Crim LR 225).

It is possible for more than one person to have the same weapon 'with them', provided you can show that they knew of its existence in the hands of another at the time (*R* v *Edmonds* [1963] 2 QB 142).

You must show that the defendant knew that he/she had *something* with him/her and that the 'something' was, in fact, an offensive weapon (*R* v *Cugullere* [1961] 1 WLR 858).

4.13.2.4 Public Place

The Prevention of Crime Act 1953, s. 1 states:

> (4) In this section 'public place' includes any highway and any other premises or place to which at the material time the public have or are permitted to have access, whether on payment or otherwise.

KEYNOTE

What is a public place is a question of fact, but whether it is capable of being a public place is a question of law (*R* v *Hanrahan* [2004] EWCA Crim 2943).

4.13.2.5 Offensive Weapon

The Prevention of Crime Act 1953, s.1(4) also states:

> 'offensive weapon' means any article made or adapted for use for causing injury to the person, or intended by the person having it with him for such use by him or by some other person.

KEYNOTE

Offensive weapons fall into three categories for the purposes of this offence, namely, articles:

- made for causing injury (offensive weapons *per se*);
- adapted for causing injury; and
- intended by the person who has them, for causing injury.

Made

Offensive weapons *per se* are those which have been manufactured for use for causing injury and include truncheons, PR-24 batons and bayonets. A swordstick has been held to be such a weapon (*R* v *Butler* [1988] Crim LR 695) as have flick-knives (*R* v *Simpson* [1983] 1 WLR 1494), butterfly knives (*DPP* v *Hynde* [1998] 1 WLR 1222) and petrol bombs (*R* v *Akhtar* [2015] EWCA Crim 176). In *Hynde* the court took notice of the fact that butterfly knives were outlawed under the Criminal Justice Act 1988, deciding that such knives were clearly 'made' for causing injury. A flick-knife that also operates as a lighter remains an offensive weapon *per se* despite its alternative function (*R* v *Vasili* [2011] EWCA Crim 615).

Adapted

In *R* v *R* [2007] EWCA Crim 3312, the Court of Appeal held that a pair of combat gloves containing powdered lead/sand in the knuckle area were designed or adapted as an offensive weapon.

Weapons *adapted* for causing injury can include virtually anything. Whether something has in fact been so adapted is a question of fact for the court/jury to decide in each case. Bottles or glasses which have been broken in order to create a jagged edge have been held to be 'adapted' (*R* v *Simpson* [1983] 1 WLR 1494), so, too, has a potato with razor blades protruding from it (*R* v *Williamson* (1978) 67 Cr App R 35). If the article itself has not been altered in any physical way (such as by putting ammonia in a 'Jif' lemon to squirt in people's eyes—*R* v *Formosa* [1991] 2 QB 1), it has not been adapted.

It is still unclear whether the adaptation has to be to cause injury to *another* person or whether its capacity for self-inflicted injury (as in a suicide attempt) is enough. It is submitted that, as it is the *adaptation* of the

---

article which is relevant, and not the *intention* of the person carrying it, the ultimate 'victim' is irrelevant (*Bryan v Mott* (1976) 62 Cr App R 71).

Intended

Weapons *intended* to be used for causing injury can also include virtually anything. Here the intention of the person carrying it *is relevant* and you must prove an intention to cause injury. An intention to cause shock can be enough to satisfy this condition (*R v Rapier* (1980) 70 Cr App R 17 and also *R v Ali* [2012] EWCA Crim 934) but simply using the article to scare potential attackers away will not (*R v Snooks* [1997] Crim LR 230). To an extent this overlaps with the issues of 'reasonable excuse' and 'has with him' discussed above. In *C v DPP* [2001] EWHC Admin 1093 the court held that it was necessary to examine how closely the adoption of the relevant object and the intention to use it occurred, along with the circumstances in which the offence took place. There is an important distinction between an article (not an offensive weapon *per se*) that is introduced into a public place with an intent to injure, and an article (already possessed lawfully and for good reason) that is used offensively to cause injury. Each case depends on its facts (*R v Tucker* [2016] EWCA Crim 13).

No Proof of Intention to Use Required

Once it has been shown that the article in question was in fact an offensive weapon, there is no need for the prosecution to show any intention to use it for causing injury (*Davis v Alexander* (1970) 54 Cr App R 398).

4.13.3 Threatening with Offensive Weapon in Public

OFFENCE: **Threatening with Offensive Weapon in Public—*Prevention of Crime Act 1953, s. 1A***
- Triable either way • Four years' imprisonment and/or a fine on indictment
- Six months' imprisonment and/or a fine summarily

The Prevention of Crime Act 1953, s. 1A states:

(1) A person is guilty of an offence if that person—
  (a) has an offensive weapon with him or her in a public place,
  (b) unlawfully and intentionally threatens another person with the weapon, and
  (c) does so in such a way that there is an immediate risk of serious physical harm to that other person.

KEYNOTE

This section creates an offence relating to the aggravated use of an offensive weapon in a public place.

The offence is committed where a person (A) has an offensive weapon with him/her and intentionally uses the weapon to threaten another (B) creating an immediate risk of serious physical harm to B. A's use of the weapon must be unlawful, allowing A to raise relevant defences to the use such as self-defence, defence of others or property, and the prevention of crime. If raised, the burden of rebutting those defences will rest on the prosecution.

In this section 'physical harm' is serious if it amounts to grievous bodily harm for the purposes of the Offences against the Person Act 1861 (s. 1A(2)). 'Public place' and 'offensive weapon' have the same meaning as in s. 1 of the 1953 Act (s. 1A(3)).

Where a person aged 16 or over is convicted of an offence under this section, the court must impose an appropriate custodial sentence (with or without a fine) unless the court is of the opinion that there are particular circumstances which (a) relate to the offence or to the offender, and (b) would make it unjust to do so in all the circumstances (s. 1A(5)). 'Appropriate custodial sentence' means:

(a) in the case of a person who is aged 18 or over when convicted, a sentence of imprisonment for a term of at least six months;
(b) in the case of a person who is aged at least 16 but under 18 when convicted, a detention and training order of at least four months (s. 1A(6)).

4.13.4 Having Bladed or Pointed Article in Public Place

OFFENCE: **Having Bladed or Sharply Pointed Article in Public Place—*Criminal Justice Act 1988, s. 139(1)***

- • Triable either way • Four years' imprisonment and/or a fine on indictment
- • Six months' imprisonment and/or a fine summarily

The Criminal Justice Act 1988, s. 139 states:

(1) Subject to subsections (4) and (5) below, any person who has an article to which this section applies with him in a public place shall be guilty of an offence.

KEYNOTE

This offence applies to any sharply pointed article or article having a blade. Folding pocket knives are excluded unless the cutting edge of the blade exceeds three inches (7.62 cm). If the knife is a lock-knife, it will be covered by this offence irrespective of whether the blade is actually locked open at the time (*Harris* v *DPP* [1993] 1 WLR 82).

Whether an article falls within the parameters of s. 139 is a question of law for the judge/magistrate(s) to determine (*R* v *Deegan* [1998] 2 Cr App R 121—a case that concerned the carrying of a folding pocket-knife that *was* locked open). In *R* v *Davis* [1998] Crim LR 564 the Court of Appeal reiterated that the question of whether an article was 'bladed' or not was a matter of law for the judge to decide. In that case the defendant had been carrying a screwdriver which, the prosecution contended, was a 'bladed' article capable of causing injury. The court decided that the test to be applied in such cases was not whether the 'bladed' article was capable of causing injury, but whether it had a cutting edge. Deciding whether or not an article was caught by the provisions of s. 139 was not a matter of interpreting the ordinary English word 'blade', but required the straightforward construction of the statute. This decision does not mean that a screwdriver can *never* fall within the type of article outlawed under s. 139 and if the screwdriver is pointed or it has been sharpened, it may still be caught by the above offence. There is no requirement for the item to be sharp as long as it has a blade. In *Brooker* v *DPP* [2005] EWHC 1132 (Admin) a blunt butter knife was held to fall within s. 139.

The fact that an article prohibited under s. 139 is part of something that has other innocuous features (e.g. a utility tool or 'Swiss army knife'), does not save it from falling under this offence if the other ingredients are present (*R* v *Giles* [2003] EWCA Crim 1287).

'Has with him' is discussed at **para. 4.13.2.3**. In *R* v *Henderson* [2016] EWCA Crim 965, where an article with a blade was found in the defendant's car when he was not in the car but in a second-floor flat some distance away, it was held that the defendant did not in law have the knife 'with him'. The need to prove that the defendant was aware that he/she had the weapon with him/her for this offence was reaffirmed by the Court of Appeal in *R* v *Daubney* (2000) 164 JP 519.

'Public place' is similar to that under the Prevention of Crime Act 1953. The front garden of a house has been held *not* to be a public place for the purposes of this offence even where that garden is very narrow and the defendant would be able to inflict injuries on passersby from within it (*R* v *Roberts* [2003] EWCA Crim 2753). It must also be determined whether public access was implied or tolerated (*Harriot* v *DPP* [2005] EWHC 965 (Admin)).

In *R* v *Monteiro* [2014] EWCA Crim 747 it was commented that cautions should be issued in accordance with the NPCC guidelines on Knife Crime Offences (2009) that indicates an expectation that 16 and 17-year olds should be charged with carrying a knife unless there were exceptional circumstances.

4.13.4.1 Defences

The Criminal Justice Act 1988, s. 139 states:

(4) It shall be a defence for a person charged with an offence under this section to prove that he had good reason or lawful authority for having the article with him in a public place.

(5) Without prejudice to the generality of subsection (4) above, it shall be a defence for a person charged with an offence under this section to prove that he had the article with him—
 (a) for use at work;
 (b) for religious reasons; or
 (c) as part of any national costume.

4.13.5   Offences and Powers Relating to School Premises

The Criminal Justice Act 1988 provides a number of offences and powers dealing with weapons on school premises. The offence under s. 139AA (below) also applies to 'public places'.

4.13.5.1   Threatening with Article with Blade or Point or Offensive Weapon

OFFENCE: **Threatening with Article with Blade or Point or Offensive Weapon**
Criminal Justice Act 1988, s. 139AA

- Triable either way • Four years' imprisonment and/or a fine on indictment
- Six months' imprisonment and/or a fine summarily

The Criminal Justice Act 1988, s. 139AA states:

(1) A person is guilty of an offence if that person—
    (a) has an article to which this section applies with him or her in a public place or on school premises,
    (b) unlawfully and intentionally threatens another person with the article, and
    (c) does so in such a way that there is an immediate risk of serious physical harm to that other person.

> (1) ... an educational institution which is outside the further education sector and the higher education sector and is an institution for providing—
>
> (a) primary education;
>
> (b) secondary education, or
>
> (c) both primary and secondary education,
>
> whether or not the institution also provides further education.

'School premises' means land used for the purposes of a school *excluding any land occupied solely as a dwelling by a person employed at the school*. This means that the provisions would not apply to someone found in the garden of a caretaker's house if that house was occupied solely as a dwelling by the school caretaker.

'Public place' has the same meaning as in s. 139.

'Physical harm' is serious if it amounts to grievous bodily harm for the purposes of the Offences against the Person Act 1861 (s. 139AA(4)).

4.13.5.2   Having Article with Blade or Point on School Premises

OFFENCE: **Having Bladed or Sharply Pointed Article on School Premises—** *Criminal Justice Act 1988, s. 139A(1)*

- Triable either way • Four years' imprisonment and/or a fine on indictment
- Six months' imprisonment and/or a fine summarily

The Criminal Justice Act 1988, s. 139A states:

> (1) Any person who has an article to which section 139 of this Act applies with him on school premises shall be guilty of an offence.

KEYNOTE

This offence applies to the same articles as those covered under s. 139(1), see para. **4.13.4**.

4.13.5.3   Having Offensive Weapon on School Premises

OFFENCE: **Having Offensive Weapon on School Premises—***Criminal Justice Act 1988, s. 139A(2)*

- Triable either way • Four years' imprisonment and/or a fine on indictment
- Six months' imprisonment and/or a fine summarily

The Criminal Justice Act 1988, s. 139A states:

> (2) Any person who has an offensive weapon within the meaning of section 1 of the Prevention of Crime Act 1953 with him on school premises shall be guilty of an offence.

KEYNOTE

For the purposes of this offence, 'offensive weapons' fall into the three categories discussed at para. **4.13.2.5**.

4.13.5.4   Defences

The defences are the same as for s. 139(1) (**see para. 4.13.4.1**), although in relation to a s. 139A(1) offence, it is a defence for the person charged to prove that he/she had the article or weapon in question for educational purposes (s. 139A(4)(b)).

4.13.5.5　Power of Entry

The Criminal Justice Act 1988, s. 139B states:

(1) A constable may enter school premises and search those premises and any person on those premises for—
   (a) any article to which section 139 of this Act applies, or
   (b) any offensive weapon within the meaning of section 1 of the Prevention of Crime Act 1953, if he has reasonable grounds for suspecting that an offence under section 139A of this Act is being, or has been, committed.

(2) If in the course of a search under this section a constable discovers an article or weapon which he has reasonable grounds for suspecting to be an article or weapon of a kind described in subsection (1) above, he may seize and retain it.

(3) The constable may use reasonable force, if necessary, in the exercise of the power of entry conferred by this section.

KEYNOTE

The PACE Code of Practice for the Exercise by Police Officers of Statutory Powers of Stop and Search (Code A) (2014) applies to searches under s. 139B of the Criminal Justice Act 1988, i.e. searches of persons for offensive weapons, bladed or sharply pointed articles on school premises (see para. 4.5.4).

4.13.5.6　Power of Members of Staff to Search Pupils for Prohibited Items

The Education Act 1996, s. 550ZA states:

(1) This section applies where a member of staff of a school in England—
   (a) has reasonable grounds for suspecting that a pupil at the school may have a prohibited item with him or her or in his or her possessions; and
   (b) falls within section 550ZB(1).

(2) The member of staff may search the pupil ('P') or P's possessions for that item.

(3) For the purposes of this section and section 550ZC each of the following is a 'prohibited item'—
   (a) an article to which section 139 of the Criminal Justice Act 1988 applies (knives and blades etc);
   (b) an offensive weapon, within the meaning of the Prevention of Crime Act 1953;
   ...

(5) In this section and section 550ZB—
   'member of staff', in relation to a school, means—
   (a) any teacher who works at the school; and
   (b) any other person who, with the authority of the head teacher, has lawful control or charge of pupils for whom education is being provided at the school;
   'possessions', in relation to P, includes any goods over which P has or appears to have control.

KEYNOTE

A person may carry out a search under s. 550ZA only if that person is the head teacher of the school, or has been authorised by the head teacher to carry out the search (s. 550ZB(1)). The search may be carried out only where the member of staff and the pupil are on the premises of the school, or they are elsewhere and the member of staff has lawful control or charge of the pupil (s. 550ZB(4)), and a person may use such force as is reasonable in the circumstances (s. 550ZB(5)).

The person carrying out a search may not require the pupil to remove any clothing other than outer clothing, must be of the same sex, and may carry out the search only in the presence of another member of staff who should be of the same sex if it is reasonably practicable (s. 550ZB(6)). The pupil's possessions may not be searched except in the presence of the pupil and another member of staff (s. 550ZB(7)).

The person carrying out a search may seize anything which that person has reasonable grounds for suspecting is a prohibited item, and any other thing which that person has reasonable grounds for suspecting is evidence in relation to an offence. Such force as is reasonable in the circumstances may be used for exercising this power (s. 550ZC(1) and (2)).

Note that the powers in relation to prohibited items only apply in England. In Wales the power of members of staff to search pupils is restricted to knives, blades, etc. and other offensive weapons (s. 550AA).

Where a person seizes an article to which s. 139 of the Criminal Justice Act 1988 applies (knives and blades etc.), an offensive weapon, or anything which that person has reasonable grounds for suspecting is evidence in relation to an offence, he/she must deliver it to a police constable as soon as reasonably practicable (s. 550ZC(8)).

The Further and Higher Education Act 1992 provides the power for members of staff of an institution within the further education sector in England to search students for prohibited items (s. 85AA). In Wales the 1992 Act restricts the power of members of staff in the further education sector to search students for knives, blades, etc. and offensive weapons (s. 85B). Members of staff at an attendance centre also have the power to search persons for knives, blades, etc. and offensive weapons (Violent Crime Reduction Act 2006, s. 47). In relation to all these powers a person who seizes anything as a result of the search must deliver it to a police constable as soon as reasonably practicable.

4.13.6 Trespassing with Weapon of Offence

OFFENCE: **Trespassing with Weapon of Offence—*Criminal Law Act 1977, s. 8(1)***
- Triable summarily • Three months' imprisonment and/or a fine

The Criminal Law Act 1977, s. 8 states:

(1) A person who is on any premises as a trespasser, after having entered as such, is guilty of an offence if, without lawful authority or reasonable excuse, he has with him on the premises any weapon of offence.

KEYNOTE

'Premises' for this purpose means:

- any building; or
- any part of a building under separate occupation;
- any land adjacent to and used/intended for use in connection with a building;
- the site comprising any building(s) together with ancillary land;
- any fixed structure;
- any movable structure, vehicle or vessel designed or adapted for residential purposes (s. 12 of the 1977 Act).

This offence is restricted to a person who has entered the relevant premises as a trespasser. It does not therefore extend to a person who, having entered lawfully, then becomes a trespasser for whatever reason (e.g. because the occupier has told him/her to leave).

The definition of 'weapon of offence' is the same as that for aggravated burglary, namely, any article made or adapted for use for causing injury to or incapacitating a person, or intended by the person having it with him/her for that use (s. 8(2)).

4.13.7 Manufacture and Sale of Weapons

The legislation restricting the sale, manufacture, hire and buying of some weapons is aimed at restricting the supply of such weapons and their availability in England and Wales.

OFFENCE: **Manufacture, Sale or Hire of Weapons—*Restriction of Offensive Weapons Act 1959, s. 1(1)***

- Triable summarily • Six months' imprisonment and/or a fine

The Restriction of Offensive Weapons Act 1959, s. 1 states:

(1) Any person who manufactures, sells or hires or offers for sale or hire or exposes or has in his possession for the purpose of sale or hire, or lends or gives to any other person—

  (a) any knife which has a blade which opens automatically by hand pressure applied to a button, spring or other device in or attached to the handle of the knife, sometimes known as a 'flick knife' or 'flick gun'; or

  (b) any knife which has a blade which is released from the handle or sheath thereof by the force of gravity or the application of centrifugal force and which, when released, is locked in place by means of a button, spring, lever, or other device, sometimes known as a 'gravity knife', shall be guilty of an offence.

OFFENCE: **Manufacture, Sale and Hire of Offensive Weapons—*Criminal Justice Act 1988, s. 141(1)***

- Triable summarily • Six months' imprisonment and/or a fine

The Criminal Justice Act 1988, s. 141 states:

(1) Any person who manufactures, sells or hires or offers for sale or hire, exposes or has in his possession for the purpose of sale or hire, or lends or gives to any other person, a weapon to which this section applies shall be guilty of an offence...

KEYNOTE

The importation of the weapons described in these offences is also prohibited (s. 141(4)).

4.13.7.1 Weapons Covered by s. 141

The weapons to which the 1988 Act applies are set out in the schedule to the Criminal Justice Act 1988 (Offensive Weapons) Order 1988 (SI 1988/2019). The weapons listed include knuckledusters, swordsticks, some telescopic truncheons, butterfly knives, a zombie knife, zombie killer knife or zombie slayer knife, samurai swords and a whole range of martial arts weapons.

KEYNOTE

The courts take notice of the fact that a weapon has been outlawed under this legislation in deciding whether or not it is 'made' for causing injury under the Prevention of Crime Act 1953.

There are a number of defences provided that include Crown servants and visiting forces (s. 141(5)–(7)), transactions made by or to museums and galleries (s. 141(8)–(11)), theatrical performances/rehearsals, and the production of films or television programmes (s. 141(11A) and (11B)). For the purpose of these defences the onus is on the defendant to provide sufficient evidence and the contrary is not proved beyond reasonable doubt (s. 141(11C)).

4.13.8 Knives

Although some knives will fall into the categories of offence covered above, there are further restrictions which apply to knives specifically:

4.13.8.1 Sale of Knives etc. to Persons under 18

OFFENCE: **Selling Knives and Articles to under 18 s—*Criminal Justice Act 1988, s. 141A***

- Triable summarily • Six months' imprisonment and/or a fine

The Criminal Justice Act 1988, s. 141A states:

(1) Any person who sells to a person under the age of eighteen years an article to which this section applies shall be guilty of an offence...

(2) Subject to subsection (3) below, this section applies to—

    (a) any knife, knife blade or razor blade,

    (b) any axe, and

    (c) any other article which has a blade or which is sharply pointed and which is made or adapted for use for causing injury to the person.

(3) This section does not apply to any article described in—

    (a) section 1 of the Restriction of Offensive Weapons Act 1959,

    (b) an order made under section 141(2) of this Act, or

    (c) an order made by the Secretary of State under this section.

KEYNOTE

This offence does not apply to folding pocket knives with a cutting edge not exceeding three inches (7.62cm), neither does it apply to certain types of razor blade in a cartridge where not more than 2mm of blade is exposed (Criminal Justice Act 1988 (Offensive Weapons) (Exemption) Order 1996 (SI 1996/3064)).

Similar to the absurdity of a butter knife falling within the definition of an offence under s. 139 of the 1998 Act, in *R (On the Application of the Royal Borough of Windsor and Maidenhead)* v *East Berkshire Justices* [2010] EWHC 3020 (Admin) it was held that a grapefruit knife is not just a gadget but a knife within the meaning of s. 141A(2)(a).

4.13.8.2 Defence

The Criminal Justice Act 1988, s. 141A states:

(4) It shall be a defence for a person charged with an offence under subsection (1) above to prove that he took all reasonable precautions and exercised all due diligence to avoid the commission of the offence.

4.13.8.3 Unlawful Marketing of Knives

OFFENCE: **Unlawful Marketing of Knives—*Knives Act 1997, s. 1***

- Triable either way • Two years' imprisonment and/or a fine on indictment
- Six months' imprisonment and/or a fine summarily

The Knives Act 1997, s. 1 states:

(1) A person is guilty of an offence if he markets a knife in a way which—

    (a) indicates, or suggests, that it is suitable for combat; or

    (b) is otherwise likely to stimulate or encourage violent behaviour involving the use of the knife as a weapon.

KEYNOTE

'Knife' for this purpose means any instrument which has a blade *or* which is sharply pointed (s. 10 of the 1997 Act).

Marketing will include selling, hiring, offering or exposing for sale or hire and possessing it for those purposes (s. 1(4)).

'Indicates or suggests' is a very loose concept requiring no *mens rea* on the part of the defendant (however, see defences at **para. 4.13.8.4**).

'Suitable for combat' means suitable for use as a weapon for inflicting injury to anyone *or causing them to fear injury*, and 'violent behaviour' means an unlawful act inflicting injury *or causing a person to fear injury* (s. 10). The elements in italics (author's emphasis) show that the legislation is intended to address the fear of the use of knives as well as their actual use.

The suggestion that knives are suitable for combat may be express or it may be implied by the name given to a product (e.g. 'commando') or by the packaging or advertisement relating to it (s. 1(3)). Therefore such packaging or advertising material, together with any surrounding advertisements, can be produced in evidence.

4.13.8.4 Defences

The Knives Act 1997, ss. 3 and 4 state:

> 3.—(1) It is a defence for a person charged with an offence under section 1 to prove that—
>   (a) the knife was marketed—
>   (i) for use by the armed forces of any country;
>   (ii) as an antique or curio; or
>   (iii) as falling within such other category (if any) as may be prescribed;
>   (b) it was reasonable for the knife to be marketed in that way; and
>   (c) there were no reasonable grounds for suspecting that a person into whose possession the knife might come in consequence of the way in which it was marketed would use it for an unlawful purpose.
>
>   . . .
>
> 4.—(1) It is a defence for a person charged with an offence under section 1 to prove that he did not know or suspect, and had no reasonable grounds for suspecting, that the way in which the knife was marketed—
>   (a) amounted to an indication or suggestion that the knife was suitable for combat; or
>   (b) was likely to stimulate or encourage violent behaviour involving the use of the knife as a weapon...

KEYNOTE

There is also the general defence under s. 4(3) for the person to show that he/she took *all* reasonable precautions and exercised *all* due diligence to avoid committing the offence.

Section 5 allows a court to issue a warrant for the entry onto premises and for the search, seizure and removal of knives (or materials where an offence under s. 2 is involved). Any knives or publications which have been seized and removed by a constable under a warrant issued under this section may be retained until the conclusion of proceedings against the suspect (s. 5(4)).

4.13.8.5 Publications Relating to Knives

OFFENCE: **Publications Relating to Knives—*Knives Act 1997, s. 2(1)***
- Triable either way • Two years' imprisonment and/or a fine on indictment
- Six months' imprisonment and/or a fine summarily

The Knives Act 1997, s. 2 states:

> (1) A person is guilty of an offence if he publishes any written, pictorial or other material in connection with the marketing of any knife and that material—
>   (a) indicates, or suggests, that the knife is suitable for combat; or
>   (b) is otherwise likely to stimulate or encourage violent behaviour involving the use of the knife as a weapon.

The Knives Act 1997, s. 3 states:

> (2) It is a defence for a person charged with an offence under section 2 to prove that—
>   (a) the material was published in connection with marketing a knife—
>   (i) for use by the armed forces of any country;
>   (ii) as an antique or curio; or
>   (iii) as falling within such other category (if any) as may be prescribed;
>   (b) it was reasonable for the knife to be marketed in that way; and

(c) there were no reasonable grounds for suspecting that a person into whose possession the knife might come in consequence of the publishing of the material would use it for an unlawful purpose.

The Knives Act 1997, s. 4 states:

(2) It is a defence for a person charged with an offence under section 2 to prove that he did not know or suspect, and had no reasonable grounds for suspecting, that the material—
    (a) amounted to an indication or suggestion that the knife was suitable for combat; or
    (b) was likely to stimulate or encourage violent behaviour involving the use of the knife as a weapon.

KEYNOTE

The offence under s. 2(1) is aimed at the publishers of advertisements rather than those who are involved in the sale and marketing of knives. A search warrant may be issued for relevant publications (s. 5).

4.13.9 Crossbows

Even though they might fit into some of the other offences discussed above, crossbows are also subject to specific legislation.

The Crossbows Act 1987 provides three summary offences:

- Selling or letting on hire a crossbow or part of a crossbow to a person under the age of 18 (s. 1);
- A person under the age of 18 buying or hiring a crossbow or a part of a crossbow (s. 2);
- A person under the age of 18 having with him a crossbow capable of discharging a missile (s. 3).

KEYNOTE

The 1987 Act provides that where a constable has reasonable cause to suspect that a person is committing or has committed an offence under s. 3, they may search that person or any vehicle for a crossbow or part of a crossbow (s. 4(1)) and detain them for the purpose of the search (s. 4(2)).

The PACE Code of Practice for the Exercise by Police Officers of Statutory Powers of Stop and Search (Code A) (2014) applies to searches under s. 4 of the Crossbows Act 1987, i.e. searches of persons and vehicles for crossbows or parts of crossbows (except crossbows with a draw weight of less than 1.4 kilograms), anywhere except dwellings (see para. 4.5.4).

For the purpose of exercising their powers a constable may enter any land other than a dwelling (s. 4(4)).

General Police Duties

4.14 Domestic Violence and Trade Disputes

4.14.1 Introduction

This chapter deals with domestic violence and abuse, and trade disputes. It is an accepted fact that domestic violence and abuse requires the expertise and associated resources to deal with criminal acts involving the abuse by one partner against another in an intimate relationship such as marriage, civil partnership, cohabitation, dating or within the family.

4.14.2 Domestic Violence and Abuse

The shared NPCC, CPS and government definition of domestic violence and abuse as contained in Home Office Circular 003/2013 is:

> Any incident or pattern of incidents of controlling, coercive or threatening behaviour, violence or abuse between those aged 16 or over who are or have been intimate partners or family members regardless of gender or sexuality. This can encompass, but is not limited to, the following types of abuse:
>
> • psychological
> • physical
> • sexual
> • financial
> • emotional
>
> Controlling behaviour is: a range of acts designed to make a person subordinate and/or dependent by isolating them from sources of support, exploiting their resources and capacities for personal gain, depriving them of the means needed for independence, resistance and escape and regulating their everyday behaviour.
>
> Coercive behaviour is: an act or a pattern of acts of assault, threats, humiliation and intimidation or other abuse that is used to harm, punish, or frighten their victim.
>
> This definition, which is not a legal definition, includes so called 'honour' based violence, female genital mutilation (FGM) and forced marriage, and is clear that victims are not confined to one gender or ethnic group.

KEYNOTE

Section 76 of the Serious Crime Act 2015 provides for an offence of 'controlling or coercive behaviour in an intimate or family relationship' (see *Crime*). Controlling or coercive behaviour is defined under this section as causing someone to fear that violence will be used against them on at least two occasions, or generating serious alarm or distress that has a substantial effect on their usual day-to-day activities.

4.14.2.1 Domestic Violence Protection Notices and Orders

A Domestic Violence Protection Notice (DVPN) is the initial notice issued by the police to provide emergency protection to an individual believed to be the victim of domestic violence and abuse.

The power to issue a domestic violence protection notice is provided by s. 24 of the Crime and Security Act 2010, which states:

(1) A member of a police force not below the rank of superintendent ('the authorising officer') may issue a domestic violence protection notice ('a DVPN') under this section.

(2) A DVPN may be issued to a person ('P') aged 18 years or over if the authorising officer has reasonable grounds for believing that—
  (a) P has been violent towards, or has threatened violence towards, an associated person, and
  (b) the issue of the DVPN is necessary to protect that person from violence or a threat of violence by P.

(3) Before issuing a DVPN, the authorising officer must, in particular, consider—
  (a) the welfare of any person under the age of 18 whose interests the officer considers relevant to the issuing of the DVPN (whether or not that person is an associated person),
  (b) the opinion of the person for whose protection the DVPN would be issued as to the issuing of the DVPN,
  (c) any representations made by P as to the issuing of the DVPN, and
  (d) in the case of provision included by virtue of subsection (8), the opinion of any other associated person who lives in the premises to which the provision would relate.

(4) The authorising officer must take reasonable steps to discover the opinions mentioned in subsection (3).

(5) But the authorising officer may issue a DVPN in circumstances where the person for whose protection it is issued does not consent to the issuing of the DVPN.

KEYNOTE

The purpose of a DVPN is to secure the immediate protection of a victim of domestic violence and abuse (V) from future violence or a threat of violence from a suspected perpetrator (P). A DVPN prohibits P from molesting V and, where they cohabit, may require P to leave those premises.

Where a DVPN has been issued, a constable must apply to a magistrates' court for a Domestic Violence Protection Order (DVPO). The application must be heard by the magistrates' court not later than 48 hours after the DVPN was served (s. 27). The DVPO is an order lasting between 14 and 28 days, which prohibits P from molesting V and may also make provision about access to shared accommodation (s. 28).

A person who breaches a DVPN may be arrested without warrant (s. 25(1)(b)) and must be held in custody to appear before a magistrates' court within 24 hours when an application for a DVPO can be heard (s. 26).

The Home Office has published a Domestic Violence and Abuse Chapter to add to the Guide on Firearms Licensing Law (July 2013) that is available on the gov.uk website. It outlines that general evidence of domestic violence and abuse will indicate that an individual should not be permitted to possess a firearm or shotgun, and all cases must be assessed by the police on their own merits. It also says that every incident of domestic violence and abuse should prompt a police review of whether a certificate holder should be allowed to hold a firearm without posing a danger to the public.

4.14.2.2 Domestic Violence Disclosure Scheme

The Domestic Violence Disclosure Scheme, also known as Clare's Law, gained momentum following the tragic case of Clare Wood, who was murdered by her former partner in 2009. Her partner had three previous convictions under the Protection from Harassment Act 1997.

The principal aim of the Scheme is to introduce recognised and consistent procedures for disclosing information which will enable a partner (A) of a previously violent individual (B) to make informed choices about whether and how A takes forward that relationship with B.

There are two distinct entry routes that may lead to a disclosure being made. The first entry route—'right to ask'—is modelled closely on the existing Child Sex Offender Disclosure Scheme, and is triggered when a person makes a *direct application* to the police for information about B. The second entry route—'right to know'—is triggered when the police receive *indirect* information or intelligence about the safety of A and where, after appropriate checks are made, the police judge that a disclosure should be made to safeguard A.

Every request made under the scheme is thoroughly checked by a panel made up of the police, probation services and other agencies such as social services who decide whether any disclosure is lawful, necessary and proportionate.

4.14.2.3 Court Orders

Any court having jurisdiction over family law matters can make an order under the Family Law Act 1996. This Act consolidated many aspects of the law regulating family proceedings. Part IV of the Act makes provisions relating to family homes and domestic violence.

4.14.2.4 Non-molestation Orders

Section 42 of the 1996 Act provides for 'non-molestation' orders. Section 42 states:

(1) In this Part a 'non-molestation order' means an order containing either or both of the following provisions—
  (a) provision prohibiting a person ('the respondent') from molesting another person who is associated with the respondent;
  (b) provision prohibiting the respondent from molesting a relevant child.
(2) The court may make a non-molestation order—
  (a) if an application for the order has been made (whether in other family proceedings or without any other family proceedings being instituted) by a person who is associated with the respondent; or
  (b) if in any family proceedings to which the respondent is a party the court considers that the order should be made for the benefit of any other party to the proceedings or any relevant child even though no such application has been made.

KEYNOTE

Non-molestation orders can be applied for even though no other proceedings have been begun and such orders do not relate just to spouses or former partners; they apply to anyone who is 'associated' with the respondent.

Under s. 62, a person is 'associated' with another person if:

(3) ...
  (a)   they are or have been married to each other;
  (aa) they are or have been civil partners of each other;
  (b)   they are cohabitants or former cohabitants;
  (c)   they live or have lived in the same household, otherwise than merely by reason of one of them being the other's employee, tenant, lodger or boarder;
  (d)   they are relatives;
  (e)   they have agreed to marry one another (whether or not that agreement has been terminated);
  (ea) they have or have had an intimate personal relationship with each other which is or was of significant duration;
  (eza) they have entered a civil partnership agreement (as defined by section 73 of the Civil Partnership Act 2004) (whether or not that agreement has been terminated);
  (f)   in relation to any child, they are both persons falling within subsection (4); or
  (g)   they are parties to the same family proceedings (other than proceedings under this Part).
(4) A person falls within this subsection in relation to a child if—
  (a)   he is a parent of the child; or
  (b)   he has or has had parental responsibility for the child.

In deciding whether or not to make such an order, the court must consider all the circumstances, including the need to secure the health, safety and well-being of the applicant or any relevant child (s. 42(5)).

4.14.2.5 Breach of a Non-molestation Order

OFFENCE: **Breach of a Non-molestation Order**—*Family Law Act 1996, s. 42A*
- Triable either way • Five years' imprisonment and/or a fine on indictment
- 12 months' imprisonment and/or a fine summarily

The Family Law Act 1996, s. 42A states:

(1) A person who without reasonable excuse does anything that he is prohibited from doing by a non-molestation order is guilty of an offence.

(2) In the case of a non-molestation order made by virtue of s. 45(1), a person can be guilty of an offence under this section only in respect of conduct engaged in at a time when he was aware of the existence of the order.

KEYNOTE

Note that there is a power of arrest for the breach of a non-molestation order under the provisions of s. 24(1) of the Police and Criminal Evidence Act 1984.

In relation to s. 42A(2), non-molestation orders made by virtue of s. 45(1) are *ex parte* orders where the respondent has not been present at the proceedings when the order was made.

Restraining orders (see para. 4.7.4.13) may be made on conviction for any offence, rather than only on conviction for offences under the Protection from Harassment Act 1997. Consequently, these orders are available to be used in cases involving domestic violence.

4.14.3 Trade Disputes

Most of the conditions regulating trade disputes can be found in the Trade Union and Labour Relations (Consolidation) Act 1992.

The areas which have historically created the greatest need for police involvement arise from the differences between those who wish to exercise their right to strike and those who wish to continue to work.

4.14.3.1 Picketing

The Trade Union and Labour Relations (Consolidation) Act 1992, s. 220 states:

(1) It is lawful for a person in contemplation or furtherance of a trade dispute to attend—
   (a) at or near his own place of work, or
   (b) if he is an official of a trade union, at or near the place of work of a member of the union whom he is accompanying and whom he represents, for the purpose only of peacefully obtaining or communicating information, or peacefully persuading any person to work or abstain from working.

(2) If a person works or normally works—
   (a) otherwise than at any one place, or
   (b) at a place the location of which is such that attendance there for a purpose mentioned in subsection (1) is impracticable, his place of work for the purposes of that subsection shall be any premises of his employer from which he works or from which his work is administered.

(3) In the case of a worker not in employment where—
   (a) his last employment was terminated in connection with a trade dispute, or
   (b) the termination of his employment was one of the circumstances giving rise to a trade dispute, in relation to that dispute his former place of work shall be treated for the purposes of subsection (1) as being his place of work.

(4) A person who is an official of a trade union by virtue only of having been elected or appointed to be a representative of some of the members of the union shall be regarded for the purposes of subsection (1) as representing only those members; but otherwise an official of a union shall be regarded for those purposes as representing all its members.

4.14.3.2 Meaning of 'Trade Dispute'

The Trade Union and Labour Relations (Consolidation) Act 1992, s. 244 states:

(1) In this Part a 'trade dispute' means a dispute between workers and their employer which relates wholly or mainly to one or more of the following—
   (a) terms and conditions of employment, or the physical conditions in which any workers are required to work;
   (b) engagement or non-engagement, or termination or suspension of employment or the duties of employment, of one or more workers;
   (c) allocation of work or the duties of employment between workers or groups of workers;
   (d) matters of discipline;
   (e) a worker's membership or non-membership of a trade union;
   (f) facilities for officials of trade unions; and
   (g) machinery for negotiation or consultation, and other procedures, relating to any of the above matters, including the recognition by employers or employers' associations of the right of a trade union to represent workers in such negotiation or consultation or in the carrying out of such procedures.

KEYNOTE

'Employment' includes any relationship whereby one person personally does work or performs services for another. 'Worker', in relation to a dispute with an employer, means a worker employed by that employer, or a person who has ceased to be so employed if his/her employment was terminated in connection with the dispute, or if the termination of his/her employment was one of the circumstances giving rise to the dispute (s. 244(5)).

4.14.3.3 Use of Violence or Intimidation

OFFENCE: **Intimidation or Annoyance by Violence or Otherwise—*Trade Union and Labour Relations (Consolidation) Act 1992, s. 241***
   • Triable summarily • Six months' imprisonment and/or a fine

The Trade Union and Labour Relations (Consolidation) Act 1992, s. 241 states:

(1) A person commits an offence who, with a view to compelling another person to abstain from doing or to do any act which that person has a legal right to do or abstain from doing, wrongfully and without legal authority—
   (a) uses violence to or intimidates that person or his spouse or civil partner or children, or injures his property,

(b) persistently follows that person about from place to place,

(c) hides any tools, clothes or other property owned or used by that person, or deprives him of or hinders him in the use thereof,

(d) watches or besets the house or other place where that person resides, works, carries on business or happens to be, or the approach to any such house or place, or

(e) follows that person with two or more other persons in a disorderly manner in or through any street or road.

KEYNOTE

'With a view to compelling' means with intent to compel. This is therefore an offence of 'specific intent'.

'Wrongfully' means a civil wrong.

Although the breach of a contract is generally not a criminal offence, this section imposes a duty on some contracted personnel not to breach their contract under certain conditions.

4.15 Protection of People Suffering from Mental Disorders

4.15.1 Introduction

The Mental Health Act 1983 provides for the care and treatment of people suffering from mental disorders and supplies powers for enforcing some of its provisions. If those powers are executed in good faith, the 1983 Act also provides some protection against criminal and civil liability for the police officers and care workers who use them (s. 139). The 1983 Act is supported by a Code of Practice that sets out guidance for the police and other agencies when dealing with people suffering from mental disorders.

4.15.2 Mentally Disordered People Found in Public Places

Section 136 of the Mental Health Act 1983 creates a power for police officers to remove such a person under certain conditions.

Section 136 states:

(1) If a constable finds in a place to which the public have access a person who appears to him to be suffering from mental disorder and to be in immediate need of care or control, the constable may, if he thinks it necessary to do so in the interests of that person or for the protection of other persons, remove that person to a place of safety within the meaning of section 135 above.

(2) A person removed to a place of safety under this section may be detained there for a period not exceeding 72 hours for the purpose of enabling him to be examined by a registered medical practitioner and to be interviewed by an approved mental health professional and of making any necessary arrangements for his treatment or care.

(3) A constable, an approved mental health professional or a person authorised by either of them for the purposes of this subsection may, before the end of the period of 72 hours mentioned in subsection (2) above, take a person detained in a place of safety under that subsection to one or more other places of safety.

(4) A person taken to a place of safety under subsection (3) above may be detained there for a purpose mentioned in subsection (2) above for a period ending no later than at the end of the period of 72 hours mentioned in that subsection.

KEYNOTE

The power places a lot of responsibility and latitude on the officer who must decide whether:

- the person is suffering from mental disorder (see below),
- the person is in immediate need of care or control, and
- it is necessary in the person's interest or for someone else's protection that he/she be removed to a place of safety,

before the power is applicable.

The definition of 'mental disorder' under s. 1(2) is very wide and means:

- mental illness;
- arrested or incomplete development of mind;
- any other disorder or disability of mind.

Under s. 135(6), a 'place of safety' is:

- residential accommodation provided by social services;
- a hospital;
- a police station;
- an independent hospital or care home for mentally disordered persons; or
- any other suitable place where the occupier is willing to receive the patient temporarily.

Home Office Circular 07/2008 states that police stations should only be used as a place of safety in *exceptional circumstances*, e.g. where the person's behaviour would pose an unmanageably high risk to other patients, staff or users of a health care setting. Nor should police stations be assumed to be the automatic second choice if the first place of safety is not immediately available. Other options such as a residential care home or home of a friend/relative should also be considered. If a police station must be used, health and social care agencies should work with the police in supporting the care and welfare of the person while in police custody, and assist in arranging, where appropriate, the transfer of the person to a more suitable place of safety.

Section 136(3) and (4) enable a person detained at a place of safety to be transferred to another one, subject to an overall time limit for detention of 72 hours.

Anyone being taken to a place of safety or detained at such a place will be treated as being in legal custody (s. 137(1)). This expression is only relevant in relation to escaping and assisting in an escape; it is very different from 'in police detention' used under s. 118 of the Police and Criminal Evidence Act 1984. A mentally disordered person removed from a public place is *not* in police detention even if taken to a police station.

Note that this power is a power of removal from a public place; it is not a power of arrest nor does it provide a power to detain/further detain someone who is already in police detention.

It is an offence to assist someone removed under s. 136 to escape (s. 128).

4.15.3 Warrant to Search for Patients

Where there is reasonable cause to suspect that a person believed to be suffering from a mental disorder has been, or is being ill-treated or neglected or is unable to care for him/herself and is living alone, a warrant may be issued by a magistrate (s. 135).

The warrant allows a constable to enter any premises specified and to remove the person to a place of safety. In doing so, the officer must be accompanied by a social worker and a doctor (s. 135(4)).

A warrant may also be issued in respect of a patient ordered to be detained by a court.

4.15.4 Power to Retake Escaped Patients

Section 138 provides a power to retake people who have been in legal custody under the 1983 Act.

A person removed to a place of safety under s. 136 or a person removed under a warrant, who subsequently escapes while being taken to or detained in a place of safety, cannot generally be retaken after 72 hours have elapsed. That time period starts either when the person escapes or when his/her liability to be detained began, whichever expires first (s. 138(3)). This means that, if the person escapes *before* reaching the place of safety, the 72 hours begins then; if the person escapes *from* the place of safety, the 72 hours begins at the time he/she arrived there.

There is also a power for a court to issue a warrant for the arrest of a convicted mental patient who is unlawfully at large (Criminal Justice Act 1967, s. 72(3)).

4.15.5 Ambit of the Mental Health Act 1983

The ambit of the Mental Health Act 1983 was reviewed in *St George's Healthcare NHS Trust* v *S* [1999] Fam 26, by the Court of Appeal. There it was held that:

- The 1983 Act should not be invoked to overrule the decision of a patient concerning medical treatment simply because that decision appears to be irrational.
- A person detained under the 1983 Act should not be forced to receive medical treatment which is not connected with his/her mental condition unless his/her capacity to give consent is seriously diminished.

4.15.6 The Mental Capacity Act 2005

The Mental Capacity Act 2005 provides a statutory framework to empower and protect vulnerable people who are not able to make their own decisions. It covers a wide range of situations in all areas of life and provides protection from legal liability for acts done in connection with care and treatment if done in a person's best interests and in keeping with the Act. Importantly, it can provide police officers with a power to act in a person's best interests, effectively as if they had the person's consent.

4.15.6.1 The Principles

The Mental Capacity Act 2005, s. 1 states:

(1) The following principles apply for the purposes of this Act.
(2) A person must be assumed to have capacity unless it is established that he lacks capacity.
(3) A person is not to be treated as unable to make a decision unless all practicable steps to help him to do so have been taken without success.
(4) A person is not to be treated as unable to make a decision merely because he makes an unwise decision.
(5) An act done, or decision made, under this Act for or on behalf of a person who lacks capacity must be done, or made, in his best interests.
(6) Before the act is done, or the decision is made, regard must be had to whether the purpose for which it is needed can be as effectively achieved in a way that is less restrictive of the person's rights and freedom of action.

KEYNOTE

Section 1 sets out key principles applying to decisions and actions taken under the Act. The starting point is a presumption of capacity. A person must be assumed to have capacity until it is proved otherwise. A person must also be supported to make his own decision, as far it is practicable to do so. The Act requires 'all practicable steps' to be taken to help the person. This could include, for example, making sure that the person is in an environment in which he is comfortable or involving an expert in helping him express his views. It is expressly provided that a person is not to be treated as lacking capacity to make a decision simply because he makes an unwise decision. This means that a person who has the necessary ability to make the decision has the right to make irrational or eccentric decisions that others may not judge to be in his best interests (see s. 3 at **para. 4.15.6.3**). Everything done, or decisions made, under the Act for a person who lacks capacity must be done in that person's best interests. In addition, the 'least restrictive option' principle must always be considered. The person making the decision or acting must think whether it is possible to decide or act in a way that would interfere less with the rights and freedom of action of the person who lacks capacity.

4.15.6.2 People who Lack Capacity

The Mental Health Act 2005, s. 2 states:

(1) For the purposes of this Act, a person lacks capacity in relation to a matter if at the material time he is unable to make a decision for himself in relation to the matter because of an impairment of, or a disturbance in the functioning of, the mind or brain.

(2) It does not matter whether the impairment or disturbance is permanent or temporary.

(3) A lack of capacity cannot be established merely by reference to—

    (a) a person's age or appearance, or

    (b) a condition of his, or an aspect of his behaviour, which might lead others to make unjustified assumptions about his capacity.

(4) In proceedings under this Act or any other enactment, any question whether a person lacks capacity within the meaning of this Act must be decided on the balance of probabilities.

(5) No power which a person ('D') may exercise under this Act—

    (a) in relation to a person who lacks capacity, or

    (b) where D reasonably thinks that a person lacks capacity,

    is exercisable in relation to a person under 16.

KEYNOTE

Section 2 sets out the Act's definition of a person who lacks capacity. It focuses on the particular time when a decision has to be made and on the particular matter to which the decision relates, not on any theoretical ability to make decisions generally. It follows that a person can lack capacity for the purposes of the Act even if the loss of capacity is partial or temporary or if his capacity fluctuates. It also follows that a person may lack capacity in relation to one matter but not in relation to another matter.

The inability to make a decision must be caused by an impairment of or disturbance in the functioning of the mind or brain. This is the so-called 'diagnostic test'. This could cover a range of problems, such as psychiatric illness, learning disability, dementia, brain damage or even a toxic confusional state, as long as it has the necessary effect on the functioning of the mind or brain, causing the person to be unable to make the decision.

Section 2(3) introduces a principle of equal consideration in relation to determinations of a person's capacity. It makes it clear that such determinations should not merely be made on the basis of a person's age, appearance or unjustified assumptions about capacity based on the person's condition or behaviour. Any preconceptions and prejudicial assumptions held by a person making the assessment of capacity must therefore have no input into the assessment of capacity. The reference to 'condition' captures a range of factors, including any physical disability a person may have. So, in making an assessment of capacity, the fact that the person in question has a learning difficulty should not in itself lead the person making the assessment to assume that the person with the learning difficulty would lack capacity to decide, for example, where to live. The reference to 'appearance' would also include skin colour.

Section 2(5) makes it clear that powers under the Act generally only arise where the person lacking capacity is 16 or over (although powers in relation to property might be exercised in relation to a younger person who has disabilities which will cause the incapacity to last into adulthood (s. 18(3)). Any overlap with the jurisdiction under the Children Act 1989 can be dealt with by orders about the transfer of proceedings to the more appropriate court (s. 21).

4.15.6.3 Inability to Make Decisions

The Mental Health Act 2005, s. 3 states:

(1) For the purposes of section 2, a person is unable to make a decision for himself if he is unable—

    (a) to understand the information relevant to the decision,

    (b) to retain that information,

    (c) to use or weigh that information as part of the process of making the decision, or

    (d) to communicate his decision (whether by talking, using sign language or any other means).

(2) A person is not to be regarded as unable to understand the information relevant to a decision if he is able to understand an explanation of it given to him in a way that is appropriate to his circumstances (using simple language, visual aids or any other means).

(3) The fact that a person is able to retain the information relevant to a decision for a short period only does not prevent him from being regarded as able to make the decision.

(4) The information relevant to a decision includes information about the reasonably foreseeable consequences of—

(a) deciding one way or another, or

(b) failing to make the decision.

KEYNOTE

Section 3 sets out the test for assessing whether a person is unable to make a decision about a matter and therefore lacks capacity in relation to that matter. It is a 'functional' test, looking at the decision-making process itself. Four reasons are given why a person may be unable to make a decision. The first three (s. 3(1)(a)–(c)) will cover the vast majority of cases. To make a decision, a person must first be able to comprehend the information relevant to the decision (further defined in s. 3(4)). Section 3(2) makes clear that a determination of incapacity may not be reached without the relevant information having been presented to the person in a way that is appropriate to his circumstances. Secondly, the person must be able to retain this information (for long enough to make the decision, as explained in s. 3(3)). And thirdly, he must be able to use and weigh it to arrive at a choice. If the person cannot undertake one of these three aspects of the decision-making process then he is unable to make the decision.

Section 3(1)(d) provides for the fourth situation where someone is unable to make a decision, namely where he cannot communicate it in any way. This is intended to be a residual category and will only affect a small number of persons, in particular some of those with the very rare condition of 'locked-in syndrome'. It seems likely that people suffering from this condition can in fact still understand, retain and use information and so would not be regarded as lacking capacity under s. 3(1)(a)–(c). Some people who suffer from this condition can communicate by blinking an eye, but it seems that others cannot communicate at all. Section 3(1)(d) treats those who are completely unable to communicate their decisions as unable to make a decision. Any residual ability to communicate (such as blinking an eye to indicate 'yes' or 'no' in answer to a question) would exclude a person from this category.

4.15.6.4 Acts in Connection with Care or Treatment

The Mental Capacity Act 2005, s. 5 states:

(1) If a person (D) does an act in connection with the care or treatment of another person (P), the act is one to which this section applies if—

(a) before doing the act, D takes reasonable steps to establish whether P lacks capacity in relation to the matter in question, and

(b) when doing the act, D reasonably believes—

(i) that P lacks clarity in relation to the matter and

(ii) that it will be in P's best interests for the act to be done.

(2) D does not incur any liability in relation to the act that he would not have incurred if P—

(a) had had capacity to consent in relation to the matter, and

(b) had consented to D's doing the act.

(3) ...

(4) ...

The Mental Capacity Act 2005, s. 6 states:

(1) If D does an act that is intended to restrain P, it is not an act to which section 5 applies unless two further conditions are satisfied.

(2) The first condition is that D reasonably believes that it is necessary to do the act in order to prevent harm to P.

(3) The second is that the act is a proportionate response to—

(a) the likelihood of P's suffering harm, and

(b) the seriousness of that harm.

(4) For the purposes of this section D restrains P if he—
  (a) uses, or threatens to use, force to secure the doing of an act which P resists, or
  (b) restricts P's liberty of movement, whether or not P resists.
(5) ...
(6) Section 5 does not authorise a person to do an act which conflicts with a decision made, within the scope of his authority and in accordance with this Part, by—
  (a) a donee of a lasting power of attorney granted by P, or
  (b) a deputy appointed for P by the court.
(7) But nothing in subsection (6) stops a person—
  (a) providing life-sustaining treatment, or
  (b) doing an act which he reasonably believes to be necessary to prevent a serious deterioration in P's condition, while a decision as respects any relevant issue is sought from the court.

KEYNOTE

This legislation provides a statutory footing for the actions of police officers when they are called to deal with an individual who lacks capacity. If an act qualifies as a 'section 5 act' then a police officer (or other relevant person) can be confident that he/she will not face civil liability or criminal prosecution as no offence has been committed by the individual. The officer can act in that person's best interests in connection with care and treatment. Where the officer has used the capacity test (set out in s. 5), force can be used to move that person from one place to another. Simply put, the 'capacity test' is the question, 'Does this person have the capacity to make this decision at this time?' If the decision is that the person lacks capacity, the officer can act in the individual's best interests.

- -

EXAMPLE

An officer on patrol finds an elderly man in the street. The man is extremely confused and is bleeding from a head injury. The elderly man refuses any assistance from the officer who is concerned for the man's welfare. The officer can consider the 'test of capacity' and if he/she decides that at that time the man lacks capacity, the officer can act in the man's best interests.

Section 6 defines restraint and before this is permitted it must be considered necessary and proportionate. The ability to restrain under s. 6 does not provide a power to remove the person to a place of safety (*R (On the Application of Sessay)* v *South London and Maudsley NHS Foundation* [2011] EWHC 2617), rather it relates to holding a person in a particular place (i.e. preventing them from leaving), or physically restraining a person so that care or treatment can be given. Where it is required to remove a person to a place of safety then the powers available under the Mental Health Act 1983 should be used.

4.16 Offences Relating to Land and Premises

4.16.1 Criminal Trespass

'Criminal' trespass can generally be categorised as:

- trespassing with the intention of disrupting or obstructing a lawful activity, or intimidating those engaged in it;
- two or more people trespassing with the purpose of residing on the land;
- residing in vehicles on land.

This chapter also includes the legislation dealing with 'criminal' trespass in relation to residential, educational and protected premises.

4.16.2 Aggravated Trespass

OFFENCE: **Trespass Intending to Obstruct, Disrupt or Intimidate—*Criminal Justice and Public Order Act 1994, s. 68***

- Triable summarily • Three months' imprisonment and/or a fine

The Criminal Justice and Public Order Act 1994, s. 68 states:

(1) A person commits the offence of aggravated trespass if he trespasses on land and, in relation to any lawful activity which persons are engaging in or are about to engage in on that or adjoining land, does there anything which is intended by him to have the effect—
   (a) of intimidating those persons or any of them so as to deter them or any of them from engaging in that activity,
   (b) of obstructing that activity, or
   (c) of disrupting that activity.
(2) Activity on any occasion on the part of a person or persons on land is 'lawful' for the purposes of this section if he or they may engage in the activity on the land on that occasion without committing an offence or trespassing on the land.

KEYNOTE

Examples of the sort of conduct envisaged would be environmental activists disrupting a building programme or disrupting the planting of genetically modified crops (*DPP* v *Bayer* [2003] EWHC 2567 (Admin)).

It must be shown that the defendant intended to bring about the effects set out at s. 68(1)(a)–(c). There is no need to specify which of the intended activities (i.e. deterring, obstructing or disrupting) in any charge and use of all three expressions is not bad for duplicity (*Nelder* v *DPP* (1988) *The Times*, 11 June). However, proof is required of both the trespassing on land *and* of some overt act, other than the trespassing, which was intended to have the effects set out at s. 68(1)(a)–(c) (*DPP* v *Barnard* [2000] Crim LR 371; *Peppersharp* v *DPP* [2012] EWHC 474 (Admin)).

In *Bauer* v *DPP* [2013] EWHC 634 (Admin) it was held that a large group of protesters, known as 'UK Uncut', protesting against tax avoidance, who occupied Fortnum and Mason's store in London for a period of nearly two and a half hours were guilty of aggravated trespass by virtue of their presence which had the intention to intimidate staff and customers within the store. It was also held that if the facts showed that people were part of the group which had committed the aggravated trespass then they were as guilty as the rest as a joint principal.

Under s. 68(5) land does not include land forming part of a highway unless it is:

- a footpath, bridleway or byway open to all traffic or road used as a public path (as defined by s. 54 of the Wildlife and Countryside Act 1981) or
- a cycle track under the Highways Act 1980 or the Cycle Tracks Act 1984.

Lawful activity is defined at s. 68(2) and is a very wide concept. This point has been determined in the context of anti-war protestors where it was argued that the war against Iraq was illegal and therefore the activities carried out by staff at airbases were also unlawful. The House of Lords determined that for the purposes of s. 68(2), an act of aggression against another State or a general crime against peace did not constitute an offence contrary to the law of England and Wales (*R* v *Jones* [2006] UKHL 16; *Ayliffe* v *DPP* [2005] EWHC 684 (Admin); *Nero* v *DPP* [2012] EWHC 1238 (Admin); *Richardson* v *DPP* [2014] UKSC 8).

4.16.2.1 Aggravated Trespass: Power to Remove Persons

The Criminal Justice and Public Order Act 1994, s. 69 states:

(1) If the senior police officer present at the scene reasonably believes—
   (a) that a person is committing, has committed or intends to commit the offence of aggravated trespass on land; or
   (b) that two or more persons are trespassing on land and are present there with the common purpose of intimidating persons so as to deter them from engaging in a lawful activity or of obstructing or disrupting a lawful activity,
   he may direct that person or (as the case may be) those persons (or any of them) to leave the land.
(2) A direction under subsection (1) above, if not communicated to the persons referred to in subsection (1) by the police officer giving the direction, may be communicated to them by any constable at the scene.

KEYNOTE

Although this power requires the senior officer present at the scene to have a reasonable *belief* as to the circumstances set out at s. 69(1)(a) or (b), the power is available as a preventive measure and as a means of dealing with the incident after it has happened.

The direction to leave the land may be communicated to the relevant people by any police officer at the scene and there is no requirement for either officer to be in uniform.

4.16.2.2 Failure to Leave Land or Re-entry to Land when Directed to Leave

OFFENCE: **Failure to Leave or Re-entry when Directed to Leave—*Criminal Justice and Public Order Act 1994, s. 69(3)***
   - Triable summarily   - Three months' imprisonment and/or a fine

The Criminal Justice and Public Order Act 1994, s. 69 states:

(3) If a person knowing that a direction under subsection (1) above has been given which applies to him—
   (a) fails to leave the land as soon as practicable, or
   (b) having left again enters the land as a trespasser within the period of three months beginning with the day on which the direction was given,
   he commits an offence…

KEYNOTE

In order to prove this offence it must be shown that the person knew of the direction and that it applied to him/her. Clearly the easiest way of ensuring both elements would be to serve a written notice on the person at the same time as communicating the direction to leave and to record any response.

It is a defence for the accused to show that he/she was not trespassing on the land, or had a reasonable excuse for failing to leave the land as soon as practicable or for again entering the land as a trespasser (s. 69(4)).

In *Nero* v *DPP* [2012] EWHC 1238 (Admin), the court quashed the appellants' convictions for failing to leave the premises as soon as practicable when so directed by the police because they were physically unable to move until they had been unchained, and had left as soon as this was done. What they did was designed to disrupt the shop's trade, not to frustrate the operation of s. 69: the fact that they had voluntarily (and deliberately) placed themselves in a situation in which they could not leave when directed was held to be irrelevant. Likewise, in *Richardson* v *DPP* [2012] EWHC 1238 (Admin), it was held that protesters tying themselves together who could not leave until untied left 'as soon as practicable'

4.16.3   Trespassing for Purpose of Residence: Power to Remove Trespassers on Land

The Criminal Justice and Public Order Act 1994, s. 61 states:

(1) If the senior police officer present at the scene reasonably believes that two or more persons are trespassing on land and are present there with the common purpose of residing there for any period, that reasonable steps have been taken by or on behalf of the occupier to ask them to leave and—

   (a) that any of those persons has caused damage to the land or to property on the land or used threatening, abusive or insulting words or behaviour towards the occupier, a member of his family or an employee or agent of his, or

   (b) that those persons have between them six or more vehicles on the land,

   he may direct those persons, or any of them, to leave the land and to remove any vehicles or other property they have with them on the land.

(2) Where the persons in question are reasonably believed by the senior police officer to be persons who were not originally trespassers but have become trespassers on the land, the officer must reasonably believe that the other conditions specified in subsection (1) are satisfied after those persons became trespassers before he can exercise the power conferred by that subsection.

(3) A direction under subsection (1) above, if not communicated to the persons referred to in subsection (1) by the police officer giving the direction, may be communicated to them by any constable at the scene.

KEYNOTE

The key features of this section can be broken down into two parts. First, the senior officer present at the scene must have a reasonable belief that:

- at least two people *are trespassing* on land *and*
- that they are there with the common purpose of residing there *and*
- that reasonable (though not *all* reasonable) steps have been taken by/on behalf of the occupier to ask them to leave.

If this is the case, the senior officer must also have a reasonable belief that:

- *any* of those people have caused damage to the land or to property on the land *or*
- *any* of those people have used threatening, abusive or insulting words or behaviour towards the occupier or a member of the occupier's family or staff or one of his/her agents *or*
- those people have between them six or more vehicles on the land.

If all the conditions under the first heading, together with any of the conditions under the second are met, the officer may direct the people to leave the land and to take their vehicles and other property with them.

Most of the terms used in this section are defined under s. 61(9). 'Land' does not include buildings other than agricultural buildings or scheduled monuments. It also has the same restrictions in relation to highways as those set out under s. 68 (see para. 4.16.2).

The damaging of property includes the deposit of any substance capable of polluting the land and property for the purposes of damage has the same meaning as under the Criminal Damage Act 1971.

'Vehicles' do not have to be in a fit state for use on a road and can include a chassis or body (with or without wheels) appearing to have formed part of a vehicle. They also include caravans (as defined under the Caravan Sites and Control of Development Act 1960).

A person may be regarded as having a purpose of residing on land even though he/she has a home elsewhere.

Where the land concerned is 'common land', any references to trespassing will be construed as acts that are an infringement of the rights of the occupier or 'commoners' rights'. Where the public has access to that common land, references to the occupier will include the local authority (s. 61(7)).

If the people concerned were not originally trespassers (e.g. because they were given limited permission to be there), the senior officer present must have a reasonable belief that the relevant conditions above came about after the people became trespassers.

Again, the direction to leave the land may be communicated to the relevant parties by any police officer at the scene and there is no requirement for either officer to be in uniform.

The Home Office provides guidance on the use of s. 61 and advises that the police must be able to demonstrate that all eviction and enforcement decisions are 'proportionate' in weighing individual harm against the wider public interest. The guidance further states that the use of this section is not prohibited by the equality legislation, providing that the police are able to show that they have properly considered the race and equalities implications of their policies and actions in relation to unauthorised encampments and unauthorised development by gypsies and Irish travellers, and can demonstrate that their policies and actions are proportionate bearing in mind all the circumstances of the case.

4.16.3.1 Failure to Leave or Re-entry to Land after Police Direction to Leave

OFFENCE: **Failure to Leave or Re-entry to Land—*Criminal Justice and Public Order Act 1994, s. 61(4)***

> • Triable summarily • Three months' imprisonment and/or a fine

The Criminal Justice and Public Order Act 1994, s. 61 states:

(4) If a person knowing that a direction under subsection (1) above has been given which applies to him—
 (a) fails to leave the land as soon as reasonably practicable, or
 (b) having left again enters the land as a trespasser within the period of three months beginning with the day on which the direction was given,
 he commits an offence...

KEYNOTE

The requirements as to proof of knowledge here are the same as those under s. 69 (see para. 4.16.2.2). This offence is the same as that under s. 69 with the exception of the word *reasonably* before practicable. This suggests that the law provides more latitude to people directed to leave the land under s. 61 than under s. 69, a suggestion that is also borne out by the wording of the respective defences.

It is a defence for the accused to show that he/she was not trespassing on the land, or had a reasonable excuse for failing to leave the land as soon as reasonably practicable or for re-entering the land as a trespasser (s. 61(6)).

A police officer may seize and remove a vehicle where he/she reasonably suspects a person, to whom a s. 61 direction applies, to be the owner or in possession or control of that vehicle. This power also applies where a person entered the land as a trespasser with a vehicle within the period of three months beginning with the day when the direction was given (s. 62).

4.16.4 Trespassing for Purpose of Residence with Vehicle(s) when Alternative Site Available: Power to Remove Trespassers and Vehicles on Land

Section 62A of the Criminal Justice and Public Order Act 1994 creates a power for a senior police officer to direct people to leave land and remove any vehicle or other property with them on that land.

Section 62A states:

(1) If the senior police officer present at a scene reasonably believes that the conditions in subsection (2) are satisfied in relation to a person and land, he may direct the person—
    (a) to leave the land;
    (b) to remove any vehicle and other property he has with him on the land.
(2) The conditions are—
    (a) that the person and one or more others ('the trespassers') are trespassing on the land;
    (b) that the trespassers have between them at least one vehicle on the land;
    (c) that the trespassers are present on the land with the common purpose of residing there for any period;
    (d) if it appears to the officer that the person has one or more caravans in his possession or under his control on the land, that there is a suitable pitch on a relevant caravan site for that caravan or each of those caravans;
    (e) that the occupier of the land or a person acting on his behalf has asked the police to remove the trespassers from the land.

KEYNOTE

As with the powers under s. 61, the key features of this section can be broken down into component parts. First, the senior officer present at the scene must have a reasonable belief:

- that at least two people *are trespassing* on the land;
- that they have at least one vehicle between them; and
- that they are there with the common purpose of residing there for any period;
- that the occupier (or person acting on the occupier's behalf) has asked the police to remove the trespassers from the land.

If it appears that a person has one or more caravans in his/her possession or under his/her control on the land, there is a further condition requiring the senior officer to consult with the local authority and ascertain that there is a suitable pitch on a relevant caravan site for that caravan or each of those caravans (s. 62A(4) and (5)).

If the above conditions are satisfied, the senior officer can direct the people to leave the land and to remove any vehicles and other property they have with them.

This direction may be communicated to the person by any constable at the scene (s. 62A(3)) and there is no requirement that the officer giving the direction be in uniform.

A person may be regarded as having a 'purpose of residing' in a place even if he/she has a home elsewhere (s. 62E(8)).

'Vehicle' has the same meaning as under s. 61 (see para. 4.16.3).

'Land' does not generally include buildings here (except for ancient monuments and certain specific types of agricultural buildings (s. 62E).

4.16.4.1　Failure to Leave Land on Police Direction after Occupier's Request

> OFFENCE: **Failure to Comply with Direction under Section 62A—*Criminal Justice and Public Order Act 1994, s. 62B***
>
> • Triable summarily • Three months' imprisonment and/or a fine

The Criminal Justice and Public Order Act 1994, s. 62B states:

(1) A person commits an offence if he knows that a direction under section 62A(1) has been given which applies to him and—
  (a) he fails to leave the relevant land as soon as reasonably practicable, or
  (b) he enters any land in the area of the relevant local authority as a trespasser before the end of the relevant period with the intention of residing there.

KEYNOTE

This section has two limbs. The first makes it an offence to fail to comply with a direction properly given under s. 62A as soon as reasonably practicable. The second limb makes it an offence, within the relevant period (three months of the direction being given—s. 62B(2)), to return to any land in the area of the relevant local authority as a trespasser with the intention of residing there.

There is a defence under s. 62B(5) if the defendant was not a trespasser or if he/she had a reasonable excuse for failing to leave or for returning to the relevant land, or if he/she was under 18 and living with a parent or guardian when the direction was given.

4.16.5　Power of Local Authority to Direct Unauthorised Campers to Leave Land

The Criminal Justice and Public Order Act 1994, s. 77 states:

(1) If it appears to a local authority that persons are for the time being residing in a vehicle or vehicles within that authority's area—
  (a) on any land forming part of a highway;
  (b) on any other unoccupied land; or
  (c) on any occupied land without the consent of the occupier,
the authority may give a direction that those persons and any others with them are to leave the land and remove the vehicle or vehicles and any other property they have with them on the land.

KEYNOTE

A person commits an offence if, knowing that a direction has been given which applies to him/her, he/she fails, as soon as practicable, to leave the land or remove from the land any vehicle or other property which is the subject of the direction, or having removed any such vehicle or property again enters the land with a vehicle within the period of three months beginning with the day on which the direction was given (s. 77(3)).

It is a defence for the accused to show that his/her failure to leave or to remove the vehicle or other property as soon as practicable or his/her re-entry with a vehicle was due to illness, mechanical breakdown or other immediate emergency (s. 77(5)).

A local authority may apply to a magistrates' court for a removal order where people continue to reside in their vehicles on land in contravention of a s. 77 notice (s. 78(1)). A person who wilfully obstructs any person in the exercise of any power conferred on him/her by an order under this section commits a summary offence (s. 78(4)).

4.16.6 Other Offences Involving Premises

There are several specific offences and provisions relating to various types of premises that impact on day-to-day policing.

4.16.6.1 Depriving Residential Occupier

OFFENCE: **Depriving Residential Occupier—*Protection from Eviction Act 1977, s. 1***
- Triable either way • Two years' imprisonment and/or a fine on indictment
- Six months' imprisonment and/or a fine summarily

The Protection from Eviction Act 1977, s. 1 states:

(2) If any person unlawfully deprives the residential occupier of any premises of his occupation of the premises or any part thereof, or attempts to do so, he shall be guilty of an offence unless he proves that he believed, and had reasonable cause to believe, that the residential occupier had ceased to reside in the premises.

(3) If any person with intent to cause the residential occupier of any premises—
   (a) to give up the occupation of the premises or any part thereof; or
   (b) to refrain from exercising any right or pursuing any remedy in respect of the premises or part thereof;

   does acts likely to interfere with the peace or comfort of the residential occupier or members of his household, or persistently withdraws or withholds services reasonably required for the occupation of the premises as a residence, he shall be guilty of an offence.

(3A) Subject to subsection (3B) below, the landlord of a residential occupier or an agent of the landlord shall be guilty of an offence if—
   (a) he does acts likely to interfere with the peace or comfort of the residential occupier or members of his household, or
   (b) he persistently withdraws or withholds services reasonably required for the occupation of the premises in question as a residence,

   and (in either case) he knows, or has reasonable cause to believe, that that conduct is likely to cause the residential occupier to give up the occupation of the whole or part of the premises or to refrain from exercising any right or pursuing any remedy in respect of the whole or part of the premises.

KEYNOTE

'Residential occupier', in relation to any premises, means a person occupying the premises as a residence, whether under a contract or by virtue of any enactment or rule of law giving him/her the right to remain in occupation or restricting the right of any other person to recover possession of the premises (s. 1(1)).

The actions envisaged by s. 1(2) are those which amount to an eviction for any length of time (*R v Yuthiwattana* (1985) 80 Cr App R 55), while anything less (e.g. changing the locks of an entrance door while the residential occupier is out) would amount to an offence under s. 1(3) (*Costelloe v Camden London Borough Council* [1986] Crim LR 249).

In addition to the defence provided by s. 1(2), there is a specific defence to an offence under s. 1(3A), namely where a person proves that he/she had reasonable grounds for doing the acts or withdrawing or withholding the services in question (s. 1(3B)).

Where these offences are committed by a 'body corporate' (e.g. a company), then the company's officers may be guilty as well as the company itself (s. 1(6)).

The Court of Appeal has refused to find that a duty of care is owed by the police to an assured tenant to prevent that tenant's eviction without the necessary court order in breach of the Protection from Eviction Act 1977 (*Cowan v Chief Constable of Avon and Somerset* [2002] HLR 44).

A caravan may amount to 'premises' for these offences (*Norton v Knowles* [1969] 1 QB 572).

4.16.6.2 Using or Threatening Violence to Secure Entry

OFFENCE: **Using or Threatening Violence to Secure Entry to Premises—***Criminal Law Act 1977, s. 6(1)*

- Triable summarily • Six months' imprisonment and/or a fine

The Criminal Law Act 1977, s. 6 states:

(1) Subject to the following provisions of this section, any person who, without lawful authority, uses or threatens violence for the purpose of securing entry into any premises for himself or for any other person is guilty of an offence, provided that—

(a) there is someone present on those premises at the time who is opposed to the entry which the violence is intended to secure; and

(b) the person using or threatening the violence knows that that is the case.

KEYNOTE

This offence is not restricted to occasions involving 'residential occupiers'.

The fact that a person has any right or interest in premises will not constitute 'lawful authority' to use violence to secure entry into those premises (s. 6(2)).

It is immaterial whether the violence used/threatened is against a person or property, or whether the purpose of the entry is to gain possession of the premises or any other purpose (s. 6(4)).

4.16.6.3 Defence to Using or Threatening Violence to Secure Entry

The Criminal Law Act 1977, s. 6 states:

(1A) Subsection (1) above does not apply to a person who is a displaced residential occupier or a protected intending occupier of the premises in question or who is acting on behalf of such an occupier; and if the accused adduces sufficient evidence that he was, or was acting on behalf of, such an occupier he shall be presumed to be, or to be acting on behalf of, such an occupier unless the contrary is proved by the prosecution.

(2) Subject to subsection (1A) above, the fact that a person has any interest in or right to possession or occupation of any premises shall not for the purposes of subsection (1) above constitute lawful authority for the use or threat of violence by him or anyone else for the purpose of securing his entry into those premises.

A 'displaced residential occupier' is defined at s. 12, which states:

(3) Subject to subsection (4) below, any person who was occupying any premises as a residence immediately before being excluded from occupation by anyone who entered those premises, or any access to those premises, as a trespasser is a displaced residential occupier of the premises for the purposes of this Part of this Act so long as he continues to be excluded from occupation of the premises by the original trespasser or by any subsequent trespasser.

(4) A person who was himself occupying the premises in question as a trespasser immediately before being excluded from occupation shall not by virtue of subsection (3) above be a displaced residential occupier of the premises for the purposes of this Part of this Act.

KEYNOTE

Section 12A defines a 'protected intending occupier' and is extremely detailed. The gist of it is that it will include someone with a freehold or leasehold interest in the premises which has at least two years left to run; where the person needs the premises for his/her own occupation as a residence; where he/she is excluded from those premises by a trespasser and where he/she has documentation to prove his/her right to occupy the premises. A co-owner of a property who has been excluded from it by another co-owner may be guilty of an offence under this section if he/she uses force to enter it while the resident co-owner is inside, and he/she cannot then claim to be a 'protected intending occupier' within the meaning of s. 12A (*Wakolo* v *DPP* [2012] EWHC 611 (Admin)).

4.16.6.4 Failing to Leave Premises

OFFENCE: **Failing to Leave Premises—*Criminal Law Act 1977, s. 7***

- Triable summarily • Six months' imprisonment and/or a fine

The Criminal Law Act 1977, s. 7 states:

(1) Subject to the following provisions of this section and to section 12A(9) below, any person who is on any premises as a trespasser after having entered as such is guilty of an offence if he fails to leave those premises on being required to do so by or on behalf of—
   (a) a displaced residential occupier of the premises; or
   (b) an individual who is a protected intending occupier of the premises.

KEYNOTE

Sections 7 and 12A of the 1977 Act provide defences in relation to s. 7(1). It is a defence for the accused to prove that he/she believed that the person requiring him/her to leave the premises was not a person as described in s. 7(1)(a) or (b), or that the premises were used mainly for non-residential purposes and he/she was not on any part of the premises used wholly or mainly for residential purposes (s. 7(2) and (3)).

It is a defence for the accused to prove that, although asked to do so at the time they were requested to leave, that person failed at that time to produce to the accused a written statement specifying his/her interest in the premises or a certificate or licence from a protected intending occupier in relation to his/her right to tenancy of occupancy of the premises (s. 12A(9)).

4.16.6.5 Squatting in a Residential Building

OFFENCE: **Squatting in a Residential Building—*Legal Aid, Sentencing and Punishment of Offenders Act 2012, s. 144***

- Six months' imprisonment and/or a fine summarily

The Legal Aid, Sentencing and Punishment of Offenders Act 2012, s. 144 states:

(1) A person commits an offence if—
   (a) the person is in a residential building as a trespasser having entered it as a trespasser,
   (b) the person knows or ought to know that he or she is a trespasser, and
   (c) the person is living in the building or intends to live there for any period.
(2) The offence is not committed by a person holding over after the end of a lease or licence (even if the person leaves and re-enters the building).

KEYNOTE

'Building' includes any structure or part of a structure (including a temporary or moveable structure), and a building is 'residential' if it is designed or adapted, before the time of entry, for use as a place to live (s. 144(3)).

For the purposes of this section the fact that a person derives title from a trespasser, or has the permission of a trespasser, does not prevent the person from being a trespasser (s. 144(4)).

Section 17 of the Police and Criminal Evidence Act 1984 gives uniformed police officers the power to enter and search premises for the purpose of arresting a person for the offence of squatting in a residential building.

4.16.6.6 Found on Enclosed Premises

It is a summary offence under s. 4 of the Vagrancy Act 1824 for any person to be found in or upon any dwelling house, warehouse, coach house, stable or outhouse or in any inclosed yard, garden or area for *any unlawful purpose*. The unlawful purpose must be to commit some specific criminal offence as opposed to simply trespassing and a purely immoral purpose, and without more will not suffice (*Hayes* v *Stevenson* (1860) 3 LT 296). Note that in *L* v *CPS* [2007] EWHC 1843 (Admin), hiding from the police is not regarded as an unlawful purpose.

Where the defendant is found on the relevant premises, he/she can be arrested elsewhere (*R* v *Lumsden* [1951] 2 KB 513). Where a defendant was found in the garden of a house peering through the window at a woman inside intending to frighten her, his conduct was held to amount to an 'unlawful purpose' (*Smith* v *Chief Superintendent of Woking Police Station* (1983) 76 Cr App R 234). Had there not been any intention to frighten, the 'unlawful' purpose would probably not have been made out.

An area may still be 'inclosed' even though there are spaces left in between buildings, arches etc. for access (*Goodhew* v *Morton* [1962] 1 WLR 210). Railway sidings have been held not to amount to 'inclosed' premises and the essential feature of yards and similar enclosed areas for the purposes of this offence would appear to be that they are small pieces of land ancillary to a building (*Quatromini* v *Peck* [1972] 1 WLR 1318). However, a room within an office building has been held not to amount to an inclosed area for the purposes of this offence (*Talbot* v *Oxford City Justices* [2000] 1 WLR 1102). It appears from the findings of the Divisional Court in *Talbot* that the expression 'inclosed' relates only to yards, gardens and areas in the open air. If the defendant is found in a *building* then that building must be a 'dwelling house, warehouse, coach house, stable or outhouse' before the offence under s. 4 can be applied. In *Akhurst* v *DPP* [2009] EWHC 806 (Admin), it was held that an 'inclosed area' had to be interpreted in a restrictive manner that took into account the wording of s. 4. In this instance the campuses of a university could not amount to an 'inclosed area'.

There is no need to show that the person intended to carry out the relevant criminal offence at the time or at that particular place. If the person is found in a building and either intends to commit certain offences there or had that intention when entering, the relevant offences of burglary may well apply.

4.16.6.7   Housing and Accommodation

In some cases the policing problems presented within a particular area will arise directly or indirectly from the area's housing. Among the legislation available to the relevant agencies in this regard are the Housing Acts of 1985, 1988, 1996 and 2004. These Acts provide local authorities with a range of significant powers where use of premises or the state of the property itself presents a nuisance or hazard to the physical or mental health of others.

Under current housing legislation, landlords may apply to the county court to evict tenants who are behaving anti-socially using the relevant 'ground for possession'. These are ground 2 of sch. 2 to the Housing Act 1985 for secure tenants (mostly tenants of local authorities) and ground 14 of sch. 2 to the Housing Act 1988 for assured tenants (tenants of housing associations and landlords in the private rented sector) respectively. These grounds are discretionary, that is, the court must be satisfied that anti-social behaviour has occurred and that it would be reasonable to grant possession.

Section 84A of and sch. 2A to the 1985 Act provide landlords with an 'absolute ground for possession for anti-social behaviour'. The relevant grounds on which a court may order repossession under these provisions are that the tenant or a person residing in or visiting the dwelling house: (a) has been guilty of conduct causing or likely to cause a nuisance or annoyance to a person residing, visiting or otherwise engaging in a lawful activity in the locality; or (b) has been convicted either of using the dwelling house or allowing it to be used for immoral or illegal purposes, or of an indictable offence committed in, or in the locality of, the dwelling house.

4.16.6.8 Nuisance on Educational Premises

In relation to nuisances on educational premises, the Education Act 1996 applies to premises that provide primary or secondary education (or both) and which are maintained by a local education authority or are grant-maintained.

OFFENCE: **Causing or Permitting Nuisance—*Education Act 1996, s. 547(1)***
  • Triable summarily • Fine

The Education Act 1996, s. 547 states:

(1) Any person who without lawful authority is present on premises to which this section applies and causes or permits nuisance or disturbance to the annoyance of persons who lawfully use those premises (whether or not any such persons are present at the time) [shall be guilty of an offence].

KEYNOTE

This offence is designed to deal with many types of nuisance, from using school playing fields inappropriately (this provision applies to playing fields and other premises for outdoor recreation of the relevant institution including playgrounds (s. 547(2)), to interrupting lessons and lectures.

  To be guilty of the above offence the defendant must be on the relevant premises without lawful authority and have caused (been directly responsible for bringing about) or permitted a nuisance or disturbance.

Police powers

The Education Act 1996, s. 547(3) states:

(3) If—
  (a) a police constable or
  (b) ..., a person whom the appropriate authority has authorised to exercise the power conferred by this subsection,
  has reasonable cause to suspect that any person is committing or has committed an offence under this section, he may remove him from the premises in question.

KEYNOTE

The nuisance or disturbance may have finished by the time the police officer gets to the premises but the wording of the subsection allows for the removal of the offender provided there is reasonable cause to suspect that he/she committed the offence.

4.16.7 Trespass on Protected Sites

The Serious Organised Crime and Police Act 2005 provides that various public access rights, as provided by the Countryside and Rights of Way Act 2000 in England and Wales, are not exercisable in relation to land forming part of a protected site.

OFFENCE: **Trespassing on Protected Sites—*Serious Organised Crime and Police Act 2005, s. 128(1)***
  • Triable summarily • Six months' imprisonment and/or a fine

The Serious Organised Crime and Police Act 2005, s. 128 states:

(1) A person commits an offence if he enters, or is on, any protected site in England and Wales . . . as a trespasser.

(1A) In this section 'protected site' means—

    (a) a nuclear site; or

    (b) a designated site.

KEYNOTE

A nuclear site means so much of any premises in respect of which a nuclear site licence (within the meaning of the Nuclear Installations Act 1965) is for the time being in force as lies within the outer perimeter of the protection provided for those premises (s. 128(1B)).

A 'designated' site means a site specified or described in an order made by the Secretary of State (s. 128(2)), and a schedule of these sites is contained in the Serious Organised Crime and Police Act 2005 (Designated Sites) Order 2005 (SI 2005/3447), which designates 13 sites of military significance, and the Serious Organised Crime and Police Act 2005 (Designated Sites under Section 128) Order 2007 (SI 2007/930 as amended by SI 2012/1769, SI 2012/2709, SI 2013/1562 and SI 2014/2263), which designates 19 sites associated with the government, security services and the Royal family. Such a 'site' means the whole or part of any building or buildings, or any land, or both (s. 128(8)(a)).

It is a defence for a person charged with an offence under this section to prove that he/she did not know, and had no reasonable cause to suspect, that the site in relation to which the offence is alleged to have been committed was a protected site (s. 128(4)).

For the purposes of this section a person who is on any protected site as a trespasser does not cease to be a trespasser by virtue of being allowed time to leave the site (s. 128(7)).

4.17 Licensing and Offences Relating to Alcohol

4.17.1 Introduction

The sale, supply and consumption of alcohol, along with the proper control and management of relevant premises, is a significant part of everyday policing.

This chapter only provides a brief overview of these matters and concentrates on the specific offences and police powers contained within the relevant legislation.

4.17.2 Licensable Activities

The Licensing Act 2003, s. 1 states:

   (1) For the purposes of this Act the following are licensable activities—
      (a) the sale by retail of alcohol,
      (b) the supply of alcohol by or on behalf of a club to, or to the order of, a member of the club,
      (c) the provision of regulated entertainment, and
      (d) the provision of late night refreshment.

KEYNOTE

A licensable activity may be carried on under a premises licence or in circumstances where the activity is a permitted temporary activity (s. 2(1)).

There is a raft of exemptions to licensable activities which include aircraft, vessels, hovercraft, ports, railway vehicles, premises occupied by the armed forces and premises exempt for national security purposes (ss. 173 to 175).

4.17.3 Licensing Objectives

The purpose of the system of licensing for licensable activities is to promote four fundamental objectives—the licensing objectives (s. 4(2)). These objectives are:

(a) the prevention of crime and disorder;
(b) public safety;
(c) the prevention of public nuisance; and
(d) the protection of children from harm.

KEYNOTE

The aim of the licensing objectives is to ensure that carrying on licensable activities on or from premises is done in the public interest. The third objective, the prevention of public nuisance, will not extend to every activity where annoyance may be caused to other people but will cover behaviour which, when balanced against the public interest, is found to be unacceptable. The fourth objective is concerned with the harm to children beyond matters relating to physical safety.

4.17.4 The Licensing System

The 2003 Act sets out a single licensing system that governs all premises used for licensable activities. The system is administered by licensing authorities that include councils of a district, county or borough within England and Wales (s. 3(1)).

The key licensing authorisations that may be issued are:

- Premises Licence
- Personal Licence
- Club Premises Certificate
- Temporary Event Notice.

Carrying on a licensable activity other than in accordance with a premises licence, club premises certificate or temporary event notice is an offence (s. 136).

4.17.4.1 Premises Licence

A 'premises licence' means a licence in respect of any premises, which authorises them to be used for one or more licensable activities (s. 11).

The Licensing Act 2003, s. 16 states:

(1) Subject to subsections (2) and (2A), the following persons may apply for a premises licence—
  (a) a person who carries on, or proposes to carry on, a business which involves the use of the premises for the licensable activities to which the application relates,
  (b) a person who makes the application pursuant to—
    (i) any statutory function discharged by that person which relates to those licensable activities, or
    (ii) any function discharged by that person by virtue of Her Majesty's prerogative,
  (c) a recognised club,
  (d) a charity,
  (e) the proprietor of an educational institution,
  (f) a health service body,
  (g) a person who is registered under Part 2 of the Care Standards Act 2000 in respect of an independent hospital, in Wales,
  (ga) a person who is registered under Chapter 2 of Part 1 of the Health and Social Care Act 2008 in respect of the carrying on of a regulated activity (within the meaning of that Part) in an independent hospital in England,
  (h) the chief officer of police of a police force in England and Wales,
  (i) a person of such other description as may be prescribed.
(2) An individual may not apply for a premises licence unless he is aged 18 or over.
(2A) An individual who is resident in the United Kingdom may not apply for a premises licence authorising premises to be used for a licensable activity within section 1(1)(a) or (d) unless the individual is entitled to work in the United Kingdom.

KEYNOTE

The premises licence will name a designated premises supervisor who holds a valid personal licence. Every supply of alcohol under the licence must be made by a personal licence holder or a person authorised by such a holder (s. 19).

A constable or an authorised person may require production of a premises licence or a certified copy of it (s. 57(5)), and a person who fails, without reasonable excuse, to produce the licence, or certified copy, commits a summary offence (s. 57(7)).

A premises licence may be reviewed by a licensing authority where it is considered a licensee is failing to take sufficient measures to prevent public nuisance, or where the police consider that measures put in place to prevent crime and disorder are not being effective.

4.17.4.2   Personal Licences

The supply of alcohol is regulated generally by the granting of a personal licence to an individual. The Licensing Act 2003, s. 111 states:

(1) In this Act 'personal licence' means a licence which—
   (a) is granted by a licensing authority to an individual, and
   (b) authorises that individual to supply alcohol, or authorise the supply of alcohol, in accordance with a premises licence.
(2) In subsection (1)(b) the reference to an individual supplying alcohol is to him—
   (a) selling alcohol by retail, or
   (b) supplying alcohol by or on behalf of a club to, or to the order of, a member of the club.

> **KEYNOTE**
>
> The licensing of individuals is separate from the licensing of premises and enables personal licence holders to move from one set of premises to another.
>
> A mainstay of the personal licensing system is the ability to refuse to grant, or to suspend/revoke the licence as a result of the applicant's or licensee's previous character or other conduct.
>
> A personal licence must be held by the designated premises supervisor and more than one individual at the licensed premises may hold a personal licence. It is not necessary for all staff to be licensed, but all supplies of alcohol under a premises licence must be made by or under the authority of a personal licence holder.
>
> A constable or an authorised person may require production of a personal licence (s. 135(2)), and a person who fails without reasonable excuse to produce the licence commits a summary offence (s. 135(4)).

4.17.4.3   Club Premises Certificate

A club premises certificate may be granted by a licensing authority in respect of premises occupied by, and habitually used for the purposes of, a club. The premises may be used by the club for one or more qualifying club activities specified in the certificate, and the club is a qualifying club in relation to each of those activities (s. 60).

The general conditions that apply for a club to qualify as a qualifying club are listed under s. 62 and are:

- persons may not be admitted to membership, or be admitted, as candidates for membership, to any of the privileges of membership without an interval of at least two days between their nomination or application for membership and their admission;
- persons becoming members without prior nomination or application may not be admitted to the privileges of membership without an interval of at least two days between their becoming members and their admission;
- the club is established and conducted in good faith as a club;
- the club has at least 25 members;
- alcohol is not supplied, or intended to be supplied, to members on the premises otherwise than by or on behalf of the club.

> **KEYNOTE**
>
> Clubs falling within this category will include the Royal British Legion, Working Men's Clubs, cricket and rugby clubs, where activities are carried on from private premises and because alcohol and entertainment are provided otherwise than for profit. Generally, 'nightclubs' do not fall within this category.
>
> Where a club holds a club premises certificate, a responsible authority or any other person may apply to the relevant licensing authority for a review of the certificate (s. 87(1)). Where conditions are imposed following a review of a club premises certificate they must be proportionate in achieving the licensing objectives (*R (On the Application of Merlot 73 Ltd)* v *City of Westminster Magistrates' Court* [2013] EWHC 3416 (Admin)).

A constable or authorised person may require production of a club premises certificate (s. 94(7)) and failure to produce a certificate without reasonable excuse is a summary offence (s. 94(9)).

A constable may enter and search the club premises where they have reasonable cause to believe that an offence under s. 4(3)(a), (b) or (c) of the Misuse of Drugs Act 1971 (supplying or offering to supply, or being concerned in supplying or making an offer to supply, a controlled drug), has been, is being, or is about to be committed there, or there is likely to be a breach of the peace there. The constable may use reasonable force if necessary (s. 97).

4.17.4.4 Temporary Event Notice

A temporary event notice, issued by the licensing authority, is required where a person (the premises user) intends to carry out a licensable activity on unlicensed premises or wishes to operate outside the terms of their existing premises licence or club premises licence (s. 100).

A 'licensable activity' is the sale or supply of alcohol, regulated entertainment (e.g. music, singing or dancing), or provisions of late night refreshment (hot food or drink between the hours of 2300 and 0500). Such activities might include a publican engaged to run a temporary bar for a wedding at a venue not licensed for the sale of alcohol, or a person not being the holder of a personal licence who may wish to run a bar and provide a band at a party to celebrate a significant anniversary.

A personal licence holder is permitted fifty temporary event notices per calendar year and an individual who is not the holder of a personal licence is permitted five temporary event notices a year.

Individual premises are limited to fifteen temporary event notices in a calendar year. A temporary event notice can last up to 168 hours (seven days) but in total the 15 temporary event notices cannot exceed 21 days in a calendar year.

A temporary event notice can only be used when the number of persons at the event (including performers) does not exceed 499 persons at any one time.

KEYNOTE

Where the police consider the temporary event notice would undermine the 'crime prevention objective' they must notify the premises user and licensing authority of their objection. The licensing authority may withdraw the temporary event notice or it may be modified so that it no longer undermines the objective (s. 104).

At any reasonable time, a constable or an authorised person may enter premises to which a temporary event notice relates to assess the likely effect of the notice on the promotion of the crime prevention objective (s. 108(1)). Obstructing a constable or authorised officer is an offence (s. 108(3)).

On the day of the event a copy of the temporary event notice and any statement of conditions attached to it following an objection, must be prominently displayed at the premises or be in possession of the premises user or their nominated representative. Failure to comply with these requirements is an offence (s. 109(4)) and failure to produce a temporary event notice when required by a constable or authorised person is also an offence (s. 109(8)).

4.17.5 Police Powers

The Act creates a number of powers for police officers and other authorised persons to enter and inspect premises, to investigate licensable activities, to investigate offences, and to require the production of documents.

4.17.5.1 Power of Entry to Investigate Licensable Activities

Where a constable or an authorised person has reason to believe that any premises are being, or are about to be, used for a licensable activity, he may enter the premises with a view to seeing whether the activity is being, or is to be, carried on under and in accordance with an authorisation (s. 179(1)). An authorised person exercising the power must, if so requested, produce evidence of his authority to exercise the power (s. 179(2)).

A person exercising the power conferred by this section may, if necessary, use reasonable force (s. 179(3)), and a person commits an offence if he intentionally obstructs an authorised person exercising a power conferred by this section (s. 179(4)).

4.17.5.2 Right of Entry to Investigate Offences

A constable may enter and search any premises in respect of which he has reason to believe that an offence under this Act has been, is being or is about to be committed (s. 180(1)), and may, if necessary, use reasonable force (s. 180(2)).

4.17.6 Regulated Entertainment

Detailed guidance on the provision of regulated entertainment is contained in sch. 1 to the Act.

Regulated entertainment covers entertainment, provided solely or partly for members of the public, or exclusively to club members and their guests, or for which a charge is made, which is provided for profit (which will include raising money for charities).

The forms of entertainment regulated by the Act include:

- plays, including both performance and rehearsal;
- films, or any exhibition of moving pictures;
- all indoor sporting events;
- outdoor boxing and wrestling matches;
- performance of live music and the playing of recorded music;
- performance of dance.

Schedule 1 provides a number of exemptions to regulated entertainment, for example, entertainment at a garden fete, Morris dancing (or dancing of a similar nature), and entertainment provided on vehicles in motion.

KEYNOTE

The Policing and Crime Act 2017, s. 134 creates an offence of possessing pyrotechnic articles at a musical event that is authorised by a premises licence issued under the Licensing Act 2003 to provide regulated entertainment in the form of a performance of live music (Policing and Crime Act 2017 (Possession of Pyrotechnic Articles at Musical Events) Regulations 2017 (SI 2017/306)). A 'pyrotechnic article' means an article that contains explosive substances, or an explosive mixture of substances, designed to produce heat, light, sound, gas or smoke, or a combination of such effect, through self-sustained exothermic chemical reactions. It does not include a match or an article specified in associated regulations. A person guilty of an offence under this section is liable on summary conviction to imprisonment for a term not exceeding 51 weeks and/or a fine.

4.17.7 Offences

The main offences with which police officers will be involved are contained in the 2003 Act. These follow a fairly common-sense approach imposing requirements and obligations on those people who could have acted to prevent the relevant conduct or who could have made the relevant request, e.g. of a disorderly person to leave licensed premises.

4.17.7.1 Unauthorised Licensable Activities

OFFENCE: **Unauthorised Licensable Activities—*Licensing Act 2003, s. 136***

- Triable summarily • Six months' imprisonment and/or a fine up to £20,000

The Licensing Act 2003, s. 136 states:

(1) A person commits an offence if—
    (a) he carries on or attempts to carry on a licensable activity on or from any premises otherwise than under and in accordance with an authorisation, or
    (b) he knowingly allows a licensable activity to be so carried on.

KEYNOTE

This offence requires that the person carried on (or attempted to carry on) the licensable activity *either* in a manner not authorised by or in accordance with an appropriate authorisation, or *knowingly* allowing the activity to be carried on in that way. Therefore the element of knowledge on the part of the defendant is essential in any case where he/she is not directly involved.

If the relevant authorisation (e.g. a premises licence) has certain conditions attached and they are not adhered to, this offence would be committed.

'Authorisation' here means a premises licence, a club premises certificate or a temporary event notice in respect of which the relevant conditions have been met. While some offences apply only to 'relevant premises', the above is wider than that and applies to any premises.

Where the licensable activity in question is the provision of regulated entertainment, a person will generally not commit an offence under this section if his/her only involvement in the provision of the entertainment is that he/she played the music, performed the dance etc. (s. 136(2)).

The statutory defence of due diligence applies to this offence.

4.17.7.2 Exposing Alcohol for Unauthorised Sale

OFFENCE: **Exposing Alcohol for Unauthorised Sale—*Licensing Act 2003, s. 137***

- Triable summarily • Six months' imprisonment and/or a fine up to £20,000

The Licensing Act 2003, s. 137 states:

(1) A person commits an offence if, on any premises, he exposes for sale by retail any alcohol in circumstances where the sale by retail of that alcohol on those premises would be an unauthorised licensable activity.
(2) For that purpose a licensable activity is unauthorised unless it is under and in accordance with an authorisation.

KEYNOTE

'Sale by retail' is specifically defined in s. 192. In essence it excludes wholesale transactions made with people (including personal licence holders) in the course of their trade and sales for consumption off the premises.

This offence concerns retail sales of alcohol on premises where to do so lawfully would ordinarily require some form of authorisation. There is no requirement for the person to have done so 'knowingly' or with any particular state of mind, neither is there a need for any *sale* actually to have taken place, and the exposing for sale under the relevant circumstances makes the offence complete.

While some offences apply only to 'relevant premises', the above is wider than that and applies to any premises.

There is a further summary offence (punishable by a fine) for a person to have in his/her possession or under his/her control alcohol which he/she intends to sell by retail or supply by or on behalf of a club to a member

---

of the club in circumstances where that activity would be an unauthorised licensable activity (s. 138). The statutory defence of 'due diligence' applies to both these offences.

The court by which a person is convicted of either of these offences may order the alcohol in question (and any container), to be forfeited and either destroyed or dealt with in such other manner as the court may order (s. 137(4)).

4.17.7.3   Defence of Due Diligence

The Licensing Act 2003 contains a specific defence of 'due diligence', and s. 139 states:

(1) In proceedings against a person for an offence to which subsection (2) applies, it is a defence that—
   (a) his act was due to a mistake, or to reliance on information given to him, or to an act or omission by another person, or to some other cause beyond his control, and
   (b) he took all reasonable precautions and exercised all due diligence to avoid committing the offence.

KEYNOTE

The offences to which this defence applies are:

- s. 136(1)(a) (carrying on unauthorised licensable activity);
- s. 137 (exposing alcohol for unauthorised sale); or
- s. 138 (keeping alcohol on premises for unauthorised sale).

The defence of due diligence has two limbs and both (a) and (b) must be shown for it to apply.

4.17.7.4   Allowing Disorderly Conduct on Licensed Premises

OFFENCE: **Allowing Disorderly Conduct on Licensed Premises etc.—*Licensing Act 2003, s. 140***
- Triable summarily • Fine

The Licensing Act 2003, s. 140 states:

(1) A person to whom subsection (2) applies commits an offence if he knowingly allows disorderly conduct on relevant premises.
(2) This subsection applies—
   (a) to any person who works at the premises in a capacity, whether paid or unpaid, which authorises him to prevent the conduct,
   (b) in the case of licensed premises, to—
     (i) the holder of a premises licence in respect of the premises, and
     (ii) the designated premises supervisor (if any) under such a licence,
   (c) in the case of premises in respect of which a club premises certificate has effect, to any member or officer of the club which holds the certificate who at the time the conduct takes place is present on the premises in a capacity which enables him to prevent it, and
   (d) in the case of premises which may be used for a permitted temporary activity by virtue of Part 5, to the premises user in relation to the temporary event notice in question.

KEYNOTE

'Relevant premises' means licensed premises, premises in respect of which there is in force a club premises certificate, and premises which may be used for a permitted temporary activity by virtue of part 5 (s. 159).

It will be important to note the distinctions between the roles of the people mentioned in s. 140(2)(a)–(d). In the case of licensed premises (and premises which may be used for a permitted temporary activity by virtue of part 5), the requirements are fairly straightforward. In such cases the holder of the premises licence, the designated premises supervisor or the premises user respectively will be liable and it will only be necessary to prove that he/she *knowingly* allowed disorderly conduct on relevant premises. In the case of premises where a club premises certificate is in effect, it will be necessary, in addition, to show that the defendant was present on the premises and in a capacity that enabled him/her to prevent the conduct.

Whether the conduct involved was disorderly will be a question of fact to be decided in all the circumstances.

4.17.7.5 Sale of Alcohol to a Person who is Drunk

OFFENCE: **Sale of Alcohol to a Person who is Drunk**—*Licensing Act 2003, s. 141*
- Triable summarily • Fine

The Licensing Act 2003, s. 141 states:

(1) A person to whom subsection (2) applies commits an offence if, on relevant premises, he knowingly—
   (a) sells or attempts to sell alcohol to a person who is drunk, or
   (b) allows alcohol to be sold to such a person.
(2) This subsection applies—
   (a) to any person who works at the premises in a capacity, whether paid or unpaid, which gives him authority to sell the alcohol concerned,
   (b) in the case of licensed premises, to—
      (i) the holder of a premises licence in respect of the premises, and
      (ii) the designated premises supervisor (if any) under such a licence,
   (c) in the case of premises in respect of which a club premises certificate has effect, to any member or officer of the club which holds the certificate who at the time the sale (or attempted sale) takes place is present on the premises in a capacity which enables him to prevent it, and
   (d) in the case of premises which may be used for a permitted temporary activity by virtue of Part 5, to the premises user in relation to the temporary event notice in question.

KEYNOTE

For 'relevant premises' **see para. 4.17.7.4.**

The people to whom this offence applies are those in the roles that would allow them to take the appropriate action in preventing the offence.

This offence is not restricted to retail sales and will cover all sales, including those for consumption off the premises.

This section applies in relation to the supply of alcohol by or on behalf of a club to, or to the order of, a member of the club as it applies in relation to the sale of alcohol (s. 141(3)).

4.17.7.6 Obtaining Alcohol for a Person who is Drunk

OFFENCE: **Obtaining Alcohol for a Person who is Drunk**—*Licensing Act 2003, s. 142*
- Triable summarily • Fine

The Licensing Act 2003, s. 142 states:

(1) A person commits an offence if, on relevant premises, he knowingly obtains or attempts to obtain alcohol for consumption on those premises by a person who is drunk.

KEYNOTE

For 'relevant premises' **see para. 4.17.7.4.**

The requirement to show that the defendant acted *knowingly* is critical to prove this offence.

The intended consumption must be on the premises where the alcohol is obtained/attempted to be obtained.

4.17.7.7 Failure to Leave Licensed Premises

OFFENCE: **Failure to Leave Licensed Premises etc.—***Licensing Act 2003, s. 143*

- Triable summarily • Fine

The Licensing Act 2003, s. 143 states:

(1) A person who is drunk *or* disorderly commits an offence if, without reasonable excuse—
  (a) he fails to leave relevant premises when requested to do so by a constable or by a person to whom subsection (2) applies, or
  (b) he enters or attempts to enter relevant premises after a constable or a person to whom subsection (2) applies has requested him not to enter.

(2) This subsection applies—
  (a) to any person who works at the premises in a capacity, whether paid or unpaid, which gives him authority to sell the alcohol concerned,
  (b) in the case of licensed premises, to—
    (i) the holder of a premises licence in respect of the premises, and
    (ii) the designated premises supervisor (if any) under such a licence,
  (c) in the case of premises in respect of which a club premises certificate has effect, to any member or officer of the club which holds the certificate who is present on the premises in a capacity which enables him to make such a request, and
  (d) in the case of premises which may be used for a permitted temporary activity by virtue of Part 5, to the premises user in relation to the temporary event notice in question.

KEYNOTE

For 'relevant premises' **see para. 4.17.7.4.**

The above offence requires that the person concerned is shown to be *either* drunk *or* disorderly.

The absence of a reasonable excuse is an important ingredient in this offence, and it should be shown that the request to leave/not to enter was both heard and understood by the defendant.

On being requested to do so by a person to whom s. 143(2) applies, a constable must:

- help to expel from relevant premises a person who is drunk or disorderly;
- help to prevent such a person from entering relevant premises.

(s. 143(4))

If requested to do so by one of the above people, a police officer is under a duty (rather than simply having a power) to help them expel anyone who is drunk or disorderly. The wording of the section means that police officers are also under a similar duty to help to prevent such a person from entering relevant premises.

In assisting the removal of an individual a police officer is entitled to use force (*Semple* v *Luton and South Bedfordshire Magistrates' Court* [2009] EWHC 3241 (Admin)).

4.17.7.8 Drunk and Disorderly

OFFENCE: **Drunk and Disorderly—***Criminal Justice Act 1967, s. 91(1)*

- Triable summarily • Fine

The Criminal Justice Act 1967, s. 91 states:

(1) Any person who in any public place is guilty, while drunk, of disorderly behaviour shall be liable...

KEYNOTE

In *Carroll* v *DPP* [2009] EWHC 554 (Admin) the court stated that drunk and disorderly was one of the most basic of offences and that it required proof of three elements: the accused was drunk; he/she was in a public place; and he/she was guilty of disorderly behaviour.

The drunkenness must be as a result of excessive consumption of alcohol; if the person's state is caused by some other intoxicant (e.g. glue solvents), the offence is not made out (*Neale* v *R.M.I.E. (a minor)* (1985) 80 Cr App R 20). The same ruling applies to a person 'found drunk' in a public place (*Lanham* v *Rickwood* (1984) 148 JP 737).

'Drunkenness' here means where the defendant has taken intoxicating liquor (alcohol) to an extent that affects his/her steady self-control (per Goff LJ in *Neale*).

Where there are *several* causes of a person's incapacitated state, one of which is alcohol, a court can find that the person was in fact 'drunk', even though some additional intoxicant had an exacerbating effect on his/her loss of 'steady self-control'.

In *McMillan* v *CPS* [2008] EWHC 1457 (Admin), it was held that where a police officer took hold of a drunken person by the arm to steady her for her own safety it was not an arrest. The circumstances entailed the officer leading the drunken person from a private garden to a public place. It was then legitimate for the officer to arrest for this offence where the accused displayed disorderly behaviour. However, this offence is not committed where a person did not commit any disorderly act until after the arrest (*H* v *DPP* [2005] EWHC 2459 (Admin)).

This offence is a 'penalty offence' for the purposes of s. 1 of the Criminal Justice and Police Act 2001. Note that a penalty notice for s. 91(1) cannot be given to a person aged under 18, and a constable giving a notice to a person other than at a police station does not need to be in uniform (Legal Aid, Sentencing and Punishment of Offenders Act 2012 (Consequential Amendments) Regulations 2013 (SI 2013/903)).

Where a person is arrested for committing this offence, under the powers contained within s. 24 of the Police and Criminal Evidence Act 1984, a constable may take him/her to an approved treatment centre for alcoholism (a 'detoxification' centre) and he/she will be treated as being in lawful custody for the purposes of that journey (see s. 34(1) of the Criminal Justice Act 1972).

The conduct of passengers who are drunk on an aircraft has a potential impact on the safety of the aircraft and the people therein, therefore they can be dealt with under s. 61 of the Civil Aviation Act 1982 and the relevant regulations made thereunder (*R* v *Tagg* [2001] EWCA Crim 1230 and Air Navigation Order 2009 (SI 2009/3015, part 19) made under the Civil Aviation Act 1982 and the Airports Act 1986).

4.17.7.9 Found Drunk

OFFENCE: **Being Found Drunk—*Licensing Act 1872, s. 12***
- Triable summarily • Fine

The Licensing Act 1872, s. 12 states:

Every person found drunk in any highway or other public place, whether a building or not, or on any licensed premises, shall be liable...

Every person who is drunk while in charge on any highway or other public place of any carriage, horse, cattle, or steam engine, or who is drunk when in possession of any loaded firearms, shall be liable to a penalty not exceeding level 1 on the standard scale or in the discretion of the court to imprisonment for any term not exceeding one month.

KEYNOTE

This offence is committed if a person is on the highway or public place and shown to be drunk. It does not matter that the person is there only briefly or of his/her own volition.

'Other public place' will include all places to which the public have access (whether on payment or otherwise).

The offence has been held to apply to the licensee when found drunk on the licensed premises, even when those premises were not open to the public (*Evans* v *Fletcher* (1926) 135 LT 153).

This offence is a 'penalty offence' for the purposes of s. 1 of the Criminal Justice and Police Act 2001.

On arresting a person for this offence, under the powers contained in s. 24 of the Police and Criminal Evidence Act 1984, a police officer may, if he/she thinks fit, take the person to an approved treatment centre under s. 34 of the Criminal Justice Act 1972. During the journey to such a treatment centre the person will be deemed to be in lawful custody. Section 34 does not allow a person to be detained at the centre and does not preclude any charge being brought in relation to the offence.

4.17.7.10   Being Drunk While in Charge of Child

OFFENCE: **Being Drunk While in Charge of Child—*Licensing Act 1902, s. 2***
- • One month's imprisonment and/or a fine summarily

The Licensing Act 1902, s. 2 states:

(1) If any person is found drunk in any highway or other public place, whether a building or not, or on any licensed premises, while having the charge of a child apparently under the age of seven years, he may be apprehended...

(2) If the child appears to the court to be under the age of seven, the child shall, for the purposes of this section, be deemed to be under that age unless the contrary is proved.

KEYNOTE

This is used for its specific purpose, i.e. the safety of young children (*R (On the Application of A)* v *Lowestoft Magistrates' Court* [2013] EWHC 659 (Admin)).

4.17.8   Children—Offences under the Licensing Act 2003

The Licensing Act 2003 makes provision for offences and breaches of the regulatory framework with the protection of children as one of its primary objectives. In summary, the key offences under the 2003 Act are:

Unaccompanied children prohibited from certain premises (s. 145). Allowing an unaccompanied child, aged under 16, on relevant premises at a time when they are open for the purposes of being used for the supply of alcohol for consumption on the premises.

Sale of alcohol to children (s. 146). The 'selling' of alcohol to a person aged under 18 *anywhere* (not just on licensed premises). It is a defence where the person charged believed that the individual was 18 or over, had taken all reasonable steps to establish the individual's age, or nobody could reasonably have suspected from the individual's appearance that they were aged under 18.

Allowing the sale of alcohol to children (s. 147). Where a person, who works at relevant premises in a paid or unpaid capacity which authorises them to prevent the sale, knowingly allows the sale of alcohol on the premises to an individual under 18.

Persistently selling alcohol to children (s. 147A). If on two or more different occasions within a period of three consecutive months alcohol is unlawfully sold on the same premises to an individual aged under 18. It is 'unlawfully sold' if the person making the sale believed the individual to be under 18 or did not have reasonable grounds for believing them to be 18 or over.

Purchase of alcohol by or on behalf of children (s. 149). This covers all forms of under-18s buying (or trying to buy) alcohol or someone else doing it on their behalf.

Consumption of alcohol by children (s. 150). A person aged under 18 knowingly consumes alcohol on relevant premises and by a person working at the premises who knowingly allows the consumption of alcohol. However, no offences are committed where the individual is aged 16 or 17, the alcohol is beer, wine or cider, the consumption is at a table meal and the individual is accompanied by an person aged 18 or over.

Delivering alcohol to children (s. 151). A person working on relevant premises knowingly delivering alcohol sold on the premises to a person aged under 18. For example, circumstances where a child takes delivery of a consignment of alcohol bought by a parent from an off-licence.

Sending a child to obtain alcohol (s. 152). A person knowingly sending an individual aged under 18 to obtain alcohol that is sold on relevant premises, for consumption off the premises. For example, where a parent sends their child to an off-licence to collect some alcohol which had been bought over the telephone. The offence will be committed regardless of whether the child is sent to the actual premises from where the alcohol is sold or supplied, or whether the child is sent to other premises to which the alcohol has been sent.

Prohibition of unsupervised sales by children (s. 153). A premises licence holder, designated premises supervisor or someone over 18 authorised by them, to knowingly allow an individual aged under 18 to make on the relevant premises any sale of alcohol, or in the case of a club, any supply of alcohol to members of the club. This does not apply to the sale or supply of alcohol to persons having table meals.

KEYNOTE

All of the offences listed above are triable summarily and punishable by a fine.

In relation to *allowing the sale of alcohol to children* (s. 147), *purchase of alcohol by or on behalf of children* (s. 149) and *sending a child to obtain alcohol* (s. 152), an offence will not be committed where the individual buys or attempts to buy the alcohol at the request of a constable or a weights and measures inspector who is acting in the course of his/her duty.

With the exceptions of ss. 146, 147A and 149, all the other offences listed refer to the offence occurring on 'relevant premises'. This means premises that are exclusively or primarily used for the supply of alcohol for consumption on the premises and include premises operating with a temporary event notice.

4.17.9 Children—Other Offences

In addition to the offences outlined above, other legislation creates specific offences in relation to children.

4.17.9.1 Persistently Possessing Alcohol in a Public Place

OFFENCE: **Persistently Possessing Alcohol in a Public Place—*Policing and Crime Act 2009, s. 30***
- Triable summarily • Fine

The Policing and Crime Act 2009, s. 30 states:

(1) A person under the age of 18 is guilty of an offence if, without reasonable excuse, the person is in possession of alcohol in any relevant place on 3 or more occasions within a period of 12 consecutive months.

(2) 'Relevant place', in relation to a person, means—
   (a) any public place, other than excluded premises, or
   (b) any place, other than a public place, to which the person has unlawfully gained access.
   ...

(4) For the purposes of subsection (2) a place is a public place if at the material time the public or any section of the public has access to it, on payment or otherwise, as of right or by virtue of express or implied permission.

KEYNOTE

In relation to s. 30 (2)(a), 'excluded premises' means premises with a premises licence or permitted temporary activity used for the supply of alcohol, and premises with a club premises certificate used for the supply of alcohol to members or guests.

The original Home Office guidance set out the steps to be taken to deter young people from drinking and possessing alcohol in public places, including engagement with their parents or guardians. It was intended that this offence be used in conjunction with s. 1 of the Confiscation of Alcohol (Young Persons) Act 1997 (**see para. 4.17.9.2**), to enable a constable to confiscate alcohol from those under 18 years of age, and to ensure that the young person was required to give his/her name and address to the constable.

4.17.9.2 Confiscation of Alcohol when Person under 18 may be Involved

The Confiscation of Alcohol (Young Persons) Act 1997, s. 1 states:

(1) Where a constable reasonably suspects that a person in a relevant place is in possession of alcohol, and that either—

    (a) he is under the age of 18; or

    (b) he intends that any of the alcohol should be consumed by a person under the age of 18 in that or any other relevant place; or

    (c) a person under the age of 18 who is, or has recently been, with him has recently consumed alcohol in that or any other relevant place, the constable may require him to surrender anything in his possession which is, or which the constable reasonably believes to be, alcohol or a container for such alcohol.

(1AA) A constable who imposes a requirement on a person under subsection (1) shall also require the person to state the person's name and address.

(1AB) A constable who imposes a requirement on a person under subsection (1) may, if the constable reasonably suspects that the person is under the age of 16, remove the person to the person's place of residence or a place of safety.

KEYNOTE

Under s. 1(6), a 'relevant place' is:

Subsections (1) and (2) do not apply where:

- any public place, other than licensed premises; or
- any place, other than a public place, to which that person has unlawfully gained access;

and for this purpose a place is a public place if, at the material time, the public or any section of the public has access to it, on payment or otherwise, as of right or by virtue of express or implied permission. Therefore the power may be exercised in any public place (as defined above) not being 'licensed premises'. It may also be exercised in any other place that is not a public place to which the person has gained access unlawfully. This second expression suggests that the person must, as a matter of fact, have gained access to the place unlawfully as opposed to the officer simply 'suspecting' or 'believing' that to be the case. It also suggests that, if the person was originally in the place lawfully but was later asked to leave, the power would not apply as the person's access would not have been 'unlawfully gained'. The section does not provide the police officer with a power of entry or a power to search.

This is a discretionary power for police officers to exercise as they deem fit.

It is unusual that the wording of the section says 'either', then goes on to give *three* instances where the power will be available. However, if one of the instances at s. 1(1)(a)–(c) applies, the police officer may require the person concerned to surrender anything that is, or that the officer reasonably *believes* to be, alcohol or a container for such alcohol.

Subsection (1AA) states the constable *shall* require the person to state his/her name and address. Subsection (1AB) was part of a government initiative intended to prevent low-level crime and disorder. Although a 'place of safety' is not defined, this may be a relative or friend, or where necessary, a police station or social services accommodation.

There is no requirement for the officer to be in uniform.

Under s. 1(2), the officer may dispose of *anything* surrendered to him/her in answer to the making of such a requirement.

4.17.9.3 Failure to Surrender Items believed to be Alcohol

OFFENCE: **Failing to Surrender Alcohol—*Confiscation of Alcohol (Young Persons) Act 1997, s 1(3)***

    • Triable summarily • Fine

The Confiscation of Alcohol (Young Persons) Act 1997, s. 1 states:

(3) A person who fails without reasonable excuse to comply with a requirement imposed on him under subsection (1)or (1AA) commits an offence.

4.17.9.4 Closure Notices for Persistently Selling Alcohol to Children

Section 169A of the Licensing Act 2003, provides that a senior police officer (of the rank of superintendent or higher), or an inspector of weights and measures, may give a closure notice where there is evidence that a person has committed the offence of persistently selling alcohol to children at the premises in question, and he/she considers that the evidence is such that there would be a realistic prospect of conviction if the offender was prosecuted for it. A closure notice can only be given within three months of the last offence (s. 169A(9)).

A closure notice will propose a prohibition on sales of alcohol at the premises in question for at least 48 hours but not more than 336 hours (s. 169A(4)), and will offer the opportunity to discharge all criminal liability in respect of the alleged offence by the acceptance of the prohibition proposed in the notice (s. 169A(2)). The premises licence holder will have 14 days to decide whether or not to accept the proposed prohibition or to elect to be tried for the offence (s. 169A(4)). Where the licence holder decides to accept the prohibition, it must take effect not less than 14 days after the date on which the notice was served at a time specified in the closure notice (s. 169A(5)).

A closure notice may be served on the premises to which it applies only by being handed by a constable or trading standards officer to a person on the premises who appears to the constable or trading standards officer to have control of or responsibility for the premises (s. 169A(7)). The closure notice can only be served at a time when licensable activities are being carried on at the premises.

4.17.10 Public Spaces Protection Order: Alcohol Prohibition

The power to make a Public Spaces Protection Order is contained in s. 59 of the Anti-social Behaviour, Crime and Policing Act 2014. It provides for an order to be made prohibiting the consumption of alcohol in designated public places, as well as dealing with any other particular nuisance or problem in a particular area.

4.17.10.1 Power to Make Orders

The Anti-social Behaviour, Crime and Policing Act 2014, s. 59 states:

(1) A local authority may make a public spaces protection order if satisfied on reasonable grounds that two conditions are met.
(2) The first condition is that—
  (a) activities carried on in a public place within the authority's area have had a detrimental effect on the quality of life of those in the locality, or
  (b) it is likely that activities will be carried on in a public place within that area and that they will have such an effect.
(3) The second condition is that the effect, or likely effect, of the activities—
  (a) is, or is likely to be, of a persistent or continuing nature,
  (b) is, or is likely to be, such as to make the activities unreasonable, and
  (c) justifies the restrictions imposed by the notice.
(4) A public spaces protection order is an order that identifies the public place referred to in subsection (2) ('the restricted area') and—
  (a) prohibits specified things being done in the restricted area,
  (b) requires specified things to be done by persons carrying on specified activities in that area, or
  (c) does both of those things.

4.17.11 Orders to Close Premises in Area Experiencing Disorder

The Licensing Act 2003, s.160 states:

(1) Where there is or is expected to be disorder in any local justice area, a magistrates' court acting in the area may make an order requiring all premises—
   (a) which are situated at or near the place of the disorder or expected disorder, and
   (b) in respect of which a premises licence or a temporary event notice has effect, to be closed for a period, not exceeding 24 hours, specified in the order.
(2) A magistrates' court may make an order under this section only on the application of a police officer who is of the rank of superintendent or above.
(3) A magistrates' court may not make such an order unless it is satisfied that it is necessary to prevent disorder.

OFFENCE: **Contravening Closure Order—*Licensing Act 2003, s. 160***
   • Triable summarily • Fine

The Licensing Act 2003, s. 160 states:

(4) Where an order is made under this section, a person to whom subsection (5) applies commits an offence if he knowingly keeps any premises to which the order relates open, or allows any such premises to be kept open, during the period of the order.
(5) This subsection applies—
   (a) to any manager of the premises,
   (b) in the case of licensed premises, to—
      (i) the holder of a premises licence in respect of the premises, and
      (ii) the designated premises supervisor (if any) under such a licence, and
   (c) in the case of premises in respect of which a temporary event notice has effect, to the premises user in relation to that notice.

4.17.12 Closure Notices for Unlicensed Premises

The Criminal Justice and Police Act 2001, s. 19 states:

(1) Where a constable is satisfied that any premises are being, or within the last 24 hours have been, used for the unauthorised sale of alcohol for consumption on, or in the vicinity of, the premises, he may serve under subsection (3) a notice in respect of the premises.

(2) Where a local authority is satisfied that any premises in the area of the authority are being, or within the last 24 hours have been, used for the unauthorised sale of alcohol for consumption on, or in the vicinity of, the premises, the authority may serve under subsection (3) a notice in respect of the premises.

(3) A notice under subsection (1) or (2) ('a closure notice') shall be served by the constable or local authority concerned on a person having control of, or responsibility for, the activities carried on at the premises.

(4) A closure notice shall also be served by the constable or local authority concerned on any person occupying another part of any building or other structure of which the premises form part if the constable or (as the case may be) the local authority concerned reasonably believes, at the time of serving notice under subsection (3), that the person's access to the other part of the building or other structure would be impeded if an order under section 21 providing for the closure of the premises were made.

(5) A closure notice may also be served by a constable or the local authority concerned on—
   (a) any other person having control of, or responsibility for, the activities carried on at the premises;
   (b) any person who has an interest in the premises.

KEYNOTE

The power provided by this section is available to any police officer irrespective of rank.

The closure notice must specify the alleged use of the premises, the grounds on which it has been issued, the steps that are required to be taken to ensure that the alleged use of the premises ceases or does not recur, and state the effects of s. 20 (s. 19(6)).

Where a closure notice has been served under s. 19(3), a constable or the local authority concerned may make a complaint to a justice of the peace for a closure order (s. 20(1)). The complaint must be made not less than seven days, and not more than six months, after the service of the closure notice (s. 20(2)). However, a complaint cannot be made under this subsection if the constable or the local authority is satisfied that the use of the premises for the unauthorised sale of alcohol for consumption on, or in the vicinity of, the premises has ceased, and there is no reasonable likelihood that the premises will be so used in the future (s. 20(3)).

Where a closure order is made by the court a constable or authorised person may enter the premises, if necessary using reasonable force, at any reasonable time to do anything necessary to secure compliance with the order (s. 25(1)). The constable or authorised person must produce identification if so required by the owner, occupier or person in charge of the premises (s. 25(2)). Intentionally obstructing a constable or authorised person is a summary offence (s. 25(3)). Permitting premises to be open in contravention of the order is an offence (s. 25(4), as is failing to comply with a closure order generally (s. 25(5)).

4.17.13 Keeping of Smuggled Goods

OFFENCE: **Keeping of Smuggled Goods—*Licensing Act 2003, s. 144***
   • Triable summarily • Fine

The Licensing Act 2003, s. 144 states:

(1) A person to whom subsection (2) applies commits an offence if he knowingly keeps or allows to be kept, on any relevant premises, any goods which have been imported without payment of duty or which have otherwise been unlawfully imported.

(2) This subsection applies—

(a) to any person who works at the premises in a capacity, whether paid or unpaid, which gives him authority to prevent the keeping of the goods on the premises,

(b) in the case of licensed premises, to—

    (i) the holder of a premises licence in respect of the premises, and

    (ii) the designated premises supervisor (if any) under such a licence,

(c) in the case of premises in respect of which a club premises certificate has effect, to any member or officer of the club which holds the certificate who is present on the premises at any time when the goods are kept on the premises in a capacity which enables him to prevent them being so kept, and

(d) in the case of premises which may be used for a permitted temporary activity by virtue of Part 5, to the premises user in relation to the temporary event notice in question.

KEYNOTE

This offence was primarily created in an attempt to control the influx of tobacco and alcohol products on which the relevant duty had not been paid, but it is far wider than that.

The requirement that the defendant acted *knowingly* is an essential element of this offence.

The court by which a person is convicted of this offence may order the goods in question (and any container for them) to be forfeited and either destroyed or dealt with in such other manner as the court may order (s. 144(4)).

4.18 | Offences and Powers Relating to Information

4.18.1 Introduction

This chapter examines the provisions of the Freedom of Information Act 2000, Computer Misuse Act 1990, Data Protection Act 1998 and the Regulation of Investigatory Powers Act 2000.

Article 8 (Right to Respect for Private and Family Life, Home and Correspondence) of the European Convention on Human Rights has implications for the law in relation to all these areas, as well as other areas contained within this Manual.

4.18.1.1 Article 8—Right to Respect for Private and Family Life, Home and Correspondence

Article 8 of the Convention states:

1. Everyone has the right to respect for his private and family life, his home and his correspondence.
2. There shall be no interference by a public authority with the exercise of this right except such as is in accordance with the law and is necessary in a democratic society in the interests of national security, public safety or the economic well being of the country, for the prevention of disorder or crime, for the protection of health or morals, or for the protection of the rights and freedoms of others.

KEYNOTE

The provisions of Article 8 extend a right to respect for a person's private life, family life, home, and correspondence.

This Article protects these features of a person's life from arbitrary interference by 'public authorities' (*Kroon* v *Netherlands* (1995) 19 EHRR 263). 'Public authorities' include a court, tribunal or groups who are concerned solely with discharging functions of a public nature or those who have some public functions (s. 6 of the Human Rights Act 1998). However, the Convention does allow for individuals to raise issues of unjustified interference with their private lives and the courts have held that even celebrities have a basic right to privacy which will be protected by Article 8 (*Campbell* v *Mirror Group Newspapers* [2004] UKHL 22); similar arguments can be found in *Theakston* v *Mirror Group Newspapers* [2002] EWHC 137 (QB).

The State is under a duty not to interfere with a person's life except in accordance with Article 8(2). Many police activities such as entry onto premises, surveillance and the seizure of property, touch upon the features covered by Article 8.

Another reason why this Article is of importance to police services is that the State also has a positive obligation to prevent others from interfering with an individual's right to private life (*Stjerna* v *Finland* (1994) 24 EHRR 194). How far the police would have to go in order to discharge this obligation is unclear, but Article 8 will be relevant in many areas and in particular community safety.

It is here that the notion of balancing the rights and freedoms of individuals against each other and against those of the community at large can be seen most acutely.

4.18.1.2 Access to Information Held by Public Authorities

The Freedom of Information Act 2000, s. 1 provides for the general right of access to information held by public authorities, and states:

(1) Any person making a request for information to a public authority is entitled—
    (a) to be informed in writing by the public authority whether it holds information of the description specified in the request, and
    (b) if that is the case, to have that information communicated to him.

KEYNOTE

Public authorities for the purposes of this section include the police, the CPS and government departments, along with National Health Service bodies, schools and colleges (s. 3 and sch. 1). These public authorities are required to adopt and maintain a publication scheme and to publish information in accordance with it that sets out their specific plans for making certain types of information available (s. 19).

Requests for information must be in writing, state the name of the applicant and an address for correspondence, and describe the information requested (s. 8(1)). A request is to be treated as made in writing where the text of the request is transmitted by electronic means, is received in legible form, and is capable of being used for subsequent reference (s.8(2)). A fee may be charged for complying with the request (s. 9). Generally, a public authority must comply with a request for information promptly and in any event not later than the twentieth working day following the date of receipt (s. 10).

A number of exemptions and qualifications are imposed by the Act on the general 'right to know' and these usually arise due to the nature or the quantity of the material sought or the excessive costs involved in providing the information.

The Act creates the role of Information Commissioner (s. 18), and places a duty on the Commissioner to promote good practice by public authorities and promote the observance of the requirements of the Act and the Codes of Practice (s. 47).

4.18.1.3 Duty to Share Information

A number of public agencies have a duty to share information under the Multi-Agency Public Protection Arrangements (MAPPA). These are statutory arrangements to assess and manage the risk posed by certain sexual and violent offenders. They are established by virtue of ss. 325 to 327 of the Criminal Justice Act 2003 and bring together the police, probation and prison services into what is known as the 'MAPPA Responsible Authority' for each MAPPA Area.

4.18.2 Offences under the Computer Misuse Act 1990

The Computer Misuse Act 1990 Act ensures the United Kingdom's compliance with the European Union Framework Decision on Attacks Against Information Systems. This compliance requires that penalties relating to 'hacking' into computer systems, unauthorised access to computer material, the intentional serious hindering of a computer system and importing tools for cyber crime, reflect the seriousness of the criminal activities that can be involved in committing these offences.

4.18.2.1 Unauthorised Access to Computer Materials

OFFENCE: **Unauthorised Access to Computer Material ('Hacking')—*Computer Misuse Act 1990, s. 1***
- Triable either way • Two years' imprisonment and/or a fine on indictment
- Six months' imprisonment and/or a fine summarily

The Computer Misuse Act 1990, s. 1 states:

(1) A person is guilty of an offence if—
    (a) he causes a computer to perform any function with intent to secure access to any program or data held in any computer;
    (b) the access he intends to secure is unauthorised; and
    (c) he knows at the time when he causes the computer to perform the function that that is the case.
(2) The intent a person has to have to commit an offence under this section need not be directed at—
    (a) any particular program or data;
    (b) a program or data of any particular kind; or
    (c) a program or data held in any particular computer.

KEYNOTE

'Computer' is not defined and therefore must be given its ordinary meaning. Given the multiple functions of many electronic devices such as mobile phones, this could arguably bring them within the ambit of the Act.

This offence involves 'causing a computer to perform any function', which means more than simply looking at material on a screen or having any physical contact with computer hardware. In the latter case an offence of criminal damage may be appropriate. Any attempt to log on would involve getting the computer to perform a function (even if the function is to deny you access!).

Any access must be 'unauthorised'. If the defendant is authorised to *access* a computer, albeit for restricted purposes, then it was originally held that he/she did not commit this offence if he/she then *used* any information for some other unauthorised purpose (e.g. police officers using data from the Police National Computer (PNC) for private gain (*DPP* v *Bignell* [1998] 1 Cr App R 1)). However, in *R* v *Bow Street Metropolitan Stipendiary Magistrate, ex parte Government of the USA* [2000] 2 AC 216 it was held that where an employee accessed accounts that fell outside his normal scope of work and passed on the information, in this instance to credit card forgers, he was not authorised to access the specific data involved.

Essentially, the purpose of this section is to address unauthorised access as opposed to unauthorised use of data, and behaviour such as looking over a computer operator's shoulder to read what is on the screen would not be covered.

In order to prove the offence under s. 1 you must show that the defendant intended to secure access to the program or data. This is therefore an offence of 'specific intent' and lesser forms of *mens rea* such as recklessness will not do.

You must also show that the defendant knew the access was unauthorised.

The Privacy and Electronic Communications (EC Directive) Regulations 2003 (SI 2003/2426) regulate the use of cookies and Internet tracking devices, along with the use of unsolicited email and text messages. Guidance in their extent and practical effect is prepared by the Office of the Information Commissioner.

The powers of entry, search and seizure under the Police and Criminal Evidence Act 1984 apply to this offence.

4.18.2.2 Definition of Terms

The 1990 Act defines a number of its terms at s. 17 which states:

(2) A person secures access to any program or data held in a computer if by causing a computer to perform any function he—
    (a) alters or erases the program or data;
    (b) copies or moves it to any storage medium other than that in which it is held or to a different location in the storage medium in which it is held;
    (c) uses it; or
    (d) has it output from the computer in which it is held (whether by having it displayed or in any other manner);
    and references to access to a program or data (and to an intent to secure such access) shall be read accordingly.

(3) For the purposes of subsection (2)(c) above a person uses a program if the function he causes the computer to perform—
   (a) causes the program to be executed; or
   (b) is itself a function of the program.
(4) For the purposes of subsection (2)(d) above—
   (a) a program is output if the instructions of which it consists are output; and
   (b) the form in which any such instructions or any other data is output (and in particular whether or not it represents a form in which, in the case of instructions, they are capable of being executed or, in the case of data, it is capable of being processed by a computer) is immaterial.
(5) Access of any kind by any person to any program or data held in a computer is unauthorised if—
   (a) he is not himself entitled to control access of the kind in question to the program or data; and
   (b) he does not have consent to access by him of the kind in question to the program or data from any person who is so entitled, but this subsection is subject to section 10.
(6) References to any program or data held in a computer include references to any program or data held in any removable storage medium which is for the time being in the computer; and a computer is to be regarded as containing any program or data held in any such medium.
   ...
(8) An act done in relation to a computer is unauthorised if the person doing the act (or causing it to be done)—
   (a) is not himself a person who has responsibility for the computer and is entitled to determine whether the act may be done; and
   (b) does not have consent to the act from any such person.

In this subsection 'act' includes a series of acts.

KEYNOTE

Securing access will therefore include:

- altering or erasing a program or data;
- copying or moving a program or data to a new storage medium;
- using data or having it displayed or 'output' in any form from the computer in which it is held.

Under s. 17(5) access is 'unauthorised' if the person is neither entitled to control that type of access to a program or data, nor does he/she have the consent of any person who is so entitled. The provision under s. 17(5)(a) was the basis for the decision in *Bow Street* (see para. 4.18.2.1). This definition does not affect the powers available to any 'enforcement officers', i.e. police officers or other people charged with a duty of investigating offences (s. 10).

4.18.2.3   Unauthorised Access to Computers with Intent

OFFENCE: **Unauthorised Access with Intent to Commit Further Offences— *Computer Misuse Act 1990, s. 2***
   - Triable either way • Five years' imprisonment and/or a fine on indictment
   - 12 months' imprisonment and/or a fine summarily

The Computer Misuse Act 1990, s. 2 states:

(1) A person is guilty of an offence under this section if he commits an offence under section 1 above ('the unauthorised access offence') with intent—
   (a) to commit an offence to which this section applies; or
   (b) to facilitate the commission of such an offence (whether by himself or by any other person); and the offence he intends to commit or facilitate is referred to below in this section as the further offence.
(2) This section applies to offences—
   (a) for which the sentence is fixed by law; or
   (b) for which a person of twenty-one years of age or over (not previously convicted) may be sentenced to imprisonment for a term of five years (or, in England and Wales, might be so sentenced but for the restrictions imposed by section 33 of the Magistrates' Courts Act 1980).

(3) It is immaterial for the purposes of this section whether the further offence is to be committed on the same occasion as the unauthorised access offence or on any future occasion.

(4) A person may be guilty of an offence under this section even though the facts are such that the commission of the further offence is impossible.

KEYNOTE

The defendant must be shown to have had the required intent at the time of the access or other *actus reus*.

The intended further offence does not have to be committed at the same time, but may be committed in future (e.g. where the data is used to commit an offence of blackmail or to secure the transfer of funds from a bank account).

The provision as to impossibility (s. 2(4)) means that a person would still commit the offence if he/she tried, say, to access the bank account of a person who did not in fact exist.

4.18.2.4   **Unauthorised Acts with Intent to Impair Operation of Computer, etc.**

OFFENCE: **Unauthorised Acts with Intent to Impair, or with Recklessness as to Impairing, Operation of Computer, etc.—*Computer Misuse Act 1990, s. 3***

- • Triable either way • 10 years' imprisonment and/or a fine on indictment
- • 12 months' imprisonment and/or a fine summarily

The Computer Misuse Act 1990, s. 3 states:

(1) A person is guilty of an offence if—
    (a) he does any unauthorised act in relation to a computer;
    (b) at the time when he does the act he knows that it is unauthorised; and
    (c) either subsection (2) or subsection (3) below applies.

(2) This subsection applies if the person intends by doing the act—
    (a) to impair the operation of any computer;
    (b) to prevent or hinder access to any program or data held in any computer; or
    (c) to impair the operation of any such program or the reliability of any such data.

(3) This subsection applies if the person is reckless as to whether the act will do any of the things mentioned in paragraphs (a) to (c) of subsection (2) above.

KEYNOTE

This section is designed to ensure that adequate provision is made to criminalise all forms of denial of service attacks in which the attacker denies the victim(s) access to a particular resource, typically by preventing legitimate users of a service accessing that service. An example of this is where a former employee, acting on a grudge, impaired the operation of a company's computer by using a program to generate and send 5 million emails to the company (*DPP* v *Lennon* [2006] EWHC 1201 (Admin)).

The intention referred to in s. 3(2), or the recklessness referred to in s. 3(3), need not relate to any particular computer, any particular program or data, or a program or data of any particular kind (s. 3(4)). An 'unauthorised act' can include a series of acts, and a reference to impairing, preventing or hindering something includes a reference to doing so temporarily (s. 3(5)).

The 'hindering' provided by this section is intended to cover programs that generate denial of service attacks, or malicious code such as viruses.

Causing a computer to record that information came from one source when it in fact came from another clearly affects the reliability of that information for the purposes of s. 3(2)(c) (*Zezev* v *USA*; *Yarimaka* v *Governor of HM Prison Brixton* [2002] EWHC 589 (Admin)).

4.18.2.5 Unauthorised Acts Causing, or Creating Risk of, Serious Damage

OFFENCE: **Unauthorised Acts Causing, or Creating Risk of, Serious Damage—**
Computer Misuse Act 1990, s. 3ZA

- Triable on indictment • Life imprisonment and/or a fine

The Computer Misuse Act 1990, s. 3ZA states:

(1) A person is guilty of an offence if—
    (a) the person does any unauthorised act in relation to a computer;
    (b) at the time of doing the act the person knows that it is unauthorised;
    (c) the act causes, or creates a significant risk of, serious damage of a material kind; and
    (d) the person intends by doing the act to cause serious damage of a material kind or is reckless as to whether such damage is caused.
(2) Damage is of a 'material kind' for the purposes of this section if it is—
    (a) damage to human welfare in any place;
    (b) damage to the environment of any place;
    (c) damage to the economy of any country; or
    (d) damage to the national security of any country.
(3) For the purposes of subsection (2)(a) an act causes damage to human welfare only if it causes—
    (a) loss to human life;
    (b) human illness or injury;
    (c) disruption of a supply of money, food, water, energy or fuel;
    (d) disruption of a system of communication;
    (e) disruption of facilities for transport; or
    (f) disruption of services relating to health.
(4) It is immaterial for the purposes of subsection (2) whether or not an act causing damage—
    (a) does so directly;
    (b) is the only or main cause of the damage.

KEYNOTE

Reference to doing an act includes a reference to causing an act to be done, and 'act' includes a series of acts. In reference to a country, this includes a reference to a territory, and to any place in, or part or region of, a country or territory (s. 3ZA(5)).

Where an offence under this section is committed as a result of an act causing or creating a significant risk of serious damage to human welfare of the kind mentioned in s. 3ZA(3)(a) or (b), or serious damage to national security, a person guilty of the offence is liable, on conviction on indictment, to imprisonment for life, or to a fine, or to both (s. 3ZA(7)).

Section 3ZA(1) sets out the elements of the offence. The _actus reus_ (or conduct element) is that the accused undertakes an unauthorised act in relation to a computer (as in s. 3(1)(a) of the 1990 Act) and that act causes, or creates a significant risk of causing, serious damage of a material kind. The _mens rea_ (namely the mental elements of the offence) is that the accused, at the time of committing the act, knows that it is unauthorised (as in s. 3(1)(b) of the 1990 Act) and intends the act to cause serious damage of a material kind or is reckless as to whether such damage is caused. An unauthorised act is defined in s. 17(8) of the 1990 Act as an act where the person doing the act does not have responsibility for the computer in question, which would thereby entitle him or her to determine whether the act is undertaken, and does not have the consent of the person responsible for the computer to commit the act.

4.18.2.6 Making, Supplying or Obtaining Articles for Use in Offences under sections 1, 3 or 3ZA

OFFENCE: **Making, Supplying or Obtaining Articles for Use in Offences under sections 1 or 3—_Computer Misuse Act 1990, s. 3A_**

- Triable either way • Two years' imprisonment and/or a fine on indictment
- 12 months' imprisonment and/or a fine summarily

The Computer Misuse Act 1990, s. 3A states:

(1) A person is guilty of an offence if he makes, adapts, supplies or offers to supply any article intending it to be used to commit, or to assist in the commission of, an offence under section 1, 3 or 3ZA.

(2) A person is guilty of an offence if he supplies or offers to supply any article believing that it is likely to be used to commit, or to assist in the commission of, an offence under section 1, 3 or 3ZA.

(3) A person is guilty of an offence if he obtains any article—

    (a) intending to use it to commit, or to assist in the commission of, an offence under section 1, 3 or 3ZA, or

    (b) with a view to its being supplied for use to commit, or to assist in the commission, of, an offence under section 1, 2 or 3ZA.

(4) In this section 'article' includes any program or data held in electronic form.

KEYNOTE

This section creates three offences designed to combat the market in electronic tools, such as 'hacker tools' which can be used for hacking into computer systems, and the increase in the use of such tools in connection with organised crime.

The Serious Crime Act 2015 amended s. 3A(3) of the 1990 Act to ensure that the offence provided for in s. 3A also applies to the making etc of hacker tools intended to be used to commit the new s. 3ZA offence. Under the existing offence, the prosecution was required to show that the individual obtained the tool with a view to its being *supplied* for use to commit, or assist in the commission of an offence under s. 1 or 3 of the Act. Subsection (3) has been extended to include an offence of obtaining a tool for use to commit a Computer Misuse Act offence (including one under the new s. 3ZA) *regardless of an intention to supply* that tool.

4.18.3   The Data Protection Act 1998

The Data Protection Act 1998 is intended to strike a balance between the rights of individuals to privacy and the ability of organisations to use data for the purposes of their business. It provides basic rules of registration for users of data and rights of access to that data for the individuals to which it related.

Data protection law applies whenever a data controller processes personal data. A data controller is the person who determines the purposes for which, and the manner in which, any personal data is, or is likely to be, processed (s. 1(1)). A typical example of a data controller is an employer. The data controller must register with the Information Commissioner who has overall responsibility to ensure that personal data is protected in observance with the Act.

The Information Commissioner provides guidance and information, resolves complaints, and prosecutes those who commit offences under the Act. The DPP may also prosecute offences or give consent to such prosecutions.

4.18.3.1   Personal Data

The Data Protection Act 1998, s. 1 states:

(1) In this Act, unless the context otherwise requires— 'data' means information which—

    (a) is being processed by means of equipment operating automatically in response to instructions given for that purpose,

    (b) is recorded with the intention that it should be processed by means of such equipment,

    (c) is recorded as part of a relevant filing system or with the intention that it should form part of a relevant filing system, or

    (d) does not fall within paragraph (a), (b) or (c) but forms part of an accessible record as defined by section 68, or

    (e) is recorded information held by a public authority and does not fall within any of paragraphs (a) to (d).

The 1998 Act seeks to protect 'personal data', that is,

> data which relate to a living individual who can be identified, (a) from those data, or (b) from those data and other information which is in the possession of, or is likely to come into the possession of, the data controller, and includes any expression of opinion about the individual and any indication of the intentions of the data controller or any other person in respect of the individual (s. 1(1)).

KEYNOTE

In *Johnson* v *Medical Defence Union Ltd (No. 2)* [2007] EWCA Civ 262 it was held that the compilation of information from various manual and electronic files in a computer-related document is not necessarily the creation of data capable of being processed under s. 1(1).

The individual must be capable of being identified from the data that the data controller has or is likely to get. This does not mean that the person's name and/or address must be known. If it is possible to distinguish the individual from other people (e.q. by email addresses which contain the person's name or from CCTV film of that person) then it may be that the above test is satisfied.

Data controllers must give data subjects the right of access to their personal data. An individual may request access to all personal data of which he/she is the subject and which is being processed by the data controller. There are exemptions from these access rules in certain limited circumstances.

'Personal data' means data which relates to a living individual who can be identified from those data, or from those data and other information which are in the possession of, or are likely to come into the possession of, the data controller. It includes any expression of opinion about the individual and any indication of the intentions of the data controller or any other person in respect of the individual.

The definition of personal data would apply to data held on police computers about suspected and convicted offenders and may well apply to other similar paper records. Personal data held on the PNC clearly falls within this category (*R* v *Rees* [2000] LTL 20 October).

4.18.3.2 Sensitive Personal Data

The 1998 Act makes special provision in relation to 'sensitive personal data' which it defines (at s. 2) as:

> personal data consisting of information as to—
> (a) the racial or ethnic origin of the data subject,
> (b) his political opinions,
> (c) his religious beliefs or other beliefs of a similar nature,
> (d) whether he is a member of a trade union (within the meaning of the Trade Union and Labour Relations (Consolidation) Act 1992),
> (e) his physical or mental health or condition,
> (f) his sexual life,
> (g) the commission or alleged commission by him of any offence, or
> (h) any proceedings for any offence committed or alleged to have been committed by him, the disposal of such proceedings or the sentence of any court in such proceedings.

KEYNOTE

Data controllers are not permitted to process sensitive data about an individual unless: the processing is in connection with current or prospective legal proceedings or consultations; or is in the substantial public interest; or the explicit, informed and freely given consent of the individual has been obtained. This consent of the individual must be in writing, he/she must be informed of what information is to be processed, and no detriment must be suffered by an individual refusing to give consent.

4.18.3.3 Data Protection Principles

A crucial element in the 1998 Act is the data protection principles set out at sch. 1. As well as introducing the principles, s. 4(4) makes it clear that it is the duty of the relevant 'data controller' to comply with those principles wherever they apply. Part I of sch. 1 sets out the principles as being:

1. Personal data shall be processed fairly and lawfully and, in particular, shall not be processed unless—
   (a) at least one of the conditions in Schedule 2 is met, and
   (b) in the case of sensitive personal data, at least one of the conditions in Schedule 3 is also met.
2. Personal data shall be obtained only for one or more specified and lawful purposes, and shall not be further processed in any manner incompatible with that purpose or those purposes.
3. Personal data shall be adequate, relevant and not excessive in relation to the purpose or purposes for which they are processed.
4. Personal data shall be accurate and, where necessary, kept up to date.
5. Personal data processed for any purpose or purposes shall not be kept for longer than is necessary for that purpose or those purposes.
6. Personal data shall be processed in accordance with the rights of data subjects under this Act.
7. Appropriate technical and organisational measures shall be taken against unauthorised or unlawful processing of personal data and against accidental loss or destruction of, or damage to, personal data.
8. Personal data shall not be transferred to a country or territory outside the European Economic Area unless that country or territory ensures an adequate level of protection for the rights and freedoms of data subjects in relation to the processing of personal data.

KEYNOTE

Under the first data protection principle, a data controller must justify its processing of personal data under one of the following conditions:

- the data subject has given his/her consent to the processing;
- the processing is necessary for the performance of a contract or the entering into of a contract to which the data subject is a party;
- the processing is necessary for compliance with any legal obligation to which the data controller is subject;
- the processing is necessary in order to protect the vital interests of the data subject;
- the processing is necessary for the administration of justice; or
- the processing is necessary for the purposes of legitimate interests pursued by the data controller provided such processing does not harm the rights and freedoms or legitimate interests of data subjects.

The 1998 Act creates certain offences from the first data protection principle. Section 55 of the Act provides that a person must not knowingly or recklessly, without the consent of the data controller, obtain or disclose data or the information contained in personal data, or procure its disclosure to another person (s. 55(1)). However, this subsection does not apply where the obtaining, disclosing or procuring was necessary for the purpose of preventing or detecting crime (s. 55(2)(a)). In *R (On the Applications of Catt and T)* v *Commissioner of the Metropolis* [2015] UKSC 9, the Supreme Court held that the retention by the police of records of an elderly and non-violent man's participation in demonstrations organised by an extremist protest group was proportionate for the purposes of Article 8 of the European Convention on Human Rights. The police's policy on the retention of data in relation to harassment cases was not unlawful.

Other exemptions from subs. (1) are contained within s. 55.

4.18.4 The Regulation of Investigatory Powers Act 2000

The Regulation of Investigatory Powers Act 2000 (RIPA) is the law governing the use of covert techniques by public authorities. It requires that when the police or other law enforcement bodies (e.g. the Serious Fraud Office or the National Crime Agency (NCA)), the security and intelligence services (MI5, MI6 and GCHQ), as well as a large number of other public bodies, including local government, need to use covert techniques to obtain private information about someone, they do it in a way that is necessary, proportionate, and compatible with human rights. Surveillance measures necessarily involve some interference with private life, but have the legitimate aim of protecting national security and economic well-being (*Kennedy* v *United Kingdom* (2011) 52 EHRR 4).

Part II of the 2000 Act and associated Codes of Practice apply to actions such as:

- intercepting communications, such as the content of telephone calls, emails or letters;
- acquiring communications data: the 'who, when and where' of communications, such as telephone billing or subscriber details;
- conducting covert surveillance, either in private premises or vehicles (intrusive surveillance) or in public places (directed surveillance);
- the use of covert human intelligence sources, such as informants or undercover officers;
- access to electronic data protected by encryption or passwords.

In a policing context, any breach of the Act's provisions, or the provisions contained in the Codes of Practice, issued by the Secretary of State under s. 71, can have three main consequences:

- any evidence obtained may be excluded by a court or tribunal as being unfair;
- proceedings may be taken under the relevant police conduct regulations; or
- a person may make a claim before the Investigatory Powers Tribunal.

4.18.4.1 Surveillance and Covert Human Intelligence Sources

The Regulation of Investigatory Powers Act 2000, s. 26 provides:

> (1) This Part applies to the following conduct—
>   (a) directed surveillance;
>   (b) intrusive surveillance; and
>   (c) the conduct and use of covert human intelligence sources.

KEYNOTE

Although only s. 26(1)(c) expressly uses the word 'covert' for the nature of the activity, it is relevant to *all three* of these areas. Part II is concerned with *covert* activity and so, as a general rule, if it is not covert, it is not covered.

Some law enforcement activities fall outside the scope of the Act, e.g. 'property interference' which is a very intrusive form of intelligence gathering such as attaching listening devices within people's homes. This type of activity is covered by part III of the Police Act 1997 and is beyond the scope of this Manual.

4.18.4.2 Covert Human Intelligence Sources (CHIS): Definition

The following, which relates to s. 26, is an extract from the Covert Human Intelligence Sources Code of Practice (Regulation of Investigatory Powers (Covert Surveillance and Property Interference: Code of Practice) Order 2014 (SI 2014/3103)), Chapter 2, which states:

Definition of a covert human intelligence source (CHIS)
2.1 Under the 2000 Act, a person is a CHIS if:
   (a) they establish or maintain a personal or other relationship with a person for the covert purpose of facilitating the doing of anything falling within paragraph b) or c);

(b) they covertly use such a relationship to obtain information or to provide access to any information to another person; or

(c) they covertly disclose information obtained by the use of such a relationship or as a consequence of the existence of such a relationship.

See section 26(8) of the 2000 Act.

2.2 A relationship is established or maintained for a covert purpose if and only if it is conducted in a manner that is calculated to ensure that one of the parties to the relationship is unaware of the purpose.

See section 26(9)(b) of the 2000 Act for full definition.

2.3 A relationship is used covertly, and information obtained is disclosed covertly, if and only if the relationship is used or the information is disclosed in a manner that is calculated to ensure that one of the parties to the relationship is unaware of the use or disclosure in question.

See section 26(9)(c) of the 2000 Act for full definition.

KEYNOTE

A purpose is 'covert' here only if the relationship (and the subsequent disclosure of information) is conducted in a manner that is calculated to ensure that one of the parties is unaware of that purpose. Therefore the definition would not usually apply to members of the public generally supplying information to the police. Similarly, people who have come across information in the ordinary course of their jobs who suspect criminal activity (such as bank staff, local authority employees, etc.) do not have a covert relationship with the police simply by passing on information.

Great care will be needed, however, if the person supplying the information is asked by the police to do something further in order to develop or enhance it. Any form of direction or tasking by the police in this way could make the person a CHIS and thereby attract all the statutory provisions and safeguards.

There are two areas to be considered when considering covert human intelligence sources: the 'use' of a CHIS and 'conduct' as a CHIS. Both areas are strictly controlled by the legislation and require the relevant authorisation if they are to be lawful. The 'use' of a CHIS involves any action on behalf of a public authority to induce, ask or assist a person to engage in the conduct of a CHIS, or to obtain information by means of the conduct of a CHIS (s. 26(7)(b)). The conduct of a CHIS is any conduct of a CHIS which falls within para. 2.1 above, that is, steps taken by the CHIS on behalf, or at the request, of a public authority (s. 26(7)(a)). Most CHIS authorisations will be for both use and conduct as public authorities usually task the CHIS to undertake covert action, and because the CHIS will be expected to take action in relation to the public authority, such as responding to particular tasking.

Generally, covertly recording conversations and other personal information about a particular person will amount to some form of 'surveillance' (and therefore will be governed by the strict rules regulating such operations). However, such use of a CHIS will not amount to 'surveillance' (s. 48(3)).

Note that, apart from the many other considerations of using a CHIS, the police owe a duty to take reasonable care to avoid unnecessary disclosure to the general public of information provided by a CHIS (*Swinney* v *Chief Constable of Northumbria (No. 2)* (1999) 11 Admin LR 811).

4.18.4.3 CHIS: General Rules on Authorisations

In relation to the authorisation of a CHIS by the police the Regulation of Investigatory Powers Act 2000, s. 29 states:

(1) Subject to the following provisions of this Part, the persons designated for the purposes of this section shall each have power to grant authorisations for the conduct or the use of a covert human intelligence source.

(2) A person shall not grant an authorisation for the conduct or the use of a covert human intelligence source unless he believes—

(a) that the authorisation is necessary on grounds falling within subsection (3);

(b) that the authorised conduct or use is proportionate to what is sought to be achieved by that conduct or use; and

(c) that arrangements exist for the source's case that satisfy—

(i) the requirements of subsection (4A), in the case of a source of a relevant collaborative unit;

…

(ii) the requirements of subsection (5), in the case of any other source; and that satisfy such other requirements as may be imposed by order made by the Secretary of State.

(3) An authorisation is necessary on grounds falling within this subsection if it is necessary—

(a) in the interests of national security;

(b) for the purpose of preventing or detecting crime or of preventing disorder;

(c) in the interests of the economic well-being of the United Kingdom;

(d) in the interests of public safety;

(e) for the purpose of protecting public health;

(f) for the purpose of assessing or collecting any tax, duty, levy or other imposition, contribution or charge payable to a government department; or

(g) for any purpose (not falling within paragraphs (a) to (f)) which is specified for the purposes of this subsection by an order made by the Secretary of State.

KEYNOTE

Note that in relation to s. 29(3)(b), preventing and detecting crime is defined in s. 81(5) and goes beyond the prosecution of offenders and includes actions taken to avert, end or disrupt the commission of criminal offences.

The following extract from the Covert Human Intelligence Sources Code of Practice, Chapter 3, explains the terms 'necessary' and 'proportionate' contained within s. 29(2):

Necessity and Proportionality

3.2 The 2000 Act stipulates that the authorising officer must believe that an authorisation for the use or conduct of a CHIS is necessary in the circumstances of the particular case for one or more of the statutory grounds listed in section 29(3) of the 2000 Act.

3.3 If the use or conduct of the CHIS is deemed necessary, on one of more of the statutory grounds, the person granting the authorisation must also believe that it is proportionate to what is sought to be achieved by carrying it out. This involves balancing the seriousness of the intrusion into the private or family life of the subject of the operation (or any other person who may be affected) against the need for the activity in investigative and operational terms.

3.4 The authorisation will not be proportionate if it is excessive in the overall circumstances of the case. Each action authorised should bring an expected benefit to the investigation or operation and should not be disproportionate or arbitrary. The fact that a suspected offence may be serious will not alone render the use or conduct of a CHIS proportionate. Similarly, an offence may be so minor that any deployment of a CHIS would be disproportionate. No activity should be considered proportionate if the information, which is sought, could reasonably be obtained by other less intrusive means.

3.5 The following elements of proportionality should therefore be considered:

- balancing the size and scope of the proposed activity against the gravity and extent of the perceived crime or offence;
- explaining how and why the methods to be adopted will cause the least possible intrusion on the subject and others;
- considering whether the activity is an appropriate use of the legislation and a reasonable way, having considered all reasonable alternatives, of obtaining the necessary result;
- evidencing, as far as reasonably practicable, what other methods had been considered and why they were not implemented.

Authorising officers are also required to take into account collateral intrusion, namely, the risk of interference with the private and family life of persons who are not the intended subjects of the CHIS activity (Code of Practice, para. 3.9). They will also need to be aware of any particular sensitivities in the local community. Consideration should also be given to any adverse impact on community confidence or safety that may result from the use or conduct of a CHIS or use of information obtained from that CHIS (para. 3.17).

4.18.4.4   CHIS: Authorisation Procedures

The regulatory framework sets out specific conditions in relation to the deployment of different types of CHIS, from undercover operatives who change their entire identity to infiltrate criminal organisations, to 'decoys' that have no direct communication with suspects.

The following extract from the Covert Human Intelligence Sources Code of Practice, Chapter 5, outlines authorisation procedures for the use or conduct of a CHIS:

Authorisation Procedures

5.4 Responsibility for authorising the use or conduct of a CHIS rests with the authorising officer and all authorisations require the personal authority of the authorising officer. The Regulation of

Investigatory Powers (Directed Surveillance and Covert Human Intelligence Sources) Order 2010 as amended by the 2013 Order, designates the authorising officer for each different public authority and the officers entitled to act only in urgent cases. In certain circumstances the Secretary of State will be the authorising officer (see section 30(2) of the 2000 Act).

5.5 The authorising officer must give authorisations in writing, except in urgent cases, where they may be given orally. In such cases, a statement that the authorising officer has expressly authorised the action should be recorded in writing by the applicant (or the person with whom the authorising officer spoke) as a priority. This statement need not contain the full detail of the application, which should however subsequently be recorded in writing when reasonably practicable (generally the next working day).

5.6 Other officers entitled to act in urgent cases may only give authorisation in writing e.g. written authorisation for directed surveillance given by an Inspector.

5.7 A case is not normally to be regarded as urgent unless the time that would elapse before the authorising officer was available to grant the authorisation would, in the judgment of the person giving the authorisation, be likely to endanger life or jeopardise the operation or investigation for which the authorisation was being given. An authorisation is not to be regarded as urgent where the need for an authorisation has been neglected or the urgency is of the applicant's or authorising officer's own making.

KEYNOTE

Authorising officers should, where possible, be independent of the investigation. However, it is recognised that this is not always possible, especially in the cases of small organisations, or where it is necessary to act urgently or for security reasons.

The Regulation of Investigatory Powers (Directed Surveillance and Covert Human Intelligence Sources) Order 2010 (SI 2010/521, as amended by SI 2013/2788), prescribes the ranks of those within the police service in England and Wales who can authorise a CHIS. The relevant rank of an authorising officer for a CHIS is a superintendent and above. However, in urgent cases, where it is not reasonably practicable to have the application considered by someone of that rank in the same organisation, an inspector may generally give the relevant authorisation (sch. 1, part 1 of the 2010 Order). Unless it is renewed, the authorisation given by a superintendent will ordinarily cease to have effect after 12 months beginning on the day it was granted (s. 43(3)(b)). If that authorisation was given orally by a superintendent in an urgent case, it will only last for 72 hours unless renewed, and where the case is urgent and the authority was given by an inspector, it will cease to have effect 72 hours later unless renewed (s. 43(3)(a)). Authorisations may also be made on an application made by a member of another police force where such a police force is party to a collaborative agreement that provides for this (s. 33(3ZA)–(3ZC)). Long-term authorisations (those exceeding 12 months) can only be given by a chief constable/commissioner and are subject to approval by an independent Surveillance Commissioner.

A single authorisation can combine two or more different authorisations (e.g. the use of surveillance and the use of a CHIS) but they operate independently of each other (s. 43(2)). This means that when one authorisation lapses, any other authorisations made at the same time do not necessarily end as well.

All deployments of undercover officers (referred to in the Order and Code as 'relevant sources') must be authorised by an assistant chief constable/commander or in urgent cases by a superintendent. Authorisations lasting more than 12 months must be approved by a chief constable/commissioner and the Office of Surveillance Commissioners must give prior approval (sch. 1, part 1A to the 2010 Order). The CHIS Code of Practice states that all police officers deployed as a relevant source must comply with the College of Policing Code of Ethics.

Special safeguards apply in relation to juveniles and vulnerable individuals. Juveniles are those under 18 years of age. On no occasion should the use or conduct of a CHIS under 16 years of age be authorised to give information against his parents or any person who has parental responsibility for him. In other cases, authorisations should not be granted unless the special provisions contained within the Regulation of Investigatory Powers (Juveniles) Order 2000 (SI 2000/2793) are satisfied. A vulnerable individual is a person who is or may be in need of community care services by reason of mental or other disability, age or illness and who is or may be unable to take care of him/herself, or unable to protect him/herself against significant harm or exploitation.

The authorisation levels for juveniles and vulnerable individuals are assistant chief constable/commander where they are to be used as sources, or chief constable/commissioner when knowledge of confidential information is likely to be acquired. Regular reviews of authorisations are required to assess whether it remains necessary and proportionate to use a CHIS and whether the authorisation remains justified. An authorisation must be cancelled if the use or conduct of the CHIS no longer satisfies the criteria for authorisation.

The Regulation of Investigatory Powers (Covert Human Intelligence Sources: Matters Subject to Legal Privilege) Order 2010 (SI 2010/521, as amended by SI 2013/2788) deals with cases where through the use or conduct of a CHIS it is likely that knowledge of legally privileged material or other confidential information will be acquired. In such cases the deployment of the CHIS is subject to an enhanced regime of prior approval. Confidential information consists of matters subject to legal privilege, confidential personal information, confidential constituent information or confidential journalistic material.

The Code of Practice sets out clear guidelines for the management of a CHIS (Chapter 6), i.e. the control and monitoring of CHIS activities, the keeping of records (Chapter 7), and the handling, storage and destruction of materials (Chapter 8).

4.18.4.5 Covert Surveillance

The Covert Surveillance and Property Interference Code of Practice, Chapter 1 provides:

The surveillance activity to which this code applies

1.8 Part II of the 2000 Act provides for the *authorisation* of covert surveillance by *public authorities* where that surveillance is likely to result in the obtaining of *private information* about a person.

1.9 Surveillance, for the purpose of the 2000 Act, includes monitoring, observing or listening to persons, their movements, conversations or other activities and communications. It may be conducted with or without the assistance of a surveillance device and includes the recording of any information obtained.
(See section 48(2) of the 2000 Act)

1.10 Surveillance is covert if, and only if, it is carried out in a manner calculated to ensure that any persons who are subject to the surveillance are unaware that it is or may be taking place.
(As defined in section 26(9)(a) of the 2000 Act)

1.11 Specifically, covert surveillance may be authorised under the 2000 Act if it is either intrusive or directed:
- Intrusive surveillance is covert surveillance that is carried out in relation to anything taking place on residential premises or in any private vehicle (and that involves the presence of an individual on the premises or in the vehicle or is carried out by a means of a surveillance device);
- Directed surveillance is covert surveillance that is not intrusive but is carried out in relation to a specific investigation or operation in such a manner as is likely to result in the obtaining of *private information* about any person (other than by way of an immediate response to events or circumstances such that it is not reasonably practicable to seek *authorisation* under the 2000 Act).

KEYNOTE

Some surveillance activity does not constitute intrusive or directed surveillance for the purposes of part II of the 2000 Act and includes:

- covert surveillance by way of an immediate response to events, e.g. where police officers conceal themselves to observe suspicious persons that they come across in the course of a routine patrol;
- covert surveillance as part of general observation activities, e.g. where plain clothes police officers are on patrol to monitor a high street crime hot-spot or prevent and detect shoplifting;
- covert surveillance not relating to specified grounds, e.g. where a specific investigation or operation does not relate to the grounds specified at s. 28(3) of the 2000 Act;
- overt use of CCTV and ANPR systems, e.g. members of the public will be aware that such systems are in use, and their operation is covered by the Data Protection Act 1998 and the CCTV Code of Practice 2008, and the overt use of ANPR systems to monitor traffic flows or detect motoring offences does not require an authorisation under the 2000 Act;

- certain other specific situations, e.g. the use of a recording device by a CHIS in respect of whom an appropriate use or conduct authorisation has been granted permitting him to record any information obtained in his presence (s. 48(3));
- the recording, whether overt or covert, of an interview with a member of the public where it is made clear that the interview is entirely voluntary and that the interviewer is a member of a public authority.

4.18.4.6   Directed Surveillance

Chapter 2 of the Covert Surveillance and Property Interference Code of Practice provides further guidance on what is directed surveillance and states:

Directed surveillance

2.2 Surveillance is directed surveillance if the following are all true:
- it is covert, but not intrusive surveillance;
- it is conducted for the purposes of a specific investigation or operation;
- it is likely to result in the obtaining of *private information* about a person (whether or not one specifically identified for the purposes of the investigation or operation);
- it is conducted otherwise than by way of an immediate response to events or circumstances the nature of which is such that it would not be reasonably practicable for an *authorisation* under Part II of the 2000 Act to be sought.

2.3 Thus, the planned covert surveillance of a specific person, where not intrusive, would constitute directed surveillance if such surveillance is likely to result in the obtaining of *private information* about that, or any other person.

KEYNOTE

Private information includes any information relating to a person's private or family life (s. 26(10)). It should be taken generally to include any aspect of a person's private or personal relationship with others, including family. Family should be treated as extending beyond the formal relationships created by marriage or civil partnership and may include professional or business relationships.

Private information may include personal data, such as names, telephone numbers and address details. Where such information is acquired by means of covert surveillance of a person having a reasonable expectation of privacy, a directed surveillance authorisation is appropriate. The fact that a directed surveillance authorisation is available does not mean it is required. There may be other lawful means of obtaining personal data that do not involve directed surveillance.

While a person may have a reduced expectation of privacy when in a public place, covert surveillance of that person's activities in public may still result in the obtaining of private information. This is likely to be the case where that person has a reasonable expectation of privacy even though acting in public and where a record is being made by a public authority of that person's activities for future consideration or analysis. Note also that a person in police custody will have certain expectations of privacy.

As with a CHIS, an authorisation for directed surveillance should not be granted unless it is believed to be proportionate to what is sought to be achieved and necessary on the specified grounds (**see para. 4.18.4.3** in relation to 'necessary' and 'proportionate'). The specified grounds, contained in s. 28(3), are:

- in the interests of national security;
- for the purpose of preventing or detecting crime or of preventing disorder;
- in the interests of the economic well-being of the United Kingdom;
- in the interests of public safety;
- for the purpose of protecting public health;
- for the purpose of assessing or collecting any tax, duty, levy or other imposition, contribution or charge payable to a government department; or
- for any purpose (not falling within paragraphs (a) to (f)) which is specified for the purposes of this subsection by an order made by the Secretary of State.

The Regulation of Investigatory Powers (Directed Surveillance and Covert Human Intelligence Sources) Order 2003 (SI 2003/3171), as amended, sets out the relevant roles and ranks for those who can authorise directed surveillance. In the case of the police the relevant rank will generally be at superintendent level and above, and the authorisation must be in writing except in urgent cases where oral authorisation may be given (s. 43(1)(a)). A written authorisation ceases to have effect after three months beginning on the day it was granted, and if given orally will only last 72 hours unless renewed (s. 43(3)). Where it is not reasonably practicable to have the application considered by a superintendent or above, having regard to the urgency of the case, then an inspector may give the relevant authorisation which will only last 72 hours unless renewed by a superintendent. For the NCA the authorising officer is a Senior Manager (Grade 2) and for urgent cases a Principal Officer (Grade 3).

Authorisations may also be made on an application made by a member of another police force where such police forces are party to a collaborative agreement that provides for them (s. 33(3ZA)–(3ZC)).

As with a CHIS the Codes of Practice provide additional procedural safeguards regarding where the material sought by the surveillance is subject to legal privilege, is confidential personal information or some journalistic material. It is of interest to note that the House of Lords has held that the 2000 Act permits covert surveillance of communications between lawyers and their clients even though these may be subject to legal professional privilege (*Re McE (Northern Ireland)* [2009] UKHL 15).

4.18.4.7 Intrusive Surveillance

The Covert Surveillance and Property Interference Code of Practice, Chapter 2, provides further guidance on what is intrusive surveillance and states:

Intrusive Surveillance

2.11 Intrusive surveillance is covert surveillance that is carried out in relation to anything taking place on residential premises or in any private vehicle, and that involves the presence of an individual on the premises or in the vehicle or is carried out by a means of a surveillance device.

2.12 The definition of surveillance as intrusive relates to the location of the surveillance, and not any other consideration of the nature of the information that is expected to be obtained. In addition, surveillance under the ambit of the 2010 Order is to be treated as intrusive surveillance. Accordingly, it is not necessary to consider whether or not intrusive surveillance is likely to result in the obtaining of private information.

KEYNOTE

'Residential premises' are considered to be so much of any premises as is for the time being occupied or used by any person, however temporarily, for residential purposes or otherwise as living accommodation. This specifically includes hotel or prison accommodation that is so occupied or used (s. 48)(1)). However, common areas (such as hotel dining areas) to which a person has access in connection with their use or occupation of accommodation are specifically excluded (s. 48(7)). The Act further states that the concept of premises should be taken to include any place whatsoever, including any vehicle or movable structure, whether or not occupied as land (s. 48(8)).

A 'private vehicle' is defined as any vehicle, including vessels, aircraft or hovercraft, which is used primarily for the private purposes of the person who owns it or a person otherwise having the right to use it. This would include, for example, a company car, owned by a leasing company and used for business and pleasure by the employee of a company (s. 48(1) and (7)).

In *R* v *Plunkett* [2013] EWCA Crim 261, in admitting evidence of statements and admissions by the accused in a police van which were covertly recorded, it was held that a police van is not a private vehicle for the purposes of s. 26(3) and that the authorisation given by a superintendent under s. 28 for directed surveillance was appropriate. Interestingly, evidence arising from the use of a bug in police transport, which was obtained in circumstances that meant there was a technical breach of the RIPA authority, was held admissible in that the officers had not acted in bad faith knowing they were exceeding their authority (*Khan* v *R* [2013] EWCA Crim 2230).

Surveillance is not intrusive if it is carried out by means only of a surveillance device designed or adapted principally for the purpose of providing information about the location of a vehicle (s. 25(4)(a)).

If the surveillance is carried out by means of a surveillance device in relation to anything taking place on the premises or private vehicle, but is carried out without that device being present on the premises or in the vehicle, it is not intrusive unless the device is such that it consistently provides information of the same quality and detail as might be expected to be obtained from a device actually present on the premises or in the vehicle (s. 25(5)).

The Regulation of Investigatory Powers (Extension of Authorisation Provisions: Legal Consultations) Order 2010 (SI 2010/461) provides that directed surveillance carried out in relation to anything taking place on any premises specified in the Order that are being used for the purpose of legal consultations shall be treated as 'intrusive surveillance'. The 'any premises' includes prisons, police stations, high security psychiatric hospitals, the place of business of any professional legal adviser; and any place used for the sittings and business of any court, tribunal, inquest or inquiry.

Authorisations for intrusive surveillance will generally be granted by chief constables/commissioners and the Director General of the NCA (s. 32), or in some cases designated deputies. As with the other authorisations under the Act the authorising officer shall not grant an authorisation for the carrying out of intrusive surveillance unless he/she believes that the authorisation is necessary on the specified grounds and that the authorised surveillance is proportionate to what is sought to be achieved by carrying it out (s. 32(2)). The specified grounds, contained in s. 32(3) are:

- in the interests of national security;
- for the purpose of preventing or detecting serious crime;
- in the interests of the economic well-being of the United Kingdom.

Subsection (3A) provides that in the case of an authorisation granted by the chairman of the Competition and Markets Authority, the authorisation is necessary on grounds falling within subs. (3) only if it is necessary for the purpose of preventing or detecting an offence under s. 188 of the Enterprise Act 2002 (cartel offence).

In relation to 'national security' a senior authorising officer or designated deputy of a law enforcement agency shall not issue an authorisation for intrusive surveillance where the investigation or operation is within the responsibilities of one of the intelligence services and properly falls to be authorised by warrant issued by the Secretary of State. 'Serious crime' is defined in s. 81(2) and (3) as crime that comprises an offence for which a person who has attained the age of 21 and has no previous convictions could reasonably be expected to be sentenced to imprisonment for a term of three years or more, or which involves the use of violence, results in substantial financial gain or is conduct by a large number of persons in pursuit of a common purpose.

Except in urgent cases, authorisation granted for intrusive surveillance will not take effect until a Surveillance Commissioner has approved it and written notice of the Commissioner's decision has been given to the person who granted the authorisation. This means that the approval will not take effect until the notice has been received in the office of the person who granted the authorisation within the relevant force or organisation (s. 35(3)(a)). When the authorisation is urgent it will take effect from the time it is granted provided notice is given to the Surveillance Commissioner (s. 35(3)(b)).

A written authorisation will cease to have effect (unless renewed) at the end of a period of three months. Oral authorisations given in urgent cases will cease to have effect (unless renewed) at the end of the period of 72 hours beginning with the time when they took effect.

Authorisations may also be made on an application made by a member of another police force where such police forces are party to a collaborative agreement that provides for them (s. 33(3ZA)–(3ZC)).

4.18.4.8 Interception of Communications

The 2000 Act creates two interception offences: one concerned with the interception of communications transmitted by either public postal or public communication systems; and the other concerned with the interception of communications transmitted by private telecommunication systems.

The Code of Practice in relation to the interception of communications provides guidance on the procedures that must be followed before interception of communications can take place under the provisions of the Act (Regulation of Investigatory Powers (Interception of Communications: Code of Practice) Order 2016 (SI 2016/37)).

4.18.4.9 Unlawful Interception of Public and Private Communications

OFFENCE: **Unlawful Interception of Public and Private Communications—**
Regulation of Investigatory Powers Act 2000, s. 1(1) and (2)
- Triable either way • Two years' imprisonment and/or a fine on indictment
- Fine summarily

The Regulation of Investigatory Powers Act 2000, s. 1 states:

(1) It shall be an offence for a person intentionally and without lawful authority to intercept, at any place in the United Kingdom, any communication in the course of its transmission by means of—
   (a) a public postal service; or
   (b) a public telecommunication system.
(1A) ...
(1B) ...
(2) It shall be an offence for a person—
   (a) intentionally and without lawful authority, and
   (b) otherwise than in circumstances in which his conduct is excluded by subsection (6) from criminal liability under this subsection,
   to intercept, at any place in the United Kingdom, any communication in the course of its transmission by means of a private telecommunication system.

KEYNOTE

Subsections (1A) and (1B) relate to monetary penalty notices that can be served on a person by the Interception of Communications Commissioner, effectively imposing a fine if the person fails to comply with a direction requiring cessation of specified interception communication.

For the offence under subs. (1) the meaning of public postal service and public telecommunications systems are broadly provided by s. 2:

- Public postal service—any postal service which is offered or provided to the public in any part of the United Kingdom.
- Public telecommunications systems—the parts of a public telecommunication service that are located within the United Kingdom.

For the offence under subs. (2) a private telecommunication system must:

- be attached (directly or indirectly) to a public telecommunication system; and
- have apparatus comprised in it which is located in the United Kingdom and is used for attaching it to that public telecommunication system.

A privately owned office telephone system in England and Wales which is locally attached to a public telecommunication system would meet the criteria, as would the type of police station payphone which is routed via the internal telephone system.

In relation to subs. (2)(b) where 'conduct is excluded by subsection (6)' this exempts some interception of private communications where the interceptor has a right to control the operation or use of the system or has the consent of such a person to intercept the communication. This means the right to authorise or forbid the operation of the system (*R* v *Stanford* [2006] EWCA Crim 258). The sort of interception envisaged here is where organisations intercept and monitor communications made on their own telecommunication systems.

The legislation applies to companies providing communications services to customers in the United Kingdom, wherever those companies are located, Internet-based services such as web-based email, messaging applications and cloud-based services are covered by the Act.

The authority of the DPP is required for a prosecution under both subss. (1) and (2) (s. 1(8)(a)).

4.18.4.10　What Amounts to Interception?

The Regulation of Investigatory Powers Act 2000, s. 2 states:

(2) For the purposes of this Act, but subject to the following provisions of this section, a person intercepts a communication in the course of its transmission by means of a telecommunication system if, and only if, he—
   (a) so modifies or interferes with the system, or its operation,
   (b) so monitors transmissions made by means of the system, or
   (c) so monitors transmissions made by wireless telegraphy to or from apparatus comprised in the system,
   as to make some or all of the contents of the communication available, while being transmitted, to a person other than the sender or intended recipient of the communication.

KEYNOTE

The expression 'in the course of its transmission' is critical in applying the extent of the definition of interception. In a case where a listening device installed by the police in the defendant's car had recorded the defendant speaking on his mobile phone, the Court of Appeal held that this did not amount to an 'interception', and mere eavesdropping on a conversation between one person at one end of a mobile telephone or two people face-to-face could not constitute communication in the course of transmission (*R* v *Allsopp* [2005] EWCA Crim 703; see also *R* v *E* (*Admissibility: Covert Listening Device*) [2004] EWCA Crim 1243).

A communication is 'being transmitted' for the purposes of this offence when it is stored on the system for the intended recipient to collect or access (s. 2(7)). This means that email messages awaiting collection/access by the intended recipient are still 'being transmitted', as are unreceived or uncollected pager messages. This also includes a situation where a voicemail message has been saved by the recipient on the voicemail facility of a public telecommunications system (*R* v *Edmondson* [2013] EWCA Crim 1026).

There is no equivalent definition for the interception of postal communications and this will presumably be a question of fact to be addressed on the merits of each case.

Having set out what the offence covers, the Act goes on to specify particular activities that will *not* be caught by this section. These include:

- the interception of any communication broadcast for general reception, which covers broadcasts such as television and radio; it does not extend to pagers and mobile phone communications and these *are* covered by the Act;
- the interception of certain types of 'traffic data' (this means certain types of information that are needed to deliver or route the communication).

4.18.4.11　Lawful Authority

The Regulation of Investigatory Powers Act 2000, s. 1 states:

(5) Conduct has lawful authority for the purposes of this section if, and only if—
   (a) it is authorised by or under section 3 or 4;
   (b) it takes place in accordance with a warrant under section 5 ('an interception warrant'); or
   (c) it is in exercise, in relation to any stored communication, of any statutory power that is exercised (apart from this section) for the purpose of obtaining information or of taking possession of any document or other property;
   and conduct (whether or not prohibited by this section) which has lawful authority for the purposes of this section by virtue of paragraph (a) or (b) shall also be taken to be lawful for all other purposes.

KEYNOTE

The conduct authorised by the warrant must be proportionate to what is sought to be achieved by it (s. 5(2)(b)).

Conduct Authorised under section 3 or 4

Section 3 of the 2000 Act authorises certain *types of interception* without the need for a warrant. In general, it covers interception where:

- both the sender and intended recipient have consented to it;
- either the sender or intended recipient has consented and surveillance by means of that interception has been authorised under part II (as to which, **see para. 4.18.4.14**)—this might cover the situation where the police are monitoring threatening telephone calls made to a victim or calls made in connection with black-mail demands;
- the interception is by/on behalf of the provider of the postal or telecommunication service for purposes connected with it (examples of this conduct would include postal workers who need to open mail in order to return it to the sender);
- the person is authorised under s. 48 of the Wireless Telegraphy Act 2006.

Section 4 of the 2000 Act sets out occasions where *other authorities* might permit the interception of certain communications without the need for a warrant such as communications to or from prisons and high security psychiatric hospitals. Section 4 also makes provision for interception of communications involving people who are (or are believed to be) outside the United Kingdom.

Interception Warrants

The issuing, exercising and oversight of interception warrants are subject to extensive statutory procedures (ss. 5 to 11). They are issued by the Secretary of State where he/she *believes* that the warrant is *necessary* on grounds falling within s. 5(3) and proportionate to what is sought to be achieved by the conduct authorised by the warrant.

Section 5(3) states that the warrant is *necessary* on grounds falling within this subsection if it is necessary: in the interests of national security; for the purpose of preventing or detecting serious crime (including the provisions of any international mutual assistance agreement); or for the purpose, in circumstances appearing to the Secretary of State to be relevant to the interests of national security, of safeguarding the economic well-being of the United Kingdom (s. 7). For the meaning of 'serious crime' **see para. 4.18.4.7**.

Stored Communication

This relates to occasions where the person is exercising a statutory power, other than s. 1 of the 2000 Act, for the purpose of obtaining information or taking possession of any document or other property *in relation to any stored communication*. The example given by the Home Office of such a situation is where police officers have recovered a pager from a person in custody and they apply to a circuit judge for an order under sch. 1 to the Police and Criminal Evidence Act 1984 to access its messages.

4.18.4.12 **Unauthorised Disclosures**

OFFENCE **Unauthorised Disclosures—*Regulation of Investigatory Powers Act 2000, s. 19***
- Triable either way • Five years' imprisonment and/or a fine on indictment
- Six months' imprisonment and/or a fine summarily

The Regulation of Investigatory Powers Act 2000, s. 19 states:

(1) Where an interception warrant has been issued or renewed, it shall be the duty of every person falling within subsection (2) to keep secret all the matters mentioned in subsection (3).

(2) The persons falling within this subsection are—

(a) the persons specified in section 6(2);

(b) every person holding office under the Crown;

...

(e) every person employed by or for the purposes of a police force;

(f) persons providing postal services or employed for the purposes of any business of providing such a service;

(g) persons providing public telecommunications services or employed for the purposes of any business of providing such a service;

(h) persons having control of the whole or any part of a telecommunication system located wholly or partly in the United Kingdom.

(3) Those matters are—

(a) the existence and contents of the warrant and of any section 8(4) certificate in relation to the warrant;

(b) the details of the issue of the warrant and of any renewal or modification of the warrant or of any such certificate;

(c) the existence and contents of any requirement to provide assistance with giving effect to the warrant;

(d) the steps taken in pursuance of the warrant or of any such requirement; and

(e) everything in the intercepted material, together with any related communications data.

(4) A person who makes a disclosure to another of anything that he is required to keep secret under this section shall be guilty of an offence ...

KEYNOTE

This offence imposes a very clear duty on the people set out in s. 19(2) and makes no specific requirement as to state of mind.

It is clearly intended to apply to police officers and others involved in an investigation, and it also extends to support staff.

Section 19(5) provides a defence for a person charged with this offence to show that he/she could not reasonably have been expected, after first becoming aware of the matter disclosed, to take steps to prevent the disclosure. Further defences exist for some communications with professional legal advisers (s. 19(6) and (7)), and other proper communications with the Interception of Communications Commissioner (s. 19(9)).

4.18.4.13 Communications Data

The Regulation of Investigatory Powers Act 2000 provides the legislative framework to cover the requisition, provision and handling of communications data. It explains the duties and responsibilities placed upon each party involved in these processes and creates a system of safeguards, reflecting the requirements of Article 8 of the European Convention on Human Rights (Right to Respect for Private and Family Life, Home and Correspondence).

4.18.4.14 Lawful Acquisition and Disclosure of Communications Data

The Regulation of Investigatory Powers Act 2000, s. 21 states:

(1) This Chapter applies to—

(a) any conduct in relation to a postal service or telecommunication system for obtaining communications data, other than conduct consisting in the interception of communications in the course of their transmission by means of such a service or system; and

(b) the disclosure to any person of communications data.

(2) Conduct to which this Chapter applies shall be lawful for all purposes if—

(a) it is conduct in which any person is authorised or required to engage by an authorisation or notice granted or given under this Chapter; and

(b) the conduct is in accordance with, or in pursuance of, the authorisation or requirement.

4.18.4.15 Obtaining and Disclosing Communications Data

The Regulation of Investigatory Powers Act 2000, s. 22 states:

(1) This section applies where a person designated for the purposes of this Chapter believes that it is necessary on grounds falling within subsection (2) to obtain any communications data.

(2) It is necessary on grounds falling within this subsection to obtain communications data if it is necessary—

   (a) in the interests of national security;

   (b) for the purpose of preventing or detecting crime or of preventing disorder;

   (c) in the interests of the economic well-being of the United Kingdom so far as those interests are also relevant to the interests of national security;

   (d) in the interests of public safety;

   (e) for the purpose of protecting public health;

   (f) for the purpose of assessing or collecting any tax, duty, levy or other imposition, contribution or charge payable to a government department;

   (g) for the purpose, in an emergency, of preventing death or injury or any damage to a person's physical or mental health, or of mitigating any injury or damage to a person's physical or mental health; or

   (h) for any purpose (not falling within paragraphs (a) to (g)) which is specified for the purposes of this subsection by an order made by the Secretary of State.

(3) Subject to subsection (5), the designated person may grant an authorisation for persons holding offices, ranks or positions with the same relevant public authority as the designated person to engage in any conduct to which this Chapter applies.

(4) Subject to subsection (5), where it appears to the designated person that a postal or telecommunications operator is or may be in possession of, or be capable of obtaining, any communications data, the designated person may, by notice to the postal or telecommunications operator, require the operator—

   (a) if the operator is not already in possession of the data, to obtain the data; and

   (b) in any case, to disclose all of the data in his possession or subsequently obtained by him.

- for the purpose of exercising functions relating to the regulation of financial services and markets or to financial stability.

The designated person cannot grant an authorisation or give a notice under s. 22(3) or (4) unless it is believed that obtaining the data in question, by the conduct authorised or required by the authorisation or notice, is *proportionate* to what is sought to be achieved by so obtaining the data (s. 22(5)).

Although the requirements for *necessity* are the same here as for interception warrants, the grounds contain significant differences. A much wider category of people can authorise the obtaining of communications data under Chapter II and there is no stipulation that 'serious crime' is involved.

The relevant public authorities who can authorise communications data to be obtained include: a police force (as defined in s. 81(1) of the Act), the National Crime Agency, HM Revenue and Customs, the Security Service, the Secret Intelligence Service, and the Government Communications Headquarters. These and additional relevant public authorities are listed in schedules to the Regulation of Investigatory Powers (Communications Data) Order 2010 together with the offices, ranks and positions of the designated persons.

Note that s. 22(2)(c) was amended by the Data Retention and Investigatory Powers Act 2014 to require that the 'interests of economic well-being' are also relevant to the interests of national security. This amendment equally applied to s. 5(3) of the Act (**see para. 4.18.4.11**).

The above is merely a summary of the key aspects of the legislation relating to communications data. To find the full extent of the powers and duties under the 2000 Act, the statutory text should be used alongside the current Codes of Practice.

4.19 Equality

4.19.1 Introduction

The Equality Act 2010 provides a framework of protection against direct and indirect discrimination, harassment and victimisation in services and public functions; premises; work; education; associations; and transport.

This chapter briefly sets out the key features of the 2010 Act together with Article 14 of the European Convention on Human Rights in relation to the 'prohibition of discrimination'.

4.19.2 Article 14—Prohibition of Discrimination

Article 14 of the European Convention on Human Rights states:

> The enjoyment of the rights and freedoms set forth in this Convention shall be secured without discrimination on any ground such as sex, race, colour, language, religion, political or other opinion, national or social origin, association with a national minority, property, birth or other status.

KEYNOTE

Article 14 simply provides a guarantee that access to the Convention's other provisions must be enjoyed equally by everyone under the jurisdiction of the particular State. The list set out in the Article is not exhaustive and other categories of people or grounds of discrimination may be added by the courts (and have been added by the European Court of Human Rights). A person claiming a breach of Article 14 must show that his/her own individual circumstances are similar to those of another person who has been treated differently in relation to the enjoyment of Convention rights.

The open-ended wording of Article 14 means that a wide range of categories of people who can be grouped by reference to their status may be protected. It makes express provision for *indirect* discrimination (see para. 4.19.4.7) and the Divisional Court has expressed considerable doubt as to whether Article 14 provides protection against indirect, as opposed to direct, discrimination (*R (On the Application of Barber)* v *Secretary of State for Work and Pensions* [2002] EWHC 1915 (Admin)).

4.19.3 Protected Characteristics

The protected characteristics covered by the Act are:

- Age
- Disability
- Gender reassignment
- Marriage and civil partnerships
- Race
- Religion or belief
- Sex
- Sexual Orientation

4.19.3.1 Age

The Equality Act 2010, s. 5 states:

(1) In relation to the protected characteristic of age—
  (a) a reference to a person who has a particular protected characteristic is a reference to a person of a particular age group;
  (b) a reference to persons who share a protected characteristic is a reference to persons of the same age group.
(2) A reference to an age group is a reference to a group of persons defined by reference to age, whether by reference to a particular age or to a range of ages.

4.19.3.2 Disability

The Equality Act 2010, s. 6 states:

(1) A person (P) has a disability if—
  (a) P has a physical or mental impairment, and
  (b) the impairment has a substantial and long-term adverse effect on P's ability to carry out normal day-to-day activities.
(2) A reference to a disabled person is a reference to a person who has a disability.
(3) In relation to the protected characteristic of disability—
  (a) a reference to a person who has a particular protected characteristic is a reference to a person who has a particular disability;
  (b) a reference to persons who share a protected characteristic is a reference to persons who have the same disability.

The Equality Act (Disability) Regulations 2010 (SI 2010/2128) contain provisions regarding who is to be considered as having the protected characteristic of disability and is a disabled person for the purposes of the Act.

In relation to s. 6(1)(b) 'ability to carry out normal day-to-day activities', in *Chief Constable of Dumfries and Galloway Constabulary* v *Adams* [2009] ICR 1034 it was held that normal day-to-day activities for a police officer included working nights. Confrontational duties were also considered a 'normal day-to-day activity' (*Hart* v *Chief Constable of Derbyshire Constabulary* [2008] EWCA Civ 929).

4.19.3.3 Gender Reassignment

The Equality Act 2010, s. 7 states:

(1) A person has the protected characteristic of gender reassignment if the person is proposing to undergo, is undergoing or has undergone a process (or part of a process) for the purpose of re-assigning the person's sex by changing physiological or other attributes of sex.
(2) A reference to a transsexual person is a reference to a person who has the protected characteristic of gender reassignment.
(3) In relation to the protected characteristic of gender reassignment—
   (a) a reference to a person who has a particular protected characteristic is a reference to a transsexual person;
   (b) a reference to persons who share a protected characteristic is a reference to transsexual persons.

KEYNOTE

A woman making the transition to being a man and a man making the transition to being a woman both share the characteristic of gender reassignment, as does a person who has only just started out on the process of changing his/her sex and a person who has completed the process.

The established legal principle in law is that gender is set at birth. If you are born male you remain male and vice versa (*Corbett* v *Corbett* [1970] 2 WLR 1306). However, in *A* v *Chief Constable of West Yorkshire and the Secretary of State for Work and Pensions* [2004] UKHL 21 it was held that it was no longer possible in the context of employment to regard a transsexual as being his/her birth gender. But public interest considerations in relation to the police service may determine that a gender-reassigned applicant is not offered employment.

4.19.3.4 Marriage and Civil Partnerships

The Equality Act 2010, s. 8 states:

(1) A person has the protected characteristic of marriage and civil partnership if the person is married or is a civil partner.
(2) In relation to the protected characteristic of marriage and civil partnership—
   (a) a reference to a person who has a particular protected characteristic is a reference to a person who is married or is a civil partner;
   (b) a reference to persons who share a protected characteristic is a reference to persons who are married or are civil partners.

KEYNOTE

People who are not married or civil partners do not have this characteristic. A married man and a woman in a civil partnership both share the protected characteristic of marriage and civil partnership.

The Marriage (Same Sex Couples) Act 2013 extended marriage to same sex couples which means that marriage has the same effect in law in relation to such a couple as it does in relation to an opposite sex couple (s. 11(1)). Section 11(2) ensures that the law of England and Wales, including all existing and new England and Wales legislation, will be interpreted in this way.

4.19.3.5 Race

The Equality Act 2010, s. 9 states:

(1) Race includes—
   (a) colour;
   (b) nationality;
   (c) ethnic or national origins.
(2) In relation to the protected characteristic of race—
   (a) a reference to a person who has a particular protected characteristic is a reference to a person of a particular racial group;
   (b) a reference to persons who share a protected characteristic is a reference to persons of the same racial group.
(3) A racial group is a group of persons defined by reference to race; and a reference to a person's racial group is a reference to a racial group into which the person falls.
(4) The fact that a racial group comprises two or more distinct racial groups does not prevent it from constituting a particular racial group.

KEYNOTE

People who have or share characteristics of colour, nationality or ethnic or national origins can be described as belonging to a particular racial group. A racial group can be made up of two or more different racial groups.

'Nationality' has been held to include citizenship acquired by birth, and in *Souster* v *BBC Scotland* [2001] IRLR 150, it was held that an English applicant can be discriminated against by a Scottish employer.

'Ethnic group' may include any group with a shared culture or history (*Mandla* v *Dowell Lee* [1983] 2 AC 548). Sikhs (*Mandla* v *Dowell Lee* [1983] 2 AC 548), Jews (*Seide* v *Gillette Industries Ltd* [1980] IRLR 427), Romany Gypsies (*Commission for Racial Equality* v *Dutton* [1989] QB 783), and Irish Travellers (*O'Leary* v *Allied Domecq Inns Ltd* (CL 950275 July 2000, Central London County Court), have all been held to be ethnic groups, but Scots, Welsh and English are however not an ethnic group (*Dawkins* v *Department of the Environment* [1993] IRLR 284).

'National origins' may overlap with nationality but the two concepts can be distinguished since 'nationality' is concerned with membership of a particular nation, and 'national origins' describes a person's connection by birth with a nation (*Ealing London Borough Council* v *Race Relations Board* [1972] AC 342).

'Racial group' includes a group of people who have or share a colour, ethnic, or national origin or nationality.

A Minister of the Crown may amend the Act so as to add 'caste' to the current definition of 'race' (s. 9(5)). The term 'caste' denotes a hereditary, endogamous (marrying within the group) community associated with a traditional occupation and ranked accordingly on a perceived scale of ritual purity, e.g. the four classes (varnas) of Hindu tradition (the Brahmin, Kshatriya, Vaishya and Shudra communities). In *Chandhok* v *Tirkey* [2014] UKEAT 0190/14/1912 it was considered that 'caste' might come within s. 9(1)(c) since 'ethnic origins' had a wide and flexible ambit, including characteristics determined by 'descent'.

4.19.3.6 Religion or Belief

The Equality Act 2010, s. 10 states:

(1) Religion means any religion and a reference to religion includes a reference to a lack of religion.
(2) Belief means any religious or philosophical belief and a reference to belief includes a reference to a lack of belief.
(3) In relation to the protected characteristic of religion or belief—
   (a) a reference to a person who has a particular protected characteristic is a reference to a person of a particular religion or belief;
   (b) a reference to persons who share a protected characteristic is a reference to persons who are of the same religion or belief.

The section provides a definition in line with the freedom of thought, conscience and religion guaranteed by Article 9 of the European Convention on Human Rights. The main limitation is that the religion must have a clear structure and belief system. Denominations or sects within a religion can be considered to be a religion or belief, such as Protestants and Catholics within Christianity.

In *Eweida* v *United Kingdom* (2013) 57 EHRR 8 it was held that prohibiting a woman from visibly wearing a cross at work amounted to an interference with her right to manifest her Christian religion and this was in breach of the positive obligation under Article 9 of the European Convention on Human Rights (Right to freedom of thought, conscience and religion). However, in three other applications in the same case, which related to practising Christians, there was held to be no breach of either Article 9 or Article 14. (The rights and freedoms set forth in the Convention shall be secured without discrimination on any ground such as religion.) These applications included: a nurse wearing a cross where the discrimination was based on health and safety rather than religious grounds; a registrar of births, deaths and marriages who believed that same-sex civil partnerships are contrary to God's law and refused to carry out civil partnerships; a Relate counsellor who refused to work with couples on same-sex sexual practices.

Religious belief can vary from individual to individual within the same religion. Jewish people believe men should wear the Kippah (skull cap) at all times; and some Muslims believe women should cover their entire body and face with the Jilbab and Burqa (*R (On the Application of Begum)* v *Governors of Denbigh High School* [2006] UKHL 15). In *Power v Greater Manchester Police Authority* [2011] Eq LR 16 where a person was dismissed on grounds of his beliefs, it was not the belief itself but the expression of those beliefs which was in part the cause of his dismissal.

The criteria for determining what is a 'philosophical belief' are that it must be genuinely held; be a belief and not an opinion or viewpoint based on the present state of information available; be a belief as to a weighty and substantial aspect of human life and behaviour; attain a certain level of cogency, seriousness, cohesion and importance; and be worthy of respect in a democratic society, compatible with human dignity and not conflict with the fundamental rights of others. For example, a belief in 'climate change' affecting how a person lived his/her life is protected by the Act (*Grainger plc* v *Nicholson* [2010] 2 All ER 253).

4.19.3.7 Sex

The Equality Act 2010, s. 11 states:

In relation to the protected characteristic of sex—
(a) a reference to a person who has a particular protected characteristic is a reference to a man or to a woman;
(b) a reference to persons who share a protected characteristic is a reference to persons of the same sex.

This provision explains that references in the Act to people having the protected characteristic of sex are to mean being a man or a woman, and that men share this characteristic with other men, and women with other women.

The Act contains provisions (ss. 66 to 70) designed to achieve equality between men and women in pay and other terms of employment where the work of an employee and his/her comparator, a person of the opposite sex, is equal. It does so by providing for a sex equality clause to be read into the employee's contract of employment. This is designed to ensure parity of terms between the employee and his/her comparator.

For work to be equal, a claimant must establish that he/she is doing like work, work rated as equivalent or work of equal value to a comparator's work (s. 65). For example, in *Blackburn* v *West Midlands Police* [2008] EWCA Civ 1208 it was held that where police officers needed to work hours compatible with their child care responsibilities they were not entitled to special payments received by officers working 24/7 shift patterns.

4.19.3.8   Sexual Orientation

The Equality Act 2010, s. 12 states:

> (1) Sexual orientation means a person's sexual orientation towards—
>   (a) persons of the same sex,
>   (b) persons of the opposite sex, or
>   (c) persons of either sex.
> (2) In relation to the protected characteristic of sexual orientation—
>   (a) a reference to a person who has a particular protected characteristic is a reference to a person who is of a particular sexual orientation;
>   (b) a reference to persons who share a protected characteristic is a reference to persons who are of the same sexual orientation.

KEYNOTE

This section defines the protected characteristic of sexual orientation as being a person's sexual orientation towards: people of the same sex as him/her (the person is a gay man or a lesbian); people of the opposite sex from him/her (the person is heterosexual); people of both sexes (the person is bisexual).

4.19.4   Discrimination

The Equality Act 2010 provides for the following six different types of discrimination which are discussed within this section:

- **Direct discrimination**: discrimination because of a protected characteristic.
- **Associative discrimination**: direct discrimination against someone because he/she is associated with another person with a protected characteristic.
- **Indirect discrimination**: a rule or policy that applies to everyone but disadvantages a person with a protected characteristic.
- **Harassment**: behaviour deemed offensive by the recipient.
- **Victimisation**: discrimination against someone because he/she made or supported a complaint under Equality Act legislation.
- **Discrimination by perception**: direct discrimination against someone because others think he/she has a protected characteristic.

KEYNOTE

In proceedings relating to contraventions of the Act (save offences), the burden of proof rests initially with the complainant. Once the complainant establishes facts from which it might be presumed that there had been discrimination, the burden of proof shifts to the respondent to prove no breach of the principle of equal treatment (s. 136).

4.19.4.1   Direct Discrimination

The Equality Act 2010, s. 13 states:

> (1) A person (A) discriminates against another (B) if, because of a protected characteristic, A treats B less favourably than A treats or would treat others.
> (2) If the protected characteristic is age, A does not discriminate against B if A can show A's treatment of B to be a proportionate means of achieving a legitimate aim.
> (3) If the protected characteristic is disability, and B is not a disabled person, A does not discriminate against B only because A treats or would treat disabled persons more favourably than A treats B.
> (4) If the protected characteristic is marriage and civil partnership, this section applies to a contravention of Part 5 (work) only if the treatment is because it is B who is married or a civil partner.

(5) If the protected characteristic is race, less favourable treatment includes segregating B from others.

(6) If the protected characteristic is sex—

    (a) less favourable treatment of a woman includes less favourable treatment of her because she is breast-feeding;

    (b) in a case where B is a man, no account is to be taken of special treatment afforded to a woman in connection with pregnancy or childbirth.

KEYNOTE

To constitute direct discrimination the treatment experienced by B must be different from that of another person. This difference is often referred to as a 'comparator'. The treatment of B must be less favourable than the treatment afforded a comparator. The comparator can be hypothetical where B can establish direct discrimination by showing that if there was another person in similar circumstances, but without B's protected characteristic, that person would be treated more favourably (for an explanation of hypothetical comparators see *Shamoon* v *Chief Constable of the Royal Ulster Constabulary* [2003] UKHL 11).

Less favourable treatment is a broad concept and any disadvantage to which B has been subject will constitute such treatment. B need not have suffered a tangible or material loss (*Chief Constable of West Yorkshire Police* v *Khan* [2001] UKHL 48) but it is not enough merely to show unreasonable treatment (*Bahl* v *The Law Society* [2004] IRLR 799).

The test of whether less favourable treatment was 'because of' a protected characteristic is an objective test of causation. The words 'because of' have the same meaning as the words 'on the grounds of' which were used in the previous legislation. This change in wording does not alter the legal meaning of the definition, but rather, is designed to make it more accessible to the ordinary user of the Act.

Less favourable treatment of a person because that person is associated with a protected characteristic, e.g. because the person has a friend or partner with a particular protected characteristic, or carries out work related to a protected characteristic, is within the scope of this section. This might include carers of disabled people and elderly relatives, who can claim they were treated unfairly because of duties that they had to carry out at home relating to their care work. For example, the non-disabled mother of a disabled child can be discriminated against because of the child's disability (*Coleman* v *Attridge Law* (Case C-303/06) [2008] IRLR 722). It also covers discrimination against someone because, for example, his/her partner is from another country. This is known as 'associative discrimination'.

The use of the words 'because of' are also wide enough to allow claims for direct discrimination where less favourable treatment is based on the claimant's perceived protected characteristics, i.e. where others think he/she has a protected characteristic (even if he/she does not). This is known as 'discrimination by perception'. For example, in *English* v *Thomas Sanderson Ltd* [2008] EWCA Civ 1421 it was held that homophobic banter amounts to unlawful harassment even when the victim's tormentors know the person is not gay.

4.19.4.2   **Discrimination Arising from Disability**

The Equality Act 2010, s. 15 states:

(1) A person (A) discriminates against a disabled person (B) if—

    (a) A treats B unfavourably because of something arising in consequence of B's disability, and

    (b) A cannot show that the treatment is a proportionate means of achieving a legitimate aim.

(2) Subsection (1) does not apply if A shows that A did not know, and could not reasonably have been expected to know, that B had the disability.

KEYNOTE

This section provides that it is discrimination to treat a disabled person unfavourably not because of the person's disability itself but because of something arising from, or in consequence of, that disability, such as the need to take a period of disability-related absence. It is, however, possible to justify such treatment if it can be shown to be a proportionate means of achieving a legitimate aim. In *Buchanan* v *The Commissioner of Police of the Metropolis* [2016] UKEAT 0112/16/RN, where a seriously injured police motor cyclist was subject to the 'Unsatisfactory Performance Procedure' it was held that he had received unfavourable treatment arising from a disability. The tribunal was required to consider whether the *treatment* was justified, as it was not sufficient to ask whether the underlying procedure was justified.

For this type of discrimination to occur, the employer or other person must know, or reasonably be expected to know, that the disabled person has a disability.

In the judgment of *Lewisham London Borough Council* v *Malcolm* [2008] UKHL 43, it was held that the previous legislative provisions no longer provided the degree of protection from disability-related discrimination that is intended for disabled people. This section is aimed at re-establishing an appropriate balance between enabling a disabled person to make out a case of experiencing a detriment which arises because of his/her disability, and providing an opportunity for an employer or other person to defend the treatment.

4.19.4.3   Adjustments for Disabled Persons

The duty to make reasonable adjustments is a key element of a range of measures intended to eliminate barriers to access and participation for disabled people.

The Equality Act 2010, s. 20 states:

(1) Where this Act imposes a duty to make reasonable adjustments on a person, this section, sections 21 and 22 and the applicable Schedule apply; and for those purposes, a person on whom the duty is imposed is referred to as A.

(2) The duty comprises the following three requirements.

(3) The first requirement is a requirement, where a provision, criterion or practice of A's puts a disabled person at a substantial disadvantage in relation to a relevant matter in comparison with persons who are not disabled, to take such steps as it is reasonable to have to take to avoid the disadvantage.

(4) The second requirement is a requirement, where a physical feature puts a disabled person at a substantial disadvantage in relation to a relevant matter in comparison with persons who are not disabled, to take such steps as it is reasonable to have to take to avoid the disadvantage.

(5) The third requirement is a requirement, where a disabled person would, but for the provision of an auxiliary aid, be put at a substantial disadvantage in relation to a relevant matter in comparison with persons who are not disabled, to take such steps as it is reasonable to have to take to provide the auxiliary aid.

KEYNOTE

The duty to make reasonable adjustments comprises three requirements which apply where a disabled person is placed at a substantial disadvantage in comparison with non-disabled people.

The first requirement covers changing the way things are done (such as changing a practice), the second covers making changes to the built environment (such as providing access to a building), and the third covers providing auxiliary aids and services (such as providing special computer software or providing a different service).

Under the second requirement, taking steps to avoid the disadvantage will include removing, altering or providing a reasonable means of avoiding the physical feature, where it would be reasonable to do so (s. 209). Where the first or third requirements involve the way in which information is provided, a reasonable step includes providing that information in an accessible format (s. 20(6)). It also makes clear that, except where the Act states otherwise, it would never be reasonable for a person bound by the duty to pass on the costs of complying with it to an individual disabled person (s. 20(7)).

The section contains only one threshold for the reasonable adjustment duty, that of 'substantial disadvantage'. Section 212(1) defines 'substantial' as more than minor or trivial.

Section 21 provides that a failure to comply with any one of the reasonable adjustment requirements amounts to discrimination against a disabled person to whom the duty is owed. It also provides that, apart from under this Act, no other action can be taken for failure to comply with the duty. The test of reasonableness is an objective one (*Collins* v *Royal National Theatre Board Ltd* [2004] IRLR 395), and will always depend on the particular circumstances in an individual case (*Archibald* v *Fife County Council* [2004] IRLR 651).

Although accepting the difficult role the police are often called upon to play, in *ZH* v *Commissioner of Police for the Metropolis* [2012] EWHC 604 (QB) it was held that the police dealing with a person who was severely autistic had a duty to make reasonable adjustments in *dealing* with that person irrespective of the fact that they acted in a well-intentioned but misguided manner.

In *Chief Constable of South Yorkshire* v *Jelic* [2010] IRLR 744 it was determined that the force had not acted 'reasonably' when it failed to allow an officer suffering from chronic anxiety syndrome to swap jobs with another officer. Also, in *Hinsley* v *Chief Constable of West Mercia Constabulary* [2010] UKEAT 0200/10/0911, it was decided that there was a breach of duty to make reasonable adjustments where there was a failure to reinstate a probationary police officer who had resigned while depressed. However, where an officer was perceived to have a dangerous mental condition, the adjustments made to ensure he did not present a danger to colleagues or to the public were considered reasonable (*Aitken* v *Commissioner of Police of the Metropolis* [2011] EWCA Civ 582). In *Cordell* v *Foreign and Commonwealth Office* [2012] ICR 280 a tribunal dismissed claims of direct discrimination and discrimination by way of failure to make reasonable adjustments where the costs of providing an English-speaking lip-speaker support for a deaf employee were about £230,000 a year.

It was held that police officers lawfully searching the home of a man whom they knew to be profoundly deaf did not have any effect on the ability of the man and the officers to communicate with each other effectively without a British Sign Language interpreter being present. Officers who had had previous dealings with the man were satisfied on the basis of these dealings that they could achieve a basic level of communication with him without the benefit of an interpreter (*Finnegan* v *Chief Constable of Northumbria* [2013] EWCA Civ 1191).

4.19.4.4 Gender Reassignment Discrimination: Cases of Absence from Work

The Equality Act 2010, s. 16 states:

(1) This section has effect for the purposes of the application of Part 5 (work) to the protected characteristic of gender reassignment.
(2) A person (A) discriminates against a transsexual person (B) if, in relation to an absence of B's that is because of gender reassignment, A treats B less favourably than A would treat B if—
    (a) B's absence was because of sickness or injury, or
    (b) B's absence was for some other reason and it is not reasonable for B to be treated less favourably.
(3) A person's absence is because of gender reassignment if it is because the person is proposing to undergo, is undergoing or has undergone the process (or part of the process) mentioned in section 7(1).

KEYNOTE

A person's absence is 'because of gender reassignment' if it is because the person is proposing to undergo, is undergoing, or has undergone gender reassignment. For example, where a female to male transsexual person takes time off work to receive hormone treatment as part of his gender reassignment, his employer cannot discriminate against him because of his absence from work for this purpose.

4.19.4.5 Pregnancy and Maternity Discrimination: Non-work Cases

The Equality Act 2010, s. 17 states:

(1) This section has effect for the purposes of the application to the protected characteristic of pregnancy and maternity of—
    (a) Part 3 (services and public functions);
    (b) Part 4 (premises);
    (c) Part 6 (education);
    (d) Part 7 (associations).

(2) A person (A) discriminates against a woman if A treats her unfavourably because of a pregnancy of hers.

(3) A person (A) discriminates against a woman if, in the period of 26 weeks beginning with the day on which she gives birth, A treats her unfavourably because she has given birth.

(4) The reference in subsection (3) to treating a woman unfavourably because she has given birth includes, in particular, a reference to treating her unfavourably because she is breast-feeding.

(5) For the purposes of this section, the day on which a woman gives birth is the day on which—
   (a) she gives birth to a living child, or
   (b) she gives birth to a dead child (more than 24 weeks of the pregnancy having passed).

KEYNOTE

Note that pregnancy and maternity are 'protected characteristics' even though they are not grouped with the other protected characteristics in the Act.

Pregnancy and maternity discrimination is excluded from the definition of direct sex discrimination (s. 17(6)) and is dealt with under this separate provision and s. 18 (work situations, see para. 4.19.4.6).

4.19.4.6 Pregnancy and Maternity Discrimination: Work Cases

The Equality Act 2010, s. 18 states:

(1) This section has effect for the purposes of the application of Part 5 (work) to the protected characteristic of pregnancy and maternity.

(2) A person (A) discriminates against a woman if, in the protected period in relation to a pregnancy of hers, A treats her unfavourably—
   (a) because of the pregnancy, or
   (b) because of illness suffered by her as a result of it.

(3) A person (A) discriminates against a woman if A treats her unfavourably because she is on compulsory maternity leave.

(4) A person (A) discriminates against a woman if A treats her unfavourably because she is exercising or seeking to exercise, or has exercised or sought to exercise, the right to ordinary or additional maternity leave.

KEYNOTE

In relation to s. 18(2), if the treatment of a woman is in implementation of a decision taken in the protected period, the treatment is to be regarded as occurring in that period (even if the implementation is not until after the end of that period (s. 18(5)).

The duration of the protected period depends on the statutory maternity leave entitlements as set out in the Employment Rights Act 1996 which defines the right to compulsory, ordinary and additional maternity leave. The protected period starts when a woman becomes pregnant and ends either:

• if she has the right to ordinary and additional maternity leave, at the end of the additional maternity leave period or (if earlier) when she returns to work after the pregnancy; or

• if she does not have that right, at the end of the period of two weeks beginning with the end of the pregnancy.

As with s. 17 of the 2010 Act, sex discrimination does not apply to treatment of a woman in so far as it is in the protected period, or it is for a reason mentioned in s. 18(3) or (4).

Unfavourable treatment suffered because of an association with a pregnant woman or because of being perceived to be pregnant are not covered by this section, though such treatment might constitute direct discrimination under s. 13.

In *Maksymiuk* v *Bar Roma Partnership* [2012] Eq LR 917 an employee who was the only one of a number of bar staff who was selected for dismissal by reason of purported redundancy only a matter of days after she had announced that she was pregnant, had her claim of discrimination on the ground of pregnancy or sickness related to pregnancy dismissed.

4.19.4.7 Indirect Discrimination

The Equality Act 2010, s. 19 states:

(1) A person (A) discriminates against another (B) if A applies to B a provision, criterion or practice which is discriminatory in relation to a relevant protected characteristic of B's.

(2) For the purposes of subsection (1), a provision, criterion or practice is discriminatory in relation to a relevant protected characteristic of B's if—

    (a) A applies, or would apply, it to persons with whom B does not share the characteristic,

    (b) it puts, or would put, persons with whom B shares the characteristic at a particular disadvantage when compared with persons with whom B does not share it,

    (c) it puts, or would put, B at that disadvantage, and

    (d) A cannot show it to be a proportionate means of achieving a legitimate aim.

KEYNOTE

Apart from pregnancy and maternity, indirect discrimination applies to all the protected characteristics.

Indirect discrimination occurs when a policy which applies in the same way for everybody has an effect which particularly disadvantages people with a protected characteristic. Where a particular group is disadvantaged in this way, a person in that group is indirectly discriminated against if he/she is put at that disadvantage, unless the person applying the policy can justify it.

When a policy would put a person at a disadvantage if it were applied, e.g. where a person is deterred from applying for a job or taking up an offer of service because a policy which would be applied would result in his/her disadvantage, this may also be indirect discrimination. Examples of indirect discrimination have included: requiring all employees to work within 'normal office hours' (*Bhudi* v *IMI Refiners* [1994] IRLR 204); requiring all workers to have short hair thereby making it difficult for some groups such as Sikhs to comply (*Mandla* v *Dowell Lee* [1983] 2 AC 548); where 100 per cent of males could comply with a policy relating to rostering of duties, but only 95.2 per cent of women were able to do so, the policy discriminated indirectly against females (*London Underground Ltd* v *Edwards (No. 2)* [1998] IRLR 364).

4.19.4.8 Harassment

The Equality Act 2010, s. 26 states:

(1) A person (A) harasses another (B) if—

    (a) A engages in unwanted conduct related to a relevant protected characteristic, and

    (b) the conduct has the purpose or effect of—

        (i) violating B's dignity, or

        (ii) creating an intimidating, hostile, degrading, humiliating or offensive environment for B.

(2) A also harasses B if—

    (a) A engages in unwanted conduct of a sexual nature, and

    (b) the conduct has the purpose or effect referred to in subsection (1)(b).

(3) A also harasses B if—

    (a) A or another person engages in unwanted conduct of a sexual nature or that is related to gender reassignment or sex,

    (b) the conduct has the purpose or effect referred to in subsection (1)(b), and

    (c) because of B's rejection of or submission to the conduct, A treats B less favourably than A would treat B if B had not rejected or submitted to the conduct.

KEYNOTE

This section defines three types of harassment.

The first type, which applies to the protected characteristics apart from pregnancy and maternity, and marriage and civil partnership, involves unwanted conduct which is related to a relevant characteristic and has the purpose or effect of creating an intimidating, hostile, degrading, humiliating or offensive environment for the complainant or of violating the complainant's dignity. In deciding whether conduct has the effect referred to

---

in s. 26(1)(b), the perception of B, the other circumstances of the case, and whether it is reasonable for the conduct to have that effect, must be taken into account (s. 26(4)).

The second type is sexual harassment which is unwanted conduct of a sexual nature where this has the same purpose or effect as the first type of harassment. In *Wadman* v *Carpenter Farrer Partnership* [1993] IRLR 374 sexual harassment was described as conduct of a sexual nature or other conduct based on sex affecting the dignity of women and men at work. This could include verbal remarks, written comments and physical contact.

The third type is treating someone less favourably because he/she has either submitted to or rejected sexual harassment, or harassment related to sex or gender reassignment. Note that harassment related to sexual orientation and religion and belief is not unlawful outside a work context.

4.19.4.9 Employees and Applicants: Harassment

The Equality Act 2010, s. 40 states:

(1) An employer (A) must not, in relation to employment by A, harass a person (B)—
  (a) who is an employee of A's;
  (b) who has applied to A for employment.

KEYNOTE

The liability of employers for third party harassment of employees (s. 40(2)–(4)) was removed by s. 65 of the Enterprise and Regulatory Reform Act 2013.

Apart from marriage and civil partnerships and pregnancy and maternity, this section extends to the other protected characteristics including the employer's liability for sexual harassment. This can include behaviour such as requests for sexual favours, lewd jokes, promises, and threats concerning a person's employment conditions in return for sexual favours.

4.19.4.10 Victimisation

The Equality Act 2010, s. 27 states:

(1) A person (A) victimises another person (B) if A subjects B to a detriment because—
  (a) B does a protected act, or
  (b) A believes that B has done, or may do, a protected act.
(2) Each of the following is a protected act—
  (a) bringing proceedings under this Act;
  (b) giving evidence or information in connection with proceedings under this Act;
  (c) doing any other thing for the purposes of or in connection with this Act;
  (d) making an allegation (whether or not express) that A or another person has contravened this Act.
(3) Giving false evidence or information, or making a false allegation, is not a protected act if the evidence or information is given, or the allegation is made, in bad faith.

KEYNOTE

Victimisation takes place where one person treats another badly because he/she in good faith has done a 'protected act', e.g. taken or supported any action taken for the purpose of the Act, including in relation to any alleged breach of its provisions. In *Chief Constable of West Yorkshire Police* v *B & C* [2016] UKEAT 0306/15/RN, two former undercover police officers were found to have been subjected to detriments for making protected disclosures that related to the inadequate supervision and support of undercover operatives. Both officers had been removed from undercover duties and assigned civilian roles.

The test to be applied in assessing whether or not victimisation has taken place is, 'was the real reason for the victim's treatment the fact that they had carried out a protected act' (*Chief Constable of West Yorkshire*

Police v *Khan* [2001] UKHL 48). In *Bayode* v *Chief Constable of Derbyshire* [2008] UKEAT 0499/07/2205 it was held that a police constable, who was black African and Nigerian by national origin, had not been victimised where his colleagues recorded any problems they encountered with him in their PNBs for fear of a race discrimination claim at some future date.

Only an individual can bring a claim for victimisation, and a person is not protected from victimisation where he/she maliciously makes or supports an untrue complaint.

4.19.5 Police Officers

The 2010 Act prohibits discrimination, victimisation and harassment in other non-employment work relationships and this specifically includes police officers.

The Equality Act 2010, s. 42 states.

(1) For the purposes of this Part, holding the office of constable is to be treated as employment—
   (a) by the chief officer, in respect of any act done by the chief officer in relation to a constable or appointment to the office of constable;
   (b) by the responsible authority, in respect of any act done by the authority in relation to a constable or appointment to the office of constable.

KEYNOTE

This section provides that police constables (and police cadets (s. 42(2))) are treated as employees. The relevant employer is either the chief officer (or, in Scotland, the chief constable) or the responsible authority (s. 43), depending on who commits the act in question. For example, if a chief officer refused to allocate protective equipment to female constables he/she would be treated as the employer in a direct discrimination claim.

Constables serving with the Civil Nuclear Constabulary are treated as employees of the Civil Nuclear Constabulary. A constable seconded to the National Crime Agency (NCA) is treated as employed by the NCA.

4.19.6 Employees and Applicants

The Equality Act 2010, s. 39 makes it unlawful for an employer to discriminate against or victimise employees and people seeking work. It applies where the employer is making arrangements to fill a job, and in respect of anything done in the course of a person's employment.

KEYNOTE

Examples of direct discrimination in relation to work have included: rescinding an officer's posting on the grounds of force policy that spouses should not work in the same Division because neither officer would be compellable as a witness against the other (*Graham* v *Chief Constable of Bedfordshire Constabulary* [2002] IRLR 239); treating a police officer of one racial group, who was under investigation for disciplinary matters, differently from another officer under such investigation belonging to a different racial group (*Virdi* v *Commissioner of Police for the Metropolis* (2000) LTL 5 February); acceding to a request by a customer not to be served by someone of a particular colour (*Eldridge & Barbican Car Hire Ltd* v *Zhang* (2001) LTL 10 May).

There are a number of exceptions and defences to the provisions of the Act but two of the more relevant defences in relation to discrimination or victimisation in employment are 'genuine occupational requirement' and 'positive action'.

The principle behind 'genuine occupational requirement' is that, in certain jobs and roles, there may well be a legitimate reason that an employee is of a particular sex or belongs to a particular racial group (sch. 1, part 1, para. 1(1)(a)). In reality there are far more potential exceptions to discrimination on the grounds of sex and sexual orientation than for reasons of the other protected characteristics.

'Positive action' refers to measures to alleviate disadvantage experienced by people who share a protected characteristic, reduce their under-representation in relation to particular activities, and meet their particular needs (s. 158). It allows for measures to be targeted to particular groups, including training to enable them to gain employment, but any such measures must be a proportionate way of achieving the relevant aim.

An employer may also take a protected characteristic into consideration when deciding whom to recruit or promote, where people having the protected characteristic are at a disadvantage or are under-represented (s. 159). This can be done only where the candidates are as qualified as each other. The aim is to help employers achieve a more diverse workforce by giving them the option, when faced with candidates of equal merit, to choose a candidate from an under-represented group.

4.19.7 Liability for Discrimination in Employment

The Equality Act 2010, s. 109 states:

(1) Anything done by a person (A) in the course of A's employment must be treated as also done by the employer.
(2) ...
(3) It does not matter whether that thing is done with the employer's or principal's knowledge or approval.

KEYNOTE

This section makes employers and principals liable for acts of discrimination, harassment and victimisation carried out by their employees in the course of employment. It does not matter whether or not the employer or principal knows about or approves of those acts. For example, where police officers engage in inappropriate sexual behaviour towards a colleague at a work-related function, the chief officer may be liable for the acts of his/her officers at that function (*Chief Constable of Lincolnshire* v *Stubbs* [1999] IRLR 81).

Employers who can show that they took all reasonable steps to prevent their employees from acting unlawfully will not be held liable (s. 109(4)).

An employee is also personally liable for unlawful acts committed in the course of employment where, because of s. 109, the employer is also liable (s. 110).

4.19.8 Public Sector Equality Duty

The Act imposes a duty, known as the public sector equality duty, on public bodies, which includes a local policing body (including the Mayor's Office for Police and Crime (Metropolitan Police) and City of London) and the College of Policing.

The Equality Act 2010, s. 149 states:

(1) A public authority must, in the exercise of its functions, have due regard to the need to—
    (a) eliminate discrimination, harassment, victimisation and any other conduct that is prohibited by or under this Act;
    (b) advance equality of opportunity between persons who share a relevant protected characteristic and persons who do not share it;
    (c) foster good relations between persons who share a relevant protected characteristic and persons who do not share it.

Appendix 4.1

Powers of Police Community Support Officers

Section 38 of the Police Reform Act 2002 (PRA) allows a chief officer to designate powers to PCSOs. In addition, there are a number of local authority bylaws which can also be designated (usually enforced by the issue of fixed penalty notices). The standard list of 20 discretionary powers was introduced in 2007 and, once trained, all PCSOs are designated with these powers. This has, therefore, created core standardisation across England and Wales while still allowing for local flexibility by individual forces to grant a range of additional discretionary powers to meet local community policing needs.

LIST OF STANDARD POWERS

Power	Relevant legislation
To issue fixed penalty notices for cycling on a footpath: power of a constable in uniform to give a person a fixed penalty notice under s. 54 of the Road Traffic Offenders Act 1988 (fixed penalty notices) in respect of an offence under s. 72 of the Highway Act 1835 (riding on a footway) committed by cycling.	Paragraph 1(2)(b) of sch. 4 to the Police Reform Act 2002.
To issue fixed penalty notices for littering: power of an authorised officer of a litter authority to give a notice under s. 88 of the Environmental Protection Act 1990 (fixed penalty notices in respect of litter).	Paragraph 1(2)(d) of sch. 4 to the Police Reform Act 2002.
To require name and address: power to require the name and address of a person whom a PCSO has reason to believe has committed a relevant offence or a relevant licensing offence. (Relevant offences are defined under subpara. 2(6) of sch. 4 to the Police Reform Act 2002 and include relevant fixed penalty offences under para. 1 of sch. 4, an offence under s. 32(2) of the Anti-social Behaviour Act 2003 (failure to follow an instruction to disperse) and an offence which appears to have caused injury, alarm or distress to another person or loss of or damage to another person's property. A relevant licensing offence is defined as a specified offence under the Licensing Act 2003). Paragraph 1A enables chief constables to designate the power to require name and address without also designating the power of detention.	Paragraph 1A of sch. 4 to the Police Reform Act 2002 (inserted by para. 2 of sch. 8 to the Serious Organised Crime and Police Act 2005).
To require name and address for anti-social behaviour: power of a constable in uniform, under s. 50 of the Police Reform Act 2002, to require a person whom he or she has reason to believe has been acting, or to be acting, in an anti-social manner to give his or her name and address. Subparagraph 3(2) of sch. 4 provides the PCSO with the power to detain (under subparas 2(3) to (5) of sch. 4). However, by virtue of para. 2(8) of sch. 4 the power to detain 'has no effect unless a PCSO has been designated with the power of detention under paragraph 2 of Schedule 4'.	Paragraph 3 of sch. 4 to the Police Reform Act 2002 (as amended by para. 3(10) of sch. 8 to the Serious Organised Crime and Police Act 2005).

Power	Relevant legislation
To require name and address for road traffic offences: enables PCSOs to be designated with the power to require the name and address of a driver or pedestrian who fails to follow the directions of a community support officer or police officer under s. 35 or 37 of the Road Traffic Act 1988.	Paragraph 3A of sch. 4 to the Police Reform Act 2002 (inserted by para. 6 of sch. 8 to the Serious Organised Crime and Police Act 2005).
To require persons drinking in designated places to surrender alcohol: requires a person whom a PCSO reasonably believes is, or has been, consuming alcohol in a designated public place or intends to do so, to not consume that alcohol and to surrender any alcohol or container for alcohol. Power to dispose of alcohol surrendered.	Paragraph 5 of sch. 4 to the Police Reform Act 2002.
To require persons aged under 18 to surrender alcohol: requires a person whom a PCSO reasonably suspects is aged under 18, or is or has been supplying alcohol to a person aged under 18, to surrender any alcohol in their possession and to give their name and address. Power to require such a person to surrender sealed containers of alcohol if the PCSO has reason to believe that the person is or has been consuming or intends to consume alcohol. Power to dispose of alcohol surrendered.	Paragraph 6 of sch. 4 to the Police Reform Act 2002.
To seize tobacco from a person aged under 16 and to dispose of that tobacco.	Paragraph 7 of sch. 4 to the Police Reform Act 2002.
To seize drugs and require name and address for possession of drugs: enables PCSOs to be designated with a power to seize unconcealed drugs or drugs found when searching for alcohol, tobacco or other items if the PCSO reasonably believes the person is in unlawful possession of them. The PCSO must retain the drugs until a constable gives them further instructions. If a PCSO finds drugs in a person's possession or has reason to believe that a person is in possession of drugs and reasonably believes such possession is unlawful, the PCSO may require that person's name and address.	Paragraph 7B of sch. 4 to the Police Reform Act 2002 (inserted by para. 8 of sch. 8 to the Serious Organised Crime and Police Act 2005).
To enter and search any premises for the purposes of saving life and limb or preventing serious damage to property.	Paragraph 8 of sch. 4 to the Police Reform Act 2002.
To seize vehicles used to cause alarm: power to stop and seize a vehicle which a PCSO has reason to believe is being used in a manner which contravenes s. 3 or 34 of the Road Traffic Act 1988 (careless and inconsiderate driving and prohibition of off-road driving) and is causing alarm, distress or annoyance under s. 59 of the Police Reform Act 2002.	Paragraph 9 of sch. 4 to the Police Reform Act 2002.
To remove abandoned vehicles under regulations made under s. 99 of the Road Traffic Regulation Act 1984. A PCSO designated under this paragraph has the power to order the removal of a vehicle under reg. 3 of the Removal and Disposal of Vehicles Regulations 1986. This relates to vehicles that have broken down or been permitted to remain at rest on a road: (a) in a position, condition or situation causing obstruction or danger to persons using the road, or (b) in contravention of a prohibition contained in sch. 1 to the regulations.	
To stop cycles: powers of a constable in uniform to stop a cycle under s. 163(2) of the Road Traffic Act 1988 when a PCSO has reason to believe that a person has committed the offence of riding on a footpath.	Paragraph 11A of sch. 4 to the Police Reform Act 2002 (inserted by s. 89(3) of the Anti-social Behaviour Act 2003).

Power	Relevant legislation
To control traffic for purposes other than escorting a load of exceptional dimensions: powers to direct traffic (for purposes other than escorting loads of exceptional dimensions) based on the powers constables have under ss. 35 and 37 of the Road Traffic Act 1988. It also gives PCSOs the power to direct traffic for the purposes of conducting a traffic survey. PCSOs designated under this paragraph must also be designated with powers under para. 3A of sch. 4 to the Police Reform Act.	Paragraph 11B of sch. 4 to the Police Reform Act 2002 (inserted by para. 10 of sch. 8 to the Serious Organised Crime and Police Act 2005).
To carry out road checks: power to carry out a road check which has been authorised by a superintendent (or a police officer of higher rank) and power to stop vehicles for the purposes of carrying out a road check.	Paragraph 13 of sch. 4 to the Police Reform Act 2002.
To place signs: enables PCSOs to be designated with the power of a constable under s. 67 of the Road Traffic Regulation Act 1984 to place and maintain traffic signs.	Paragraph 13A of sch. 4 to the Police Reform Act 2002 (inserted by para. 11 of the Serious Organised Crime and Police Act 2005).
To enforce cordoned areas: under s. 36 of the Terrorism Act 2000.	Paragraph 14 of sch. 4 to the Police Reform Act 2002.
To stop and search in authorised areas: powers under the Terrorism Act 2000 in authorised areas to stop and search vehicles and pedestrians when in the company and under the supervision of a constable.	Paragraph 15 of sch. 4 to the Police Reform Act 2002.
To photograph persons away from a police station: enables PCSOs to be designated with the power to photograph a person who has been arrested, detained or given a fixed penalty notice away from the police station.	Paragraph 15ZA of sch. 4 to the Police Reform Act 2002 (inserted by para. 12 of sch. 8 to the Serious Organised Crime and Police Act 2005).

LIST OF DISCRETIONARY POWERS THAT CAN BE DESIGNATED BY CHIEF OFFICERS

Power	Relevant legislation
To issue penalty notices in respect of offences of disorder: power of a constable in uniform to give a penalty notice under chapter 1 of part 1 of the Criminal Justice and Police Act 2001 (fixed penalty notices in respect of offences of disorder).	Paragraph 1(2)(a) of sch. 4 to the Police Reform Act 2002.
To issue fixed penalty notices for truancy: power of a constable to give a penalty notice under s. 444A of the Education Act 1996 (penalty notice in respect of failure to secure regular attendance at school of registered pupil).	Paragraph 1(2)(aa) of sch. 4 to the Police Reform Act 2002 (inserted by s. 23 of the Anti-social Behaviour Act 2003).
To issue fixed penalty notices for excluded pupil found in a public place: power of a constable to give a penalty notice under s. 105 of the Education and Inspections Act 2006 (penalty notice in respect of presence of excluded pupil in public place).	Paragraph 1(2)(ab) of sch. 4 to the Police Reform Act 2002 (inserted by s. 107(2) of the Education and Inspections Act 2006).
To issue fixed penalty notices for dog fouling: power of an authorised officer of a local authority to give a notice under s. 4 of the Dogs (Fouling of Land) Act 1996 (fixed penalty notices in respect of dog fouling). This power (and the 1996 Act) have now been repealed in relation to England and Wales by s. 107 of and sch. 5 part 5 to the Clean Neighbourhoods and Environment Act 2005. However, the power continues to have effect in respect of any land which remains designated land under the 1996 Act.	Paragraph 1(2)(c) of sch. 4 to the Police Reform Act 2002.

Power	Relevant legislation
To issue fixed penalty notices for graffiti and fly-posting: power of an authorised officer of a local authority to give a notice under s. 43(1) of the Anti-social Behaviour Act 2003 (penalty notices in respect of graffiti or fly-posting).	Paragraph 1(2)(ca) of sch. 4 to the Police Reform Act 2002 (inserted by s. 46 of the Anti-social Behaviour Act 2003).
To issue a fixed penalty notice for relevant bylaw offence: power of an authorised officer of an authority which has made a bylaw to which this section applies has reason to believe that a person has committed an offence against the bylaw.	Paragraph 1ZA of sch. 4 to the Police Reform Act 2002 (inserted by s. 133 of the Local Government and Public Involvement in Health Act 2007).
To detain: power to detain a person whom a PCSO has reason to believe has committed a relevant offence who fails to comply with a requirement under para. 1A(3) to give name and address or who gives an answer which the PCSO reasonably suspects to be false or inaccurate, for up to 30 minutes for the arrival of a police officer (or to accompany that person to a police station if he or she elects to do so on request). Under para. 2(2) (as amended by sch. 8 to the Serious Organised Crime and Police Act 2005), a PCSO may only be designated with the power to detain if they have also been designated with the power to require name and address under para. 1A of the Police Reform Act 2002.	Paragraph 2(3) of sch. 4 to the Police Reform Act 2002. Paragraph 3(2) of sch. 8 to the Serious Organised Crime and Police Act 2005.
To enforce bylaws: the Serious Organised Crime and Police Act 2005 provides that offences committed under relevant bylaws are relevant offences under para. 2(6) of sch. 4 to the Police Reform Act 2002. A relevant bylaw is one from a list of bylaws that has been agreed between a chief constable and a relevant by law-making body. As well as being able to require name and address for breach of a bylaw, PCSOs can also enforce a bylaw by removing a person from a place if a constable would also have the power to enforce a bylaw in that way.	Paragraphs 1A, 2(3A), 2(6)(ad), 2(6B), 2(6C), 2(6D), 2(6E) and 2(6F) of sch. 4 to the Police Reform Act 2002 (see paras 2, 3(4), 3(7) and 3(8) of sch. 8 to the Serious Organised Crime and Police Act 2005).
To deal with begging: the Serious Organised Crime and Police Act 2005 makes offences under ss. 3 and 4 of the Vagrancy Act 1824 into relevant offences. It also gives PCSOs a power to detain a person whom they have required to stop committing an offence under ss. 3 and 4 of the Vagrancy Act and who has failed to comply with the requirement.	Paragraphs 2(6)(ac) and 2(3B) of sch. 4 to the Police Reform Act 2002 (see paras 3(4), 3(5), 3(6) and 3(7) of sch. 8 to the Serious Organised Crime and Police Act 2005).
To enforce certain licensing offences: the Serious Organised Crime and Police Act 2005 establishes a set of relevant licensing offences. These offences are sale of alcohol to a person who is drunk, obtaining alcohol for a person who is drunk, sale of alcohol to children, purchase of alcohol by or on behalf of children, consumption of alcohol by children and sending a child to obtain alcohol. Where these offences apply specifically to clubs, they are not relevant licensing offences. PCSOs may require name and address but may not detain for those relevant licensing offences that are most likely to be committed by licence holders.	Paragraph 2(6A) of sch. 4 to the Police Reform Act 2002 (see paras 3(3) and 3(8) of sch. 8 to the Serious Organised Crime and Police Act 2005).
To search detained persons for dangerous items or items that could be used to assist escape: enables PCSOs to be designated with the same powers as a constable under s. 32 of PACE to search detained persons for anything that could be used to cause physical injury or to assist escape. A PCSO must comply with a police officer's instructions on what to do with the item.	Paragraph 2A of sch. 4 to the Police Reform Act 2002 (inserted by para. 4 of sch. 8 to the Serious Organised Crime and Police Act 2005).

Power	Relevant legislation
To use reasonable force to prevent a detained person making off: either when waiting for the arrival of a constable or when accompanying a detained person to a police station.	Paragraph 4 of sch. 4 to the Police Reform Act 2002.
To disperse groups and remove persons under 16 to their place of residence: where a designation applies this paragraph to a person, that person has within the relevant police area the powers conferred on a constable by s. 35 of the Anti-social Behaviour, Crime and Policing Act 2014.	Paragraph 4A of sch. 4 to the Police Reform Act 2002 (inserted by s. 40(3) of the Anti-social Behaviour, Crime and Policing Act 2014).
To remove truants to designated premises etc.: enables a PCSO to be designated with the power of a constable under s. 16(3) of (3ZA) of the Crime and Disorder Act 1998 to remove a truant or excluded pupil found in a specified area (as specified in a direction under s. 16(2) of the 1998 Act) to designated premises or (in the case of a truant) to the school from which the truant is absent.	Paragraph 4C of sch. 4 to the Police Reform Act 2002 (inserted by s. 8 of the Police and Justice Act 2006).
To use reasonable force in relation to detained persons: para. 2(4A) of sch. 4 to the Police Reform Act 2002 places a duty on PCSOs to remain with a police officer when transferring a detained person to his or her custody until the police officer has control of the detained person. Paragraph 2(4B) places a PCSO accompanying a detained person to a police station under a duty to remain at the police station until he or she has transferred control of the detained person. If a PCSO is designated with para. 4ZB of sch. 4 then he or she may use reasonable force in complying with duties under para. 2(4A) and (4B). If a PCSO is designated with para. 4ZA then he or she may use reasonable force when exercising powers under para. 2(3B), 2(4), 7A(8) or 7C(2)(a).	Paragraphs 2(4A), 2(4B), 4ZA and 4ZB of sch. 4 to the Police Reform Act 2002 (see paras 2, 3 and 4 of sch. 9 to the Serious Organised Crime and Police Act 2005).
To search for alcohol and tobacco: where a person has failed to comply with a requirement under para. 5 or 6 or has failed to allow a PCSO to seize tobacco under para. 7 of sch. 4 to the Police Reform Act 2002 and a PCSO reasonably believes that the person is in possession of alcohol or tobacco, a PCSO may search them for it and dispose of anything found. It is an offence to fail to consent to be searched and PCSOs can require name and address for this offence. As specified in para. 3(10) of sch. 8 to the Serious Organised Crime and Police Act 2005, a PCSO may only detain a person for failure to give an adequate name and address if he or she has been designated with powers under para. 2 of sch. 4 to the Police Reform Act.	Paragraph 7A of sch. 4 to the Police Reform Act 2002 (inserted by para. 8 of sch. 8 to the Serious Organised Crime and Police Act 2005).
To seize drugs and require name and address for possession of drugs: builds on the standard power to seize drugs and require name and address under para. 7B and enables PCSOs to detain a person on failure to comply with the requirement to provide name and address. See list of standard powers.	Paragraph 7C of sch. 4 to the Police Reform Act 2002 (inserted by para. 8 of sch. 8 to the Serious Organised Crime and Police Act 2005).
To enforce park trading offences: enables a PCSO to seize non-perishable items from a person which the PCSO reasonably suspects have been used in the commission of a park trading offence under the Royal Parks (Trading) Act 2000. This power can only apply to PCSOs in the Metropolitan Police Force.	Paragraph 7D of sch. 4 to the Police Reform Act 2002.
Limited power to enter licensed premises: enables PCSOs to be designated with a power to enter licensed premises under s. 180 of the Licensing Act 2003 for the purposes of investigating relevant licensing offences. They may not enter clubs and must enter all premises with a constable unless the premises are licensed for the sale of alcohol off the premises.	Paragraph 8A of sch. 4 to the Police Reform Act 2002 (inserted by para. 9 of sch. 8 to the Serious Organised Crime and Police Act 2005).

Power	Relevant legislation
To stop vehicles for testing: powers of a constable in uniform to stop vehicles for the purposes of testing under s. 67 of the Road Traffic Act 1988.	Paragraph 11 of sch. 4 to the Police Reform Act 2002.
Power to direct traffic for the purposes of escorting abnormal loads.	Paragraph 12 of sch. 4 to the Police Reform Act 2002.
Power to serve closure notice for licensed premises persistently selling to children.	Paragraph 5A of sch. 4 to the Police Reform Act 2002 (as inserted by s. 24(6) of the Violent Crime Reduction Act 2006).

LIST OF DISCRETIONARY POWERS INTRODUCED BY VIRTUE OF THE ANTI-SOCIAL BEHAVIOUR, CRIME AND POLICING ACT 2014

Power	Relevant legislation
To issue a fixed penalty notice for cycling without lights: power of a constable to issue a fixed penalty notice for failing to comply with s. 42 (lighting equipment or reflectors for cycles) of the Road Traffic Act 1988.	Schedule 4 to the Police Reform Act 2002 as inserted by para. 2(3)(f)(i) of sch. 10 to the Anti-social Behaviour, Crime and Policing Act 2014.
To issue a fixed penalty notice for failing to comply with traffic signs: enables a PCSO to issue a fixed penalty notice for failing to comply with the indication given by a red traffic light under s. 36 of the Road Traffic Act 1988.	Schedule 4 to the Police Reform Act 2002 as inserted by para. 2(3)(e) of sch. 10 to the Anti-social Behaviour, Crime and Policing Act 2014.
To issue a fixed penalty notice for carrying a passenger on a cycle: enables a PCSO to issue a fixed penalty notice under s. 24 of the Road Traffic Act 1988 for the offence of more than one person on a one-person bicycle.	Schedule 4 to the Police Reform Act 2002 as inserted by para. 2(3)(c) of sch. 10 to the Anti-social Behaviour, Crime and Policing Act 2014.
To issue a fixed penalty notice to a cyclist for failing to comply with a traffic direction: gives PCSOs the power of a constable to issue a fixed penalty notice the rider of a cycle under s. 35 of the Road Traffic Act 1988, failing to comply with traffic directions.	Schedule 4 to the Police Reform Act 2002 as inserted by para. 2(3)(d) of sch. 10 to the Anti-social Behaviour, Crime and Policing Act 2014.
To issue a fixed penalty notice for parking in a restricted area outside schools: enables PCSOs to issue a fixed penalty notice for contravention of a prohibition or restriction that relates to stopping, waiting or parking at or near a school entrance under s. 5(1) or 8(1) of the Road Traffic Regulation Act 1984. Paragraph 3 of the Anti-social Behaviour, Crime and Policing Act 2014 requires a chief officer to consult the local authority prior to designation of this power.	Schedule 4 to the Police Reform Act 2002 as inserted by paras 2(3)(b)(i) and 3 of sch. 10 to the Anti- social Behaviour, Crime and Policing Act 2014.
To issue a fixed penalty notice for failing to stop for a police constable: gives PCSOs the power to issue a fixed penalty notice under s. 163 of the Road Traffic Act 1988 for the offence of failing to stop a vehicle or cycle when required to do so by a constable or traffic officer.	Schedule 4 to the Police Reform Act 2002 as inserted by para. 2(3)(g) of sch. 10 to the Anti-social Behaviour, Crime and Policing Act 2014.
To issue a fixed penalty notice for driving the wrong way down a one-way street: gives the power of a constable to issue a fixed penalty notice under s. 5(1) or 8(1) of the Road Traffic Regulation Act 1984 for contravention of a prohibition or restriction that relates to one-way traffic on a road.	Schedule 4 to the Police Reform Act 2002 as inserted by para. 2(3)(b)(ii) of sch. 10 to the Anti-social Behaviour, Crime and Policing Act 2014.

Power	Relevant legislation
To issue a fixed penalty notice for sounding a horn when stationary: enables a PCSO to issue a fixed penalty notice for an offence under s. 42 of the Road Traffic Act 1988.	Schedule 4 to the Police Reform Act 2002 as inserted by para. 2(3)(f)(iv) of sch. 10 to the Anti-social Behaviour, Crime and Policing Act 2014.
To issue a fixed penalty notice for sounding a horn on a restricted road at night: enables a PCSO to issue a fixed penalty notice for an offence under s. 42 of the Road Traffic Act 1988.	Schedule 4 to the Police Reform Act 2002 as inserted by para. 2(3)(f)(iv) of sch. 10 to the Anti-social Behaviour, Crime and Policing Act 2014.
To issue a fixed penalty notice for not stopping engine when stationary: under s. 42 of the Road Traffic Act 1988, PCSOs will have the power of a constable to issue a fixed penalty notice for the offence of failing to comply with a construction or use requirement about stopping the action of a stationary vehicle's machinery.	Schedule 4 to the Police Reform Act 2002 as inserted by para. 2(3)(f)(iii) of sch. 10 to the Anti-social Behaviour, Crime and Policing Act 2014.
To issue a fixed penalty notice for causing unnecessary noise: under s. 42 of the Road Traffic Act 1988, PCSOs will have the power of a constable to issue a fixed penalty notice for the offence of failing to comply with a construction or use requirement about the use on a road of a motor vehicle that causes excessive noise.	Schedule 4 to the Police Reform Act 2002 as inserted by para. 2(3)(f)(ii) of sch. 10 to the Anti-social Behaviour, Crime and Policing Act 2014.
To issue a fixed penalty notice for contravening bus lane: PCSOs will have the power of a constable under s. 5(1) or 8(1) of the Road Traffic Act 1984 to issue a fixed penalty notice for a contravention of a prohibition or restriction that relates to lanes or routes for buses.	Schedule 4 to the Police Reform Act 2002 as inserted by para. 2(3)(b)(iii) of sch. 10 to the Anti-social Behaviour, Crime and Policing Act 2014.
To issue a fixed penalty notice for opening door so as to cause injury/danger: under s. 42 of the Road Traffic Act 1988, PCSOs will have the power of a constable to issue a fixed penalty notice for the offence of failing to comply with a construction or use requirement about opening a vehicle's door on a road so as to injure or endanger a person.	Schedule 4 to the Police Reform Act 2002 as inserted by para. 2(3)(f)(v) of sch. 10 to the Anti-social Behaviour, Crime and Policing Act 2014.
Power to seize and retain: PCSOs will, when lawfully on a premises, have the same power as a constable under s. 19 of the 1984 Act (general powers of seizure) to seize things. They will also have the power to impose a requirement by virtue of subs. 4 in relation to information accessible from the premises and subs. 6 (protection for legally privileged material from seizure). Section 21(1) and (2) (record of seizure), ss. 21(3) to (8) and 22 (access, copying and retention) of the 1984 Act have effect.	Schedule 4 to the Police Reform Act 2002 as inserted by para. 4 of sch. 10 to the Anti-social Behaviour, Crime and Policing Act 2014.
To confirm the identity of a charity collector: PCSOs will have the power of a constable under s. 6 of the House to House Collections Act 1939 to require name, address and signature, and under section 4 to produce their certificate of authority.	Schedule 4 to the Police Reform Act 2002 as inserted by para. 5 of sch. 10 to the Anti-social Behaviour, Crime and Policing Act 2014.
To issue a fixed penalty notice to an unlicensed street vendor: PCSOs will have the power of an authorised officer of a borough council to give notice under s. 15 of the London Local Authorities Act 2004 in respect of an offence under s. 38(1) of the London Local Authorities Act 1990 or s. 27(1) of the City of Westminster Act 1999 (unlicensed street trading).	Schedule 4 to the Police Reform Act 2002 as inserted by para. 2(2)(cb) of sch. 10 to the Anti-social Behaviour, Crime and Policing Act 2014.
To stop cycles: the standard power to stop a cycle is extended to those listed in para. 1(2B)(a) to (e), (f)(i) or (g).	Schedule 4 to the Police Reform Act 2002 as inserted by para. 6 of sch. 10 to the Anti-social Behaviour, Crime and Policing Act 2014.

Power	Relevant legislation
To disperse persons from a specified area: enables a PCSO (once authorised by a police inspector) to require a person committing or likely to commit anti-social behaviour, crime or disorder to leave an area for up to 48 hours. A PCSO may also confiscate any item that could be used to commit anti-social behaviour, crime or disorder. A person under 16 can be taken home or to a place of safety. A direction cannot be given to someone under 10 years old.	Schedule 4 to the Police Reform Act 2002 as inserted by para. 2 of s. 40 of the Anti-social Behaviour, Crime and Policing Act 2014.
To issue a community protection notice (CPN): following the issue of a written warning, a PCSO can issue a CPN against any person aged 16 or over, business or organisation committing anti-social behaviour which spoils the community's quality of life.	Schedule 4 to the Police Reform Act 2002, as amended by ss. 43 and 52 of the Anti-social Behaviour, Crime and Policing Act 2014.
To issue a fixed penalty notice for failure to comply with a community protection notice: s. 53 of the Anti-social Behaviour, Crime and Policing Act 2014 gives designated PCSOs power to issue a fixed penalty notice for breach of the terms of a community protection notice, provided that the conduct has taken place in the relevant police area.	Schedule 4 to the Police Reform Act 2002, as inserted by s. 53 of the Anti-social Behaviour, Crime and Policing Act 2014.
To require a person not to consume alcohol and/or to surrender alcohol where a Public Spaces Protection Order (PSPO) is in place: designated PCSOs have the power to require a person reasonably believed to have been consuming alcohol in breach of a PSPO: 1. Not to consume alcohol or anything reasonably believed to be alcohol. 2. To surrender any alcohol or alcohol container.	Schedule 4 to the Police Reform Act 2002 as amended by para. 2 of s. 69 of the Anti-social Behaviour, Crime and Policing Act 2014.
To issue a fixed penalty notice for failure to comply with a Public Spaces Protection Order: following the implementation of a PSPO by the local authority, a designated PCSO can issue a fixed penalty notice to an individual who fails to comply with a PSPO. Under this power, PCSOs can also issue a fixed penalty notice for failure to comply with a request to cease drinking or surrender alcohol or an alcohol container.	Schedule 4 to the Police Reform Act 2002 as amended by ss. 63, 68 and 69 of the Anti-social Behaviour, Crime and Policing Act 2014.

Appendix 4.2

Disorder Penalty Notices

PART I   OFFENCES ATTRACTING PENALTY OF £90 FOR PEOPLE 16 AND OVER, OR £40 FOR PEOPLE UNDER 16

Offence creating provision	Description of offence
Section 80 of the Explosives Act 1875	Throwing fireworks in a thoroughfare
Section 5(2) of the Criminal Law Act 1967	Wasting police time or giving false report
Section 91 of the Criminal Justice Act 1967	Disorderly behaviour while drunk in a public place
Section 1 of the Theft Act 1968	Theft
Section 1(1) of the Criminal Damage Act 1971	Destroying or damaging property
Section 5(2) of the Misuse of Drugs Act 1971 so far as relating to the following—Possession of cannabis etc. cannabinol, cannabinol derivatives (within the meaning of part 4 of sch. 2 to that Act), cannabis or cannabis resin (within the meaning of that Act), any stereoisomeric form of a substance specified in any of paras (a) to (c), any ester or ether of a substance specified in para. (a) or (b), any salt of a substance specified in paras (a) to (e), any preparation or other product containing a substance or product specified in any of paras (a) to (f), not being a preparation falling within para. 6 of part 1 of sch. 2 to that Act.	Possession of a controlled drug
Section 5 of the Public Order Act 1986	Behaviour likely to cause harassment, alarm or distress
Section 141 of the Licensing Act 2003	Sale of alcohol to a person who is drunk
Section 146(1) and (3) of the Licensing Act 2003	Sale of alcohol to children
Section 149(3) and (4) of the Licensing Act 2003	Purchase of alcohol on behalf of children
Section 151 of the Licensing Act 2003	Delivery of alcohol to children or allowing such delivery
Section 127(2) of the Communications Act 2003	Using a public electronic communications network in order to cause annoyance, inconvenience or needless anxiety

Offence creating provision	Description of offence
Section 11 of the Fireworks Act 2003	Contravention of a prohibition or failure to comply with a requirement imposed by or under fireworks regulations or making false statements
Section 49 of the Fire and Rescue Services Act 2004	Knowingly giving a false alarm to a person acting on behalf of a fire and rescue authority

PART II OFFENCES ATTRACTING PENALTY OF £60 FOR PEOPLE 16 AND OVER, OR £30 FOR PEOPLE UNDER 16

Offence creating provision	Description of offence
Section 12 of the Licensing Act 1872	Being drunk in a highway, other public place or licensed premises
Section 2(1) of the Parks Regulation (Amendment) Act 1926 so far as it creates an offence against the Parks Regulation Act 1872 relating to any of the following provisions of the Royal Parks and Other Open Spaces Regulations 1997:	Failing to comply with, or contravening those regulations by—
(a) reg. 3(3)	Dropping or leaving litter or refuse except in a receptacle provided for the purpose
(b) reg. 3(4)	Using a pedal cycle, a roller blade etc. except on a Park road or designated area
(c) reg. 3(6)	Failing to remove immediately any faeces deposited by an animal of whom that person is in charge
Section 55 of the British Transport Commission Act 1949	Trespassing on a railway
Section 56 of the British Transport Commission Act 1949	Throwing stones etc. at trains or other things on railways
Section 87 of the Environmental Protection Act 1990	Depositing and leaving litter
Section 12 of the Criminal Justice and Police Act 2001	Consumption of alcohol in designated public place
Section 149(1) of the Licensing Act 2003	Purchase or attempt to purchase alcohol by children
Section 150 of the Licensing Act 2003	Consumption of alcohol by children or allowing such consumption

Appendix 4.3

PACE Code of Practice for the Exercise by Police Officers of Statutory Powers of Stop and Search; Police Officers and Police Staff of Requirements to Record Public Encounters (Code A), Annexes A–C

A thick grey line down the margin denotes text that is an extract of the PACE Code itself. This material is examinable for both Sergeants and Inspectors.

ANNEX A—SUMMARY OF MAIN STOP AND SEARCH POWERS

THIS TABLE RELATES TO STOP AND SEARCH POWERS ONLY. INDIVIDUAL STATUTES BELOW MAY CONTAIN OTHER POLICE POWERS OF ENTRY, SEARCH AND SEIZURE

Power	Object of Search	Extent of Search	Where Exercisable
Unlawful articles general			
1. Public Stores Act 1875, s. 6.	HM Stores stolen or unlawfully obtained.	Persons, vehicles and vessels.	Anywhere where the constabulary powers are exercisable.
2. Firearms Act 1968, s. 47.	Firearms.	Persons and vehicles.	A public place, or anywhere in the case of reasonable suspicion of offences of carrying firearms with criminal intent or trespassing with firearms.
3. Misuse of Drugs Act 1971, s. 23.	Controlled drugs.	Persons and vehicles.	Anywhere.
4. Customs and Excise Management Act 1979, s. 163.	Goods: (a) on which duty has not been paid; (b) being unlawfully removed, imported or exported; (c) otherwise liable to forfeiture to HM Revenue and Customs.	Vehicles and vessels only.	Anywhere.

Power	Object of Search	Extent of Search	Where Exercisable
5. Aviation Security Act 1982, s. 24B. *Note: This power applies throughout the UK but the provisions of this Code will apply only when the power is exercised at an aerodrome situation in England and Wales.*	Stolen articles or articles made, adapted or intended for use in the course of/in connection with conduct which constitutes an offence in the part of the UK where the aerodrome is situated or would so do, if it occurred there.	Persons, vehicles and aircraft. Anything in or on a vehicle or aircraft.	Any part of an aerodrome.
6. Police and Criminal Evidence Act 1984, s. 1.	Stolen goods.	Persons and vehicles.	Where there is public access.
	Articles made, adapted or intended for use in the course of or in connection with, certain offences under the Theft Act 1968, Fraud Act 2006 and Criminal Damage Act 1971;	Persons and vehicles.	Where there is public access.
	Offensive weapons, Bladed or sharply-pointed articles (except folding pocket knives with a bladed cutting edge not exceeding 3 inches);	Persons and vehicles.	Where there is public access.
	Fireworks: Category 4 (display grade) fireworks if possession prohibited, Adult fireworks in possession of a person under 18 in a public place.	Persons and vehicles.	Where there is public access.
7. Sporting events (Control of Alcohol etc.) Act 1985, s. 7.	Intoxicating liquor.	Persons, coaches and trains.	Designated sports grounds or coaches and trains travelling to or from a designated sporting event.
8. Crossbows Act 1987, s. 4.	Crossbows or parts of crossbows (except crossbows with a draw weight of less than 1.4 kilograms).	Persons and vehicles.	Anywhere except dwellings.
9. Criminal Justice Act 1988 s. 139B.	Offensive weapons, bladed or sharply pointed article.	Persons.	School premises.

Evidence of game and wildlife offences

Power	Object of Search	Extent of Search	Where Exercisable
10. Poaching Prevention Act 1862, s. 2.	Game or poaching equipment.	Persons and vehicles.	A public place.
11. Deer Act 1991, s. 12.	Evidence of offences under the Act.	Persons and vehicles.	Anywhere except dwellings.
12. Conservation of Seals Act 1970, s. 4.	Seals or hunting equipment.	Vehicles only.	Anywhere.

Power	Object of Search	Extent of Search	Where Exercisable
13. Protection of Badgers Act 1992, s. 11.	Evidence of offences under the Act.	Persons and vehicles.	Anywhere.
14. Wildlife and Countryside Act 1981, s. 19.	Evidence of wildlife offences.	Persons and vehicles.	Anywhere except dwellings.
Other			
15. Paragraphs 6 & 8 of Schedule 5 to the Terrorism Prevention and Investigation Measures Act 2011.	Anything that contravenes measures specified in a TPIM notice.	Persons in respect of whom a TPIM notice is being served or is in force.	Anywhere.
16. Paragraph 10 of Schedule 5 to the Terrorism Prevention and Investigation Measures Act 2011.	Anything that could be used to threaten or harm any person.	Persons in respect of whom a TPIM notice is in force.	Anywhere.
17. *Not used*			
18. *Not used*			
19. Section 60 Criminal Justice and Public Order Act 1994.	Offensive weapons or dangerous instruments to prevent incidents of serious violence or to deal with the carrying of such items or find such items which have been used in incidents of serious violence.	Persons and vehicles.	Anywhere within a locality authorised under subsection (1).

ANNEX B—SELF-DEFINED ETHNIC CLASSIFICATION CATEGORIES

White	**W**
A. White–British	W1
B. White–Irish	W2
C. Any other White background	W9
Mixed	**M**
D. White and Black Caribbean	M1
E. White and Black African	M2
F. White and Asian	M3
G. Any other Mixed Background	M9
Asian/Asian–British	**A**
H. Asian–Indian	A1
I. Asian–Pakistani	A2
J. Asian–Bangladeshi	A3
K. Any other Asian background	A9
Black/Black–British	**B**
L. Black–Caribbean	B1
M. Black African	B2
N. Any other Black background	B9

Other	O
O. Chinese	O1
P. Any other	O9
Not Stated	NS

ANNEX C—SUMMARY OF POWERS OF COMMUNITY SUPPORT OFFICERS TO SEARCH AND SEIZE

The following is a summary of the search and seizure powers that may be exercised by a community support officer (CSO) who has been designated with the relevant powers in accordance with Part 4 of the Police Reform Act 2002.

When exercising any of these powers, a CSO must have regard to any relevant provisions of this Code, including section 3 governing the conduct of searches and the steps to be taken prior to a search.

1. *Not used*

2. Powers to search requiring the consent of the person and seizure

A CSO may detain a person using reasonable force where necessary as set out in Part 1 of Schedule 4 to the Police Reform Act 2002. If the person has been lawfully detained, the CSO may search the person provided that person gives consent to such a search in relation to the following:

Designation	Powers conferred	Object of Search	Extent of Search	Where Exercisable
Police Reform Act 2002, Schedule 4, paragraphs 7 and 7A.	(a) Criminal Justice and Police Act 2001, s. 12(2).	(a) Alcohol or a container for alcohol.	(a) Persons.	(a) Designated public place.
	(b) Confiscation of Alcohol (Young Persons) Act 1997, s. 1.	(b) Alcohol.	(b) Persons under 18 years old.	(b) Public place.
	(c) Children and Young Persons Act 1933, s. 7(3).	(c) Tobacco or cigarette papers.	(c) Persons under 16 years old found smoking.	(c) Public place.

3. Powers to search not requiring the consent of the person and seizure

A CSO may detain a person using reasonable force where necessary as set out in Part 1 of Schedule 4 to the Police Reform Act 2002. If the person has been lawfully detained, the CSO may search the person without the need for that person's consent in relation to the following:

Designation	Power conferred	Object of Search	Extent of Search	Where Exercisable
Police Reform Act 2002, Schedule 4, paragraph 2A.	Police and Criminal Evidence Act 1984, s. 32.	(a) Objects that might be used to cause physical injury to the person or the CSO. (b) Items that might be used to assist escape.	Persons made subject to a requirement to wait.	Any place where the requirement to wait has been made.

4. Powers to seize without consent

This power applies when drugs are found in the course of any search mentioned above.

Designation	Power conferred	Object of Search	Where Exercisable
Police Reform Act 2002, Schedule 4, paragraph 7B.	Police Reform Act 2002, Schedule 4, paragraph 7B.	Controlled drugs in a person's possession.	Any place where the person is in possession of the drug.

Index

M

Mentally vulnerable/disordered persons
  statutory protection
    ambit of MHA 1983 4.15.5
    care and treatment 4.15.1
    persons found in public place 4.15.2
    persons lacking capacity 4.15.6
    retaking of escaped patients 4.15.4
    search warrants 4.15.3
Misconduct
  see also **Unsatisfactory performance**
  appeals
    Police Appeals Tribunal 4.2.9
    preliminary procedure 4.2.7
  death or serious injury cases 4.2.4
  fair and open procedures 4.2.5
  fast track ('special cases') procedure 4.2.8
  initial assessment of allegations 4.2.5.2
  investigations
    interviews during 4.2.5.5
    purpose 4.2.5.4
    report and supporting documents
      4.2.5.6
  meetings and hearings
    absence of officer concerned 4.2.6.6
    action prior to 4.2.5.7
    alternative procedures 4.2.6
    attendance of complainant at
      hearing 4.2.6.13
    documents for 4.2.5.8
    IPCC powers 4.2.6.14
    joint meetings 4.2.6.5
    non-senior officers 4.2.6.3
    procedure 4.2.6.7
    public hearings by default 4.2.6.4
    purpose 4.2.6.2
    standard of proof 4.2.6.8
    timing 4.2.6.1
    witnesses 4.2.5.9
  outcomes
    expiry of warnings 4.2.6.12
    notification 4.2.6.11
    overview 4.2.6.9–4.2.6.10
  role of police friend 4.2.3
  Standards of Professional Behaviour 4.2.2
  suspension or change of duty 4.2.5.1
  vicarious liability of Chief Officers 4.3.15
  written notification to officer 4.2.5.3
Mode of trial *see* **Offences, penalties and**
  mode of trial
Multi-Agency Public Protection
  Arrangements (MAPPAs) 4.18.1.3

N

Necessity
  arrest (Code G) 4.4.5.3–4.4.5.4
Noise 4.8.8
Non-molestation orders 4.14.2.3–4.14.2.5
Nuclear sites
  prevention of terrorism 4.10.6.3
  trespass on 4.16.7
Nuisance
  causing nuisance on NHS premises
    4.11.9
  Community Protection Notices 4.8.6
  on educational premises 4.16.6.8
  housing-related conduct 4.16.6.7
  public nuisance
    defence 4.8.6.3
    injunctions 4.8.6.4
    offence 4.8.6.2

O

Offences, penalties and mode of trial
  alcohol and licensing
    allowing disorderly conduct 4.17.7.4
    children 4.17.8–4.17.9
    closure notices and orders 4.17.11
    drunk and disorderly 4.17.7.8
    exposing alcohol for unauthorised
      sale 4.17.7.2–4.17.7.3
    failure to leave premises 4.17.7.7
    failure to surrender suspected
      items 4.17.9.3
    found drunk 4.17.7.9
    keeping smuggled goods 4.17.13
    obtaining alcohol for person
      drunk 4.17.7.6
    sales to drunken persons 4.17.7.5
    unauthorised activities 4.17.7.1
    unlicensed premises 4.17.12
  alcohol at sports grounds
    alcohol at sports grounds 4.12.7.4
    sale on trains 4.12.6
    travelling to or from 4.12.5
  animal research organisations
    interference with contractual
      relations 4.10.11.1
    intimidation of connected
      persons 4.10.11.2
  anti-social behaviour
    Community Protection Notices 4.8.5.4
    criminal behaviour orders 4.8.3.7
    public nuisance 4.8.6.2
  begging 4.8.10
  breaches of non-molestation
    order 4.14.2.5
  causing nuisance on NHS premises 4.11.9
  communication services
    improper use of public
      communications 4.9.6
    increasing importance 4.9.1
    malicious communications 4.9.5
    misuse and obstruction of postal
      services 4.9.4
    placing or sending material 4.9.2
    threats, noxious substances and false
      information 4.9.3
  computer misuse
    supplying or obtaining articles for
      use 4.18.2.6
    terminology 4.18.2.2
    unauthorised access 4.18.2.1
    unauthorised access with
      intent 4.18.2.3
    unauthorised access with intent to
      impair operation 4.18.2.4
    unauthorised risk of serious
      damage 4.18.2.5
  excessive noise 4.8.8
  failure to remove clothing when
    requested 4.5.4.14
  fireworks 4.8.7.5
  football matches
    designated and regulated matches 4.12.3
    failure to appear before
      magistrates 4.12.4.7
    failure to comply with banning
      order 4.12.4.4
  harassment 4.7.4
  hate offences
    racial and religious hatred 4.7.2
    sexual orientation 4.7.2
  interception of communications

    'interception' 4.18.4.10
    public and private
      communications 4.18.4.9
  litter 4.8.9
  nuisance on educational premises 4.16.6.8
  offensive weapons
    crossbows 4.13.9
    having knives in public place 4.13.4
    knives 4.13.8
    manufacture and sale 4.13.7
    possession in public place 4.13.2
    possession on school premises 4.13.5
    trespassing with offensive weapon 4.13.6
  police misconduct
    causing disaffection among
      police 4.3.17.3
    impersonation offences 4.3.17.2
    improper exercise of police
      powers 4.3.17.4
    misconduct in public office 4.3.17.1
  processions and assemblies
    advance notice requirements 4.11.10.1
    breaking up a public meeting 4.11.10.7
    trespassory
      assemblies 4.11.10.5–4.11.10.6
  public disorder
    affray 4.11.5
    fear or provocation of violence 4.11.6
    harassment, alarm or distress 4.11.8
    intentional harassment, alarm or
      distress 4.11.7
    riot 4.11.3
    violent disorder 4.11.4
  putting people in fear of violence 4.7.5
  sporting events
    fireworks 4.12.7.5
    ticket touts 4.12.8
  stalking 4.7.6.1
  terrorism
    encouragement etc. 4.10.6.1
    explosive substances 4.10.9
    funding and fundraising 4.10.3
    making and possessing explosive
      devices 4.10.6.3
    membership of proscribed
      organisations 4.10.2.1
    preparatory acts and training 4.10.6.2
    summary of other key offences 4.10.5
    unlawful disclosure of information 4.10.4
  trade disputes 4.14.3.3
  trespass
    aggravated trespass 4.16.2
    being found in enclosed
      premises 4.16.6.6
    depriving residential occupiers 4.16.6.1
    on designated sites 4.16.7
    failing to leave 4.16.6.4
    failure to leave 4.16.3.1, 4.16.4.1
    for purpose of residence 4.16.3
    squatting in residential premises 4.16.6.5
    using threats or violence to secure
      entry 4.16.6.2
Offensive weapons
  crossbows 4.13.9
  entry, search and seizure (Code B) 4.6.3.5
  having knives in public place 4.13.4
  introduction 4.13.1
  knives
    sale to juveniles 4.13.8.1–4.13.8.2
    unlawful marketing 4.13.8.3–4.13.8.4
  manufacture and sale 4.13.7
  possession in public place 4.13.2
  possession on school premises 4.13.5

T

Temporary event notices 4.17.4.4
Terrorism
    defined 4.10.2
    entry, search and seizure (Code B) 4.6.3.5,
        4.6.7, 4.6.11
    importance of communication
        offences 4.9.1
    offences
        encouragement etc. 4.10.6.1
        explosive substances 4.10.9
        funding and fundraising 4.10.3
        making and possessing explosive
          devices 4.10.6.3
        membership of proscribed
          organisations 4.10.2.1
        preparatory acts and training 4.10.6.2
        summary of other key offences 4.10.5
        unlawful disclosure of information 4.10.4
    police powers
        arrest without warrant 4.10.7.1
        cordons 4.10.7.5–4.10.4.7
        of persons 4.10.7.2
        prevention and investigative
          measures 4.10.8
        searches of vehicles 4.10.7.3
        stop and search in specified
          locations 4.10.7.4
    stop and search (Code A)
        detention of persons 4.5.4.14
        reasonable grounds for suspicion 4.5.4.3
Ticket touts 4.12.8
Tipping off 4.10.4
Tobacco smuggling 4.17.13
Trade disputes
    defined 4.14.3.2
    picketing 4.14.3.1
    statutory provisions 4.14.3
    use of violence or intimidation 4.14.3.3
Trade unions
    Police Federation 4.1.8
Travellers *see* **Trespass**

Trespass
    aggravated trespass 4.16.2
    being found in enclosed premises 4.16.6.6
    depriving residential occupiers 4.16.6.1
    on designated sites 4.16.7
    failing to leave when directed 4.16.6.4
    failure to leave 4.16.2.2
    with offensive weapon 4.13.6
    for purpose of residence
        basic offence 4.16.3
    scope of criminal law 4.16.1
    squatting in residential premises 4.16.6.5
    trespassory assemblies 4.11.10.5–4.11.10.6
    unauthorised campers 4.16.5
    using threats or violence to secure
        entry 4.16.6.2–4.16.6.3
Trials and hearings
    police misconduct hearings
        absence of officer concerned 4.2.6.6
        attendance of complainant at
          hearing 4.2.6.13
        joint meetings 4.2.6.5
        non-senior officers 4.2.6.3
        procedure 4.2.6.7
        public hearings by default 4.2.6.4
        purpose 4.2.6.2
        standard of proof 4.2.6.8
        timing 4.2.6.1

U

Unsatisfactory performance
    applicability 4.3.2
    attendance issues 4.3.7
    formal action 4.3.7.2
    general principles for management 4.3.5
    improvement notices 4.3.8
    ongoing reviews 4.3.3
    performance issues 4.3.6
    regulatory framework 4.3.1
    seconded officers 4.3.14
    sources of information 4.3.4
    UPP procedure

first stage 4.3.9
    ill health 4.3.12
    second stage 4.3.10
    third stage 4.3.11
    use of records 4.3.13
Use of force
    accredited persons 4.1.20
    arrest (Code G) 4.4.3.3
    designated police employees 4.1.20
    entry, search and seizure (Code B)
        4.6.3.5
    preservation of public order 4.11.2.3

V

Vagrancy 4.8.10
Vicarious liability
    discrimination 4.19.7
    misconduct 4.3.15
Victimisation 4.19.4.10
Violent disorder 4.11.4
Vivisection *see* **Animal experiments**
Voluntary attendance at police
    station 4.4.11

W

Warnings
    police misconduct 4.2.6.12
Warrants
    arrest (Code G) 4.4.10
    entry, search and seizure (Code B)
        application procedure 4.6.4
        general principles 4.6.3.1–4.6.3.10
        indictable offences 4.6.3.7
    interception of communications 4.18.4.11
    searches
        mentally vulnerable persons 4.15.3
Weapons *see* **Offensive weapons**
'Whistle blowing' 4.1.21–4.1.22
Wireless interceptions 4.18.4.10
Witnesses
    police misconduct hearings 4.2.5.9